The
Manhattan
Family
Guide
to
Private
Schools
and
Selective
Public
Schools

The Manhattan Family Guide to Private Schools

and Selective Public Schools

Victoria Goldman and Catherine Hausman

Revised by Victoria Goldman

SOHO

Published by
Soho Press, Inc.
853 Broadway
New York, NY 10003

Library of Congress Cataloging-in-Publication Data

Goldman, Victoria, 1958–
The Manhattan family guide to private schools and selective public schools /
Victoria Goldman and Catherine Hausman, revised by Victoria Goldman.
ISBN 1-56947-389-7

Fifth Edition

Acknowledgments

This book could not have been written without the help of many people in the independent school community: the parents, students and alumni who answered extensive questionnaires and shared their experiences, and the nursery school directors, heads of schools, admissions and development office personnel, educators and psychologists who offered their expertise and insight. And, of course, Laura Hruska, whom I thank for her patience (and red pencil).

Authors' Note

Over a decade ago, my co-author and I underwent the nursery school admissions process and found it daunting. When it came time to make applications for our children to ongoing (elementary or elementary/secondary) schools we again found ourselves overwhelmed by the number of choices and intimidated by the admissions process. We vowed that the next time around, we would know better. We hardly thought then that our research would lead to independent careers in educational journalism, countless columns, articles and books, culminating in five editions of this book, the only guide to independent schools in New York City in which the text is *not* controlled by the schools.

Touring the schools and scrutinizing brochures, annual reports, handbooks, curriculum guides and student publications became routine and we interviewed admissions directors, heads of schools, educators, IQ test administrators, child psychologists, students, alumni and parents. Originally, a letter and questionnaire was mailed to all of the heads of schools describing the project. Now, updated information is requested and, in most cases, promptly sent; when appropriate school visits and revisits are made.

It should not surprise parents that the schools that were most open to questions are also the most secure about their missions and the directions in which they are moving, and are the most welcoming to parents in general. While it is easy to understand the reluctance of the schools to disclose the inner workings of their admissions decision-making processes, many heads of schools, admissions directors and administrators continue to be very generous with their time and advice and I thank them for their cheerful cooperation.

Victoria Goldman
www.VictoriaGoldman.net

Table of Contents

PRIVATE SCHOOL LOCATOR MAP

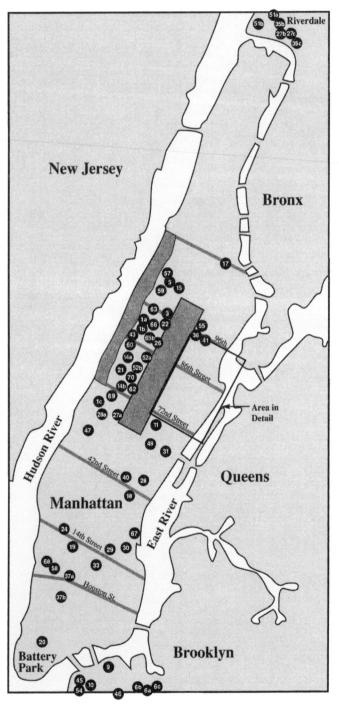

1. The Abraham Joshua Heschel School
   a. 3's–5th Grade
   b. 6th–8th Grade
   c. 9th–12th Grade
2. Abraham Lincoln School
3. Alexander Robertson School
4. The Allen-Stevenson School
5. Bank Street School for Children
6. The Berkley Carroll School
   a. Lower School Brooklyn, NY
   b. Elementary School Brooklyn, NY
   c. Middle and Upper School Brooklyn, NY
7. The Birch Wathen Lenox School
8. The Brearley School
9. Brooklyn Friends School, Brooklyn NY
10. The Brooklyn Heights Montessori School
11. The Browning School
12. The Buckley School
13. The Caedmon School
14. The Calhoun School
    a. Lower, Middle, Upper Schools
    b. Lower School
15. The Cathedral School
16. The Chapin School
17. The Children's Storefront
18. The Churchill School and Center
19. City & Country School
20. Claremont Preparatory School
21. Collegiate School
22. Columbia Grammar and Preparatory School

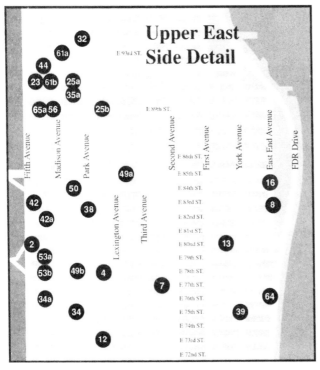

Upper East Side Detail

E 93rd ST.

E 89th ST.

E 86th ST.
E 85th ST.
E 84th ST.
E 83rd ST.
E 82nd ST.
E 81st ST.
E 80th ST.
E 79th ST.
E 78th ST.
E 77th ST.
E 76th ST.
E 75th ST.
E 74th ST.
E 73rd ST.
E 72nd ST.

Fifth Avenue
Madison Avenue
Park Avenue
Lexington Avenue
Third Avenue
Second Avenue
First Avenue
York Avenue
East End Avenue
FDR Drive

WHAT'S SO PRIVATE ABOUT PRIVATE SCHOOLS?

INTRODUCTION

The "private"° school admissions season begins the day after Labor Day when New York City parents start to drag their children, through four months of touring and testing, then wait in a state of suspended animation until the middle of that bleak wintry day in February or March when a thick or thin envelope arrives in the mail. (Thick envelopes contain a contract; thin, a non-acceptance letter). Parental egos are either elated or deflated, but for those who are disappointed, it's still not too late to go house hunting.

There are over seventy independent schools in the New York City area; these include some of the best schools in the nation. There are schools with religious affiliations, schools for children with learning disabilities, Montessori Schools and a Waldorf School: There really is an independent school for everyone, but it just might not be the one you have your heart set on. Applying to New York City's independent schools has not gotten less stressful over the years; the city's demographics significantly impact the admissions game. Although ten years ago just under 2,000 children were applicants for prekindergarten and kindergarten places, 2,354 children were recently tested by the Educational Records Bureau (ERB) for these openings.

What Is an Independent School?

All of the member schools of the Independent Schools Admissions Association of Greater New York (ISAAGNY) are not for profit, racially nondiscriminatory, have their own board of trustees, are chartered by the New York State Board of Regents and accredited by the New York State Association of Independent Schools or the Middle-States Association of Colleges and Schools. Independent schools have six basic characteristics: 1) self-governance, 2) self-support, 3) self-defined curriculum, 4) self-selected students, 5) self-selected faculty, 6) small size.°° Private schools, on the other hand, are owned by individuals who may derive profits or incur losses from school operations.°°°

°In New York City most "private" schools are either "independent" (nonprofit) or privately owned and operated for profit. Most of the schools discussed in this book are actually independent schools.
°°*Independent Schools, Independent Thinkers,* edited by Pearl Rock Kane (Jossey-Bass Publishers, San Francisco, 1992), pp. 6–17.
°°°"Independent School Myths and Realities," a newsletter published by NAIS (National Association of Independent Schools), revised March 1994.

Teachers in these schools do not need to be certified by the state. They are, however, likely to be experts in their fields, for example, a historian teaching history or a drama department head who is a playwright and director when he's not teaching. Most independent school kindergarten teachers have a master's in early childhood education.

Perhaps the most important difference between independent and public schools is that the formers' "fundamental freedom from state and local governments' regulation has allowed independent schools to develop outside of the ferment that has rocked the public schools."[*] And, of course, public schools do not charge tuition and every child is entitled to placement in such a school (subject to residence requirements and other such prerequisites).

Each school has its own unique character, with a board of trustees that appoints the head of school, who ensures that the school fulfills its educational mission. The headmaster (in conjunction with the development office) assumes the role of CEO and major fund-raiser. Every independent school has its own philosophy of education, its "statement of mission" (the primary aims of the school). This mission statement is always included in the school's literature, but you sometimes have to read between the lines to find it. Each independent school is accountable to its students and their parents; if the parents are not happy with the fulfillment of the school's mission they can remove their children and find another that suits them better. If enough parents do so, the school will fail.

A good reputation is so vital to independent schools that although some myths about a school such as "having the brightest kids" or admitting "only the most terrific families" or "getting the most kids into the top Ivy League colleges" are misleading and often false, they do attract applicants. And some school admissions personnel, perhaps inadvertently, help perpetuate these "positive" myths. (Increasingly, independent schools have created a position for a "communications director" or a director of public relations to deal with the media and to shape their public profiles.) The fact is, independent schools are much more mixed than anyone admits. (We found that siblings and legacies were the great equalizers.) As the New York State Association of Independent Schools Guide to Choosing a School states, while SAT scores and college admissions records are "good indicators of the quality of the student body, not necessarily of the school . . . the schools of worth are those whose students, facile or not, are helped to realize their

[*]*Independent Schools, Independent Thinkers, supra.*

4

highest potential, develop a lifelong love of learning and forge good character."[*]

The level of work, the pressure, pace of learning and challenge, hours of homework and amount of remedial support provided by the school all contribute to designation as "very selective." The qualities a child needs to get in and stay in one of these schools are strong academic potential, an outgoing nature, intensity, good self-esteem, independence, maturity and perseverance. A less competitive, more nurturing school would be better for a child with an average IQ, a known learning disability, a very creative or artistic nature or a nonconformist or shy personality. A desire not to subject a child to externally imposed requirements at an early age and a belief in a child's innate abilities, which, given time to flower, will lead him to a happier, more fulfilling life militate against the choice of a highly pressured school experience.

There truly is a school for your child, but it is not true that if you can pay, your child can go to the school of your choice. The apparent arbitrariness of admissions decisions is hard for many successful, ambitious and influental Manhattan parents to accept. Said one admissions director: "After all, they got into an Ivy League school, joined the sorority/fraternity of their choice, landed the job of their dreams and they expect the same for their child too." The baby boom echo is making admissions at all levels very competitive. In response, many schools are expanding their enrollments, adding an extra kindergarten or first grade class that will continue up through the school. But the bottom line is: seats are limited and tuition costs between $20,000 to $28,000 a year.

In the past few years, schools that give preference to siblings and legacies (descendants of former students) have often had more applicants than places, and have been forced to make some difficult decisions. Your child's year might be a year in which many siblings apply at the school of your choice but take heart: If your child doesn't get into your first-choice school in kindergarten, you might try again in a few years, by which time attrition will probably have occurred due to divorce and families relocating to other cities and the suburbs. Because more families are now staying in the city, fewer places may be available in the earliest years. Places do become available in sixth and ninth grades at many schools that go through twelfth grade.

[*]"Choosing a School—A Guide For Parents," a pamphlet published by the New York State Association of Independent Schools (NYSAIS), *infra* pp. 485–486.

Changes in School Services

Gone are the days when women volunteers devoted their time exclusively to serving on school committees, chaperoning field trips and organizing fund-raisers. The two-career family is now the norm (and you are as likely to see a fifty-year-old father attending the school play or walking afternoon safety patrol as a mother). There is an increased need for after-school, vacation and summer programs, and working parents are often happiest if those programs are located at their children's own schools. Most schools now have after-school programs. Caedmon School was the first to introduce "child-minding" until 6:00 P.M. Even the Collegiate School and The Brearley School added their own after-school programs, recognizing that working families depend on these services and if they want all types of diversity in their schools they have to provide support for them. (Parents are continually scheduling after-school activities such as sports, music and religious instruction, in addition to playdates, for younger children while older children often stay at school until five-forty-five or later and then have hours of homework, as well as other lessons or activities. Some of our children work longer days than their parents!

One outcome of working parents' desire to have their children in school for longer hours is that the Guild of New York Independent Schools agreed to extend the independent school year from 160 days to 170 days (still ten days or more short of the public school schedule). Schools also agreed to open their doors earlier in the fall, closer to the Labor Day holiday weekend. A handful of schools still give "travel days" on either side of spring break, a vestige of the era in which families routinely packed a trunk for Europe. Now many of these families travel to snow country in Utah or Colorado.

Financial Pressures

The question of the affordability of private school education is becoming more acute as tuition for Manhattan day schools, which doubled in the past decade, continues to rise. Now parents can expect to pay at least $20,000 or more for third-grade tuition. In addition, the gap between income generated by tuition, rising operating costs, and capital improvements has widened and all schools count upon voluntary giving and annual fund-raising revenues. "Schools are under more pressure for outside fund-raising from corporate and private sources than at any time in the past," according to an administrator of educational grants at a prestigious foundation. "Capital campaigns seem to come around as often as White Sales these days," says one beleaguered family. We know a couple who received a solicitation letter from their son's school announcing a new capital campaign with a return card enclosed showing a suggested contribution of $10,000. The next day the couple marched into the development office and asked, "Do you expect this much every year?" They were informed that they could pay in monthly installments over a five year period. The pressure to give can be especially intense when the class representative tells you they are hoping for 100% participation. What most parents don't realize is that there is no threshold for annual giving. Parents are asked to give whatever they can; contributions within a given class may range from $5.00 to $25,000. Of course only a contribution of $20,000 or more will earn you inclusion in "The Headmaster's Circle", the new millennium's equivalent of The Social Register.

The economic boom has allowed the independent schools to make capital improvements and raise the bar academically; tuitions have steadily gone up. While endowments have doubled or more since the late 90's, a deep recession could strain a school's finances. (However, parents who are concerned about the financial health of a prospective school should not ask for the annual report until *after* their child has been accepted.) A healthy endowment shouldn't be the only reason to pick a school. But, unless a school has a substantial endowment, current parents will be the school's prime source of revenue.

Many parents do not know that tuition covers only about 80 percent of a school's operating expenses and budget, much of this going toward teacher salaries and other benefits. Capital improvements, new technology and science labs, and improvements and repairs to existing facilities, are necessary to keep the schools competitive. Adding to this pressure is the increased need for tuition assistance of parents whose children are already in the schools.° "A tremendous increase in the amount of money raised by annual giving and capital fund programs over the past decade" has helped schools make ends meet, according to Fred Calder, Executive Director of the New York State Association of Independent Schools. Thus it doesn't hurt to have families who manage charitable foundations in the parent body. As one admissions director confided, "We *are* a business, you know."

°See "Applying for Financial Aid," p. 44, *infra*.

There is increased concern about socioeconomic stratification within school populations as many middle and upper middle income families find that they are unable or unwilling to pay approximately $300,000 for thirteen years of private school tuition. Most schools are seeing an increase in families with high income levels applying for financial aid. According to the Director of Financial Aid Services at NAIS, "Families may well have financial need from their perspective, but does the school have the financial aid available to meet the needs of *all* families applying?" Schools are being forced to make tough decisions about which families to support. "The decisions they make illustrate the school's attitude toward socioeconomic diversity and their desire to have it."

Following the national trend in public schools towards eliminating junior high schools in favor of middle schools (serving grades 6–8), Community School Districts 2 and 3 on the Upper East and West sides of Manhattan recently decided to end their elementary schools at fifth grade. A number of very bright and highly motivated fifth grade public school students now apply to the private schools for entrance at sixth grade. Many of the top private schools are making space for them, while at the same time, reserving places for kids in various scholarship programs who enter at seventh or ninth grade. Some schools surveyed, such as Trinity School, say that because of the way their schools are structured and/or because of space restraints, openings in sixth grade at those schools would depend upon attrition and reorganization. Others, including The Brearley School, Horace Mann, Riverdale Country and The Dalton School said they had already expanded their sixth grades to accommodate public school applicants.

As tuitions climb and the competition for places in the most exclusive schools becomes more intense, the private schools face growing resentment from full-tuition paying families who find that their hard earned tuition dollars are subsidizing increasing numbers of scholarship students. However, NAIS statistics reveal that the numbers of students receiving *full* scholarship is in fact declining. Schools find it is more cost effective to support two families on partial assistance (each paying $6,000 or more toward tuition, for example) thus achieving a greater diversity of families for the same investment. In another instance of how elementary and secondary private school admissions parallel admissions at the college level, some middle class families of color, Hispanic and Asian families, (all of whom are historically underrepresented in private schools), cognizant of their marketability, find that they are able to shop around for the best deal.

Parents should keep in mind that there is a significant difference between applying for financial assistance at the elementary and secondary levels and applying at the college level where federal assistance is available in addition to institutional assistance. Parents of elementary and secondary school age children also have another viable option—public school. More middle and upper middle class parents are considering select city public schools for a portion of their child's education. Although Hunter Elementary is under the aegis of Hunter College of the City of New York, acceptance to this highly selective tuition-free school is often considered as desirable as acceptance to the most prestigious private school. The specialized high schools such as Stuyvesant, Bronx Science and Brooklyn Tech are still magnets for many private school students beginning in ninth grade.

Technology

To remain competitive and up-to-the-minute, schools are under increasing pressure to spend more of their budgets on technology and related programs. In addition, many schools are running "computer initiative" capital campaigns to further augment their technology programs. One school hosted a "cybercarnival" to give the school's technology program a boost.

Upgrading hardware, adding high speed wireless connections to the Internet and buying the latest CD-ROMS, "smartboards" and other software is just a part of the expense. The best technology in the world is useless without people; almost every comprehensive independent school now has a Director of Technology. Many schools also find it essential to have a full-time "network administrator" to maintain the system.

And that's not all. A good educational technology program requires trained faculty to integrate all this "stuff" into the curriculum in meaningful ways. Staff training, whether through an outside workshop or an "in-house" technology coordinator, is fundamental—and expensive.

According to one technology seer, the day when "machines are the hand-maiden of cognition in the classroom" is not far off. Now, many lower school classrooms have the latest technology. Students at many schools tote laptops to and from school in their backpacks and use the computer in every subject class as a "transparent tool"—as they would use pencil and paper. Students at most schools already have access to a school "intranet" or internal website that allows students to access homework assignments, read school notices, join in school conferences, communicate with faculty and send in their homework via e-mail.

The Internet has become a primary research tool and nearly every school library is now on-line. Schools subscribe to several services that allow students to search an extensive database of full-text articles from thousands of periodicals, including *The New York Times* and many magazines, via the World Wide Web. At The Nightingale-Bamford School, students in a Constitutional Law elective learn how to conduct keyword searches on these Web-based services for information related to their study of a particular amendment. Furthermore, students can use the Web to access legal cases that are currently before the Supreme Court. And an English teacher at York Prep uses the Internet to look up the lyrics of Bob Dylan's songs for a course on the Romantic poets.

Desktop publishing gives students "ownership" of the publication process. For instance, The Brearley School offers desktop publishing workshops and an interactive design class for aspiring student editors. Students in their own Student Publications Office also produce a literary magazine and The Brearley School Yearbook.

At Convent of the Sacred Heart a young woman in a biology class used special motion, temperature, pH and pressure probes attached to a laptop computer to record and graph laboratory data, allowing her to fine-tune her experiment.

Learning literally "comes alive" when students create multi-media projects. At The Nightingale-Bamford School students created an interactive tour of a medieval village as part of a third grade social studies unit on the Middle Ages. This "virtual village" was then displayed on a touch-screen computer in the school's lobby. By clicking on different characters, such as "Minstrel Martin" or "Sir William," students could learn about that individual's role in society.

It is not enough that students acquire basic computing *skills* such as word-processing, computer graphics, desktop publishing, databases and simulation. "Computer literacy means knowing how to use the computer as a tool to help create and think, to manage information, to solve problems, to express ideas and to communicate with others."[°]

°*Ibid.*

Parents looking at a prospective school should discreetly find out:

- Does the school have a Technology Mission Statement?
- How much of the technology budget is devoted to faculty support and training?
- How is technology integrated into all subject areas, not just the obvious ones?

An educational technology consultant suggested parents look at how the computer is used. Does the school use the computer as an "electronic playbook" or as a creative tool involving high level thinking? Do students spend computer time visiting the computer lab to play games or do they create something of their own?

In the most developed programs the classroom teacher initiates projects using different applications to solve problems, so students think in new ways. One fifth grade homeroom teacher at Little Red School House and Elisabeth Irwin High School asserts, "All the hardware in the world can't beat a good curriculum idea." For a unit on the study of ancient civilizations, he created a project that looks at the problems faced by archeologists in the interpretation of artifacts. The project integrates science, math, writing, computer, history and art and culminates in the creation of a classroom museum of artifacts as well as a "computer museum."

Not all students have access to a home computer, and those who do may not have the latest software applications or a connection to the Internet. Schools are devising their own solutions to this issue of equity. Some have purchased computers for scholarship students, others are keeping their computer labs open and staffed until late afternoon. Some independent schools bridge the gap by opening the school to public school students on Saturdays. Most NYC public libraries provide Internet access free of charge.

Faculty

In addition to the composition of the student body, another essential component in measuring the quality of a school is the calibre of the faculty. Teachers in the independent schools do not have the bargaining power of a union and can be hired and fired at the will of the administration. However, teachers in independent schools do have the ability to design the curriculum and have flexibility in their choice of approach to their subject, books, grades, and materials. The advantage for schools is that they can handpick teachers who conform to the school's philosophy and style.

In some cases, independent school teachers receive pay parity with public school teachers; in other cases they are paid significantly less. For instance, the head of the English department at an independent school told us that she earns about $10,000 less than her suburban public school counterpart. The exact figures vary from school to school. Heads of schools contend that it is health and other benefits for staff that really eat into the budget. Still, in order to keep the best teachers, schools are under constant pressure to offer faculty inducements such as housing and stipends for study and travel. Many schools have named scholarship funds earmarked for this purpose.

Multiculturalism and Diversity

New York City is the most multicultural city in the country, and many parents and educators believe that its independent schools should reflect that "metropolitan mix" in their student bodies. Despite programs such as Early Steps, a program that promotes diversity at the kindergarten and first grade levels, the lower schools (K–5) have remained remarkably homogeneous. Prep for Prep prepares talented junior high school students of color for entrance into New York City's independent upper schools where there is more abundant scholarship money. The so-called "progressive" schools have always been in the vanguard of new thinking, while more "traditional" schools adapt at their own pace, especially regarding the thorny issues of diversity and multiculturalism. Schools such as The Ethical Culture Fieldston Schools, Friends Seminary and United Nations International School have always welcomed and encouraged a diverse student body. Some of the older, more traditional schools did not always do so but many of these schools now actively seek cultural diversity.

During the new millennium the pace of change is likely to become more rapid for two reasons: 1) The changing college admissions profile—in recent years, bright and able students of color and other minorities have fared particularly well in gaining admissions to the elite Ivy League colleges and universities; since a large part of an independent school's status derives from the number of students they feed to the Ivy League, this trend has inevitably trickled down to kindergarten admissions. 2) The schools do not want to give the appearance of "elitism."

A faculty commitment to diversity is important. Diversity training for faculty is on the rise and many independent school teachers spend time at anti-bias retreats and conferences related to these themes. The parent body also influences the pace of change. Many of the independent schools have a parent committee on diversity. Some parents prefer to have their children in a more homogeneous setting and therefore may choose a different sort of school.

Students at New York City's independent schools, along with the rest of the nation, are struggling with the issues of race and ethnicity and the meaning of "difference." Active recruiting and competition for children of color makes some educators uneasy, fanning fears of tokenism and concern for the schools' sensitivity to these students' needs once they are enrolled. A former Parents Association president illustrated this attitude by saying "We want to see our kids in a school with a healthy scholarship program, but of course, we will bring *them* up to our level." Support groups for families of color and students of color (some adopted students of color are not from families of color) abound. In addition, many schools now have anti-bias groups, Cultural Awareness Days and clubs such as Students Aware of Multicultural Ethics (S.A.M.E.). There is an Interschool Multicultural Coalition. Yet even in schools with diverse student bodies there are problems. For example, younger children who commute from Upper Manhattan and the boroughs find it difficult to reciprocate playdates. In some instances parents have been mistaken for baby sitters. In the upper grades there are "scholarship cliques" and tensions have been aired in school assemblies or focus groups.

The independent schools, particularly the girls' schools, are also concerned about gender issues. A 1992 study commissioned by the American Association of University Women (AAUW) carried out by the Wellesley College Center for Research on Women, entitled "How Schools Shortchange Girls" documented the subtle gender bias in schools and how girls are steered away from pursuing careers in math, science and technology. The AAUW report showed that young women were not receiving the "same quality or quantity of education as their brothers."[*]

---

[*]*The AAUW Report: How Schools Shortchange Girls,* the AAUW Educational Foundation and the National Education Association, Washington, D.C., 1992 (p. v.).

The AAUW issued a new report in 1998 which took a critical look at the value of single-sex education for girls and found no evidence that girls were better off in separate schools: "What the research shows is that separating by sex is not the solution to gender inequity in education. When elements of a good education are present, girls *and* boys succeed." A press release from the AAUW states, "No learning environment, single-sex or coed, provides a sure escape from sexism. Sound teacher training is key to reducing sex stereotyping in both the coed and single-sex programs." Ninety-five per cent of America's schoolchildren attend coed public schools. The press release also states that there is debate about whether the benefits of some single-sex programs (such as a heightened regard for math and science among girls) derive from factors unique to single-sex programs or factors that promote good education such as small classes and schools, intensive academic curriculum and a disciplined environment. (See also AAUW, *infra* p. 483).

Some independent schools have special programs to deal with sex bias. For example, The Dalton School has a parent-sponsored committee that reviews sex-equity issues in the school. The Berkeley Carroll School has a faculty sex-equity study group that meets regularly; Manhattan Country School received a five-year "gender equity grant" for $100,000 from a private family foundation in Washington; The Riverdale Country School holds a series of parent education evenings on gender issues.

In response to gender equity concerns, many schools have reevaluated their curricula, either adding or revising courses that include other perspectives including electives such as "Africa in America: an Examination of the Literature of the Men and Women Who Shaped Contemporary Black American Culture" and "Reform Movements: The Advent of Feminism, Black History and Civil Rights." Certainly there are still some schools where the DWEM (Dead White European Males) curriculum predominates, and for some parents a classic curriculum in a traditional setting is just fine. That's what freedom of choice is about.

In recent years, single-sex, established, traditional schools (many of which have ample endowments) once again became very attractive to many well-to-do parents. Even though both parents might have high-powered careers, these "new traditionalists" are reassured by structured classrooms, the old-fashioned values and a traditional curriculum, as well as the status that acceptance into these schools still confers. But today even the so-called traditional schools are sometimes

14

hard to tell apart from the progressive schools.° Some schools have a unique educational philosophy such as Bank Street School for Children, Fieldston Lower School, The Dalton School, The Rudolf Steiner School and City & Country School; many traditional schools have incorporated what were once considered "progressive" approaches to elementary education into their curricula. Schools are moving away from teacher-directed classrooms and toward encouraging classrooms where collaborative learning is stressed and where different learning styles and different rates of development are accommodated. There is increased integration of subject matter; most elementary programs favor using the experiential or hands-on approach to learning for everything from science to social studies. Parents should be aware that it is at the middle and upper levels that the schools are most different from one another. When they look at a kindergarten they should look at the upper school as well.

New York City's independent schools are not the ivory towers they once were. Although still exclusionary financially, certain schools are more inclusive in the makeup of their student bodies than they ever have been. When schools renovate, they must now make accommodations for the disabled. But as a former associate director of the Educational Records Bureau reminded us, "Private school education is still a privilege, not an entitlement." The private, independent schools of New York City are still distinguished by their ability to select . . . and exclude.

SELECTING A SCHOOL

Choosing an independent school in New York City is like dating. As one admissions director said, "The chemistry has to be right on both sides." Respect the judgment of the admissions personnel; they really know which children will be successful in their type of program. In making the final decision, a former Parents League president and leader of a toddler group advises, "There should be a commonality between home and school" and, in the final decision, "Use your gut feeling. The decision should be 98 percent stomach and heart and 2

°We have noted the schools where uniforms are prescribed. This is often a clue for parents: it can be argued that uniforms diminish dress competition but usually coed progressive schools do not require them.

percent head." Through it all remember that your child is unique. And be wary of the Trophy Child Syndrome. As David Elkind writes in *Miseducation: Preschoolers at Risk*, "The social pressure on contemporary parents to use their children as symbols of economic surplus and status is powerful, even if parents are not fully aware of it." Misguided parents believe that "a successful child is the ultimate proof of one's own success."* As one Director of Admissions advised us, "Consider your *child's* comfort level" when selecting a school.

Factors to consider

1. **Location: City or "Campus"**
   Note that a campus school (located outside of Manhattan) may require busing or other transportation, which can cost up to $3,000 annually. The child attending a school far from his immediate neighborhood spends many hours in travel over the course of his education. Parents of young children may choose a campus school so that they can experience a clean outdoor environment for relaxation and recreation daily, and so that, when they are older, they may enjoy grassy playing fields and tree-shaded quads. There is always a late bus to accommodate children enrolled in after-school activities. But for some children there may be better uses for this time. Many adjust with no problem, even in the early years; others find the extra travel draining.

2. **Single Sex or Coed****
   In the younger grades, many children do not seem to value friendships with members of the opposite sex. Later, this changes drastically. Parents sometimes prefer a single-sex school where girls may feel more encouraged to be leaders and where their competitive instincts may be less fettered.

3. **Philosophy of School (Educational Practices and Values)**
   A school's goals are spelled out in its mission statement. Look at the history of the school, at its founder and his or her philosophy of education. Is the parents association active and inclusive? Does the school strive for a diverse student body? Are multicultural perspectives included in the curriculum? Are classes formal or

Miseducation: Preschoolers at Risk, by David Elkind (Knopf, New York, 1987), p. 78
**Brearley, Browning, Chapin, Collegiate, Dalton, Nightingale-Bamford, Spence and Trinity are members of the coeducational Interschool Program. Students from member schools can participate in after-school activities, academic courses, intramural sports,

16

informal? How much homework is given? How much support is provided to students who are struggling? Is there enrichment for those who need it? Is community service required (or incorporated into the curriculum)? Perhaps the most important question parents of a kindergarten applicant can ask is "How are developmental differences handled in the early years?" Ask your nursery school teacher about your child's learning style to determine what type of learning environment would be best for him or her.

4. **Religious Affiliation**

Is the school presently affiliated with a religious institution? Many schools were founded in church buildings and later became independent entities, although they may retain the name of the church. In some cases, a representative of the church continues to serve on the board of trustees. Some Jewish schools are associated with a congregation. Is there mandatory prayer or chapel attendance? Which religious holidays are recognized on the school calendar?

5. **Parent Body**

How well will you fit in? Remember that you have to live with these people for the next eight or more years and their children will form your child's peer group.

6. **Size of School**

Consider your child's "comfort level." Will he or she fare better in a smaller, more nurturing environment? Are there programs a larger school may be able to offer that will be important to your child's fulfillment?

7. **After-School Programs, Early Bird Programs, Vacation Programs and Child Minding**

These programs are of particular interest to many parents, those who work as well as those who don't.

8. **Grade at Which School Ends (sixth, eighth, ninth or twelfth)**

Pick the school that will be right for your child at the outset. Schools without a high school may put more emphasis on the lower grades and offer more leadership opportunities at an earlier age, such as student council president or editorship of the yearbook. Students say that exposure to the behavior of older adolescents, with the concomitant possibilities of experimentation with sex, drugs and alcohol, is more limited at a school without a high school. On the other hand, a parent may breathe a sigh of relief

community service projects and other activities and clubs. Weekend and holiday dances are an adjunct to single-sex schooling.

17

when his kindergartner begins at a school that continues through twelfth grade. But bear in mind that while the child *may* complete his or her education at this school that is not always the case. Further school applications may still lie in wait.

9. **Pace and Expectations of the Academic Program**

How academic is the kindergarten? Certain New York City schools such as Horace Mann, Dalton, Trinity, Fieldston, Collegiate, Chapin, Brearley and Spence are considered the most demanding of their students and are often categorized as "very selective." However, parents should note that the pace and expectations vary greatly amongst the lower schools at these "top tier" institutions. But a child develops at his or her own pace. Not every child who enters such a school is happy as it becomes more academically demanding; yet many who are not "ready" at the age of five blossom in the later years.

10. **Consider Your Own Family Pattern**

If your family enjoys ski weekends be aware that some schools require more work on weekends and vacations than others. On the other hand, if your academic expectations are traditional you won't be comfortable waiting until your child *wants* to learn a subject you feel is important.

11. **Birthday Cut-Off**

It's important to know whether your child is the appropriate age for entrance to the school.

Feeder Schools

Many New York City parents are concerned about getting their children onto the "Harvard Track"; they believe that if a child is accepted into the right nursery school, then he/she will get into the right ongoing school and will eventually be accepted at a prestigious Ivy League college. A "feeder school" is a nursery school that channels its graduates to a specific ongoing school. Twenty or more years ago, certain schools preselected their applicant bodies. When parents called a nursery school for an application, they would have a "chat" with the admissions director after which an application might or might not be forwarded.

Today, the reality is that each season, certain nursery schools have a large number of applicants to certain ongoing schools but acceptances are narrowing. Some are siblings of the students already enrolled, some live nearby, some are following the fashion at that nursery school. And, over the years, certain nursery school directors have developed relationships with the admissions directors at the ongoing schools. They can communicate to those schools whether or not certain children would be good candidates for their programs. There is absolutely no guarantee that even at the "right" nursery school, your child will get into your number-one choice ongoing school. An educational consultant and former admissions director told us: "Kindergarten admissions have become terribly arbitrary over the past couple of years."

Even the most traditional schools, which used to take children predominantly from the Upper East Side or Upper West Side, now accept children from all parts of New York City. Admissions directors are having to go farther and farther afield to look at candidates these days. Commonly, in a class of forty-four children at Collegiate School, roughly twenty-five or more different preschool programs are represented. One year, The Chapin School had applicants from sixty nursery schools and enrolled children from twenty.

At nursery schools with a large number of applicants to a particular ongoing school, the director of admissions or a member of the admissions department of an ongoing school will go and observe the applicants in their nursery-school environment. This is an advantage because a child is more relaxed and natural when interacting with his peers in his own familiar classroom. (Most ongoing schools, however, still require that a parent bring the child in for additional testing at the school interview.)

Keep in mind that some ongoing schools have their own nursery or pre-K programs, most of which were originally set up as a service for the children of alumni. Now, these pre-K programs predominantly serve siblings and the children of faculty members. But Friends Seminary and Dalton recently dropped their pre-K programs, and Horace Mann dropped its youngest twos, in response to limitations on classroom space and the recognition that it is too difficult to pick a two- or three-year old who will ultimately succeed in a demanding academic environment.

The bottom line is, select a nursery school program based on proximity to your home, philosophy and schedule.

THE APPLICATION

Parents of kindergarten applicants should telephone to request school applications immediately after Labor Day of the year their child is four years old (applicants to the upper grades can wait a little longer). Typically, applications should be filed no later than the first week of December. This deadline is getting earlier and earlier due to the huge number of applications that the schools have to process. Most New York City independent schools have a birthday cutoff date of September 1 (your child must turn five before entering kindergarten). But since the first step in the application process is to make tentative selections of the schools to which you may apply by consulting your nursery school director and other sources, you must start thinking about school far earlier, perhaps the spring before you are going to apply. Some schools give spring tours.

If your child is in a nursery school program, the school's director will usually set up a meeting with each family to discuss proposed choices for further schooling. If you need more information than you have been able to obtain about a school or its suitability for your child, you should request a meeting with the director to further discuss ongoing schools.

In early Fall, the Parents League sponsors Independent School Day. Most of the New York City independent schools attend, staff a table and set out their literature. Usually a school's admissions director is there to answer brief questions. Be prepared: It's a little like Macy's at Christmastime. But going, picking up brochures and asking questions will save you a lot of time and phone calls.

Try to be organized. We recommend starting a file (some parents use Excel spreadsheets), with each school in a separate folder, to keep track of correspondence and appointments. Have some nice wallet-size photos on hand because some applications require a photograph. (Although one family that sent a nude photo of their toddler to a crusty but prestigious school received an acceptance.)

Type or write your application legibly. The sooner you return your application, the sooner you will get your appointments for tours and/or interviews. It's a good idea to seek an early appointment; in case your child is ill the day of the interview, you will still have time to reschedule.

Some applications, like those for Dalton and Friends, contain essay questions. Read the school catalog very carefully and be familiar with the program before you write your essay. But remember that the essay is about your child, not about your many accomplishments or great expectations. For some parents, the most difficult part of the entire admissions process can be this essay, as it requires a real knowledge of your child, objectivity and verbal ability.

Don't send anything with the application except a letter(s) of recommendation *if* requested by the school. And if the school doesn't ask for an essay or photograph, don't send one unless you are a genuinely talented writer or photographer.

Early Notification

If your family is connected to a school (that is, if there is a sibling already enrolled, or if the child is a "legacy") then you are eligible for the Early Notification Program. These families will be notified approximately a month earlier than others not so connected. If your child is accepted and you accept the school, then you are required to withdraw your application to all other schools. You may wait until you have heard from all of the other schools on the regular ISAAGNY reply date, but you are not then guaranteed a place at the school that offered early admission.

A word of advice to parents of boys and some girls with spring or summer birthdays: There is a mistaken assumption that these children are immature. As a result, many parents hold their children back a year, so that quite a few turn seven during the kindergarten year. Discuss with your nursery school director whether or not it would be best to hold your child back. If you think your child is ready, trust your instincts.

THE INTERVIEW

After the school receives your application you will be contacted to set up an appointment for your child's interview. Independent schools like to see both parents at tours and parent interviews as a demonstration of their commitment to their child's education. Parents usually meet with the head of school or the director of admissions. The requirements are different for every school so be sure to read the instructions on your admissions packet carefully.

Most schools, but the single-sex schools in particular, like to meet with both parents together though at some schools, school personnel only meet parents as members of a tour group. Does this mean they are looking more carefully at the parents at some schools than others? Absolutely. Be prepared to talk in detail about your child. One mother was asked the following sequence of questions at a prestigious school, "When did you wean? When did he walk? When did he talk? Where do you go on weekends?" One admission director simply asks, "Tell me about your child." Parents have asked if it matters whether they are interviewed by the admissions director or a junior staff member or even a parent. The schools say it makes no difference who conducts the interview, the important thing is open and honest communication.

Nursery school and admissions directors say, "Dress your child comfortably" for the interview. If your child is fussing with his suspenders or playing with her hair it will detract from the interview. Long hair should be pulled back and off the child's face. And keep in the mind the style of the school—that is, whether or not there is a uniform or dress code. For example, when applying to Dalton, Ethical Culture, Riverdale, Friends Seminary, Village Community School or Calhoun, where most of the students will be casually dressed, play clothes are quite acceptable for your child. However, at Buckley, Chapin, St. Bernard's, Spence, or Convent of the Sacred Heart, children will be dressed more formally, and your child should be too: boys in a cardigan, collared shirt, slacks and shoes; girls in a not too fancy dress. Parents should also consider the style of the school and dress accordingly.

For kindergarten admissions, the interview may be conducted individually or in a group. The interview might be conducted by one of the following: the kindergarten teachers, the head of the lower school or the director of admissions, who will record their observations of your child at play. At some schools your child will be asked to complete specific tasks, or take the school's own age-appropriate test. Children are frequently asked to draw a picture and we found that it does help if he/she can recognize and write his/her name.

You can form an idea about whether or not the school is child-centered during the admissions process, says Grace Ball, an educational consultant. "Who is the admissions director focusing on, you or your child? Is your child addressed by name? Are they really getting down to the child's level? After the interview is over do they give you any feedback about your child? Some admissions directors give parents a few minutes after the interview," she says.

How to Prepare Your Child For the Interview

The day or night before your child's interview is enough advance notice to give him or her. Don't communicate your anxiety to the child. Tell your child as specifically as possible what to expect; for example, if he or she will be accompanying you on a tour or will be joining a group, or will be meeting with a member of the admissions staff alone. The nature of the interview is usually described in the admissions packet but if you are not sure, call the school and ask so that you can prepare your child.

If your child wakes up with a runny nose, looking under the weather, it's a judgment call whether or not to cancel your interview. Some schools are so booked that you might not get another chance. But never miss your appointment without calling the school to notify them!

If you notice during the interview that your child is really feeling and behaving oddly, and later that day the child is diagnosed with a double ear infection, call the school and let them know. They might either invite you back or take it into consideration. These are teachers; they can tell when children are not up to par.

To Bribe or Not to Bribe

Parents who are desperate to get their child to perform well at an important interview may be tempted to use bribes. This can backfire. According to an early-childhood consultant, if you really want to offer an inducement to cooperate, promise your child quality time, such as playtime in the park with you, lunch with daddy or mommy or grandpa at the office or a visit to grandma's, rather than a material reward like a trip to the toy store or that expensive toy car he's always wanted.

What if your child won't separate? We observed a fair amount of leg hanging and weeping at interviews. Please don't feel bad if your child won't go off willingly with a stranger, even though you've explained that it's a teacher. Remember he/she won't be going to kindergarten for another full year! How the school handles the separation is a good indicator of how much independence and maturity will be expected during the following year. For example, at one very selective school we were told if your child doesn't separate easily "it doesn't bode well." At other schools parents were invited to come and sit with their children during the group interview.

You should of course encourage and reassure your child that he or she is able to go with the teacher and that you'll be waiting right there for him or her to come back. The separation at the interview can be the most anxiety-producing part of the touring/interviewing process. And don't pay attention to other parents who boast about their child's easy separation. This is only one of many factors, and we know plenty of leg hangers who went on to all of the best schools.

Letters of Recommendation/Thank You Notes/First Choice Letters

Directors of admissions at nearly every school advised us that letters of recommendation should be written by someone who really knows the family and the child. One admissions director said she could wallpaper her office with letters from celebrities and politicians. The most valuable recommendation comes from a parent of a child already in the school who knows you well. Never send more than two letters. But bear in mind, things can and do get lost in the shuffle. Always keep a copy on hand just in case.

If you know a trustee at the school, now may be the moment to let him know you have an applicant, but be advised that if your child is accepted at that school you are morally obliged to enroll the child there. You have asked for a favor and it would be rude to act otherwise.

After your interview, admissions directors agree that a thank you note is nice. "I keep it in the file; it never makes or breaks a decision; when we look back, after the child is in, it shows that this is a nice parent and we were right," says consultant Grace Ball. But one admissions director said she was already inundated with mail and didn't want any more! If *you* receive a nice note from a school after the interview don't necessarily think the school is recruiting your child. Some schools send handwritten thank you postcards to *everyone* who looks at the school, even if they don't apply.

If parents have a clear first choice they can convey this information to the school in several ways: 1) Write a *brief* note to the admissions director. 2) Tell your nursery school director, who will tell the school for you. 3) Have a friend, already in the school, write a first choice note for you. There is no consensus about the effectiveness of first choice letters. Some schools say it helps them calculate their yield, others say they don't pay any attention to them because some families have been known to write first choice notes to many schools! That is unethical, as well as unwise, since schools do talk and you might need to apply to those schools again in the future.

DO'S AND DON'TS

Do

1) During the summer before you're going to apply, start to make a list of schools in which you are interested. Right after Labor Day, call these schools for a brochure and application.
2) Give your current school director the school report form from the admissions packet. Note: Some schools send this form directly to the nursery school once they have received your completed application.
3) At the same time, make sure that you have requested the required admissions testing from the Educational Records Bureau; promptly fill out the form and return it to the ERB with your check.
4) Read the brochure before your tour and interview.
5) Call ASAP if you are going to miss an appointment, whether for a group tour or your child's interview.
6) Pose thoughtful, not provocative, necessary or important questions, that show you've really read the material and know the school. Know at what grade the school ends.
7) Say something nice about the school during the parent interview, and turn off your cell phone or beeper, and don't look at your watch.
8) Ask whom you might contact if you have any additional questions during the admissions process. Being able to call a parent in the school is very helpful.
9) Call the ERB to make sure your child's test scores have been sent to all of the schools to which you have applied, and call each school in early January to make sure your file is complete. The file should contain: 1) your completed application, 2) letters of reference if requested, 3) school report from your nursery school, 4) results of ERB testing.
10) Use discretion when discussing ERB testing results and

acceptances. Feelings get hurt and friendships ruined by boasting.

11) If you genuinely have a first-choice school, let your nursery school director know and let the school know (in writing from you or a parent in the school who knows you). But realize that if you are accepted, your child is morally obliged to attend.

12) Do use pull if you have it *before* completing the application process. Don't wait until after your child is rejected; negative decisions are rarely changed. But use discretion; the thicker the file, the thinner the candidate.

13) If you are totally bewildered use an advisory service, but be discreet about it—some schools frown on consultants.

14) After admissions decisions have been made, call or write every school at which you have been wait-listed to let them know: 1) that you are still very interested or 2) that you have accepted a place elsewhere.

15) Revisit the school after your child has been accepted, and have your child sit in on classes if you need more information before making a decision.

16) Ask for a copy of the school's annual report only after your child has been accepted.

17) Recognize that you have the right to call a school and (politely) find out why your child was not accepted.

18) Realize that kindergarten is a transition year, and reevaluate your choice of schools every three to five years.

19) Be a supportive parent, try to see your child realistically, know his strengths and weaknesses, be his advocate.

20) Remember that there is no such thing as a perfect parent, a perfect child *or* a perfect school.

21) Realize that you don't know how good a school really is until you have a problem.

Don't

1) Pick a school because your husband's law partner and/or your best friend send their children there.

2) Coach your child for the ERB (WPPSI). (You can prepare your child for upper-level testing (ISEE or SSAT.)

3) Be late or miss an appointment without calling.

4) Send a personal essay, photos or any more recommendations than the school requests.

5) Ask for special treatment during the admissions process. Even celebrities have to take the group tour.

6) Ask them to convince you as to why you should send your child to their school.

7) Stand out on the tour by asking too many questions or taking notes as if you were writing an article or a book.

8) Brag about your achievements.

9) Offer money to or otherwise try to bribe the admissions director.

10) Think that you can change the basic style of the school.

11) Tell a school that it's your first choice unless you intend to enroll your child there.

12) Make the elitist assumption that all students of color are on scholarship.

13) Select a school solely on the basis of how many children get into Ivy League colleges. Do look at the range of schools to which students are accepted.

14) Forget that you're an applicant, not a supplicant.

THE ERB

The Educational Records Bureau
220 East 42nd Street (The Daily News Building)
Suite 100
(near Second Avenue)
New York, NY 10017
(212) 672-9800, FAX (212) 370-4096
website: www.erb.org

Sharon Spotnitz, Ph.D., Executive Director

If your child is applying for admission to an independent school, he or she will be asked to take the "ERB's". In fact, ERB is not the title of the admissions exam. It stands for the Educational Records Bureau, a national, nonprofit agency that serves approximately 1,350 independent and public schools nationally and internationally, which administers and interprets different types of tests for children from preschool all the way through high school. The ERB employs fifty psychologists (examiners) during the admissions season. According to the ERB: "All of the examiners are at least Masters' level school or clinical psychologists, many of them are doctoral level candidates, and some are Ph.D's. They are all experienced examiners. The ERB has been under contract with ISAAGNY (Independent Schools Admissions Association of Greater New York) for over thirty years. For New York City independent schools, the ERB administers a collection of tests that sound like kitchen appliance attachments: the WPPSI for preschool through first grade; the WISC for grades two, three, four, and five; and the ISEE for applicants to grades six through twelve. The ISEE is administered in three levels. The lower level: entrance to sixth grade, the middle level: entrance to grades seven and eight, and the upper level: entrance to grades nine through twelve. Practice questions are included in the back of the student guide. The ISEE takes approximately three hours. The ERB tests on the premises of approximately sixty nursery schools. Tests are also administered at the ERB's offices, as well as at other locations throughout Manhattan. The cost of the WPPSI is $345. (There is an ISAAGNY Fee Waiver Program for students requiring financial aid.)

If you are considering applying to Hunter Elementary or a New York City public school program for gifted and talented you'll have to go to an approved testing service for Stanford-Binet testing (approximately $125). (See Programs for Gifted and Talented Students, page 471, *infra*.)

Having a central testing agency administer one test to all children is intended to "eliminate repetitive testing and thus minimize the strain on children and parents." Prior to the selection of the ERB, parents used to take their children for formal testing at each school to which they applied. However, many schools still require up to an hour of their own "informal testing," so you can still expect your child to be thoroughly scrutinized everywhere he or she goes. It seems to parents that it is the strain on the schools that has mostly been alleviated since they can now see many more than one child at a time.

At some nursery schools, says one parent, "the fall semester of the four-year-old group is like 'Stanley Kaplan' for the ERB." The students get worksheets for practicing matching skills, copying geometric shapes and tracking mazes. They are drilled in their colors, taught to write their names and play with parquetry blocks (for spatial relations). Some children even bring *Weekly Readers* home to work on.

The WPPSI determines strengths and weaknesses and where along the developmental scale a child falls. The head of an elementary school described the ERB to touring parents as "a measuring stick against which all the children stand." The WPPSI was not devised as an admissions test, and a national sampling, not an independent school norm, is the measuring standard. It is an evaluation of the child's development in language and visual/motor skills. Like all standardized tests, it is a snapshot of the child's development taken on one day.

Children are compared with others their age; there is no advantage in holding off testing with the idea that "they will know more." In fact, they are expected to do more as they become older; in some cases the younger child may have a slight edge. Also, the later in the year it is, the more likely it is your child may have a cold or other illness. In fact, ERB introduced the option of spring testing in 1992. If your nursery school director thinks your child is ready "and will separate readily" the spring might be better. Each report is individually written, carefully reviewed and mailed in the order of the test date. Remember to schedule well in advance of school deadlines. It usually takes three to four weeks to receive the ERB report.

Parents are sent a copy of the confidential ERB report. You can discuss the results with your nursery school director or you may schedule a private consultation with the ERB.

The WPPSI is composed of four verbal and four nonverbal (or performance) sections. Children *do not* have to read or write to take this test.

Verbal

Comprehension: Commonsense; social awareness.
Vocabulary: Word knowledge; expressive skills.
Similarities: Ability to perceive relationships between things and ideas.
Word Reasoning: Deductive reasoning, social awareness.

Performance

Matrix Reasoning: Sequencing skills; non-verbal reasoning.
Coding: Visual motor speed and accuracy; short term memory.
Block Design: Ability to perceive and analyze patterns.

Picture Concepts: Non-verbal ability to perceive relationships between pictures.

It is common belief that some of the very selective schools have a fixed cutoff score below which they will not admit a candidate. This is simply not true. Admissions directors have said, "You wouldn't believe some of the scores we have here," and we know some children with astronomical scores who were not admitted. But some schools are more likely to take an "at-risk child" (with very scattered scores) than others.

Every parent fears that on the day of the test the child will be ill or otherwise not his normal self. "Schools, either nursery or ongoing, will know if a given test isn't reflective of their observations of the child, and if they determine it is necessary they can request a retest," says Dr. Spotnitz. Retesting is usually done at the request of the ongoing school. (But, of course, results of both tests will be under consideration by the school(s) to which application is being made.) It is rarely requested.

Some directors of admission place more weight on the narrative portion of the test (the second page of the ERB report), which describes the child's test-taking behavior. One admissions director told us, "It's a personality thing."

The parent must fill out a form requesting that the test results be sent to the ongoing schools to which a parent has applied. Results are routinely sent to parents, the child's current school when indicated and five participating ongoing schools. There is a $15 additional charge for each group of up to three schools and all requests must be in writing to the ERB. Be sure to follow up with the schools to make sure they received the results.

In sum, says Dr. Spotnitz, "Have faith in your own child. You know him or her better than anybody else does. In the vast majority of cases your child will look on paper exactly as he or she actually is."

And remember, ERB reports are just one piece of your child's admissions application. Your child's interview, the evaluation form from your present school and the application are all given serious consideration.

SETTING THE STAGE

In preparing your child to take the ERB, don't say he or she is going to play games or be in a room with other children. Do tell your child,

"You are going to work with someone like a teacher who wants to see the kinds of things you know. There'll be some new things and you'll get a chance to learn."

If your child attends one of the participating schools, the test is administered in the relaxed atmosphere of that school. Whenever possible, children should be tested in the familiar setting of their own school. The test is usually presented as enjoyable "special work." You might reinforce this gently beforehand if your child raises questions—but be light and casual.

You may use the same explanation if you are bringing your child to the ERB. Explain that he or she will do "special work" with someone like a teacher who is eager to see what 4, 5, or 6 year olds are able to do. Let your child know that you will be in the waiting room with other parents.

If the child is reluctant to separate from you, have your spouse or a caregiver bring him or her.

ERB will not test a child who is unhappy or reluctant. The anticipation of a pleasant experience is the best preparation for being tested.

The all-important question facing anxious parents is whether and how much to prepare (or coach) their child for intelligence testing. Administrators at the ERB, say emphatically, "Don't do it!" If your child has been coached, it is immediately apparent. One four year old walked into the tester's office and blurted, "I forgot it all!" The tester is looking for how spontaneous the child is in responding to a question never heard before, and for his problem-solving strategy as well as level of information.

Admissions directors at the on-going schools have their antennae out for any signs of familiarity with the test and if they suspect that your child has been coached; if, for instance, all of the scores are very high and this performance does not match the nursery school report or the informal testing done at the school, then the application will be compromised. There are plenty of other families about whom they do not have ethical qualms.

We are sympathetic to parents who feel they have to do something, to prepare their child, if only to ease their own anxiety, so we have listed below some age-appropriate activities that you and your child can enjoy doing together. Remember to keep it fun and it will be a treat for your child to have Mom or Dad's individual attention. When your child gets tired or fidgety, stop.

Playing with wooden blocks, LEGO blocks, connect-the-dot books and puzzles strengthen children's visual spatial abilities. Tessellation puzzles are fun and challenging. You can make your own unusual cutout images, and then ask your child to reassemble them.

Tic-Tac-Toe, "Quick Chess" (simple three-minute chess games for the super intelligent 4-year-old) and strategic board games also enhance visual spatial coordination (Keep in mind that some pre-schoolers get very upset if they lose—this is normal—and it's okay to let them win now; they'll learn about sportsmanship later.)

Reading aloud to your child increases his vocabulary and develops his pictorial imagination. There are poetry and non-fiction books that are appropriate for preschoolers, in addition to picture books. While you are reading ask your child questions based on the content, such as, "What do you think he's feeling?" "Where are they going?" "What do you think is going to happen next?" After you finish a simple story, ask your child to "tell" it back to you. Help him to put the events in order. Draw a simple picture story, or have him dictate his own stories to you. Another way to increase a child's vocabulary is to ask, "What do you call . . . (name things/identify objects)," also ask, "What do you do if . . . ?"

Incentive Publications, booklets that are available at Barnes & Noble, tap into preschoolers' verbal and math skills. *Scholastic* also publishes games for preschool children in reading, writing, learning and math. Phonemic-based books like Dr. Seuss's "Hop on Pop," and most of his other books, correlate sounds with the shape of a word in a simple way. There are CD-ROMs like "Reader Rabbit" that help develop early pre-reading skills. But whatever you do, don't push the reading! Learning to decode occurs when the child's brain is ready, not before; it's a little like losing teeth.

Always have lots of art materials on hand—crayons, paint, pipe cleaners, beads, markers, clay, stickers, etc.—for open-ended play. Children should learn how to hold a pencil correctly (there are special soft grips you can buy at any stationery store) and use it to try to write their names, run mazes and connect the dots. *McGraw Hill Spectrum,* (as well as other companies) publishes workbooks that focus specifically on fine motor control. Also, sewing with yarn, threading a big needle and beading (threading large beads on a pipe cleaner, for instance) help preschoolers' fine motor control.

A field of mass media called "edutainment" began with the Learning Company's CD-ROMs, which include "Math Blaster," "Millie's Math House" and "Math Rabbit" bolster young childrens' math skills. Parents should ask their child to count, use flash cards, play board games (Sorry, Trouble, Candyland, Chutes and Ladders) and simple card games like preschool Uno. You can make up games too. Bake and cook with your child to increase his awareness of simple addition, subtraction, fractions and percentages.

There's no substitute for experience and a trip to a museum, lollipop concert, a farm, the children's zoo, the bakery and the grocery store, can all be opportunities for learning and will increase a child's general knowledge (ability to share and get along with others, form an appropriate relationship with the teacher, work independently, follow directions, and show "maturity"). In the past, kindergarten might be a child's first school experience, but today most children have been in a preschool program for two to three years and prior to that, countless parenting classes. "Kindergarten has become an experience for which children need to be ready when they arrive."[*] However, this does *not* mean that parents should or have to teach their preschoolers to read. There are some children who will learn to read before kindergarten (you know who they are because parents of such children will invariably boast about their "little geniuses"). However, educators stress that the majority of children are ready for formal reading instruction in first grade or when they are approximately six and a half years old. Admissions directors do not expect candidates for kindergarten to read, nor should you.

A good evaluation of a child, in the words of one nursery school director, is "Verbal, curious, good self-esteem, ability to concentrate, not fidgety, has enough to give to others." Then there is an intangible measurement dubbed "the likability factor" by an early-childhood consultant we know. We'd all like to think our children have it.

ADVISORS, TESTERS AND TEST PREPARATION

Aside from this book and the director of your nursery school, there are other useful resources in Manhattan to help you select the right independent school for your family. Keep in mind that the best source of information is the school itself. Ask if the school you are interested in has spring tours. Perhaps you can rule out a school or take a second look in the fall when you apply. Once the fall admissions process gets rolling you will usually not be able to take a second look until your

[*]*Kindergarten, It Isn't What It Used to Be,* by Susan Golant and Mitch Golant, Ph.D. (Lowell House, Los Angeles, 1990)

child is accepted to the school. Advisory services (or educational consultants) help parents approach the independent school admissions process in an organized manner and provide reassurance and advice to apprehensive parents.

Parents, whether you choose to use a consultant or not, please be advised that some independent schools admissions officers have admitted that they do not look kindly on applicants who use the services of consultants. So if you choose to use one, don't broadcast it during your interview.

All except two of the services listed below require a fee; fees vary widely.

ADVISORS

1. THE PARENTS LEAGUE OF NEW YORK, INC., 115 East 82nd Street, New York, NY 10028 (212) 737-7385, website: www.parentsleague.org
Patricia Girardi, Executive Director

The Parents League was founded in 1913 and is a nonprofit organization of parents and independent schools. Annual membership fee: $90 for one year or $230 for three years. The Parents League offers a School Advisory Service for member parents who need advice about the process of applying to schools and information about the schools. Please call for an appointment. The advisors are volunteers who have all served in the independent school community and are also trained in-house.

The Parents League distributes the *New York Independent Schools Directory*, published by the Independent Schools Admissions Association of Greater New York (ISAAGNY). Anybody can purchase the book for an additional $20.00 at the office, $23.00 by mail or online. *Please be aware that the entries in this book are written by the schools themselves.*

The Parents League sponsors Independent School Day, held in the fall, at which parents can pick up printed material, including brochures and applications, from various city independent schools; representatives from the independent schools are available to answer *brief* questions. Be prepared for a mob scene, but it will save you countless phone calls.

The Parents League sponsors a Forum on Admissions, at which admissions directors from five or six independent schools speak and then answer questions from the audience about the admissions process. It offers a summer advisory service and a special education advisory service. You must be a member of the Parents League to participate; there are no additional fees.

2. IVYWISE KIDS, Nina Bauer, MA, 140 West 57th Street, Suite 3D, New York, NY 10019 (212) 262-1200, website: www.ivywise.com, e-mail: nbauer@ivywise.com.

Ms. Bauer has a Masters in early childhood education and has taught in both public and private schools. She offers a very personalized service to families who have children applying to nursery, kindergarten and high schools in Manhattan, as well as students who wish to transfer schools. Ms. Bauer guides parents through every aspect of the admissions process while helping them choose the right school for their child. There is a range of fees; initial consultation $650 for two hours, a flat rate of $4000 covers unlimited hours for the entire process for nursery and $5,000 for kindergarten. Ms. Bauer does pro bono work for eligible students. College and graduate school consulting is also provided by Dr. Katherine Cohen, Ph.D., (212) 262-3500.

3. SMART CITY KIDS, Roxana Reid, 251 East 77th Street, New York, NY 10021, website: www.smartcitykids.com, (212) 979-1829

Ms. Reid, a former kindergarten teacher with a Masters in social work, specializes in kindergarten and nursery school admissions. She holds workshops with guest speakers, and private sessions that prepare parents and children for every aspect of the admissions process—how to handle interviews testing, skill requirements, applications and essays. She also offers a Caregiver Workshop that suggests activities for caregivers and their charges, ages 3 and 4 years old. Fees are approximately $150 an hour, workshops are two hours, call for exact rates.

4. VIRGINIA J. BUSH & ASSOCIATES, 444 East 86th Street, New York, NY 10028 (212) 772-3244

Since 1975, Mrs. Bush has been advising families on secondary school and college options.

5. SCHOOLS & YOU, Sarah D. Meredith, 328 Flatbush

Avenue, Suite 372, Brooklyn, NY 11238, (718) 230-8971, website: www.schoolsandyou.com

Ms. Meredith provides information and consultations on school choices from nursery through eighth grade for both public and private schools in both Manhattan and Brooklyn. She will consult at your home or workplace. Resource materials accompany every consultation.

6. HOWARD GREENE & ASSOCIATES, The Educational Consulting Centers, 39A East 72nd Street, New York, NY 10021, (212) 737-8866, website: www.greenesguides.com

The Educational Consulting Center was founded in 1969 by Howard Greene, former admissions counselor at Princeton University. Originally known for their college admissions counseling, Howard Greene & Associates will also advise parents about secondary independent schools. There is a range of fees.

7. SCHOOL CONSULTANTS ON PRIVATE EDUCATION (SCOPE), 309 East 87th Street, New York, NY 10128, (212) 534-6531, or (888) 214-6590 (toll free), website: www.summer scope.com, e-mail: camps4u@aol.com

Director Elaine Vipler, M.S.Ed., is the director of SCOPE, an advisory service that helps families select appropriate school and summer programs for their children. Ms. Vipler assists parents with every aspect of the admissions process. There is no fee for summer programs.

8. THE INDEPENDENT EDUCATIONAL CONSULTANTS ASSOCIATION, 3251 Old Lee Highway, Suite 510, Fairfax, VA 22030 (703) 591-4850 or (800) 808-IECA (4322), website: www.iecaonline.com

The Independent Educational Consultants Association will send a directory of listings in the New York City area, free of charge.

9. GREENBERG EDUCATIONAL GROUP INC., 344 West 86th Street, Suite 1A, New York, N.Y. 10024, Tel (212) 787-6800 FAX (212) 579-8200

Greenberg Educational Group, run by a Fieldston School and Wharton Business School graduate, Eric Greenberg, provides test preparation, tutoring and educational advising. Financial aid is available.

10. ABACUSGUIDE.COM provides listings and links for private, public, and parochial schools in the NYC area. You can e-mail

questions about particular schools to info@abacusguide.com. Emily Glickman, founder and director of the Abacus Guide, helps families navigate the school selection and admissions process.

11. EDCHOICES CONSULTING, 255 West End Avenue, Suite 1A, New York, N.Y. 10023, Tel (212) 560-2575, e-mail: EdChoices@aol.com

New to the advisory business, directors Colleen Berge who holds a M.A. in Teaching and Lizabeth Sostre, an experienced educator, who holds a Masters in Education, walk parents through all every aspect of the admissions process for grade levels, public and private, through ninety-minute workshops and individual counseling.

TESTERS

There are many testers; here are just a few names to consider:

1. LOIS BERMAN, Ph.D., 177 East 87th Street, Suite 502, New York, NY 10128, (212) 722-0250

Dr. Berman was the psychologist at Trinity School for seventeen years and has worked with many independent school families. As a licensed psychologist, Dr. Berman administers psychoeducational evaluations to children with suspected learning disabilities.

2. LANA F. MORROW, Ph.D., 365 West End Avenue, New York, NY 10024, (212) 799-0636

Dr. Morrow administers neuropsychological evaluations and remediates children who have learning disabilities. She advises families as to which independent school will be best suited for their child.

3. SUSAN SCHWARTZ, Ph.D., 1160 Fifth Avenue, Suite 109, New York, NY 10029, (212) 426-0232, FAX (212) 427-0612

Dr. Schwartz administers comprehensive neuropsychological and psychological assessments that measure intelligence, academic achievement, attention, language, memory, and more. She also meets with school specialists and family members to discuss and plan remedial strategies.

4. NYU CHILD STUDY CENTER, 577 First Avenue, New York, NY, 10016 (212) 263-6622, website: www.aboutyourkids.org

TEST PREPARATION

Many New York City parents have their older children tutored, either privately or in a group, for the ISEE (Independent School Entrance Exam for grades 6–12), the Hunter High School Entrance Exam (sixth grade), the SSAT, the Specialized High Schools Exam (Stuyvesant, Bronx Science, Brooklyn Tech) and the SAT I (the reasoning test) and II (the subject tests). *What to expect on the ISEE* is a review book published by the ERB that includes practice exams and exact directions for the test. The ERB does not encourage or sanction tutoring for any child who is going through the admissions process.

Candidates for grades six and above should begin to review and refresh their knowledge several months preceding the exam using either a review book and/or a suitable tutor or review class. At the very least, students should look at the sample questions included in the registration materials.

Ideally, tutoring should boost a child's confidence in his/her abilities, familiarize the student with the kind of questions he will find on the test (multiple choice or essay type), teach test taking strategies and hone essay writing skills. It should be preparation that enables students to go into the testing situation thinking, "Hey, I know this stuff, I can do my best." Cramming for any exam the week or two before only results in a sleep-deprived and anxious candidate. Make sure your child has a good night's sleep and something to eat/drink before the test, and because most of these tests are over three hours long, bring a drink and a snack that doesn't make crumbs.

The best way to find a tutor is through inquiries at the child's present school or through word-of-mouth. In some cases the city offers review courses such as The Math/Science Institute (see pp. 476, *infra.*) National test preparation companies such as Princeton Review have offices in Manhattan. Parents have recommended the following resources to us; rates vary widely so be sure to ask how much it will cost before you sign up!

- **GRF Test Preparation,** Richard Geller, (212) 864-1100, 50 West 97th Street, apt. 11T, New York, NY 10025. Test prep for the specialized science high school entrance exam (Stuyvesant, Bronx Science, Brooklyn Tech), ten three-hour sessions, offered at two locations in Manhattan, also in Riverdale and Queens. Cost: approximately $700.
- **S & S PREP,** Alan Silver. (845) 634-3128, S&S PREP's large

group review for the Hunter High School exam is offered at Wagner Middle School, 226 East 76th Street.

- **School Skills, Inc.,** (212) 861-5083, Dianne Karlstein DeVizcaino, "Mrs. D." 210 East 73rd Street. Maybe it's the airheads and pretzels she keeps on her desk, or her thirty-plus years experience in teaching, but many children we know enjoy going to "Mrs. D." In demand for ERB and Hunter test preparation, Mrs. D. also provides basic skills review, city-wide test preparation and college application essay writing.
- **Advantage Testing,** (212) 744-8800, 241 East 86th Street, Suite 2B. Individual tutoring in your home. SSAT, ISEE and SAT specialists and graduate test prep for GMAT, MCAT and LSAT.
- **Inspirica,** (formerly Stanford Coaching, Inc.) (212) 245-3888, website: www.inspirica.com, FAX: (212) 245-3893, 850 Seventh Avenue. Inspirica provides one-on-one tutoring in most academic subjects, specialized programs for HSEE/ISEE, PSAT, SATs and other highly individualized programs, and also admissions consulting.

THICK OR THIN

Admissions decisions are usually made by committee (although the Director of Admissions acts alone at some schools.) The members of these committees vary from school to school. At some schools someone from the development office sits in, and sometimes parents of students are on these committees. There is usually a core group of children comprising siblings and legacies who are definite admissions and the committee tries to put together a balanced class around this core. Schools want a balance of personalities as well; they don't want all leaders or followers. If it is a coed school they need an equal number of boys and girls. So your chances vary from year to year depending on what kind of sibling year it is, or for unpredictable reasons. For example, in a recent year at Riverdale Country School, more applications were received than in any previous year, "over five hundred for approximately seventy spots," according to the Director of Lower School Admissions. So a rejection one year might well have been an acceptance the following year. Try not to take it as a judgment of your child.

Do admissions directors talk? The independent school world is small; admissions directors go to lunch and phone calls go back and forth during the admissions process. Usually, they will not talk about specific families. They will discuss whether the "pool" is up or down for girls or boys this year and so forth. But somehow, if you tell each school that it is your first choice, it will get around. So don't say it unless you mean it.

The yield figure is a mathematical formula, different at each school, which attempts to predict the number of children who, having been accepted to the school, will actually enroll. Anyone whose child is in an over-enrolled kindergarten class knows that this is an inexact method.

There are three elements that make up your child's file:

1) **ERB Testing Results**

   The examiner prepares an individual report for each child. Each report is carefully reviewed by a child psychologist for accuracy and clarity. Parents and schools receive the identical report.

2) **The Nursery School Report**

   A confidential report (parents never see it) that discusses your child in depth: his growth, maturity, strengths and weaknesses usually over the past (three) years as well as information about the family such as how supportive the parents are, how promptly they pay tuition, if they have donor potential and so on. Nursery school directors have to be honest in this report; as a former Parents League president put it: "Report plus rapport equals respect." An honest report plus a relationship between the nursery school director and the director of admissions at the ongoing school equals respect for the nursery school director's recommendation. Admissions directors know how to read between the lines of these reports and the notation "Call me for additional information" implies there is more to the story than what's written on the page. An early-childhood consultant told us that "for an unconnected family without significant means, it's essential that your nursery school director have an established relationship with the admissions director at the ongoing school and be able to really go to bat for you." It certainly can't hurt to be active and involved in your nursery school, and if you're unsure whether to give time or money, give both.

3) **Child's Interview**

   An admissions director who's been in the business for twenty-seven years says, "I never read a file until I meet the child." The child's profile should fit together like a jigsaw puzzle, says a representative from Ethical Culture admissions. "The nursery school report should correspond to behavior in the interview, the ERB reaffirms both. If a piece doesn't make sense, then we have to look further."

If you've got three out of three you're accepted (provided there's room), and a contract will usually be included with the acceptance letter (thick envelope). Two out of three and you might be accepted or wait-listed. One out of three is usually a nonacceptance (thin envelope containing only a nonacceptance letter). This is not gospel; there are mitigating factors and if the child is outstanding in some way that might outweigh one of the other factors.

MULTICULTURAL/SCHOLARSHIP PROGRAMS

A Better Chance
National Office
240 West 35th Street
9th floor
New York, NY 10001
(646) 346-1310 or (800) 562-7865 FAX (646) 346-1311
website: www.abetterchance.org

Founded in 1963 by twenty-three independent schools in the Northeast, A Better Chance, Inc. is the oldest national, nonprofit academic talent-search organization for minority secondary school students. The membership comprises approximately 225 independent day and boarding schools. Students are recruited and admitted to these schools on the basis of high academic achievement and personal initiative. The majority of students apply in the eighth or ninth grade. Applicants must take the SSAT or the ISEE. Financial aid is provided by the member schools. A Better Chance provides ongoing counseling and support. A Better Chance has an Affiliated Colleges Program of approximately 100 colleges and universities that have demonstrated a commitment to increase their minority enrollment.

The Albert G. Oliver Program

The School at Columbia University
556 West 110th Street
3rd floor
New York, NY 10025
(212) 851-4223 FAX (212) 851-2730
website: www.theoliverprogram.org

Johan Johnson, Executive Director

The Albert G. Oliver Program, named after an outstanding New York City educator, is a nonprofit organization founded in the 1980s to help talented black and Hispanic youngsters gain access to day and boarding schools at the high school level. The brochure says "A primary goal of the Oliver Program is to nurture the hearts of these gifted young people so they develop a sense of caring, love and responsibility that will make a positive impact on the lives of others." The Albert G. Oliver Program is unique in offering a mandatory community service program (150 hours total) and a summer internship program. Each year up to fifty black and Hispanic students are placed in independent day and boarding schools that offer strong support services including financial assistance. Oliver graduates attend many Ivy League colleges and other top universities.

Member Day Schools:

The Berkeley Carroll School
The Brearley School
Brooklyn Friends School
Collegiate School
The Dalton School
The Elisabeth Irwin High School
The Fieldston School
Friends Seminary
Horace Mann School

The Nightingale-Bamford
  School
The Packer Collegiate Institute
The Riverdale Country School
St. Bernard's School
The Spence School
Trevor Day School
Trinity School

Early Steps

540 East 76th Street
New York, NY 10021
(212) 288-9684 FAX (212) 288-0461

Ms. Jacqueline Y. Pelzer, Executive Director

Early Steps is a membership organization, created in August 1986, to increase the number of students of color in city independent day schools at the kindergarten and first grade levels. Early Steps was an outgrowth of an Independent Schools Admissions Association of Greater New York (ISAAGNY) Minority Affairs Committee study that identified the need for schools to pool resources for the recruitment of younger students of color.

Early Steps provides counseling and referral services for families of color looking for and enrolled in city independent schools. Financial aid is available but families should be prepared to pay a portion of the tuition. Some families pay full tuition.

Prep for Prep

163 West 91st Street
New York, NY 10024
(212) 579-1470 FAX (212) 579-1459
website: www.prepforprep.org

Ms. Aileen Hefferren, Executive Director

The Prep for Prep program is a nonprofit educational organization founded in 1978. Some of the original group of Prep for Prep students attended Trinity School. Today, Prep for Prep identifies academically talented students from minority group backgrounds, provides fourteen months of intensive academic preparation and places these students in leading city independent schools and boarding schools with scholarships that are based on financial need and academic performance. The program is highly selective and rigorous. Once enrolled, students are provided with ongoing counseling and leadership development opportunities until high school graduation. The Prep for Prep community includes thousands of students and alumni.

The TEAK Fellowship

16 West 22nd Street
3rd Floor
New York, NY 10010
(212) 288-6678
website: www.teakfellowship.org

Justine Stamen Arrillaga, Founder and Executive Director

The TEAK Fellowship prepares talented students from low-income families for admission to top public, private, and parochial high schools. Teak has a colorblind admissions process and accepts 25 low income, high achieving students per year. The program begins in seventh grade and follows students through their high school graduation, providing personal as well as academic support through tutoring and mentoring, test preparation, internship opportunities, leadership training and community service.

APPLYING FOR FINANCIAL AID

The rigorous process of qualifying for private school tuition assistance makes kindergarten admissions look easy. After your child has been accepted to an independent school, or if your child is already enrolled in an independent school and you are requesting tuition assistance (such needs may arise because of a divorce or the loss of a spouse's job) your first step is to contact the financial aid administrator in your child's school. The financial aid officer will give you a Parent Financial Statement or PFS which you must complete. Be forewarned that the PFS asks applicants to list all of their assets and expenses, including their country house, boats, family car(s) club memberships, lessons, summer camp, and vacations. The completed form must be returned to the SSS—The School and Student Service for Financial Aid. The SSS, an affiliate of the National Association of Independent Schools, is a nationwide service that assists independent schools in processing scholarship applications. The SSS is administered by the Educational Testing Service (ETS). Parents are usually asked to submit a copy of *both* parents' W-2 forms and the previous year's joint or separate Federal Income Tax returns in support of their application. If there are no young children at home, the SSS will impute an income for a non-working parent.

In processing the PFS the SSS uses national guidelines set for independent schools; families who live in one state might be applying for financial aid from a prep school which is located in another state. A copy of the PFS is then sent back to the school with a recommendation from the SSS of how much tuition that particular family can afford to pay. The school then recalculates; some use specific software for this purpose, taking into account the cost of living in Manhattan. The final decision rests with the school. Most schools have a scholarship committee which reviews each application and then makes "recommendations to the family" as one administrator put it. It is up to each family to decide the financial sacrifices or lifestyle changes it is willing to make. Some families start out on financial aid and eventually become full-tuition paying families and vice versa. Some families choose to "live on peanut butter" and make other sacrifices, others will consider a move to the suburbs, or begin to look at public school options.

TRANSPORTATION

Once your child has been accepted into school, whether public or private, your next consideration is how to get him or her to school and back each day, safely and conveniently. If they live nearby, many parents walk their children to and from school. Those who live further away must rely on a bus service. There are different types of bus service, free and public, or private requiring payment. Depending on the size of your child's school, you might have a limited choice of transportation services. Some parents combine services, depending on their needs.

1. ATLANTIC EXPRESS SERVICE: (A/E or yellow school bus service):

    Administered through the office of pupil transportation within the Board of Education, (718) 585-8592.

    Atlantic Express has an excellent safety record and is free to public school students within the district who attend a gifted or magnet program school, and private school students attending participating schools. Students must apply through their own school. To qualify, students in kindergarten through second grade must live 1/2 mile or more from school. Students in third through sixth grades must live 1 mile or more from school. In early September, the school provides students with a list of designated bus stops (usually along the avenues) and times for pick-up and drop-off. Students using A/E bus service *do not* receive a bus pass for use on city buses. Middle and high school students are provided with subway and bus passes.

2. PRIVATE BUS SERVICE: The private schools contract with a bus company (such as SuperTrans NY INC. (914) 968-3300, FAX (914) 968-5455, 60 Alexander Street, Yonkers, NY 10701, website: www.supertrans-ny.com) which provides pickup and drop off at specific times and many locations. This service is the most convenient and also costly. Roundtrip starts at approximately $1500 per child per year.

3. SCHOOL VAN: Various private schools run their own van service which usually picks up and drops off at designated bus stops. The cost is less than for private van service.

Students attending a regularly scheduled after-school program one or more times a week often arrange with their school for private van service for dropoff to these activities.

EXTRA-EXTRACURRICULAR ACTIVITIES

There are a number of organized after-school athletic programs which feature quality coaching and team play and provide transportation from school to the program and home. Some schools have established relationships with one of these programs, or a number of other families in the school participate. Some are co-ed, others single-sex, fees vary, but the programs that include transportation are usually costly. Advertisements and listings for many of these programs are often found in community newspapers and other local parent publications.

Boys and girls who attend the traditional single sex schools have limited social contact with the opposite sex. This is somewhat ameliorated by coed theater and musical productions, interschool classes and activities. But what could be more fitting for the offspring of the socially prominent than charity dances for the pubescent set to introduce them not only to each other but to philanthropy as well? Miniature charity balls, sponsored by organizations such as Yorkville Common Pantry and Goddard Riverside Community Center, are usually held at one of the private schools and the money raised benefits a variety of local causes. These dances for teenagers attending Manhattan's exclusive schools are a quaint but benign form of organized dating for many 11 and 12 year olds as well as a time for parents to enjoy their last vestige of social control because before they know it their teenager will be out and about.

The "White Glove" social organizations listed below are traditionally "by invitation only." However, you no longer need the proper pedigree to participate; after all, good manners are for everyone.

The Barclay Classes are headquartered in Westfield, New Jersey, (908) 232–8370. For 70 years, the Barclay Series has offered classes to children in the social graces, proper party attire and ballroom dancing. The classes meet once weekly. Spit and polish is the order of the day and young ladies wear white gloves until sixth grade. There are real parties twice a year, usually with a theme. Children enjoy the classes because refreshments are served and prizes are awarded. You must contact the Barclay Series to request an invitation if one has not already been sent. There is a waiting list for girls and boys. There is a sibling policy as well.

Dancing lessons offered by **The Knickerbocker Cotillion** begin in fourth grade and children must be invited to attend; unlike the Barclay Series, The Knickerbocker Cotillion is a not-for-profit organization, an older and some say, more exclusive group. The group's coordinator usually forwards applications to those who call; however, it is the organization's policy to refrain from publicity.

The Knickerbocker Greys: An after-school cadet program for boys and girls. Telephone: (212) 585-1881. Once upon a time children from Manhattan's best families bought their school uniforms at Alex Taylor and their other clothes at Best & Company; the girls took dancing classes at Mrs. DeRhams' Dancing School at the Colony Club or if you were Jewish, at Viola Wolfe's, while their brothers drilled with the Knickerbocker Greys at the 67th Street Armory. Originally linked with Patriotic and Historical Societies such as the National Society of Colonial Dames and the Society of Mayflower Descendants this organization appeals to any child who simply likes history and tin soldiers. Since 1881 the Knickerbocker Greys has offered boys (and now girls) ages 6–16 the opportunity to participate in parades, reviews and civic ceremonies in New York City. (Remember when you had to join the Girl Scouts just to march in the Memorial Day parade?) The Greys is not a military organization but they use precision drill and the "pomp and circumstance of beautiful old uniforms." Meetings are held twice a week, attendance is required only one of the two days.

GLOSSARY

Alternative Forms of Testing: Testing that is not standardized, but rather a measure of an individual child's capabilities and progress relative to himself, not to other children. The most popular trend in alternative testing is portfolio assessment: A child will select his best work from the whole semester or year, and submit this work instead of taking a standardized test. This gives the child's judges the ability to gauge the child's progress over the course of the term, and gives them a fuller picture of the child's abilities, rather than a brief snapshot from a test taken on one particular day.

Child-Centered Program: A program in which learning in the classroom is facilitated by the teacher and directed by the students. Activities require active learning and motivation on the part of the student; the teacher does not lecture to a passive class. The phrase "child-centered program" is also used to describe a program in which a child is presented with age-appropriate, meaningful curricula.

Chicago Math: Chicago Math is a program developed at the University of Chicago that teaches children to reason logically, see mathematical patterns and relationships, and understand the usefulness of math in everyday life. Manipulatives, math games and literature are woven into the curriculum to develop abstract mathematical thinking while reinforcing computational concepts.

Classic Curriculum: Featured in traditional schools. A classic curriculum always includes Shakespeare, Virgil and the Greeks. The goal is "a cultured mind nourished by the humanist tradition."

Collaborative Learning: In a classroom that subscribes to collaborative learning, the students work in groups. It is assumed an individual student will be motivated to work because he or she will feel responsible to the group, that a student will learn to clarify his thinking through the need to articulate and debate his ideas within the group, and further, that he will learn new ways of thinking when he analyzes the ideas of other group members.

Cum Laude Society: The Cum Laude Society is an honor society modeled on Phi Beta Kappa, which has member chapters in several New

York City independent high schools. The purpose of the Cum Laude Society is the encouragement and recognition of academic excellence. Many chapters (particularly at schools that no longer rank students or do not give grades) make selections by such criteria as character, honor and integrity. New York City independent schools with member chapters and year of induction are: Berkeley Carroll School, Brooklyn, 1989; Collegiate School, 1922; Horace Mann School, 1951; Packer Collegiate Institute, Brooklyn, 1976; Poly Prep Country Day School, Brooklyn, 1908; The Riverdale Country School, 1922; Trinity School, 1934.

D'Nealian Handwriting Method: Using the D'Nealian method young children are taught to form print letters with loops and rounded angles so that the transition to cursive writing later on is easier and more natural.

Departmentalization: When students leave their homeroom classroom to go to specialists for core subjects.

Different Learning Styles: This phrase refers to the idea that students learn in different ways, and under different conditions. Some students learn best from reading in a quiet room; other students learn best when engaged in debate. Teachers who subscribe to this theory will try to provide experiences that will accommodate different kinds of learners.

Experiential Learning: Learning through hands-on activities and first-hand experiences.

Integrated Curriculum: A curriculum organized around a central theme. All areas of study (reading, writing, math, science, social studies, art and music) are used to investigate this theme. In this way, the children learn process and content within a unified context. "Core curriculum" is a term that is often used synonymously.

Interage, Mixed-Age or Flexible Class Grouping: Classes that are not grouped according to calendar age. There might be a two-year age span within the class composed of children with "a diversity of achievement, capacity, talent and style, but who have enough intellectual and social congruence to work well together" (Bank Street School for Children brochure).

International Baccalaureate: The I.B. is an internationally recognized curriculum and examination. The I.B. diploma is required for admission to many foreign universities. The I.B. program is administered from Geneva, Switzerland, and taught in over four hundred secondary schools in thirty-eight countries. It is a rigorous and demanding program; students must master a minimum of six subjects and demonstrate the ability to think clearly and communicate effectively. Many colleges and universities in the United States offer advanced placement and/or a year of college credit for superior performance on the I.B. Lycée Français and a very few other schools, all in Manhattan, offer an I.B. program.

Interschool: A consortium of eight New York City independent schools—Brearley, Chapin, Nightingale-Bamford, Spence (girls' schools); Browning and Collegiate (boys' schools); Dalton and Trinity (coed schools)—which share academic, extracurricular and administrative components.

Invented Spelling: What we all do when we try to spell a word: We make an educated guess. The use of this method allows children the freedom to write the words they may not know how to spell, instead of "dumbing down" their writing to avoid making mistakes. Invented spelling is used in a classroom for rough drafts; students must use the correct spellings of words for final copies.

ISAAGNY: Acronym for the Independent Schools Admissions Association of Greater New York. Composed of admissions directors and heads of early childhood programs, ISAAGNY was founded in 1965 in order to simplify and coordinate admissions procedures among independent schools in the New York Metropolitan area. It is now composed of approximately 150 member schools. ISAAGNY contracted with the Educational Records Bureau to administer uniform admissions testing. ISAAGNY also developed a uniform school report form and sets common notification and reply dates.

Kwanzaa: A seven-day African-American cultural holiday similar to traditional African harvest festivals. Kwanzaa means "first fruits" in Swahili. Kwanzaa coincides with the celebration of Chanukah and Christmas.

Learning Disability, Learning Disorder (LD or Learning Difference): The term currently used to describe a handicap that is neurological in origin, which interferes with a person's ability to store, process or produce information. The impairment can be quite subtle and may go undetected throughout life. The primary characteristic of a learning disability is a significant difference between overall intelligence and achievement in some areas according to the National Center for Learning Disabilities. If you or a school suspects that your child has a learning problem, your child will probably be asked to get an extensive psychoeducational evaluation.

Montessori Method of Education: Based on Dr. Maria Montessori's scientific observations of the behavior of young children who were orphaned, disadvantaged or, for other reasons, institutionalized. The Montessori approach encourages active, self-directed learning in a non-competitive environment. The Montessori classroom features multi-aged, multi-graded heterogenous groups and is based on the principle of freedom within limits. Children are free to work at their own pace with materials they have chosen, either alone or with others. Individual mastery is balanced with small group collaboration within the whole group community. The teacher relies on his or her observations of the children to determine which new activities and materials he may introduce to an individual child or to a small or large group. Several NYC Montessori schools that are members of the American Montessori Assocation, use an "eclectic" or "modified" approach, a comfort to those who think "pure" Montessori is too doctrinaire or rigid.

Multiculturalism: In the classroom, multiculturalism introduces subjects and authors that are not typically considered a part of the Western cultural canon. It is a theory of inclusion that allows many cultures a place in the curriculum, with the aim of increasing respect and understanding for the diverse populations of the world.

Multiple Intelligences: Intelligence is not restricted to a score on an I.Q. test but can encompass many areas of life. Some people may excel in music, some in leadership. These are not necessarily testable qualities, but they are forms of intelligence nonetheless.

People of Color (Children of Color) and Cultral Diversity: Inclusive terms of respect agreed upon by the National Association of Independent Schools' Committee on Diversity for people usually described as non-white ethnic minorities, including: African-Americans, Latinos,

51

Asian-Americans, Native Americans, Pacific Islanders and natives of Alaska.

Progressive vs. Traditional School: These terms are in disrepute these days. Many of the traditional schools have incorporated elements of progressive education into their elementary school classrooms. Progressive schools remain in the vanguard in their use of innovative educational practices. A traditional classroom may have a teacher at the front of the room lecturing to students sitting in rows; children are grouped homogeneously by ability level and generally work on the same material at the same time. A progressive school is more likely to have an informal or seminar-style classroom with more discussion and is one in which children work in small groups independently. We found that traditional schools tend to be the older, established single-sex schools, which have a Latin motto, concentrate on the Western or classical canon, have a dress code or uniform, a handbell choir and "quaint" traditions.

Revolving Loan: At a school without a significant endowment parents are asked to give an interest-free loan to the school, refundable when the student graduates or leaves for any reason.

Waldorf Education: The Waldorf method is based on the scientific observations and pedagogical insights derived by Rudolf Steiner (1861–1925), an Austrian scientist, philosopher, artist, and educator. At the heart of the Waldorf philosophy is the belief that education is an artistic process. Innovative teaching methods address the whole child, working to develop clarity in thought, balance in feeling, and conscience and initiative in action. In a pure Waldorf school, students stay with the same teacher from grades one through eight and create their own Main Lesson Books for their core subjects. Students create their own textbooks based on classroom instruction. There is an emphasis on using natural materials and the arts. The program includes knitting, folklore, crocheting and woodcarving usually reserved for the afternoons. A typical Waldorf curriculum offers phonics, grammar, English, two foreign languages (in many schools German is one of the languages), music, eurythmy (a form of music and movement), mythology, drama, art, crafts, science, math and world history. The school aims to encourage close human relationships that help students develop a strong sense of themselves and an awareness of others.

52

Whole Language: A practical body of ideas about education that originated in New Zealand with the seminal work of Sylvia Ashton-Warner. The connections between reading, writing and speaking are made complete in the Whole Language classroom. Students in a Whole Language classroom read literature (not basal readers) and write stories, plays and poems (instead of filling out workbooks). A Whole Language classroom uses an integrated curriculum, so learning centers around one subject. In this way, students learn both process (the mechanics of learning, like long division) and content (long division is used to answer a question about the subject under study) simultaneously. Learning becomes relevant to the student, and ceases to be an abstraction. There is some controversy surrounding Whole Language. Some educators would like to see more of the "old-fashioned methods," particularly an emphasis on phonics, included in any Whole Language program, and on drills for matters that must be remembered and reproduced quickly and accurately (such as multiplication tables, spelling, grammar).

Writing Across the Curriculum: Teachers who believe in writing across the curriculum will not confine writing to language arts; instead they will provide writing experiences throughout the curriculum. This will help students refine their writing and will demonstrate that writing can serve a variety of purposes and is used in many disciplines.

Writing Process or *Writers' Workshop:* The teaching of writing in which students are taught to discover what they think about the topic in question and to clarify those thoughts through the process of writing, editing, rewriting and publishing: 1) drafting (brain drain), 2) revising (sloppy copy), 3) editing (neat sheet), 4) finalizing (final fame). Grammar, usage and spelling are taught within the context of the individual student's writing needs rather than in isolation.

THE PRIVATE
SCHOOLS

The Abraham Joshua Heschel School

(Nursery–5th grade)
270 West 89th Street
New York, NY 10024
(212) 595-7087
website: www.heschel.org

(6th–8th grade)
314 West 91st Street
New York, NY 10024
(212) 595-7817

(9th–12th grade)
20 West End Avenue
New York, NY 10023
(212) 246-7717

Coed
Accessible

Ms. Roanna Shorofsky, Head of School
Ms. Marsha Feris, Director of Admissions

Birthday Cutoff   Children entering nursery school must be 3 by August 31
Children entering kindergarten must be 5 by August 31

Enrollment   Total enrollment: 640
Nursery 3's places: 25
Pre Kindergarten places: 16–18
Kindergarten places: 12–16
Graduating class size: approximately 40

Tuition Range 2005–2006 $15,990 to $25,000, Nursery 3's (1/2 day)–12th grade
Additional fees: for student activities and supplies, are approximately $500 to $675
Capital fund contribution: $850

After-School Program   Heschel After-School Program: until 5:30 P.M.; creative and recreational activities; an additional payment is required

The Heschel School was founded in 1983 by a group of Jewish educators and laymen. Named for a prominent scholar, philosopher and colleague of Martin Luther King, the school is not affiliated with a synagogue. The student body is composed of a broad spectrum of families from unaffiliated reform to modern orthodox. "Heschel is a Jewish school as opposed to a religious school," that uses a "holistic, child-centered approach." Girls participate fully in all aspects of the school.

Interest in Heschel is increasing because, one parent surmised, "Heschel is the answer to the current quest for spiritual renewal without being doctrinaire or rigid." Heschel is committed to Jewish ethics and values. There are social action projects on every level throughout the year. For instance, Pre-K children participated in the Common Cents penny harvest for the homeless; seventh graders collected blankets and brought them to Hale House.

Parents: A parent told us: "Heschel has a very West Side feeling even to a West Sider." According to her, "There are many professionals and lots of academics with Ph.D's—the type who subscribe to *Tikkun* magazine." Admissions looks for the child who is "bright, inquiring and verbal, who can contribute to the Heschel community." There is no dress code except for the yarmulke which must be worn during meals and Judaic studies.

Program: The Heschel School is rigorous and structured. Each class has two teachers all the way through fifth grade, and classes often break into many small groups; grades six through eight are departmentalized. Formal Hebrew and Judaic studies begin in first grade. Heschel's dual curriculum is composed of Jewish history, culture, and Hebrew language integrated with language arts, math, science, social studies and the arts. "The Jewish and secular curricula are intertwined in an organic and relevant way," parents say. Experiential learning is stressed and there is an emphasis on creativity and critical thinking. Computer projects are integrated into many curriculum areas.

The high school, opened in 2002, is housed in a state of the art facility that includes a chapel, full-sized gym, three science labs, library and art, music and dance studios. Every student has a laptop; the classrooms are wireless, as is the entire building. Students from Manhattan, Brooklyn, Queens, New Jersey and Westchester Jewish schools comprise most of the student body. The *sha'ar* program for students who have not previously attended a Jewish school offers intensive courses in Hebrew language, Bible and Jewish history. The dual (Jewish and general studies) curriculum is integrated with college prep. There is no specific community service requirement as service is an integral part of the school's culture.

The Abraham Lincoln School For Boys
The Abraham Lincoln School For Girls

12 East 79th Street
New York, NY 10021
(212) 744-7300, FAX (212) 744-5876
website: www.abrahamlincoln.org

Nursery–8th grade
partially accessible

Mr. William Fox, Headmaster
Mrs. Jennifer Merced, Director of Admissions
Mrs. Kathleen Kigel, The Ark Nursery School, Director

Birthday Cutoff   Children entering nursery school must be 3 years old by September 1
Children entering kindergarten must be 5 years old by September 1

Enrollment   50

Grades   Anecdotal reports and checklists starting in kindergarten

Tuition Range 2005–2006 $11,450 to $14,150, Nursery–8th grade

Financial Aid/Scholarship   25% of the student body receives some form of aid

After-School Program   Weekdays for AL students only from 3:15 P.M. to 4:30 P.M. An additional fee is required.

————

The Abraham Lincoln School is part of a worldwide group of associated schools that share the same values. The oldest of these is the St. James School in London, founded in 1975. The choice of name reflects a recognition of "the needs and traditions of America" according to the school's literature. The school building is an elegant landmark limestone townhouse which houses The School of Practical Philosophy in the evening. William Fox, the school's headmaster, was affiliated with the St. James Independent School before coming to New York.

Getting in: The school hosts an open house in the Fall. After applying, parents tour and meet with the director of admissions. Applicants are interviewed on a separate date; the ERB is required for kindergarten.

Program: Like The Ark Nursery School, now under its aegis, The Abraham Lincoln School is closely connected to The School of Practical Philosophy (a non-profit organization chartered by the Board of Regents of the State of New York). According to the brochure, The School of Practical Philosophy "draws upon the timeless teachings of both Western and Eastern traditions to discover the unifying principles that underlie human existence. The emphasis is on the practical application of these teachings."

Beginning in kindergarten, students learn the eighteen virtues over a two year cycle. Topics include, goodness, compassion, honesty, loyalty and truthfulness.

The teachers at the Abraham Lincoln School are all members of The School of Practical Philosophy: "All teachers have attended the School's teachers group for many years studying both teaching and their particular subject."

Many subjects are taught in separate boys and girls classes in the belief that boys and girls learn better when taught separately.

The school offers students such traditional subjects as reading, writing, mathematics, science, history, Latin and Spanish as well non-traditional studies: philosophy, scripture, and Sanskrit (the oldest extant language known to man and a model for the study of language in general.) The development of strong language skills is emphasized, with particular care given to the clear development of speech. Students examine the universal themes and principles found in the world's great philosophic and religious traditions in weekly philosophy classes.

Central Park is used for recreation and exercise.

Traditions   Abraham Lincoln Day, Speech Day, Penny Harvest, Festival of Lights, Book Fair, Holiday Concert, Field Day, Awards Day

The Alexander Robertson School

3 West 95th Street
New York, NY 10025
(212) 663-6441
e-mail: info@alexanderrobertson.com
website: www.alexanderrobertson.com

Coed
(Kindergarten–5th grade)
Not accessible

Rev. Leslie Merlin, Headmistress
Mrs. Cheryl Vasios, Director of Admissions

Birthday Cutoff Flexible

Enrollment Total enrollment: 75
Kindergarten–1st grade places: 15
1st grade places: 5
Graduating class size: Approximately 10

Grades Four terms
Letter grades begin in 4th grade

Tuition Range 2005–2006 $15,000 for all grades

Financial Aid/Scholarship There are no full scholarships; aid is available

Endowment N/A

After-School Program A variety of creative and recreational activities from 3:00 P.M. until 6:00 P.M. Monday through Friday, operated by Oasis Day Camp. A separate fee is required.

Summer Program The school acts as a host for the Oasis Day Camp.

Founded in 1789, The Alexander Robertson School is one of the oldest coeducational schools in the city. The school is named for its founder, a prosperous Scottish businessman and member of the

61

Second Presbyterian Church. Among the original students were immigrants and freed slaves. Although The Alexander Robertson School is still owned and operated by the Second Presbyterian Church, it is nonsectarian "while strongly espousing Judeo-Christian values and traditions." In 1998 the Reverend Leslie Merlin became Head of School. The Reverend Merlin was Associate Pastor of The Brick Presbyterian Church for eighteen years, and as such was closely associated with the Brick Church School. She taught in the U.S. and abroad before entering Princeton Seminary, where she received her Master of Divinity degree in 1976.

The student body represents the diversity of the surrounding neighborhood. The ERB is required for entering students. The style of the school is traditional and structured. The program follows a logical sequence through all grades with emphasis on basic skills and study habits. Teachers are sensitive to individual learning styles and differences.

The pre-first class focuses on socialization, exploration of the neighborhood and world, and beginning academic foundations. Reading through phonics is emphasized in first grade, with greater proficiency encouraged in second grade. Basic math skills are taught using traditional methods and manipulatives. Creative and critical thinking and writing skills are introduced and cultivated in the middle grades leading to clear, concise, expository writing, including reports in social studies and science in the upper grades. ARS's art program has earned awards for its students both locally and nationally. The music program includes movement, Orff instruments, recorder instruction, theory, introduction to the classics and vocal training. French is taught in all grades. Students bring their own lunch. The school has its own gym and also uses Central Park for recreation and science.

The Allen-Stevenson School

132 East 78th Street
New York, NY 10021
(212) 288-6710, FAX (212) 288-6802
website: www.allen-stevenson.org

All boys
Kindergarten–8th/9th grade
Not accessible

Mr. David R. Trower, Headmaster
Ms. Ronnie R. Jankoff, Director of Admissions

Uniform   Lower School: Allen-Stevenson polo shirt with emblem, pants (no jeans), sneakers allowed kindergarten–3, no sneakers grades 4–9
Middle and Upper Schools: blazer, dress shirts, tie and pants (no jeans)

Birthday Cutoff   Children entering kindergarten must be 5 by September 1
Children entering 1st grade must be 6 by September 1

Enrollment   Total enrollment: 380
Kindergarten places: approximately 42–45
Graduating class size: approximately 22–25

Grades   Semester system in the Lower School
Trimester system in the Middle and Upper Schools
Lower School students receive anecdotal reports and checklists
Letter grades begin in 5th grade
Departmentalization begins in 6th grade
Practice exam given in 6th grade
First final exam given in 7th grade

Tuition Range 2005–2006 $25,525 to $26,830, kindergarten–9th grade
All fees are included in the tuition
An alternative payment plan is offered through the Key Tuition Plan

Financial Aid/Scholarship Approximately 12%–14% of the student body receive some form of aid
$950,000 available

Endowment Approximately $16.4 million

Diversity Prep for Prep, Early Steps and Boys Club students are enrolled
Multicultural Committee for parents
Multicultural elements are incorporated into the curriculum at all levels

Homework Kindergarten: none
1st–3rd: 15–30 minutes
4th–6th: 1 to 1½ hours
7th–9th: 2½ to 3 hours

After-School Program Alligator Soup: open to A-S students only, with selected classes offered to Nightingale-Bamford students; kindergarten through 6th graders, 3:30–5:00 P.M., fall, winter and spring; a variety of creative and recreational activities; an additional payment is required
Middle School and Upper School intramural program
Junior varsity and varsity sports

Summer Program June Club: A 2-week sports and trip program open to A-S students and siblings from other schools; last 2 weeks in June. The 6-week summer day camp program is for kindergarten through 3rd grades. Second and 3rd graders may participate in either June Club or Summer Day Camp. The camp program offers a variety of creative and recreational activities; an additional payment is required.

The Allen-Stevenson School was founded in 1883 by Mr. Francis Bellows Allen, who was later joined by Mr. Robert Alston Stevenson as administrative head of the school. Allen-Stevenson was originally located in a brownstone next door to The Chapin School on East 57th Street. During this time, a group of A-S boys once climbed across the roof of the building and into the proper girls' school next door and were severely punished. Perhaps to avoid unnecessary temptation, in

1924 the A-S school moved uptown to its present location on East 78th Street. In the 1920s, A-S boys would roller skate and roll hoops to school whereas now they scooter. A-S is a traditional school with an emphasis on hands-on learning within a structured setting. A-S has always had an emphasis on physical hardiness, music and language arts. Parents say that A-S graduates are very well-rounded and well-mannered.

Allen-Stevenson is located on the Upper East Side. It has a neighborhood school character; parents say the school provides a small and warm community. As of Fall 2005, Allen-Stevenson will have completed a major renovation that will increase its physical space by fifty percent. Each division of the school now has its own level with flexible "town centers" for divisional meetings. There's also a new multi-purpose auditorium that holds up to four hundred people, a large library/media center, a separate Lower School library, a "Smart" classroom, an additional science lab, a science suite, a new music area, and art and woodworking space.

Getting in: The number of applications to A-S has increased over the past few years resulting in a much more competitive admissions process. After an application has been filed, parents tour the school with a parent tour guide. Parents meet individually with the director of admissions, then parents are invited back with their sons for a small group visit (six to eight boys). While the boys are busy in a classroom with members of the admissions staff, parents are invited to the library to watch a video about the school and to talk with the headmaster and the head of the Lower School. The visit lasts about one hour. The school maintains an active wait list and there is a sibling and legacy policy, but admission is not automatic. The most important criteria for admission is a good fit between the school, the boy and the family.

Parents: Parents are very comfortable at A-S. One parent described it as "an open, warm environment, a wonderful place." She described the parent body as "low key, with a lot of professional people." Another parent said, "It's a normal cross-section of independent school families." Annual class cocktail parties are held in the fall at parents' apartments. Fund-raising events include a Holiday Raffle, Book Fair and spring fund-raiser. There are annual holiday and spring concerts. New parents are invited to an evening reception at the school to meet the Lower School teachers and administrators. The school has no religious affiliation.

Program: Headmaster David Trower, who came from the Collegiate School, is credited with revising and updating the curriculum and attracting good faculty. Parents say, "Mr. Trower's door is always open and he goes out of his way to know you and your son," "He shakes every parent's and boy's hand." In a recent issue of *The Lamplighter* Mr. Trower is quoted on the tone of Allen-Stevenson: "Our strong academic expectations of the boys are set within a nurturing context. This combination makes Allen-Stevenson unique."

Allen-Stevenson has a very strong music program and boasts one of the finest elementary school orchestra programs in New York City. All students learn to sing and read music. The Middle School Chorus has sung on the White House Ellipse.

The Artist-in-Residence Program during Book Fair Week at A-S features an artist or writer with a specialty. One year while the kindergarten boys worked with a paper maker, older boys made beautiful bound-book covers. Artwork frequently coordinates with other subjects. For instance, fifth grade boys study ancient civilizations in history and in art class, reinterpreting the art of ancient civilizations: they make ceramic vessels based on ancient Greek vases decorated with narrative scenes or patterns. Trips to the museums support the study of "Ancients" in both art and history. The shop program is extensive and combines art and math skills. Beginning in seventh grade students select an elective arts course during the three weekly "creative" periods.

Public speaking and the dramatic arts are also important at A-S. Upper School boys participate in the annual public speaking contest. Every year there is a Middle School play with a student cast and crew. The popular fifth through ninth grade annual Gilbert and Sullivan production often includes faculty in cameo roles or chorus. A classic American play is produced by seventh graders. Girls from the Nightingale-Bamford School play the female roles in the annual Upper School Shakespeare production as well as the sixth grade and seventh grade plays.

At A-S technology is used to enhance teaching and learning. Boys are taught how, when and why to use computer systems beginning in kindergarten and technological tools are appropriately used by teachers and students in every grade as aids for thinking, producing and presenting work in all areas of the curriculum.

The Lower School at A-S is composed of grades kindergarten through third. Parents say that the Lower School has a non-pressured approach to learning. The teachers employ an eclectic array of materials to teach basic concepts and skills. Reading, writing and math skills are taught in small, fluid groups. There are computers in all of the classrooms. In addition to their classroom teachers, boys interact regularly with a science specialist, art and music teachers, computer teachers and the Physical Education staff. Artwork displayed throughout the school reflects A-S's commitment to the integration of the art into the overall curriculum. At the first of many science fairs, Lower School boys participate in "The Invention Convention," an exercise in problem solving. One boy solved the problem of soap sinking in the bathtub (he inserted a cork), another solved the problem of the spoon sinking into the sauce pot with a magnetic spoon holder. Seventh through ninth graders participate in the annual Science Fair while fourth through sixth graders have their own Science Festival each winter.

Middle School at A-S is composed of grades fourth through sixth. The boys now wear navy blue blazers with the school emblem on the pocket, a dress shirt and tie. Toward the end of third grade, the boys are invited by the fourth grade to a special "tie ceremony" where they are taught how to knot a tie.

The goal of the Middle School program is to develop a student's abilities and self-confidence so that he can begin to take more responsibility for his own learning. Critical thinking is emphasized in English. Science instruction encourages investigation, observation and interpretation of information. In mathematics boys now explore conceptualization, problem solving and logical interpretation of math facts. Fourth graders study map skills and geography as it applies to explorers and exploration as well as current events. The fifth grade history program covers The "Ancients": Near East, Egypt, Greece and Rome, integrating art, music and literature. Sixth graders begin the study of American history which continues into seventh grade. The school library is completely computerized with CD-ROM, on-line access, and a variety of on-line data base subscriptions. Middle and Upper School boys use the computer for writing and research. The Learning Resource Center offers support to students needing extra help in acquiring study skills and strategies as well as enrichment at all levels.

The level of work becomes more demanding in the Upper School (grades seven through nine) as the boys prepare for secondary school admissions. Critical reading of both classical and contemporary literature is emphasized. The boys also complete large "theme projects" such as "Facing History," an inter-disciplinary program dealing with the social implications of the Holocaust. The history curriculum incorporates geography and covers the study of the U.S. and the world.

Upper School mathematics covers the study of algebra, geometry and introductory trigonometry. The science curriculum is designed to develop scientifically literate, independent researchers who are ecologically aware and informed about global issues. Weekly labs provide hands-on experience in life science, physical science and biology.

Study of a contemporary foreign language is introduced in sixth grade with a choice between French or Spanish. Language fundamentals are made clear through the study of Latin, introduced in third grade. The Arts are taught by professional artists and musicians. Art and music courses are required through seventh grade; afterward they are offered as electives.

In keeping with the longstanding emphasis on physical hardiness at A-S, there is ample opportunity for exercise. Boys in the Lower School go to Central Park for "field" three times a week. There is gym on the other days. "A certain level of fitness is expected," said one parent. Another parent said, "The A-S boys are sports-minded but it's not a jock school." A-S offers ice hockey at Chelsea Piers and swimming at the Asphalt Green Aquatic Center. Team sports begin in Middle School. Upper School boys go to Randalls Island four times a week in the spring and fall. School colors are blue and gold. One of Allen-Stevenson's big rivals is The Buckley School, just down the avenue.

Allen-Stevenson has traditional Lower School weekly assemblies that feature a variety of guest speakers, class performances, poetry readings and so forth. At Middle and Upper School weekly "morning meetings" a member of the faculty will discuss subjects of concern to the A-S community. Topics have included the AIDS epidemic, community service projects and alternatives to watching television.

Project Charlie, the anti-drug program, begins in first grade. Education about health issues is part of the curriculum in grades seventh through ninth, including AIDS prevention. Seventh through ninth graders attend an advisory period once a week to discuss a variety of issues.

Boys participate in special projects in community service throughout their years at A-S. Ninth graders hold Community Service Week and are required to perform twenty hours of community service.

Extracurricular activities in the Upper School include: orchestra, theatre, yearbook, chorus, photography, painting, woodworking, printmaking, newspaper and student council. (Music rehearsals are scheduled so that they don't interfere with other extracurricular activities.)

Special privileges for ninth graders include overnight trips, the use of the seminar room and permission to leave school for lunch once a week.

There are numerous awards in recognition of excellence at A-S. The Anthony G. Couloucoundis Memorial Award is presented to a sixth grader for "scholastic excellence; all-around participation in athletics, the arts and community service and above all, the gift of friendship." Other awards distributed on Prize Day include the Alumni Medal, DAR Medal, an athletic award, the Charles E. Horman Award for Independence of Spirit and for Citizenship as well as awards in many of the academic disciplines, creative writing, public speaking, Latin, music, shop, art and drama. Closing ceremonies are held in the upper gym.

Graduates attend a variety of New York City independent secondary schools and boarding schools.

Traditions Founders' Day, Grandparents' Day, Mother's Day Lunch, Father/Son Breakfast, Father/Son Dinner, Holiday Concert, Spring Concert, Headmaster for a Day, Dinosaur Parade, Field Day, Science Fair, Book Fair, Arts Festival, Middle and Upper School picnic, annual Gilbert and Sullivan production, annual Shakespeare play, Young Alumni Day

Publications Alumni publication: *The Lamplighter*
Lower School literary magazine: *Rabbit Pie*
Middle School literary magazine: *What We Write*
Upper School literary magazine: *Pages*
Newspaper: *The Allen-Stevenson Weekly*
Yearbook: *The Unicorn*

Community Service Requirement Special projects in Middle and Upper School; 20 hours in 9th grade; 9th grade Community Service Week

Hangout The steps outside school

Bank Street School For Children

610 West 112th Street
New York, NY 10025
(212) 875-4420 (main number)
(212) 875-4433 (admissions), FAX (212) 875-4454
website: www.bankstreet.edu

Coed
3's–13's (interage groupings)
Accessible

Mr. Reuel Jordan, Dean of Children's Programs
Ms. Betsy Hall, Director of Admissions

Birthday Cutoff   September of the year of entry

Enrollment   Total enrollment: 430 in 2004–2005
Nursery 3's places: 16
4's places: 25
5's places: 5–10
Graduating class size: approximately 40–44

Grades   Semester system
No letter or numerical grades
Bi-yearly parent conferences and reports
Departmentalization begins in the 10's (beginning of Upper School)
No formal exams or testing but there are "curriculum tests" and standardized tests in the Upper School

Tuition Range 2005–2006 $20,595 to $23,200, Nursery 3's–13's
Tuition payment plan available

Financial Aid/Scholarship   Approximately 33% of the student body receive some form of aid

Endowment $1.3 million; Bank Street's capital campaign exceeded its goal of $25 million

Diversity   Approximately 34% of the student body is diverse; Parents Multicultural Committee; Parents of Children of Color group;

Teachers of Children of Color Group; Teacher of Color Group; Kids of Color Group; The Buddy Program
Prep for Prep students and Early Steps students enrolled

Homework   6/7's: When appropriate
7/8's: 30 minutes, builds to 3 nights a week
8/9's: 45 minutes, 4 nights a week
9/10's: 1 hour, 5 nights a week
10/11's, 11/12's: 1½–2 hours, 5 nights a week
12/13's, 13/14's: 2–2½ hours, 5 nights a week
There are group and individual assignments

After-School Program   Bank Street After-School Program: for children ages 4 and up; 3:15–6:00 P.M., five days a week
Children 5 years and older have a variety of activities to choose from including: sports, art, violin, woodworking, puppetmaking, theater, judo, flute and quilt making
An extended day program of supervised play is available from 4:30 P.M. until 6:00 P.M.
School vacation program: Bank Street operates a full day program of activities for children age 4 and older
These programs require an additional payment

Summer Program   Bank Street Summer Camp: during the last weeks of June and the month of July

---

The Bank Street School, a demonstration school for children, is part of the prestigious Bank Street College of Education which also includes an independent Graduate School of Education, a Division of Continuing Education and the Bank Street Bookstore. The Bank Street School uses the "developmental interaction" approach to education, which is based on the views of visionary educator Lucy Sprague Mitchell.

Lucy Sprague Mitchell, the founder of the Bureau of Educational Experiments (which later became Bank Street) was part of a group of educators in the 1920s who believed that children learn best "when they are involved in the process of learning, in a developmentally appropriate environment." Concurrent with this philosophy is the belief that children construct meaning out of interaction with the world—they learn best from direct experience. Mitchell's vision of the "classroom as a

71

community" was very different from the nineteenth-century "factory worker model" for schools. Today at Bank Street these elements of "progressive" education are put into practice with a diverse group of children, backed up with a dedicated and highly skilled staff.

Lucy Sprague Mitchell also believed that when children learn to be members of classroom groups that work together and care about each other's welfare, this lesson will extend to caring about the welfare of the society in which we live. The Bank Street College of Education was involved in designing the Civil Rights Act of 1965 and the Head Start and Follow Through Programs.

Getting in: By November, parents should call for the dates of the Fall open houses and register for one. At the open house we attended in early November, the school's spacious auditorium was packed. Parents are shown a video that illustrates the philosophy of the school. This video was unique—not a public-relations tool but a real snapshot of classroom life. A tour of the school is given after the open house and parents sit in on classes as part of the admissions process once they apply. If you then decide that this school would be right for your family, call for an application. The WPPSI is not required for admission to the Lower School but ERB testing is required for admission to the Upper School starting at age ten. Parents bring their child to Bank Street for a small group interview (approximately four to five children); separation is handled gently. Parents observe two classrooms for about ten to fifteen minutes while their child is being interviewed. The final step in the process is the parent interview in which there is an exchange of information. The interviewer will share what she observed about your child. Parents might be asked, "What are you looking for in the next twelve years?" In addition to a diverse student body, the brochure says the school "seeks children who give evidence of becoming adventurous learners and who will use the school experience well." An admissions committee of eight staff members makes the final decision.

Parents: Parents describe the atmosphere at Bank Street as informal: "Everyone is on a first-name basis." Many professors from nearby Barnard College and Columbia University send their children to Bank Street. Although one parent said, "There's more money at Bank Street now than there was before," Bank Street is committed to a diverse student body and 33 percent of the student body receive some form of financial aid. Parents are welcome everywhere in the school. "In Lower School you might see ten parents listening in at morning meeting," a mother told us. The cafeteria is the gathering place for parents in the morning. Potluck breakfasts and dinners are held. Parents often serve on committees or task forces; for example, recently both the music curriculum and the Spanish program were reviewed. Parent education is an important component of Bank Street. The school conducts a series of evening classes for parents about how math is taught to their children. Parents say that the administration is always "looking, questioning, improving" the school.

The Parents Association consists of four elected officers and a president and vice-president for each division (Lower, Middle and Upper). In addition, the class parents meet with the dean of children's programs. There are a number of fund-raising activities undertaken in an effort to boost teacher's salaries.

Since holidays are not celebrated at Bank Street, the Bank Street Winter Fest is an eagerly anticipated community celebration. Each year a central theme is chosen for the event (a celebration of the winter solstice). The whole school gets involved by writing skits, creating scenery and costumes, and performing. Tickets are free for this three-night event. There is also a Fall Fair and Auction.

Program: The program at Bank Street requires a lot of student initiative but the teachers are there to back students up. "They have an amazing amount of energy for the children," a parent said. Graduate students from the Bank Street College of Education do their student practicum within the classrooms. There are two teachers in every classroom until fifth grade, then two core teachers for math and humanities. One-third of the teachers at Bank Street are men. A typical 4/5's classroom of twenty-one children has a head teacher (who holds a master's degree), a full-time assistant, one or two graduate assistants, lots of blocks, puzzles, books, art materials, snails, and plants.

The teachers at Bank Street "lead from behind" rather than lecturing in front of the classroom. They are actively involved with the students, guiding them in their choices. "The teaching is always adapted to the child's style, that's what they pride themselves on," a parent told us. Teachers are encouraged to derive much of the curriculum from student interests and from the students' cultures or environments.

The Lower School is composed of ages three through six. Flexible or mixed-age groupings are used throughout Bank Street. In addition to the 3's, there are two 4/5's classrooms and two 5/6's classrooms. There is typically a 14 month age span within the classroom groupings. Smaller groups are formed for reading and math. Activities are geared to the appropriate developmental level of the child. For instance, "pre-operational" thinkers are not pushed to master a task that will come naturally at age seven. The brochure says "the creation of meaning is the central task of childhood." In practice, children make sense out of concrete experience using concrete materials. (Bank Street students were among the first to use the Cuisenaire rods, unifix cubes and pattern blocks that have become standard materials used to teach math in many elementary school classrooms.) These are noisy, productive classrooms—there is the time and space for exploration, and a forty-five minute "block-time" is built into each day. There is, however, an underlying structure. Each day begins with a meeting at which students exchange ideas and learn to listen to each other. All of the students have classroom "jobs" that they take very seriously. Parents say students learn organizational skills right from the beginning.

The daily schedule posted in the meeting area usually includes reading, writing, math, music, movement, gym time and recess and Spanish exposure. (By sixth grade students choose Spanish or French.) The youngest children play on the deck for one hour each day. Older students use Riverside Park. In the Lower School, movement, gymnastics and imaginative improvisation are all part of the physical education program. Students ten and older participate in interschool teams in soccer, basketball and softball.

The writing program includes teaching of reading from a literature-based program and involves all areas associated with language: listening, speaking and writing. (The Bank Street Readers were the first multiracial readers geared to young children growing up in an urban environment.) Recently, a 4/5's class visited the Bank Street Bookstore and then made their own bookstore in the classroom that they ran for one week as a real store. They sold library books and homemade books and ordered books by telephone. Other classes and parents came in. The money they made was donated to a charity.

The Middle School at Bank Street comprises ages six through ten. Students leave the classroom for woodworking, art, music and gym. The class often breaks into half groups; one-half of the class will go to computer lab while the other half does math in the classroom. In these years, students make the connection between the use of the concrete materials (Cuisenaire rods, unifix cubes and blocks) and the use of symbols.

In science students conduct experiments with natural and synthetic matter; they learn about simple machines. They examine hermit crabs and salamanders, and they experiment with the Nile Delta Stream table.

Beginning in first grade, the students break into student-led reading response groups in which four to five students read the same book and discuss it. Parents say, "At Bank Street the children's opinions are really valued." By the 7/8's "they're picking magnificent books to read by themselves." Students write and revise their own work with their peers acting as gentle "critics." Using the computer the students then "publish" their work, which becomes part of the classroom library. There are two computer labs with Macintosh and PC computers and students begin writing on the computer in the 7/8's. Parents say there is a lot of independent reading and writing under the watchful eye of the teacher(s). Because of the low student-teacher ratio, learning difficulties are recognized quickly and a reading specialist works with children in the classroom.

Field trips are often integrated into the writing program. All students write in notebooks every day.

Beginning with the 6's, students visit the art studio and woodworking shop. Students are introduced to many media including: sculpture, weaving, batiking and printmaking. Art is frequently integrated into the curriculum. Murals are done in groups—we saw an impressive "Egyptian" collaborative mural.

In the Lower School the social studies curriculum expands from the study of neighborhood and community to the study of how people work in New York City.

Middle Schoolers completed a core study of the Hudson River. A class of 6/7's studied buildings around the city and the students created their own neighborhood complete with video store, pizza shop, and grocery store, all made from wooden crates which they painted and furnished. This "crate city" was then peopled with handmade puppets.

A group of 7/8's studying the evolution of Central Park learned about the original design of the park, talked with the present day Parks Commissioner, and drew their own maps. The unit culminated in the creation of a huge papier-mâché model of Central Park displayed in the school's lobby.

The music program is multicultural and the Orff method is used. The 7/8's learn to play the recorder. There are instrumental ensembles and chorus in the Middle and Upper School, and a new string program.

The Upper School is composed of ages ten through thirteen. For Upper School students, a team comprising the Core (social studies and language arts), and math and science teachers provide the home base for each class. In addition to content, these teachers serve as advisors and are first in line to speak with family members or other support people. Students leave their classrooms for art, woodworking, music, drama and Spanish in the 8/9s and 9/10s. Science is taught to the 9/10s three times a week. All older children elect Spanish or French and go to those rooms for instruction. They have physical education four times a week and in addition to the arts that are integrated into the academic subjects, students also study art, shop and music. As in the rest of the school, students learn using both traditional and experimental methods. Each age group takes day trips and an overnight trip. Each learns how to do research and participates in role-playing and simulations based on this research. For example, the 13's/14's participate in a Mock Congress, and go on a four-day trip to Washington, D.C. during which they speak directly with members of Congress. Classes publish and share their research projects via handmade books, displays, "coffee houses," newspapers and magazines. Each year, in Science Expo, teams of students conduct real scientific investigations and share their results with the community. One student wrote about "our debt to the Greeks" after her Washington trip.

The 13's may leave the school building for lunch only.

Bank Street graduates attend a variety of independent day schools (Fieldston and Dalton are popular choices) and New York City public schools.

Traditions   Fall Fair, potluck dinners and breakfasts, theatre party, parents' fund-raiser dance, Tuesday morning meetings, overnight class trips (beginning with the 9/10's), Washington, D.C., trip for 13's, Winter Fest (celebration of the winter solstice), 13's play/musical, Spring Concert, alumni reunions, Arts Day

Publications   Student Literary Magazine: *The Cornucopia*
Newsletter: *School for Children Network*
Yearbook
Various publications of Bank Street College Parents Association:
PA Newsletter: *Connections*

Community Service Requirement   None; the Upper School students have community service projects within the school

Hangouts   Famiglia Pizza, Samad's Deli, New Nacho, Mama's, (Students often bring back food to eat in the cafeteria)

The Berkeley Carroll School

Lower Division (Pre-Kindergarten–Grade 4)
701 Carroll Street
Brooklyn, NY 11215
(718) 638-1703

Middle and Upper Divisions (Grades 5–12)
181 Lincoln Place
Brooklyn, NY 11217
(718) 789-6060, FAX (718) 398-3640
website: www.berkeleycarroll.org
e-mail: bcs@berkeleycarroll.org

Coed
Pre-Kindergarten–12th grade
Not accessible, Lower Division
Accessible for 5th–12th grade

Dr. Richard F. Barter, Headmaster
Henry Trevor, Associate Head of School for Institutional Advancement

Birthday Cutoff   Children entering kindergarten should be 5 by September 30 but readiness is key

Enrollment   Total enrollment: 750
  Pre-K places: 40
  Kindergarten places: 15
  1st grade places: 10
  6th grade places: 10
  9th grade places: 15
  Graduating class size 2004: 48

Grades   Trimester system, Pre-K through 12.
  In all grades, extensive narrative written reports twice a year, as well as family conferences. Beginning in 7th grade, students accompany parents at conferences.
  Letter grades and Honor Roll begin in 6th grade
  Departmentalization in English, History and Math begins in 5th grade

78

Required foreign language study begins in 5th grade
First final exam begins in 8th grade

Tuition Range 2005–2006 $11,000 to $22,950, Pre-K (1/2 day)–12th grade
Lunch fee for grades 5–11: $890

Financial Aid/Scholarship   Approximately 30% of the student body receives some form of aid

Endowment $2.5 million

Diversity   14 Prep for Prep students as of Fall 2004
Early Steps participant
Seeking Educational and Diversity Program: A reading and discussion group for faculty and parents
Perspectives on Diversity Committee of Parent Association: Sponsors cultural activities
Faculty Study Group on Equity & Diversity: Advises the school on ways to insure student gender equity in all disciplines, as well as multicultural studies; vigorous recruitment of faculty applicants of color

Homework   Kindergarten: Begins in the spring with "think about" assignments one night per week
1st: Twice a week, 15–30 minutes
2nd–4th: nightly, Monday–Thursday, 30–60 minutes, lengthening as age increases.
4th: all assignments are given at the beginning of the week to facilitate longer-range planning. Longer term projects are added
5th/6th: 1$1/2$ hours per night
7th/8th: 2–2$1/2$ hours per night
9th/12th: 3 hours per night

After-School Program   Extended day program and early morning (7:30 A.M.) for Berkeley Carroll students only: for Lower Division, from 3:00 P.M. until 6:00 P.M. A variety of academic, creative and recreational activities; an additional payment is required
Interscholastic and intramural athletic competition for Grades 5–12
Music and voice instruction available

Summer Program   The Berkeley Carroll Summer Programs run from mid-June through mid-August and are open to students from other schools; an additional payment is required for all summer programs

Summer Day Camp: for Pre-K–4th graders; a variety of creative and recreational activities including swimming trips and weekly BBQ

Creative Arts Camp: for 8–14 year olds; a variety of creative and recreational activities with an emphasis on the performing and visual arts

---

The Berkeley Institute, named in honor of Bishop George Berkeley, was founded in 1886. Bishop Berkeley envisioned a white glove school in which the classics were taught along with the arts. One hundred and ten years later the Bishop's vision is only a tintype memory. In 1982 the institute merged with the Carroll Street School, a growing Montessori-based elementary school. In 1996, The Berkeley Carroll School was one of four independent schools in the NYC area to be designated a Blue Ribbon School by the U.S. Department of Education.

Tucked away in the heart of Brownstone Brooklyn, within walking distance of the Brooklyn Botanic Garden, the Brooklyn Museum and Prospect Park, the Berkeley Carroll School's four coed divisions are housed on two campuses only four blocks apart. "Class Links" programs provide opportunities for the youngest toddlers to mingle with senior students, for activities such as crafting pottery or a walk in the park.

A capital campaign completed in 1992 nearly doubled the space of the Lincoln Place (Middle and Upper School) campus and the award-winning classroom complex also houses administrative offices, a student commons, and floor-through Visual Arts Center. In 1994 a new Media Center was added, a new athletic center opened in 2001 and BC just added a child care center for 1 to 3 year olds.

Getting in: Parents can attend one of the many open houses that are offered in the Fall which include a tour of the school and Q and A sessions with current parents. The school's Parent Ambassador program links prospective families with other BC parents in their neighborhood.

All Lower School applicants are tested and interviewed on site by the Admissions Director. Candidates for grades kindergarten through four must be tested by the ERB. Berkeley Carroll looks for students who are a good match for the program, "A child who is bright and motivated and demonstrates an interest in learning and doing." Middle and Upper School Admissions Director Christopher Weeks told us: "Every student we enroll brings distinctive strengths so that students may excel in all areas—academics, the arts and athletics."

Parents: Parents automatically become members of the Parent Association. The PA sponsors parenting workshops and a speakers bureau to which two speakers are invited each year. Recent guests include Terry Anderson, Anna Quindlen, Terry McMillan and Jonathan Kozol. Parents are also welcome to assist in the classroom, serve on committees, volunteer at the library, and accompany children on trips. At BC parents have a real voice in how their school is run because they serve on the school's 25 member Board of Trustees where they comprise the majority of members. But Dr. Zubay, the former head, was quick to note that the school is "not a parent co-op." The Administration remains firmly in charge of academic direction, class placement and faculty appointments.

Parents who are also authors (and there are quite a few) sign their latest books at the two PA book fairs. Parents created the elementary division's Law Day, helping students stage mock trials at one of which the appropriate sentence for the Wolf in Little Red Riding Hood was adjudicated. Parents also organize and participate in Career Day at which students have the opportunity to create architectural models, write legal briefs and so on. Parents are involved in the social life of the school from planning a year-end trip for graduating seniors to organizing the fifth grade bowling party.

Program: Active hands-on learning is the credo of the Berkeley Carroll School and there is an emphasis on writing, both expository and creative. In a pre-school classroom you might see several children stroking the ears of the class rabbit while charting its growth with pencil and paper. Others will be working independently on a classic Montessori activity such as fitting cylindrical shapes into self-correcting slots or might be gathered around the head teacher, mastering the "M" sound by carefully tracing the shape of a sand-paper letter. Children in grades kindergarten through fourth have swimming classes twice a week.

Reading activities begin in kindergarten in a self-paced instructional setting. Many learning styles are accommodated; worksheets are available for those children who gravitate to them. Phonics and whole-language approaches are used to teach reading and all children work one-on-one with the Head Teacher. To complete a book is more than an exercise in pronouncing the words: children master vocabulary and answer reading comprehension questions after which they are "given" the book as part of their personal "library." By the end of the year, some six-year-olds have acquired a library of 12 books or more, testament to their diligent efforts.

The Lower School at BC is housed in two buildings. There is a weekly assembly program. Students receive a solid grounding in the basics through an integrated approach to learning. A first-grade unit on "community" might include activities related to the history of the school, and include field trips to several social service organizations. Second grade students studying Native-American cultures might play Inuit games in physical education. Third graders studying China make Chinese puppets. Parents praise Maxine Barnett, a third grade teacher, for her "incredible ability to reach all children, whether it's a child in the middle, lower or upper portion of the class. She excels with every child." According to tradition, fourth graders studying the history of the American experience in the Westward Expansion, transform their classroom into a 19th century schoolroom for Caddie Woodlawn Day.

The teaching of writing begins with journals in first grade and progresses to include the use of dialogue, appropriate punctuation and grammar skills. In science, Lower School students study the life cycle of myriad creatures, make life-sized models of the human body complete with all the internal organs, and create papier-mâché models of the solar system.

Field trips are an integral part of the curriculum beginning in pre-school with visits to pumpkin farms and to dramatic performances. Starting in fifth grade all students take a full-week trip away from the BC campus. Fifth-graders journey to Nature's Classroom in Rhode Island for an adventure in team-building, scientific exploration and dramatic play.

After-school programs in music includes instruction in virtually all instruments and voice. Older children can select from a large variety of mini-courses including: cooking, quilting, chess, puppet-making, fencing, and gardening. The Lower School division participates year-round in the nationally recognized Hands-on-Science program.

The Middle School program at BC "recognizes that children are going through major developmental hurdles. We watch and guide children in every aspect of this development." In fifth grade students have three teachers for the five major subjects, with English/history and science/math taught as core subjects. A mandatory foreign language, either French or Spanish is then added. By sixth grade, students are grouped according to skill level in foreign language and math. Latin is an option beginning in seventh grade. English and history are still taught as "core" subjects. By seventh grade, the curriculum is entirely departmentalized. Subjects are explored in depth and often involve multi-week projects. Sixth graders, for example, stage a December Aztec Day, during which one classroom is turned into a marketplace and another becomes a temple. Visitors meet Montezuma and Cortez as well as a priestess who explains the unusual 20-month calendar. Eighth graders use a study of Robinson Crusoe to discuss utilization of natural resources. During a symposium on tropical rain forest supervision, students play the roles of farmers, rubber tappers, eco-tourism developers, miners and environmentalists, all struggling to co-exist. Historical novels supplement the curriculum. All eighth graders take a full-year world history and geography course.

The fifth grade writing curriculum stresses the conventional five paragraph essay. Middle School students gradually master expository and creative writing. At all grade levels, revision is a major component of the writing process and there is extensive peer and teacher review. The foundation of the Middle School math curriculum is mastery of the basics with an emphasis on creative problem solving, such as finding the most efficient route for a city sanitation crew. Advanced students finish algebra by the end of eighth-grade—some more quickly than others. Seventh graders study tessellations and their relationship to Islamic art. Pi Day (not coincidentally on 3/14 of each year) allows students to derive an approximation of pi using a "human" circle chain.

Science courses in the Middle Division begin with general science in fifth grade, life science in sixth, physical science in seventh and earth science in eighth grade with lab work at the core of each year's curriculum. There are several computer labs at BC. All campuses are hooked up to the Internet and the school's e-mail system allows for virtual links among teachers and between teachers and parents. The libraries are fully automated and use CD-ROMs.

In the Upper Division students model calculus derivatives on state-of-the-art calculators and computers. In 1996 the Upper Division science curricula were redesigned to put greater emphasis on bio-chemistry in the mandatory biology course. As a result, physics is taught in ninth grade, chemistry in tenth, and biology in the junior year. More than three quarters of the students take AP courses.

Choice within structure best summarizes the Upper Division at BC and students have several options in arts and athletics. A highly motivated student might play varsity baseball in the afternoon and sing in the choir at night. From ninth through twelfth grades, students take five core academic courses: history, science, English, math and foreign language. They also enroll in two rotating semester electives. (Fifteen electives are offered in everything from chamber orchestra and jazz band to photography and ceramics.) There are often multiple ways of meeting the course requirements—some more rigorous, others explore an interesting aspect of a familiar subject. For instance, juniors may opt for AP American History or select a course on Democracy in America or American Social and Cultural History.

Freshmen take a three period a week mandatory writing course in addition to English class. Sophomores must enroll in a twice-weekly health course; juniors and seniors have a mandatory college counseling requirement. All seniors participate in an internship program to explore an area of professional interest. The school helps them with placement and contacts; internships range from finance and medicine to photography, music, fashion and advertising. Foreign exchange opportunities are available for those who prefer a more far-flung experience. Each spring students from a school outside Paris spend two weeks with Berkeley Carroll tenth graders. BC students make a return trip to France. A companion program with a Spanish institution is another option. BCS is the first independent day school in the metropolitan area to host a small group of international students who will be enrolled for a full year at the school and live with BC families.

Athletics are an important part of the program at BC but this is not your typical "jock" school. Berkeley Carroll has won first place for four of the past five years in the independent schools judo championship. In the Middle Division, interscholastic teams are fielded in coed soccer, coed track, cross country, girls' volleyball, and there are strong boys' and girls' basketball teams. The girls' softball team posted undefeated seasons in recent years. Berkeley Carroll's varsity baseball team won the Baseball League of Independent Schools championship for five of the past six years.

Community service starts in the preschool years with food drives for Thanksgiving. Older children devise their own community service projects. By the time students reach the age of 18 they are volunteering in soup kitchens, geriatric centers or on park clean-up crews. Upper Schoolers are required to perform 50 hours of community service but many graduate with more than 200 hours.

Popular College Choices   Tufts, New York University, Wesleyan, Vassar, Syracuse, Columbia, University of Pennsylvania

Traditions   All-School Theme Write-In (recent topics include gender differences, justice and fairness, and leadership), Arch Day, Lower Division Spring Festival, Thanksgiving Sharing Assembly, Holiday Candle Lighting Ceremony, Middle and Upper Division Prize Day, Parent Association Speakers Bureau, Halloween Party, Sesame Place Trip and Annual Auction

Publications   Lower School quarterly creative-writing compendium: *Explorations*
Newspaper: *Blotter*
Literary magazine: *Reflections*
Yearbook: *The Lion*

Community Service Requirement   80 hours minimum for Upper Division students; all students participate

Hangout   Ozzie's Coffee Bar, Roma's Pizza, Prospect Park playing fields

The Birch Wathen Lenox School

210 East 77th Street
New York, NY 10021
(212) 861-0404
website: www.bwl.org

Coed
Kindergarten–12th grade
Accessible-elevator

Mr. Frank J. Carnabuci, Headmaster
Ms. Julianne Kaplan, Director of Admissions

Uniform   Lower School: *Boys* (grades K–5): Tan or gray trousers, white shirt with BWL logo; Wednesdays (dress-up day): dress tie and navy blazer with BWL logo; dress shoes. *Girls* (grades K–3): Early Fall and Spring, pink uniform jumper, white shirt with BWL logo, dress blouse or collared polo. Late Fall and Winter, dark blue and green plaid uniform jumper. *Girls* (grades 4 and 5): Early Fall and Spring, pink uniform skirt, white top with BWL logo; late Fall and Winter, dark green and blue plaid skirt, white top with BWL logo, dress shoes.

Middle School (grades 6–8): *Boys:* dress slacks or pants (not jeans), dress shoes, collared shirt or turtleneck; *Girls:* collared shirt or turtleneck, dress skirt (must be longer than fingers of extended arm) dress slacks or pants (no jeans); dress shoes, loafers, or docksiders.

Birthday Cutoff   No specific cutoff; most children entering kindergarten have turned 5 by the beginning of school

Enrollment   Total enrollment: 440
Kindergarten places: 30
Graduating class: approximately 35

Grades   Semester system in the Lower School and Upper Schools
Trimester system in the Middle School
Letter grades begin in 6th grade
Departmentalization begins in 6th grade

Tuition Range 2005–2006 $22,974 to $26,199, K–12th grade
Additional fees: for trips, books, lunch, PA dues, and activity fees, approximately $1,200. Lunch program ($1,200) is optional for 10th through 12th graders; there is a 12th-grade graduation fee of $585

Financial Aid/Scholarship   19% of the student body receive some form of aid

Endowment $5.2 million

Diversity   18% children of color

Homework
1st: 15–30 minutes, increasing during the year
2nd: approximately 30–45 minutes per night
3rd: and 4th: approximately 1 hour per night
5th: 1½ hrs per night
6th–8th: 20 to 40 minutes per subject per night
9th–12th: 3–4 hrs per night

After-School Program   Open to Birch Wathen Lenox students only; a variety of creative and recreational activities; extended day until 6:00 P.M. daily for Lower School; an additional payment is required
Junior varsity and varsity teams

Summer Program   none

———

In 1991, the Birch Wathen Lenox School was created by the merger of two established schools: The Lenox School (founded 1916) and The Birch Wathen School (founded 1921). The sale of the former Birch Wathen and Lenox School buildings created a substantial endowment enabling the school to weather the transition. Headmaster Frank Carnabuci, who had been the assistant head at The Dalton School for eleven years, brings administrative skills and enthusiasm to the job. He has been at the school for more than ten years. Parents say he knows every student by name and has implemented interesting new programs such as the Russian exchange, the overseas study program, and yearly schoolwide themes such as "The Year of

87

Mythology," "The Year of the Headline," and "The Year of New York City as a Classroom."

Getting in: The ERB is required for admission to the school. Parents tour and student interview/assessments are also part of the process.

The Birch Wathen Lenox school is a traditional school with a nurturing atmosphere.

Birch Wathen Lenox's strength is the ability to individualize the curriculum to fit the child. The student to teacher ratio is very small. Parents say, "Nobody falls through the cracks." Specialists work with tutors and parents to resolve learning difficulties.

The school has expanded by adding a new theater and renovating the gymnasium, and classrooms. An extra elevator will be installed and at least eight extra classrooms will be added to the school.

The BWL School offers a traditional, comprehensive academic program that features small classes (average of 12 students per class) and serves a range of students. The school is able to meet the needs of a wide range of abilities through the use of an academic tracking system that separates students into groups based on their ability levels in specific subject areas. Tracking is a method familiar to most baby boomers but has long been out of favor with educators and is considered by many to be "politically incorrect." BWL, bucking the trend, says, "An academic tracking system allows students to progress at a pace that appropriately challenges them, while ensuring the greatest degree of success."

The school is fully networked, with a T1 connection to the Internet. Computers are introduced in kindergarten. Students begin the study of French language and culture in fourth grade. Departmentalization begins in sixth grades in Middle School, where a traditional core of studies, including English, mathematics, history and science, and foreign language, are rounded out with computer science, music and art. In the Upper School, a traditional college preparatory program allows students more choices and independent study opportunities. Recently, three AP courses were added along with a nationally recognized Peer Leadership program.

BWL offers an overseas study program during spring break that enables students to go to France, Italy, Spain, Britain and various other locations. The program is linked to the school curriculum; daily assignments and a travel journal are required.

The extra-curricular athletic program is broad and includes championship teams in girls' volleyball and tennis, and championship boys' basketball, softball and soccer teams. The Middle School athletic program offers soccer, softball, basketball, track and field, tennis, ice hockey, golf, and swimming.

Popular College Choices   Princeton, Dartmouth, Cornell, Columbia, Connecticut College, Emory, Harvard, Washington University, RISD

Traditions   "Great food," Holiday Pageant at All Souls Church, Arch Day, Field Day, Spring Fair, "Year of" theme, Senior Art Calendar, Fall Convocation, 100 Nights Dinner, Harrison Moore Award, International Night

Publications

Lower School newspaper:	*The Upbeat*
Middle School Newspaper:	*The Black and White Ledger*
Upper School newspaper:	*The Clarion*
Alumni Magazine:	*The Banner*

Community Service Requirement

Middle School:	Grades 6,7,8	30 hours
Upper School	Grades 9,10	30 hours
	Grades 11,12	30 hours

The Brearley School

610 East 83rd Street
New York, NY 10028
(212) 744-8582 (main number) (212) 570-8600 (admissions)
website: www.brearley.org

All girls
Kindergarten–12th grade
Accessible–elevator

Dr. Stephanie J. Hull, Head of School
Ms. Winifred Mabley, Director of Lower School Admission
Ms. Joan Kaplan, Director of Middle and Upper School Admission
and Financial Assistance
e-mail: admission@brearley.org

Uniform   Lower School: navy blue jumper, socks and shirt can be any color, sneakers permitted but no clogs or boots
Middle School: navy-blue skirt, shirt or blouse (with sleeves), shoes or sneakers, sweat pants on cold days
Upper School: none

Birthday Cutoff   Girls entering kindergarten must have reached their 4th birthday on or before September 1 of the year in which they apply

Enrollment   Total enrollment: 675
Kindergarten places: 50–52
Graduating class size: approximately 45–50

Grades   Semester system
Kindergarten: parent conferences twice a year
Classes I–III: fall parent conference; spring narrative report
Class IV: fall parent conference; midyear and spring anecdotal reports with grades
Classes V–XII: marks are given in every subject with comments and suggestions
Classes V and VI: receive marks and comments four times a year
Classes VII and VIII: receive marks and comments three times a year
Departmentalization in science, music, physical education, library

and art begins in Lower School; math departmentalization begins in class IV; computer departmentalization in Class III
Exams: before class VII, classroom tests are informal and marks are averaged with the term's work; once-a-year examinations begin in class VII and are held in March

Tuition Range 2005–2006 $27,650 to $28,150, K–12th grade, which includes fees for books, supplies, trips, food, and/or snacks

Financial Aid   21% of the student body receives some form of aid; approximately $3 million was awarded in 2003–2004

Endowment   Market value as of June 30, 2004: $71,000,000

Diversity   28% of the student body; Brearley enrolls students from Prep for Prep, TEAK, The Oliver Program, A Better Chance, and Early Steps; Parent/Faculty Diversity Forum which meets weekly and holds a Festival of Cultures twice a year; Upper School students hold discussions about diversity led by elected student representatives

Homework   Lower School families are expected to read aloud with their children from kindergarten on; when girls have learned how to read they are expected to spend 1/2 hour per night reading, as well as being read to
Classes II and III: weekly spelling assignments, math facts and puzzles, 20–30 minutes, plus nightly reading
Class IV: 30 minutes on weekdays, 60 minutes over the weekend, plus nightly reading
Class V–VI: 2 hours
Classes VII and VIII: 2–21/2 hours daily
Classes IX–XII: 21/2–4 hours daily

After-School Programs   Afternoon program: *The Clubhouse,* a joint after-school program with Chapin for girls in Kindergarten through Class VI; a variety of activities including sports, crafts, homework help from 2:30 P.M.–5:45 P.M., an additional payment is required, financial aid is available; additional activities for older students include Fall Drama, Winter Musical, Spring Senior Drama, all including boys from a variety of city schools; in Middle School there is the Class VII Gilbert and Sullivan, and Class VIII drama, technical and design work all year long afternoons and weekends; debate, ceramics, and photography, work on the school newspaper, literary magazine, yearbook and 14 student-run clubs and committees

Summer Program SummerStart, for children grades K–VI; 2 weeks in June; creative and recreational activities for an additional fee; open to children in the community
Basketball Camp for grades V–XII held at the Field House at East 87th Street
Upper School students are eligible for summer study scholarships and exchange programs and can choose from a range of study/travel programs in the U.S., Europe (including Turkey and Greece) and Asia.

Brearley was founded by Harvard and Oxford-educated Samuel A. Brearley, Jr. so that girls could receive a college preparatory education comparable to that offered at the independent boys' schools. Brearley opened its doors in 1884, originally serving many of New York's socially prominent families, including those of German Jewish background. Today's diverse enrollment is a vibrant cross section of New York City. Since 1930 the school has had only five heads: Millicent Carey McIntosh (who later became Barnard's first president); Jean Fair Mitchell, Head of School for twenty-eight years, who guided the school through the turbulent sixties and early seventies; Evelyn J. Halpert, a Brearley alumna, who succeeded Miss Mitchell in 1975 and served until her retirement in 1997; and Dr. Priscilla Winn Barlow. Brearley's current head, Dr. Stephanie J. Hull comes to Brearley from Mount Holyoke College where she served as Assistant to the President. In her first address to graduates, Dr. Hull commended the class members for all of their hard work and unpretentious ways.

Located steps from tranquil Carl Schurz Park, Brearley's twelve-story red brick building on East 83rd Street overlooks the East River. Two floors were added in 1995 providing 10 percent more space. In September 1997, Brearley opened a 12,000 square foot Field House on East 87th Street, a short walk from the school. From the windows of the refurbished library in the school building on East 83rd Street, you can watch the sailboats and barges slip through the waves.

Although at first sight Brearley might appear staid, when the girls are bustling through the halls or speaking forthrightly in class, informality reigns. There are no bells to signal the changing of classes. The atmosphere is relaxed; as you walk down the halls you can feel it. Here girls receive a superb education in an environment characterized by intellectual rigor, tolerance and social activism. A parent characterized the school as being "like my kindergartner's indestructible Brearley tunic: sturdy, practical, and essential. It might come home encrusted with flour, paint, or papier-mâché but it washes clean and ready to go the next day." Brearley is not, as rumored, all work and no play. Frivolity prevails at the annual Lower School family fun nights; at Middle School social events such as the Class VIII Carnival and Class VIII Dance and at many Upper School events that are sponsored by the Self-Government Association and student clubs and committees. Brearley girls are just as well mannered as "the green and yellow 'ladies' down the street at Chapin," and also strong, brainy, confident, poised and prepared. "These aren't shrinking violets; everyone has a distinct personality," says a parent.

Getting in: Brearley's catalog is a very understated, small white book, whose only decoration is the Brearley school seal bearing the motto, "By Truth and Toil" emblazoned on the front cover. The catalog is complemented by *Images*, an equally understated, but beautifully photographed view book of school life. Applications must be filed by December 1 for Lower School and December 15 for Middle and Upper School. It is not imperative to apply before you tour the school, but one parent advised that you make your tour appointment by early October. And both parents should come. Tours for Middle and Upper School applicants are given by Upper School students. Parents of Lower School applicants are given tours by admissions office personnel. One prospective parent said, "It looks like a school: wide hallways, bright classrooms and everything is up to date and spotless." After your tour you meet with with an admissions officer. There is plenty of time for parents to describe their daughters and ask questions. Brearley attracts and enrolls candidates from a broad base; in a recent year the kindergarten class came from 32 different nursery programs. What are they looking for? "Eagerness to learn, a sense of curiosity and the willingness to take learning risks," says an admissions officer. "We don't expect the girls to come to us as finished products. We nurture each girl in her individual development, while instilling values of simplicity, generosity of spirit and respect for others."

During the child's visit, the school looks for the beginnings of critical thinking skills and at how the child approaches a challenge. "Above all, we want to be sure that students can take full and joyous advantage of all that Brearley has to offer."

Interview appointments for applicants are made from mid-September to mid-January, and a very helpful letter is sent prior to the interview to describe the process in detail. When you arrive with your daughter there are children's books in the waiting room (no squirm test here) and the children go into a classroom with age-appropriate materials. Children might be asked to play a game, tell a story, complete a puzzle or draw a picture while chatting with a teacher. The parents meet with the head of the Lower School faculty, giving them an opportunity to learn more about the school. One parent inferred, "They are also looking at the parents." Financial aid is available beginning in kindergarten; it is need-based, and individual family circumstances are taken into account. Preference is given to siblings and legacies, but they are not automatically accepted.

For applicants to Classes I–V, tours are for parents only and are given in the morning and last about an hour. After the admissions office has received a completed application, there is a small group interview for applicants, which includes an assessment of the student's academic abilities. For students applying to Class VI and above, tours are given to applicants and their parents by Upper School students and last about forty minutes. An admissions officer or division supervisor interviews applicants and parents also only after the admissions office has received a completed application. If a family submits an application before seeing the school, then the tour and interview can be scheduled on the same day. A standardized exam (ISEE) and teacher references are required. Candidates also sit for Brearley entrance exams whose dates of administration can be found at the back of the school catalog. What are they looking for? "We are looking for intellectual agility and stamina, eagerness, resourcefulness, kindness, humor and the wit to differentiate the essential from the extraneous," says one representative from the admissions staff.

Parents: The parent body at Brearley, according to one alumna, is eclectic, and hard to stereotype. "Investment bankers, Wall Streeters, doctors, health care workers, police officers, civil servants, recent immigrants, lawyers, architects, academics, actors, artists, writers and musicians are all included. The Brearley community includes families from every part of the city, and all feel welcomed and comfortable," says a parent. There is an active Parents Association, a monthly parents' newsletter and a Brearley family website.

The Parents Association benefits at Brearley are the best in the city. "One-of-a-kind" is a recurring theme. In 1999, the benefit "Brearley on Broadway" brought talent together for a nostalgic look at the school through the music of former notable Brearley fathers, Irving Berlin, Leonard Bernstein, Frank Loesser and Richard Rodgers. More recently, benefits have featured The Bacon Brothers in 2001, The Flying Karamazov Brothers in 2002, and violinist Robert McDuffie and others at Alice Tully Hall in 2003, followed by a dinner at Tavern on the Green.

Over the years, Brearley has made connections to the families of the girls. "They know a tremendous amount about each girl, but they don't intrude, they feel that the school isn't a parent," said a former teacher. Beginning in Lower School, the girls learn to be their own advocates in social and academic matters, parents report. A parent said she was surprised "at how tremendously observant and psychologically astute the teachers and administration are about each girl."

Program: The Brearley kindergarten has fifteen to eighteen girls in each classroom. Separation is handled gradually. Monday through Thursday dismissal is 2:00, 12:30 on Fridays. Kindergarten girls have specialist teachers for library, music, science, dance and physical education. In music they sing, move and use percussion instruments. In Class III, girls are introduced to a stringed instrument or recorder and hand bells. Lower School girls sing together at Assembly each week and recorder and hand bells are played by Class IV girls at various assemblies as well as at the Winter Assembly and Last Day. Although not "academic" in the traditional sense, the kindergarten year at Brearley is rich with creative learning experiences that are carefully designed to enrich language and math and thinking skills. One of the three kindergarten classes studied breads from around the world, made flour from wheat stalks, baked bread and sold bread from their classroom "bakery." In another kindergarten class each girl had a chance to bring Paddington Bear (and his knapsack with pj's and toothbrush) home overnight along with a journal in which they recorded his every experience. During the year the girls get to know each other as they meet in half groups for gymnastics, PE, music, or play with balls, bikes and wagons on "the pier" or playroof and in Carl Schurz Park.

Formal academics begin in Class I and II. In Class I reading is taught in small groups. One parent said the atmosphere is more relaxed than at some of the other very selective schools and "There is free time in the morning during snack to visit other grades and classrooms." The aim of these early years, according to the brochure, is to help each girl to "form good work habits and to encourage her to be adventurous, responsible and kind." Emphasis is on cooperation, not competition. In Lower School, there is also an emphasis on public speaking with opportunities to recite poems and act in plays. One parent said girls get the sense that "everyone is good at something and the school fosters a sense of security and independence."

In Classes II and III homework includes a "math puzzle of the week" and some spelling words as homework. Starting in Class IV homogeneous math groups are formed but there is movement between groups and the girls all learn the same material, albeit at different paces.

Lower School girls have their own science lab where members of the science department oversee a hands-on approach: To study aerodynamics girls make parachutes and paper helicopters. One of the strengths of Brearley is that all of the faculty teach across the grades so they get to know the girls as they grow.

In Class II, the girls are introduced to formal computer classes once a week, twice a week in Class III. The Lower School Computer Room is fully equipped and staffed by computer teachers. The girls learn how to keyboard, create graphics, do word processing and work in multimedia. Computer teachers work closely with homeroom teachers to integrate computer activities with other subjects. Students in Class IV visit the computer room twice a week for a Creative Writing Workshop that focuses on word processing, concept mapping, timelines, and creating a multimedia slide show.

Taking into account the fact that students learn at different rates, students may take a modern language or a reading and writing skills class in Middle School. New students or continuing students can have a skills class in Class VI, or can take beginning French in Class VII. French, Spanish, and Mandarin Chinese may begin in Class V and can be continued through the Upper School. A structured advisory program in the middle and upper schools helps to create dialogues among teachers and students to better monitor student's progress and their workloads. Advisory groups are small with approximately eight to ten girls per advisor and meet weekly. Latin is required in Classes VII and VIII and there are also introductory classes in modern languages or Asian languages offered at Class VII or IX for entering students.

The curriculum in the Lower School is integrated with close coordination among the subjects. Frequently, English readings are related to topics in history and geography. One parent gave an example: "For a unit on China they studied the music, language, history, culture, customs, arts and foods of that country. The walls of the Lower School were lined with all things Chinese."

The Music Department offers private instrumental study to students in Classes II through XII on a variety of intruments. A girl may choose from almost any instrument, from the recorder to the double bass or harp. There is an additional fee, but financial aid is available for those who qualify.

Middle School at Brearley consists of Class V through Class VIII. A quaint tradition at Brearley is the stuffed animal mascot for each class handed down from Class XII to the upcoming Class V. (This is not to be confused with the official Brearley mascot, the beaver.) By Class VI all subjects are fully departmentalized. Attention is still paid to individual learning styles, placement and pace. Some coordination of subject matter continues. In sixth grade English the girls read "The Odyssey" while they are studying Greek and Roman history as part of a broader course in the History of the Ancient World. In sixth and seventh grades, the work load increases. A parent said, "By seventh grade expectations are high and the girls are well aware of their strengths and weaknesses." The parent of a seventh grader said that "reading selections are two years ahead of other schools, and high-level, sophisticated written work is required. Papers are returned with many red lines, sometimes with comments as long as the paper, but their work is the better for it."

In Class VII the girls are reading Dickens and Shakespeare and studying global medieval history, including an introduction to European, Islamic, East Asian, South Asian, and African civilizations. In the spring term they perform a Gilbert and Sullivan operetta. Drama, music and studio art classes are held once or twice a week.

Girls in Class VI take human biology, in which they study all the systems of the body including reproductive, as well as nutrition, drugs, alcohol and cigarette use. Health issues are addressed again in Class VIII to fulfill the New York state requirement. Students also take a one-semester community service course in Class IX, and volunteer in school or in the community throughout their Upper School years.

Teams in gymnastics, volleyball, soccer, softball, basketball, swimming, track and lacrosse are formed at this point.

The Upper School: The catalog says that Brearley students need nineteen credits to graduate but most leave with twenty or more. For students who qualify, two classes may be taken in the same discipline. Students have about four to five frees (free periods) a week. Homework now averages four lessons a day of fifty minutes to one hour each. Formal testing begins in Class VII.

Advanced Placement (AP) exams are usually offered in at least seventeen subjects. Almost no "AP" or "honors" courses are offered but most girls take a number of AP exams based on the preparation they get in regular Brearley courses. Math is required through Pre-Calculus though most girls go on to Calculus, and most students take more than three Upper School lab science courses. Those with proficiency in science can participate in the Columbia Science Honors Program. Any student can choose from five science courses in Classes XI and XII.

As an example of how the spirit of intellectual inquiry thrives at Brearley, a 1996 spring science project presented a challenge: "Identify a problem in the community and use science and technology to solve it." Two seventeen-year-old Brearley juniors focusing on the transmission of HIV by the sharing of infected hypodermic syringes, designed a non-reusable syringe. The Brearley students triumphed over 470 other student team projects at the NYNEX Science and Technology Awards in Boston and each girl was awarded a $15,000 scholarship and they became eligible for $250,000 in seed money to develop their invention. Two Brearley students have been recognized recently as Intel Science Competition Semi Finalists. And, in 2004, a senior was honored for her research in a medical school lab with respect to a gene that repairs DNA.

Seventh graders learn LOGO-programming in math class; students in Clases V-XII are required to have access to a computer at home with Microsoft Office, Geometer's Sketchpad (provided by the school), and an Internet connection. Financial aid is available for this program. There is no computer science requirement as such, but keyboard proficiency is expected by eighth grade and computer use is an on-going component of Lower, Middle and Upper School math, science, history and language classes. The Upper School offers two computer electives for eleventh and twelfth grade students: "Web Design and Multimedia" and "Computer Programming" are offered in alternating years. Greek courses are also offered. A pilot project that uses

Apple's i-Pods in the teaching of modern languages and the classics brings language and culture alive in innovative ways.

Class IX English is devoted to close readings of complex texts. In addition to such classics as Jane Austen and Shakespeare, the girls explore their own voices as writers. All students take a course in Twentieth century World History. In Class X students take "American Literature From the Puritans to the Moderns" and "United States History Survey." Their studies culminate in a trip to Washington, D.C.

In Classes XI and XII there is a winter requirement of Sophocles' Theban tragedies and Shakespeare's *King Lear*. Spring electives in English are determined by student interest, but even when given a choice, Brearley girls don't seem to stray too far from the classics. Past choices include: Dostoyevsky, modern British fiction and Milton's *Paradise Lost*. More recent electives have been African-American fiction and Virginia Woolf. History electives in Class XI and XII include: "Comparative Political Systems," "Issues in World Politics," "History of China and Japan," "Political and Social Philosophy," and "Modern European History."

Students take art, music or drama throughout the Middle School and continue in one or more of these disciplines in the Upper School. Class VII performs an annual Gilbert & Sullivan operetta and Upper School students perform in three main stage plays including a coeducational musical comedy production (*My Fair Lady* and *Grease* are recent examples), as well as numerous class drama productions.

For students who are still developing their reading and writing skills, the Brearley Reading and Testing Department provides support. In addition to the Lower School's reading program, there are small classes in the Middle School for girls who need significant help in some aspect of language. In the Upper School, a few girls continue to benefit from the individual attention that is offered by this department.

All students have a homeroom teacher and Brearley now has a full-time school counselor who, with the school nurse and a part-time psychologist, form the Brearley health team. There is also a peer leadership program to keep a finger on the pulse of the student body. Seniors who have completed one trimester of training during their junior year serve as a resource for younger students under the supervision of the school counselor and school psychologist.

In the spring term seniors have several options. They can choose independent study—for example, an extracurricular project, job or internship. A recent project was a student written, directed and performed ensemble production. Girls are also encouraged throughout the Upper School to do volunteer work. Girls in Class IX have a year-long community service requirement and select a project or agency they will work with for an entire year. One opportunity is "Bridges to Learning": a highly successful student-run effort that organizes five or six Saturday programs in the Spring for students from P.S. 102 who come to Brearley for a day of arts, crafts, carpentry, computer and other activities. In addition, there are numerous community service drives throughout the year at Brearley, including the Annual Mitten Drive in which mittens are bought and donated to a food pantry. Brearley supported and raised funds for the Asphalt Green Aqua-Center.

There are opportunities to nurture the adventurous spirit of the Brearley girl. In addition to Mountain Day, a day of outdoor activities for Classes V through XII at Bear Mountain, Class XI girls may spend a semester at the Mountain School program of Milton Academy in Vermont, or attend the Maine Coast Semester program of the Chewonki Foundation. They can apply to spend a term at the John F. Kennedy Schule in Berlin or at the American International School in Vienna. Students may also apply to study in China, France, Spain or Italy under the School Year Abroad Program. Other exchanges include London for Class IX; Kansas City, Missouri for Class X; Australia for Classes XI and XII, and Japan for Classes X-XII. Numerous scholarships for summer study and travel abroad are awarded to girls in the Upper School.

While academic pressure is a fact of life at Brearley, steps have been taken to ease some of the pressure and provide more support for students. Classes in the Middle School continue to run for 40 minutes, but in the Upper School, the new schedule allows for flexibility in the way that class time is structured. Language classes in Classes IX and X continue to meet for 40 minute periods, but a Class IX history course will configure its classes to meet fewer times per week and for a longer period. In addition, the school has taken steps to help students manage their assignments. In the Upper School, there are only three "major assignments" (papers, tests, and lab reports) a week and only one on any given day. In Classes XI and XII, students may make individual arrangements with faculty members when there is a schedule conflict.

Dr. Hull, the division heads, and the department heads coordinate the curriculum and homework and test schedules. Dr. Hull says that "each student will be appropriately challenged, in an environment that feels supportive enough to encourage intellectual curiosity and experimentation with ideas." "The school has taken a lot of steps to help students manage pressure and address social and emotional needs," says a parent.

Course titles don't tell you everything. One alumna said that "there is an international excitement to classes, especially English and history. All subjects are thought through; students are taught to be skeptical of assumptions. Teachers are sensitive to classroom diversity concerns. The goal of Brearley's multicultural efforts is to create an inclusive community, and to develop on-going programs to continue the process.

Students at Brearley are aware of gender issues, and most girls are appreciative of the many benefits of single-sex education. All Brearley students and faculty read a common book each summer and then meet in small groups and discuss it in the fall. Recently, the book was *All Girls* by Karen Stabiner about an all-girls school. In one first grade class a mother who is a pilot for American Airlines came in to talk about her nontraditional occupation. At a Brearley's Parents Association benefit, columnist Anna Quindlen explained what she saw as one of the great strengths of a girls' school: "Because each day when they walk into class they see a smart woman at the front of the room and, on each side a smart girl, and that means that never in their lives will they be able to believe any of the nonsense about all the things girls can't do." The school's emphasis on the written word is evidenced by the thick Bibliography of Alumnae Authors.

Two topics which propel ongoing debate and self-evaluation are diversity and leadership. Differences of opinion are respected at Brearley. There is a leveling of socio-economic differences at Brearley because of the emphasis on intellectual achievement. "Brearley girls never want to appear too rich, too social or too fancy. There's an inverse snobbism," says an alumna.

There is recognition that Brearley girls need more opportunities to socialize. As one parent said, "It's not a party school; your socializing is postponed for another time." The school does arrange a number of activities with the opposite sex. Friday night dances start in Class VIII and The Middle School Orchestra performs with two local boys' schools during each year. Coeducational activities for the Upper School students include drama department productions, joint chorus concerts with a boys' school near Philadelphia, and with Collegiate, and there are events planned by various student clubs. There is a

Holiday Semi-Formal in December and seniors may invite boys or go solo to the "Six Schools" prom held each year at the Waldorf Astoria.

The Class X trip to Frost Valley with five other single-sex schools from Interschool, including boys' schools, is very popular. Also, Brearley is a member of Joint Schools, which plan co-ed activities including an art show, poetry readings and community service days.

Student government is called Self-Government. In the Upper School, two girls form a team and they run for the positions of co-presidents. There are at least fourteen school clubs, some for Class V and up, some only for Classes VII through XII. The Service Committee organizes toy, book and mitten drives, and sponsors a child. The Tech Club builds sets for plays. Other popular clubs include the Harvard Model U.N., Asian Awareness and Harvard Model Congress. The Brearley Environmental Action Committee is an active organization that is spearheading student involvement in the N.Y.C. Department of Sanitation's WasteLe$$ program in which Brearley was one of three schools invited to participate. The students have performed a vital role in data collection and focus the attention of the school community on environmental issues such as recycling.

Brearley offers all students a wide-ranging health program. From the Lower School self-advocacy program, PREPARE, to the Middle and Upper School advisory programs, and extending to the Class IX health course, diversity discussions, seminars for juniors and seniors, decision-making, and nutrition courses, guest speakers, and more, Brearley covers all the bases.

In the Senior Seminar, all Class XII members learn about life skills, business letter writing, interviewing, health care in college, money management, basic auto mechanics, and cooking. Dr. Hull's senior seminar focuses on ethical issues raised by current events.

Outstanding sports teams are tennis, cross country and the gymnastics team, which recently was undefeated for the season and won the AAIS championship. Soccer and track teams have captured AAIS championships five years in a row and the lacrosse team (a new sport) won its first AAIS championship in Spring 1998.

A music faculty made up of approximately thirty outstanding performing musicians offer group and private lessons to Brearley students and performs regularly at the school throughout the year.

There is praise for an extraordinary faculty. A building was purchased in 1987 on East 77th Street for faculty housing. Appreciation for the gifted faculty is evident from the numerous (nineteen) chairs and faculty awards provided. The school's Professional Development Fund helps to defray a portion of graduate tuition for the faculty and the cost of short courses and workshops. There are also annual professional development days. One class bestowed the Faculty Award Fund (recipients nominated by the senior class) in recognition of "the extraordinary commitment of the Brearley faculty to their students and to the entire Brearley community." At the end of the year the students write thank-you notes to their teachers.

Parents praise the faculty as one of the best among the city's top private schools: "Brearley's greatest strength is its faculty members, who combine experience and skill with genuine warmth and attentiveness to the girls as individuals. Our teachers do an excellent job of conveying not only the concepts in their classes, but also their own love of learning and teaching," and Dr. Hull concurs.

The school has continued its emphasis on providing a rigorous classical education while continually reviewing its academic and extracurricular offerings to keep them relevant. "Brearley's academic program," says Dr. Hull, "with its emphasis on self-thinking, self-expression, and both individual and collaborative problem-solving, has a proven tradition of preparing students to succeed at whatever they choose to pursue."

Brearley makes use of many graceful euphemisms as noted by the co-presidents of the Self-Government in their "Last Days" speech: "We don't have AP courses—our courses are just impossible. We don't wear underwear—we wear bloomers. We don't get 91's—we get Very Good minus minus plus slash good plus plus minuses. And we don't graduate—we Last Day Exercise." White dresses are worn at Last Day. There is an Awards Assembly at which school prizes in all subjects and scholarships for study and travel are presented. Students are recognized for community service work, and artwork from each class is placed in the school's permanent Kunz Collection. There is also a "Head's Award" for contributions to the school community.

In the late nineteenth century when college choices for women were extremely limited, Brearley prepared girls almost exclusively for Bryn Mawr College. Since then, Brearley has been very successful over the years in matching its students with excellent colleges and universities. Ms. Melanie W. Choukrane, who has extensive experience in college admissions and as a high school college advisor, became Brearley's college advisor in 2004.

Does Brearley churn out a yearly crop of super women? Former Head of School Evelyn Halpert had said that the school's objective is to "turn out young women who will be good citizens in a democratic society . . . whether successful by the standards of our society or not. It would be wrong, I think, to suggest that we want everybody who leaves this school to be a leader or a powerful person. We want all our students to leave this school happier and stronger because of the experiences they've had here and what they've learned."

Legacies say, "I'm Brearley born and Brearley bred"; "Alumnae gatherings are so exciting, there's never a boring person"; "College was disappointing after Brearley." An alumna writes of her years at Brearley: "A superb education and a permanent love of learning. Friendships that last a lifetime." From the Last Day speech in 2004 by the co-heads of Self-Government: "Brearley teaches us to respect one another. It becomes second nature to care about each other and to get along despite our differing backgrounds, experiences and politics. Brearley brings people together, though everyone here is unique, we share a common bond. The ties formed here are wound tight with so many remarkable experiences that they will never unravel." The process of learning is lifelong and many Brearley girls become distinguished scholars, writers, journalists, scientists and professionals of all kinds. An alumna now heads The Ford Foundation and another is head of the Philadelphia Museum of Art.

Popular College Choices   Yale, Harvard/Radcliffe, Brown, Princeton, Amherst, Stanford, Dartmouth, University of Chicago, University of Pennsylvania, Vassar

Traditions   "The best food of all the independent schools," Field Day, Mountain Day, Father's Chorus Performing at Winter Assemblies, Biannual Festival of Cultures, Prom, seventh-grade Gilbert and Sullivan production, eighth-grade Carnival with a surprise theme, Book Fair, Brearley General Store, Lower School Family Nights, Last Day Exercises

Publications   Student Newspaper: *The Zephyr*
Literary Magazine: *The Beaver*
Yearbook
Parents Association: Monthly newsletter: *News From Brearley*, *The Brearley Bulletin*, website for families and alumnae

Community Service Requirement for Class IX only, a one-semester community service course Brearley's coordinator of community service helps Class IX students to secure a year-long community service commitment with various social service agencies

Hangouts The Mansion (a diner at 86th and York), the library, the "Promenade"

Brooklyn Friends School

375 Pearl Street
Brooklyn, NY 11201
(718) 852-1029, FAX: (718) 643-4868
e-mail: bfs@brooklynfriends.org
website: www.brooklynfriends.org

Coed
Toddler–12th grade
Accessible

Dr. Michael Nill, Head of School
Ms. Sara Soll, Director of Admissions, Preschool
Ms. Jennifer Knies, Director of Admissions, Kindergarten
through 12th grade

Birthday Cutoff   Children entering the Family Center must be 20 months old by September 1
Children entering preschool must be 4 by October 1
Children entering kindergarten must be 5 by October 1

Enrollment   Total enrollment: 590
Kindergarten places: approximately 15
Graduating class size: 40

Tuition Range 2005–2006 $8,200 to $24,300, Preschool (Family Center, 2's)–12th grade
For grades 4–12 lunch is included

After-School Program   A variety of creative and recreational activities are offered from 3:00 to 6:00 P.M.; an additional payment is required

Summer Program   Summer camp: From mid-June through Mid-August. For children from preschool through 2nd grade, an additional payment is required

———

Brooklyn Friends School is a Quaker college preparatory school founded in 1867 by the Brooklyn Meeting of the Society of Friends. The school is housed in a seven-story art deco building. When you enter through the brass doors you are greeted by lobby displays of student work, from digital photos to paper mâché. In addition to classrooms, four science labs and two libraries, the school boasts a darkroom, music, art, sculpting, ceramics and dance studios, a woodshop, three computer labs, a video production and editing room, two gyms, a roof top playground and a 300 seat theater. The style of the school is informal and there is no dress code.

The school is guided by the ideals of tolerance, equality and the peaceful resolution of conflict. Although Quaker traditions permeate the school parents say that the school is not in the least sectarian. "It manages to provide an enriching academic experience while fostering the sense that there is not a dichotomy between the secular and spiritual aspects of our lives." Students meet in silence for weekly Quaker Meeting and courses in ethics and social justice are offered in the Upper School.

Head of School Dr. Michael Nill is a graduate of Fordham, Johns Hopkins, Columbia University's Teachers College and the University of Texas at Austin.

Getting in: Open house tours give prospective applicants a chance to meet parents and faculty. A personal interview is required for all applicants. ERB's are required for kindergarten through fifth grade applicants. The ISEE is required for application to sixth through eleventh grades. One-third of the student body receives some form of financial assistance.

Parents: The parents at Brooklyn Friends are an eclectic mix of artists, office workers, lawyers, educators, physicians and Wall Street professionals who share a common philosophical commitment. According to one parent: "We looked for a private school that reflected and fostered our moral values, where the students were aware of their advantages but were not elitist." The parents play an important role in the school as class parents, library volunteers, and as members of the PTA, they engage in fundraising and community building.

Program: Experiential learning is emphasized in the pre- and lower schools. All classes are actively engaged in creating, hypothesizing and building. The pre-school curriculum is based on the idea of play as "the work of young children" and fosters independence and the development of language and self-expression through the arts, dance and music. Students work to develop and increase basic skills as well as taking part in art, dance, music, library and physical education. Computer science, woodworking, community service, and Japanese language and culture are also part of the Lower School program.

The Middle School is made up of fifth through eighth grade

students. Fifth and sixth graders stay in the classroom for reading, language arts, and social studies. They see specialists for science, math and foreign language. Latin instruction begins in fifth grade; students can select from Spanish, French or Latin thereafter. Seventh and eighth grades are fully departmentalized. The humanities program includes ancient history, the Middle Ages, the Renaissance and the Age of Exploration and American history. Environmental studies and discussions of new technologies enrich the traditional science curriculum. The school has ability groupings to ensure students are challenged in math; there are several new computer labs.

Upper Schoolers (grades 9–12) take four years of English, math, and physical education; three years of social studies, a foreign language, science, and art; one each of computer literacy and application, Quakerism and ethics. AP classes are also offered in math, foreign language, science and history.

Computers are integrated into the classroom curriculum from the Lower School through Upper School. The school recently installed a T1 line for Internet access throughout the building. In addition to classroom computers, students have access to six computer labs with Dell Optiplex systems. Upper Schoolers edit, write and explore scientific and mathematical formulas through a number of software programs. Brooklyn Friends has a website that is up and running.

Four days of community service are integrated into the school's calendar for group projects. Students also perform one hundred hours—80 outside, 20 inside—of service.

Many high school students play on a sports team. For a relatively small school, the teams are quite successful. BFS recently won the volleyball league championships and a New York State Independent School Soccer Championship title. Athletics are seen as an opportunity to build skills and develop good sportsmanship; despite their recent successes, BFS is not a "jock" school; sports are seen as an opportunity to do one's best.

From second grade through the Upper School, students take overnight trips to develop peer leadership skills, for academic study and for personal growth.

All High School students have an advisor who remains with them until they graduate. Recently, high school students began an exchange program with the Ackworth School, a Quaker boarding school in England.

For six weeks, at the end of senior year, all students engage in internships in areas of academic or personal interest.

Popular College Choices   Amherst, Barnard, Brown, Drexel, FIT, George Washington, Wesleyan, NYU, Sarah Lawrence, Skidmore, Smith, Saint Lawrence, SUNY Purchase, Vassar

Traditions   Holiday Crafts Fair, Dance Concert, All-School Art Show, Middle School Sports Night, Drama Productions, Sports Dinner, Spring Gala and Auction

Publications   Pre/Lower School Poetry Magazine; Middle School Literary Magazine; Middle School Newsletter; Upper School Literary Magazine; Yearbook; School Journal; Parents Notes Newsletter; *Traditions,* Alumni Newsletter; *E-News*, a weekly online publication

Community Service Requirement   All students take part in community service from pre-school through Upper School. Upper School students are required to complete 20 hours of community service in school and 80 hours outside of school in order to fulfill graduation requirements

The Brooklyn Heights Montessori School

185 Court Street
Brooklyn, NY 11201
(718) 858-5100, FAX (718) 858-0500
website: www.bhmsny.org

Coed
2-year-olds–8th Grade
Accessible

Mr. Dane L. Peters, Head of School
Molly Foran, Director of External Relations

Birthday cutoff For the 2's Program, the child must be 2 by August 31 in year of entry; for preschool through 8th grade, child must be of age by October 31

Enrollment Total enrollment: 282
Pre-K and kindergarten places: 114
Grades 1–3: 48
Grades 4–6: 48
Grades 7 and 8: 32
Little Room: 30
Little Room Kindergarten: 10

Tuition Range 2004–2005 $5,300 to $19,700, 2s–8th Grade

Financial Aid/Scholarship 7% of the Preschool budget is allotted for scholarships
11% of the Elementary and Middle School budget is allotted for scholarships
The Little Room is entirely funded by the Board of Education

Endowment None

After-school Program A variety of recreational and creative activities are offered including: chess, art, drama, athletics, soccer and more; additional payment is required.

Summer Program The summer program offers a wide range of creative and recreational activities, including weekly trips, overnight camping and beach days. Early morning drop off at 8:15 A.M. and "after camp" until 5:30; an additional payment is required

———

The Brooklyn Heights Montessori School opened its doors on October 1, 1965 with twenty children attending the one-room school in the First Presbyterian Church on Henry Street in Brooklyn Heights. Since then the school has expanded and moved to the Cobble Hill section of Brooklyn. The school recently completed an award-winning 32,000 square foot expansion, which includes not only spacious light-filled classrooms, but also a library, gymnasium and a multi-purpose performance space.

Getting in: After the school tour, a parent classroom observation, a parent interview, and a student visit are required of all applicants. Upper Elementary and Middle School applicants must submit ERB scores.

Parents: Parents play an important role in the school's community. In fact, the school's board of trustees is primarily composed of parents. The Parents Association sponsors a Speakers Forum to which a number of speakers are invited each year. There are morning coffees throughout the year, a harvest square dance, and a Valentine's Day card making event. Other activities help raise money to support special projects for the school. The PA also teams up with the diversity committee to sponsor an International Festival and Cultural Diversity Potluck.

Program: There are currently three divisions of BHMS: the Montessori Preschool, the Montessori Elementary and Middle School Program and the Little Room.

All learning at BHMS is designed to happen within the Montessori model of mixed-age classrooms which are carefully prepared environments organized to offer children a wide range of experience and to facilitate the growth of their skills and confidence. Independent work, depth of study, critical thinking, respect for and understanding of others, are all emphasized by a supportive and developmentally oriented staff at all age levels. At each stage of learning, technology is used to enhance skills, share creative ideas and communicate thoughts. BHMS emphasizes developing a sense of responsibility for the ethical considerations inherent in the use of new technology.

In the preschool and kindergarten classrooms the environment is nurturing and supportive. The educational philosophy and the teaching materials developed by Maria Montessori provide the underlying structure for the program. The BHMS faculty is concerned with the overall growth of each child, so teachers regard social, physical and emotional development as going hand in hand with intellectual growth.

In the Elementary Program, the curriculum integrates all subject areas. Studying other cultures and countries helps children to understand themselves and their community in relation to the larger world. Cultures are studied in a three-year cycle, and a unit related to the United States is included each year. Older elementary students expand the level of study by viewing cultures from a historical perspective. Problem solving provides a primary focus for the math and science programs.

The Middle School Program (grades seven and eight) focuses on conceptual modules like revolutions, building a democracy, ethical responsibility and conflict, and their impact on this country. Students deepen their exploration of math, science and technology, and apply what they have learned to real life projects, including a year-long research-intensive "expert project." Middle School students also explore ways that they can contribute to the larger community.

The Little Room is a special educational program (Preschool through First grade) which serves children with speech and learning difficulties. Housed in its own space at BHMS, the Little Room shares much of the Montessori educational philosophy and practices. Integral to the Little Room is a unique mainstreaming program (the oldest in the city for preschoolers) which has been extremely successful in helping students move on to "typical" class placements.

Students in the mainstream classrooms also gain an opportunity to become comfortable with differences in people by participating in mainstreaming activities with the children in The Little Room Program.

Publications   Newsletter *Handprints*
Weekly Bulletin

Community Service Requirement   The Upper Elementary and Middle School students perform community service each week. Assignments range from working with younger children in the classrooms, to writing articles for the school newsletter to planting trees in Prospect Park.

The Browning School

52 East 62nd Street
New York, NY 10021
(212)838-6280, FAX (212) 355-5602
website: www.browning.edu

All boys
Kindergarten–12th grade
Not accessible

Dr. Stephen M. Clement, III, Headmaster
Ms. Jackie Casey, Director of Admissions

Uniform   Dress code for all grades (coat and tie with an option of polo shirt or turtleneck shirt in the Lower School)

Birthday Cutoff   Boys entering Kindergarten must be 5 by September 1

Enrollment   Total enrollment: 371
Kindergarten places: 30
Graduating class 2004: 28
12 Prep for Prep students as of Fall 2003

Grades   Trimester system
Letter grades begin in 5th grade
Departmentalization begins in 7th grade
Two reports per trimester

Tuition Range 2005–2006 $24,415 to $25,415, K–12th grade
Additional fees: for books and lunch and PE uniforms, approximately $2,000
Tuition payment plan available

Financial Aid/Scholarship   Approximately 15% of the student body receives some form of aid

Endowment $10 million

Homework   Kindergarten: approximately 10 minutes each night
Lower School: increases to 1 hour each night
Middle School: about 2 hours each night
Upper School: about 3 hours each night

After-School Program The Browning After-School Encore Program offers a wide variety of creative and recreational activities for boys in Kindergarten through sixth grades until 5:00 P.M. Popular activities include chess, computer, science, after-school study
The Browning Sports Club (Intramurals)
Junior varsity and varsity athletic competition

Summer Program There is a two week recreational program available for the Lower School in June

---

The Browning School was founded in 1888 with five boys as a college preparatory school by John A. Browning. It is a traditional school, at one time very socially exclusive in its student body. Today, Browning boys are culled from a more diverse population and the school stresses "the importance of developing well-rounded gentlemen." Parents say Browning offers a small, nurturing, supportive environment. "They are extraordinarily understanding and caring about the development of boys," said a parent. "It's a gem that people haven't discovered." Browning has completed a renovation and has a new library, three new science labs, a new arts center, and a new physical fitness area.

Getting in: Parents should call the school and schedule a tour. Once families apply, a member of the admissions staff will call to schedule appointments for tours and interviews. Parents of kindergarten applicants take a tour of the school with a parent tour guide. After touring, the Director of Admissions meets with parents while a teacher interviews their son. Middle and Upper School families take small group tours with the Director of Middle and Upper School Admissions and a current student. After touring boys meet with the division heads for an interview and parents meet with the Admissions Director. Upper School applicants are required to schedule an additional visit to observe morning classes and an interview with the Head of the Upper School.

Parents: "I thought it would be very Muffy and Buffy, which it is," said a parent. "But, in my son's class of fifteen children, there's a family from England, one from Thailand and one African-American. In the other class, there's a South American family and an Italian family." Parents can volunteer for the Parents Association which sponsors a variety of events that support the school. The Parents Association also offers summer study stipends to support professional development.

Program: Browning is composed of three divisions: Lower School (kindergarten through Fourth), Middle School (fifth through Form II)and Upper School (Form III [ninth grade] through Form VI [twelfth grade]). Foreign language study begins in fifth grade with a choice of French or Spanish. Latin is offered in seventh and eighth grades. There is an annual Shakespeare play and public speaking contest. Browning fields strong teams in soccer, cross country, track, basketball, baseball and tennis. Field Day is a popular annual event.

The Lower School at Browning "lets boys be boys, and is structured, but nurturing. My son needed the structure and the small classes. I am beyond thrilled with the school," one parent said. The program is integrated; there are computers in every classroom. Formal reading instruction begins in first grade.

The Middle School program focuses on strengthening study and organizational skills. By fifth grade the program is fully departmentalized. In music, boys are invited to sing in the Middle School choir.

In the Upper School, there are required classes in English, math, history, science, computer science, art, music and physical education. Advanced placement courses are offered in all subjects.

Browning is a member of Interschool and beginning in fifth grade Browning boys participate in a variety of activities with a number of girls' schools including exchange days, field trips, concerts, joint assemblies, dramatic productions and community service projects.

College advising begins in Form IV (grade 10) and Forms V and VI (grades 11 and 12) take an annual trip to visit a broad selection of colleges and universities. Personalized guidance enables each student to maximize his college potential.

Hot lunch is served daily in "Ruby's kitchen"—the school cafeteria.

Popular College Choices   Boston College, Brown, Cornell, Vanderbilt, George Washington University, Hamilton College, Haverford, Yale

Traditions   Father/Son Dinner, Public Speaking Competition, Brother's Breakfast and Picture, New Parent Dinner, Book Fair, Field Days, Grandparents Days, Annual Art Show, Middle School Shakespeare play, Upper School play, Three Day College Trip, annual fundraising auction, Alumni Day, Middle School Overnight trips.

The Buckley School

113 East 73rd Street
New York, NY 10021
(212) 535-8787
website: www.buckleyschoolnyc.org

All boys
Kindergarten–8th/9th grade
Accessible

Mr. Gregory J. O'Melia, Headmaster
Mrs. Jo Ann E. Lynch, Director of Admissions

Uniform   Beginners (Kindergarten): prescribed knit blue or white Buckley polo shirt, pants (no jeans), leather shoes, no sneakers
Grades I–IX: jacket, tie, slacks and leather shoes

Birthday Cutoff   Children entering kindergarten must be 5 by September 1

Enrollment   Total enrollment: approximately 350
Kindergarten places: 40
8th grade graduating class size: approximately 35; more than half will choose to attend New York City independent day schools, the rest will stay for grade IX and then most attend boarding schools
9th grade class size: approximately 15–17; most will attend boarding schools

Grades   Trimester system
Kindergarten through 3rd grade students receive anecdotal reports and checklists
Letter grades begin in 4th grade (6 times a year)
Departmentalization begins in 6th grade, there are practice finals in 6th grade in most subjects
First final exam given in 7th grade

Tuition Range 2005–2006 $27,500, K–9th grade

Financial Aid/Scholarship   9% of the student body received some form of aid in 2003–2004
$493,000 in financial aid was awarded in 2003–2004

Endowment   Capital fund valued at $14 million (as of March 2004)

Diversity   Children of color represent 10% of the student body

Homework   Beginners: none
Class I: approximately 20 minutes, weekly spelling tests
Class II: approximately 1/2 hour, daily
Class III: 45 minutes–1 hour
Class IV: approximately 1 1/2 hours
Class V: approximately 2 hours
Classes VI and VII: 2–2 1/2 hours
Classes VIII and IX: 3–4 hours

After-School Program   Classes I through IX are required to participate in a variety of after-school sports
Interscholastic athletic competition in the Manhattan Private School League, the Metropolitan Middle School Track and Field Association, and with some schools outside of these leagues.
Friday Afternoon Lower and Middle School Gymnastics and a Middle and Upper School Basketball program
Saturday Sports Club (10 A.M.–12 P.M. in the Buckley gym)
Vacation Sports Club (10 A.M.–12 P.M. in the Buckley gym)

Summer Program   The Buckley June Program; 2 weeks in June: swimming, computers, arts and crafts, games and sports at Buckley and Ward's Island; an additional payment is required

---

Founded in 1913 by educator B. Lord Buckley, historically The Buckley School has groomed the sons of New York's captains of industry (including a few Vanderbilts, Rockefellers and their latter-day counterparts) for the elite boarding schools. Today, "leadership, citizenship and academic excellence" are still valued at The Buckley School, which is traditional in the best sense of the word, but the student body now includes children culled from a variety of socioeconomic backgrounds—more than a few from neighborhoods far beyond the toney Upper East Side. While most of the current graduates still go on to schools like Groton and Deerfield, many of the boys now attend New York City independent day schools such as Trinity and Riverdale.

Some elements of the past remain: Buckley still has "travel days" on either side of the spring vacation, a formal tea complete with finger sandwiches is served at Exhibition Day, the male teachers and athletic instructors are addressed as "Sir" and female teachers are addressed as either Miss, Mrs., or Ms. The boys are served by the kitchen staff family-style (the rumored white-gloved waiters are merely an apparition of days gone by).

The Buckley School is far removed from the turmoil rocking the public schools. Prospective parents who have toured Buckley are impressed by the sense of clarity and order. Lower School Director Mrs. Sonja Robinson says, "Clear goals make clear kids." The emphasis on a classic curriculum, the strict dress code and unabashed respect for God and country have tremendous appeal to this generation of parents dubbed "the new traditionalists." Applications to The Buckley School have been at record levels in recent years.

Is there a typical Buckley boy? Parents say: "A boy who is very interested in sports, very smart, follows directions." What is most important is that the boy will be able to handle the work, because by fourth and fifth grades the curriculum is demanding. Buckley boys are well rounded: Touring parents might see boys with their ties tucked into their smocks painting in the airy art room with classical music playing in the background. First graders recite poetry, Lower School boys perform in the annual rhythm band assembly, all classes put on a class play. Unfortunately, parents don't tour Ward's Island, where the extensive outdoor afternoon sports program (Fall and Spring) harnesses the boys' more aggressive instincts.

Getting in: An important criterion is "a match in values between school and home." Although many of the boys (including legacies and siblings) still hail from nursery schools like Park Avenue Christian, Madison Avenue Presbyterian and Episcopal, the kindergarten class is composed of boys from many different nursery programs.

Admissions at Buckley consists of four components. After the application is received comes 1) the tour, which is preceded by a group meeting with the headmaster, 2) the parents' interview with the director of admissions, 3) the applicant's group interview and 4) the ERB and nursery school report. Decisions are made on the basis of the group interview, observation at the child's preschool, ERB and school report. Both parents are requested to attend the interviews and the tour; parents have an interview with Jo Ann Lynch, Director of Admissions. As part of the tour, parents meet the Head in small groups. The school will accommodate scheduling difficulties and meet with the parents separately, if necessary. The group interview is about one hour long (during which the boys are observed playing a variety of "games"). One mother said her son enjoyed the experience so much he drew a picture of himself going to Buckley while at his Trinity interview.

What are they looking for? According to Jo Ann Lynch a boy with "a love of learning, good self-esteem, not a little old man, rather, a curious child who is fun to be with." They are also looking at how the boy socializes in a group. According to Mrs. Robinson, the ERB is "a measuring stick against which all the boys stand." And of course, they also look at the family. There is a sibling and legacy policy (some boys' fathers or even grandfathers attended Buckley); however, the school will not automatically admit a child who they feel would not do well there. Buckley does maintain a wait list.

Mr. Gregory J. O'Melia, a Boston-born Harvard man, succeeded Brian Walsh as headmaster in July 2001. Mr. O'Melia, though youthful in appearance, has extensive experience teaching and coaching in a range of private schools, including the Brooks School in North Andover, Massachusetts.

Middle School pins are given largely for academic excellence. Grades in core subjects are averaged over the year—top boys receive pins. It is acknowledged that Buckley boys are very competitive, but the belief is that this competitiveness can be positive (and a great motivator) if used appropriately. The highest awards at graduation exercises are for character, not the highest G.P.A. Of course, any school is only as good as its teachers, and at Buckley there is tremendous respect for teachers and teaching. Approximately 80 percent of tuition goes toward faculty and staff salaries and benefits. Teachers are evaluated by division directors with the assistance of the headmaster.

Parents: The first Buckley Parents' Committee was started (in 1982) for the purpose of "service and communication." There is only one officer—the president. Class representatives are selected by the homeroom teachers and division directors. The Parents' Committee meets once a month, in a closed meeting, and the minutes are distributed to all parents. Parents praise the Buckley mothers, who are "time givers to benefit the school, a cohesive group of women working towards a common goal." School benefits are well organized and well staffed.

The tone at Buckley is definitely formal and very Upper East Side. The parents are Wall Street bankers, lawyers and doctors, with a sprinkling of writers and business people. But as one parent said, "It's a cosmopolitan mix of French, Chinese, Japanese, African-American,

Jewish and Muslim." Another parent had a different perspective: "Boring, old money, coupon clipping . . . they are more dressed in the morning than Brearley parents are in the evening." Parents dress for all school events (don't even think about wearing blue jeans). The class cocktail party is usually held in a parent's elegant Upper East Side apartment.

The school has no formal church affiliation—Christmas and Chanukah songs are sung at the Beginners' Christmas party. The Nativity play for Classes I and II is an annual event, and after the pledge of allegiance, everyone recites the Lord's Prayer at assemblies. However, families of many faiths are comfortable here; the commonality seems to be a basic conservatism.

Traditions are important at Buckley. The used clothing sale and preview party, where parents can purchase gently worn Brooks Brothers pants and blazers for their sons, is a popular event. The Father-Son Overnight (kindergarten through ninth grade) is an annual rite, and the Fathers' Committee selects the Saturday night entertainment. The boys have a marvelous time playing tennis, fishing, throwing a football with Dad (substitute dads are available). One father recalls his first overnight when bedded down in his tent well after midnight, he heard a group of fathers singing "Kumbaya" around a distant campfire. Older boys attend the annual Father-Son Adventure Dinner, which features an explorer or adventurer as speaker. In addition, the annual Father-Son Day at Shea or Yankee Stadium and family skating party help to bond the Buckley community.

Programs: Buckley's main facility consists of two fully renovated connected buildings on East 73rd and East 74th Streets. The adjacent townhouse was purchased in 1996. It has been completely rebuilt to provide additional classroom space for small group instruction and technology. It will also house some of the facilities now in the 74th Street building which is to be renovated for additional classroom space. In addition, a new Assembly Room with a balcony has been constructed providing more seating space and doubling the stage area of the old facility. The Hubball Building, two blocks away, named for James M. Hubball, headmaster for thirty-two years, houses three full-size gymnasiums plus the two beginners' classrooms. Parents like the fact that the beginners have their own little world, although they travel to "Big Buckley" for Friday assemblies each week. There is a Big Brother Program to help integrate the boys into Big Buckley. Lower School boys write "fan mail" to boys in other grades after watching them perform in a school production.

The Lower School at Buckley is composed of kindergarten through grade 3. Each year the two classes are reshuffled so the boys relate to different friends. "Kindergarten at Buckley is a gentle transition into grade school," parents say. Mondays and Fridays are short days, so there is time for play dates and for just settling in. "Except for a few leftover nursery school cliques, friendships seem to shift weekly in the kindergarten year," said one parent. The Friday afternoon gymnastics and basketball clubs (for an additional charge) are "more social than athletic" and most of the boys attend. Boys who want to learn gymnastics routines can attend afternoon sessions at the school beginning in first grade. After school several boys attend art classes at the Metropolitan Museum of Art, others go to religious school, take Chinese, piano or karate, and if they haven't had enough sports already, some Lower School boys attend the Cavaliers after-school sports program.

The Beginners' classroom is traditional, with block and LEGO corners, listening center, library corner and an adjoining outdoor play roof. On three extended days (until 2:45 P.M.), the boys alternate among gym, creative movement and outdoor play. They also have science and library every week. The kindergarten day is organized but not overly structured. Parents say, "They are really tuned into the rates at which little boys develop. Throughout Buckley the boys are challenged, but they are given the skills to meet those challenges." Kindergartners end the year with the Teddy Bear Picnic, to which boys bring their favorite stuffed bear (or other well-worn animal).

Beginning in first grade boys wear a jacket and tie to school, changing into their "Buckley blues" for after-school sports each day. The day is structured and the boys leave the classroom for art, crafts, music, science and library. First through third graders go to the science lab twice a week. There is a recess in the mornings and in the afternoon an hour of sports. Project Charlie is an anti-drug program in the Lower School that fosters good self-esteem and responsible decision-making.

Each boy is challenged, fundamental skills are taught in small groups and there is never the expectation that all the boys should be at the same skill level at the same time. Homework is given to teach study skills and responsibility. Parents say that "by third grade the pace is quicker, there is serious traditional work, a certain amount of maturity is expected." Third grade boys know how to use the library, and also have access to the New York Society Library on East 79th Street.

The emphasis at Buckley has always been, and remains, on a

"sound traditional curriculum." The Buckley School brochure is notable for its brevity regarding the yearly curriculum, but there is more here than meets the eye. Social studies in the Lower School incorporates multicultural viewpoints. Boys learn to work in collaborative groups as well as individually. There are workbooks that reinforce reading, math and handwriting skills. Journal writing begins in kindergarten and first graders write daily. Formal reading instruction begins in first grade—boys break into reading groups based on ability. There is a lot of movement between these groups. Lower School Head Mrs. Sonja Robinson explains that the reading program is literature based and includes the teaching of phonics. Buckley is quick to identify learning problems before a boy's self-esteem is affected. The Skills and Language Arts Program (SLA) provides support where needed. There is a learning specialist for each division of the school. Cathy Bose, a popular teacher "who really taught the boys how to think," is now the Lower School math specialist and she is introducing new methods of teaching using manipulatives (Cuisinaire rods, blocks, etc.) and a hands-on approach. There is a computer in the kindergarten classrooms that is used for games. Boys in the Lower School "publish" their own books using the computer and there is a Lower School literary magazine that is a desktop publication.

Computer classes and related technology at Buckley includes learning to create websites and researching information on-line. Subject teachers collaborate with computer teachers to support the curriculum.

Throughout the Lower School art is frequently integrated into the curriculum. For a unit on the Middle Ages kindergarten boys went to the Arms and Armor Exhibit at the Met and to the Cathedral of St. John the Divine to see and sketch Gothic architecture. Kindergartners make stick puppets and papier-mâché masks. First graders study the cultures of ancient Mexico and Japan. They study Mayan culture, make their own pottery, pictographs, patterns and write illustrated stories. (One drawing had the caption "I am going to sacrifice you"). After visiting the Brooklyn Botanic Garden, one class designed their own Japanese gardens. The Japan unit culminates in a visit to the Urasenke Center for a traditional tea ceremony. Second graders make papier-mâché skyscrapers, study immigration and make a map of Manhattan.

The range of the art program at Buckley is visible on Exhibition Day. Works range from terra-cotta dinosaurs to seascapes inspired by Monet, from jungles à la Rousseau to multimedia sculptures and computer projects. There are collaborative murals and freedom quilts. The older boys make actual-size self-portraits of what they would like to be when they grow up; paint from still lifes on canvas, and learn the art of basic printmaking, creating dry point and mono prints. In crafts, the projects range from letter openers, toys, small benches and finely crafted, wooden bowls. Boys spend their final year at Buckley creating a carved wooden plaque of a motif that they would like to be remembered by. The plaques grace the walls of the school's lobby.

Middle School at Buckley is composed of fourth grade through sixth grade. Fourth graders enter through the 74th Street door and on the first day mothers must say goodbye downstairs as their sons find their own classrooms. Homework requires more sophisticated thinking and time, parents say (between forty-five minutes and two hours). There are more long-term assignments. Letter grades begin in this year. Boys choose a book for their book report (one self-described nonconformist told us he chose Stephen King's *Nightshift*). The boys study the ancient world and write research reports. They have their own Olympic games. French and Spanish are offered; Latin is required beginning in seventh grade.

The fifth graders study the Middle Ages, culminating in a Medieval Feast. Parents dress in luxurious costumes, the boys make banners, shields and stained glass windows. One parent said by fifth grade the work is more interesting and there is more discussion than in the Lower School. Middle Schoolers study earth science, physical science, human systems and write carefully researched history papers.

Buckley takes athletics seriously and offers a highly organized, competitive sports program. Blue championship banners line the walls of the Hubball Building and the trophy case is full. The brochure says: "Physical fitness and skill development are emphasized." Per von Scheele, the director of athletics at Buckley for over thirty years, rollerblades to school and leads ski trips to Italy during spring vacation. In fall and spring the boys travel to Ward's Island for field sports. There are weekly assessments to determine progress and the membership in the Strength Club, the Super Strength Club or Gladiators bestowed in "recognition of achievement of athletic strength at a level several years beyond a boy's grade level." Those who meet certain standards get a T-shirt.

By seventh grade, afternoon sports are seventy-five minutes long and one mother told us "the boys come home around 5:00 P.M., do a load of work and go to bed." Not every boy needs to be a jock but the boy who is totally uninterested in athletics will not be happy here (although the boys do receive an effort grade in athletics on their report cards). Boys who love to compete and are talented will thrive. Buckley gym birthday parties are popular and parents must book them about a year in advance.

There are Middle School intramural leagues and beginning in seventh grade there are Varsity A and B teams. All boys must participate in one sport each trimester. In fifth grade the boys begin playing football. The Buckley Blue Demons are a source of tremendous pride and school spirit, they score on almost every possession and have been league champions for 27 of the league's 30 year existence. In addition to football, Buckley has championship teams in soccer, wrestling, gymnastics, baseball, lacrosse, basketball and track and field. At the end of each season awards are given out recognizing outstanding individual and team achievement. At the end of the year, the most physically fit boy in Classes IV and up is given special effort recognition.

At the Middle School closing assembly eight different awards are bestowed. Pins are awarded for achievement in the areas of French, athletics, English composition and positive attitude. The Gold Founder's Pin is awarded for the student who made the greatest progress during Middle School, and the George Lane Nichols Award is given for "courage, loyalty, helpfulness and reliability."

The Upper School at Buckley consists of grades seven through nine. In classes VII and VIII boys read *The Iliad*, tackle algebra, hone their lab skills and study American and European history. They continue their study of French and Latin. During the spring term, seventh grade boys write a 2,000-plus-word research paper on a topic of their choice in American history (subject to teacher's approval). Classroom discussions in the Upper School become increasingly animated. In eighth grade the boys read more classics: *The Great Gatsby, Julius Caesar, To Kill a Mockingbird;* they complete another spring research paper and study modern European history up to the Franco-Prussian War.

According to the handbook, ninth grade "readings are chosen for their relevance to the student's developing sense of ethics and justice." They read *The Catcher in the Rye, Huckleberry Finn* and more

Shakespeare. There is a weekly debating period. Boys study Euclidean geometry, physics and modern European history through the present. Ninth graders take trips to Boston and Washington, D.C. (where the boys visit the Lincoln and Jefferson Memorials and Arlington National Cemetery, as well as the Holocaust Museum). Ninth graders complete two major research papers during the year.

The annual class play, a tradition at Buckley, starts in kindergarten. The boys soon become very comfortable onstage. Every boy participates in making scenery and has a small speaking part. First graders perform in the Nativity play and a poetry recital. The annual class plays become more sophisticated in the Middle and Upper Schools; many of these productions offer a contemporary twist on the classics, for example: *A New York Yankee in King Arthur's Court* or *Sherlock Meets the Phantom.* For the Upper School spring operetta, girls from one of the independent girls' schools often play the female roles, but in Middle School, boys play all operetta roles. In the annual Jack Woodruff Public Memorial Speaking Contest for seventh and eighth graders, boys must go through four rounds speaking from four to five minutes on controversial current issues. Recent topics have included the rise of democracy in Russia, educational vouchers and immigration restrictions. The boys are judged on delivery and content.

Ninth graders take a year-long class in debating and engage in a formal debate before the student body. There are two classes in the Upper School that focus on current issues as well as a Class IX leadership class taught by Mr. O'Melia. Ninth graders drop one language and take only five academic courses. They have the privilege of leaving school for lunch on Wednesdays during winter term so that they can use local libraries to work on their term papers, and they also spend Wednesday afternoons on field trips.

The student council for grades four through nine is elected by popular vote, with some officers appointed by faculty. Other extracurricular activities include the popular Glee Club, which gives three concerts a year as well as the Upper School operetta and an annual Middle School operetta. Boys can elect to work on the literary magazine *The Dawn* (named by Mr. Buckley after *The Salutation of the Dawn*, from the Sanskrit), the Upper School newspaper *The Shield* or join the Environmental Club. Community service activities include Glee Club Concert visits to the Mary Manning Walsh Residence, but there is no hourly requirement.

At Upper School closing exercises the Gold Pin is awarded for academic achievement. There is a first and second honor roll, a student athlete award, as well as individual awards in most subject areas. The Harrison S. Kravis Award is given by the Lewis Eisenberg family in recognition of "progress, citizenship, participation in school activities, generosity of spirit." Four major athletic awards, most of them emphasizing character, effort and sportsmanship, are given.

Every graduating Buckley boy carves his own wooden plaque, which is affixed to the school walls. On her tour one parent noticed that in the sixties the plaques featured the occasional *Playboy* Bunny or peace sign, but by the late seventies returned once again to traditional subjects like sailboats, horses, guns, golf clubs, and shields. Nineties plaques show more diverse interests.

Buckley boys have good manners, excel at sports and speak well in public. Parents say that they are well prepared for the most rigorous secondary schools in the nation: "Buckley is prepping our son for life, with high standards in many ways," an alumnus parent says. Whereas a decade ago nearly every Buckley boy went to boarding school, now almost half go to New York City–area day schools. Deerfield, Hotchkiss and Groton lead the recent boarding school choices; Trinity, Riverdale, and Collegiate are popular day school choices.

Traditions Friday assemblies, Father-Son Overnight at Camp Sloane in Lakeville, Connecticut, Father-Son Beginners' Breakfast, Father-Son Adventure Dinner, A Day at Yankee Stadium, Grandparents' Day, Book Fair, Buckley Skating Party, Class V Medieval Feast, Rhythm Band Assembly, Spring Exhibition and Tea, Glee Club operetta, Field Day, Nativity play, Holiday Concert, Annual Jack Woodruff Memorial Public Speaking Contest, Class IX trips to Boston and Washington, D.C., Fathers' Committee softball game vs. Class IX graduates, used clothing and book sale and preview party, theatre benefit, alumni party

Publications Lower School literary magazine: *A World of Stories*
Literary magazine: *The Dawn* (since 1926)
Upper School newspaper: *The Shield*
Yearbook: *Horizons*
Annual report
School and alumni news: *The Buckley Letter*

Community Service Requirement   No hourly requirement; past activities include Yorkville Common Pantry, Clown Care Unit at New York Hospital, and the Association to Benefit Children.

Hangouts   The Buckley Gym, EJ's Luncheonette

The Caedmon School

416 East 80th Street
New York, NY 10021
(212) 879-2296, FAX (212) 879-0627
website: www.caedmonschool.org

Coed
Nursery 2's–5th grade
Not accessible

Carol Gose DeVine, Head of School
Erica Lowenfels, Admissions Director

Birthday Cutoff   Children entering the beginners' group must be 3 by November 31
Children entering kindergarten must be 5 by September 1

Enrollment   Total enrollment: 200
Nursery 3's places: 18–20, largest point of entry
Kindergarten places: 5–8
Graduating class 2004: 14

Grades   Semester system
Detailed anecdotal reports 2 times a year and three conferences, one of which is a portfoio review where 3rd–5th grade students are present; three conferences and one anecdotal report in Early Program (2.9–5 year olds)

Tuition Range 2005–2006 $10,500 (1/2 day), $16,800 (full day), $20,450 for K–5th grade

Financial Aid/Scholarship   14% of the student body receives some form of aid

Endowment   N/A

Diversity   20% students of color

Homework   First grade, 20 minutes written work plus reading. Homework increases as children get older
Third grade and above: 1–1½ hours daily plus long term projects

128

After-School Program   An additional fee is required for all Caedmon after-school programs; open to Caedmon students only. For working parents, child-minding is available, Monday through Friday, until 6:00 P.M.

The after-school program for 4's–5th grade, Monday through Thursday from 3:30 P.M. to 5:30 P.M. offers a variety of creative and athletic activities

Clubs for 1st–5th graders meet every Wednesday until 5:30 P.M.

Afterschool instrumental music program: private lessons in piano, classical guitar, violin and voice are available Monday–Friday

Summer Program   None

The Caedmon School was founded in 1962 by a group of parents interested in the philosophy of Maria Montessori; Caedmon offers a "modified Montessori" program. The school is housed in a five-story building and classrooms are bright and airy. The outside courtyard, sheltered from the street, has a safety surface playground. There is a large lunchroom with a full kitchen, which serves hot lunch to everyone.

Head of School Carol DeVine points out that Caedmon differs from the classical Montessori mold in the Early Program because "Caedmon utilizes and provides materials for fantasy play and there is an emphasis on group work and relaxed socialization amongst the children. There are many more differences in the elementary program, especially in the materials used."

An "attitude of compassion," community service, multicultural respect and acceptance are woven into Caedmon's curriculum. Mrs. DeVine stresses that "we teach the child, not just the curriculum." Twenty-five percent of the student body is international; many parents work at the U.N. missions. One parent said, "My husband is with the U.N.; we move constantly and coming to New York City was overwhelming. Caedmon became an oasis for our whole family." Parents say that Caedmon is "warm and accommodating; they are very responsive to children's differing rates of development." There is praise for an "experienced, superb teaching staff" and for the "creative, well thought out homework assignments."

Getting in: The school has a fall admissions procedure; the application deadline is in November 30. Applications are processed in the order in which they are received. The application fee is $50.00. Parents are welcome to attend an evening open house held in the Fall, or they can attend a morning group tour. Children are interviewed in small groups and parents are interviewed on a separate day.

Parents: Caedmon parents range from artists to investment bankers. The Board of Trustees has twenty-one elected members, seven of whom may be present parents. The Parents' Auxiliary is close knit and dedicated. The PA hosts a "Back to School" night at the beginning of the year to introduce parents to their children's teachers and provide an opportunity for new parents to meet each other. An auction fund-raiser is held in March every year. A wine-tasting party for international parents is held in the fall and another in the spring for in-coming parents. Early morning "Coffee and Curriculum" work-shops are held throughout the year. Parents are encouraged to talk to their child's teacher either directly or on the phone. Formal conferences are held three times each year.

Program: Classes are small and the overall student/teacher ratio is 8:1. The atmosphere is academic but nurturing. Children are placed into small groups for academic instruction. Beginners start at two years and nine months; the Early Program is composed of children three to five-years-old and the Elementary Program consists of kindergarten through fifth grade. Specialists work closely with classroom teachers balancing the curriculum with science, Spanish, library/research skills, computer, music, art, gym, yoga, and community service projects.

The Early Program utilizes mixed-age classrooms and children frequently work together in small groups. The modified Montessori approach emphasizes Montessori materials and activities but also encourages creativity. Children on a full-day schedule have lunch and a nap. The afternoon activities include visits to the science room and library. There is also an art class in addition to the art activity that is available during the mornings.

In kindergarten, the focus is on language-rich reading and writing curriculum with particular emphasis on basic skills. The math program stresses the use of numbers, words (solving word problems) and graphic measurements. Using manipulatives, the students learn concepts and establish a strong foundation for learning more complex skills. Kindergarten prepares five-year-olds for the more teacher-directed and academic demands of Caedmon's Elementary Program. "The teacher really understands that my five-year-old is both a playful child and a budding student," observed one parent.

The Elementary Program offers an integrated curriculum. For example, a social studies class was studying immigration and the students' countries of origin. The music teacher wrote a play along with his class called *Making Tracks in America* with jazz and blues music taken from eighteenth century African-American spirituals and other American musical traditions. In art class, the students created various immigration scenes for the set.

Math is also integrated with other subject matter. Every year, during National Mathematics Month, the entire staff puts together a special all-day math event for the children. A different theme is selected each year with a variety of activities that demonstrate the practical applications of math.

Computer skills begin in kindergarten and the children have access to computers in the computer lab, library and every classroom.

Art and music at Caedmon are exceptionally strong. Artwork by Caedmon students has been exhibited in the Monmouth County Museum (New Jersey), the Manhattan Children's Museum, WNET Channel 13 Student Arts Festival, WNET Channel 13 Student Arts International Exchange, and many other places. Original musical productions are put on twice a year; children from kindergarten through fifth grade participate.

The Head of School works very closely with each graduating student and their family on on-going school placement to ensure success.

Popular Secondary School Choices   Allen-Stevenson, Brearley, Browning, Birch Wathen Lenox, Calhoun, Columbia Grammar & Preparatory School, Convent of the Sacred Heart, Dalton, Dwight, Hewitt, Horace Mann, Manhattan Country School, Marymount, Nightingale-Bamford, Poly Prep, Rudolf Steiner, Riverdale, Trevor Day School, UNIS, York Prep

Traditions   Caedmon Meeting (weekly meeting of entire Elementary community), student musicales, Back to School Night, Elementary apple-picking trip, all-school picnic in Central Park, all-school Thanksgiving feast, Caedmon Chorus holiday performance at Lord & Taylor, Holiday Assembly, international parent wine tasting party, fundraising auction, Grandparent/Special Friend Day, Parent breakfasts, Mathland, upper level over-night trip, annual Spring beach trip (Elementary), annual Spring park day and picnic (Early Program), and new parent cocktail party.

Community Service   Community service is an integral parent of the curriculum in fifth grade. Students explore issues related to their community service projects through interdisciplinary thematic units of study.

The Calhoun School

Robert L. Beir Lower School
160 West 74th Street
New York, NY 10023
(212) 497-6550 (main number)
(212) 497-6575 (admissions)
FAX (212) 721-2025
website: www.calhoun.org

(2nd grade–12th Grade)
433 West End Avenue (at 81st Street)
New York, NY 10024
(212) 497-6500 (main number)
(212) 497-6510 (admissions)
FAX (212) 497-6530
website: www.calhoun.org

Coed
Preschool–12th Grade
Not accessible at 160 West 74th Street;
Not fully accessible at 433 West End Avenue

Mr. Steven J. Nelson, Head of School
Ms. Nancy Sherman, Director of Admissions, 81st Street
Ms. Robin M. Otton, Director of Lower School Admissions, 74th Street
Ms. Jenny Eugenia, Assistant Director of Admissions, 81st Street

Birthday Cutoff   Children entering preschool must be 3 by September 1
Children entering kindergarten must be 5 by September 1

Enrollment   Total enrollment: 660
Preschool 3's places: 48, largest point of entry
Kindergarten places: 12
Graduating class 2004: 43

Grades   Semester system
Letter and number grades begin in 8th grade
Foreign language begins in preschool 3's with Spanish. French and Latin are added in Middle School

133

Departmentalization begins in 2nd grade (2nd through 4th graders move in homeroom or "cluster" groups to specialists in all subjects.) Full departmentalization begins in 5th grade
Timing of first midterm or final exam varies

Tuition Range 2005–2006 Approximately $16,700 to $26,700, Preschool (1/2 day 3's)–12th grade (includes lunch for 2nd through 12th grades and all materials and books)
Additional fees: for trips (5th–9th grades, ranges from $100–$400); Parents Association fees, $50
Tuition plan of 10 monthly payments can be arranged

Financial Aid/Scholarship 20% of the student body receives financial aid

Endowment N/A

Diversity Membership in Early Steps, The Albert G. Oliver Program, Prep for Prep, and Faculty Diversity Search.

Homework Preschool–1st grade: none
2nd–4th: approximately 15–45 minutes
5th–8th: 1–3 hours
9th–12th: approximately 2–4 hours

After-School Program Calhoun ASP: a variety of classes offered each school day in both buildings, Monday–Friday, 3–5 P.M. daily daycare (74th street), 3–6 P.M. (81st street), with a homework help program and a variety of activities including flower arranging, knitting, chess, fencing, yoga, digital video, ceramics, oil painting, electronic music production, and driver's education; karate, computer, cooking; an additional payment is required

Summer Program Summercare: a six-week day camp program for children ages 3–7, directed and staffed by members of the Calhoun School faculty; from the third week in June through July, 8:30 A.M.–2:30 P.M.

Founded in 1896 as the Jacobi School, Calhoun soon became an all girls school, and was renamed in 1924 for Head of School Mary Edwards Calhoun. It became completely coeducational in 1971. Calhoun has always been a forward-looking institution known for its innovative curriculum, individualized attention and small class size. Within each division of the school, there are few walls or doors and no rows of desks, but rather areas assigned to each discipline. Although the tone is informal, there is a strong underlying academic structure. Parents say, "Calhoun prepares students well for college because they have learned how to be independent thinkers and achievers."

Calhoun has two locations: Since 1989, preschool through first grade have been housed in the Robert L. Beir Building on West 74th street. Since 1975, grades two through twelve have been located in a modern building at West 81st Street and West End Avenue. In 2004, four additional floors were added to the 81st Street building. The new floors house a full-size athletic center, a state-of-the-art performance center, studio art workshops, science labs and language labs. The school is organized into three divisions, each with its own director.

Parents have a high regard for the teaching staff at Calhoun. Parents describe Calhoun as a community consisting of administrators, teachers, children and parents. Teachers and administrators are called by their first names. Under the inspired leadership of Dr. Neen Hunt, a gifted educator and former head of school, Calhoun attracted a dedicated and caring staff, some of whom have developed its innovative award-winning curriculum. Faculty incentives such as the Professional Development Program, a grant from the Edward Ford Foundation and the Faculty Enrichment Grant allow teachers at Calhoun to continue to grow and learn. Parents say, "At Calhoun children see good values that are reinforced by example." Current Head of School, Steven J. Nelson, came to Calhoun in 1998, with experience in a variety of private school and college settings, and with a deep belief in the value of a progressive education. In describing his philosophy, Mr. Nelson says, "We need to think about education in America in a new way . . . We should identify and nurture the rich mix of intelligences that accompany each child through the schoolhouse door. We should value the abstract painting as much as we value the calculation of compound interest."

Getting in: Parents interested in learning more about Calhoun can attend an open house in the Fall before applying. The application fee is $45. There are some short essay questions on the application, such as "Briefly describe your child's personality . . . distinctive qualities, temperament . . . special interests." The school views the ERB as just one component used to evaluate the match between the child and the school. Calhoun selects students with a broad range of interests and talents who have the potential to be focused and self-motivated and the intelligence necessary to meet the demands of their program. A kindergarten applicant's school visit is low-keyed, its aim is to get a sense of the child's personality and interests and to assess facility with basic skills and concepts. Parents meet with admissions personnel to see if Calhoun's philosophy and parental expectations for their child's education are compatible. The preschool program is very popular and the largest point of entry. There are some spaces each year for new four year olds, and space also opens up at the kindergarten level. Calhoun gives preference to siblings whenever possible.

Parents: Socially, Calhoun is low-key. The primary focus is always on the child, not the parent or social scene. Calhoun counts on parents to be active in their child's educational life, and the school in turn is very supportive of parents. There are frequent conferences, and parents are invited to call or visit when they need to. Annual Parents Association activities include the Lower School Halloween Fest, Book Fair at Barnes & Noble, the PA Spring Carnival and meetings on parenting and educational philosophy. Some of the more informal events for parents include Wednesday evening volleyball games and theatre parties, some of which are for families. Many parents say they feel a connection to Calhoun even after their children have graduated, and they continue to attend school events.

Program: At the Robert L. Beir Lower School building (preschool through first grade), classrooms are bright and airy. A strong, cohesive team of teachers collaborate to create an impressive curriculum that integrates art, music, theater, science, computers, Spanish, and physical education. Lower School Director Kathleen Clinesmith has worked with young children for many years and is a strong proponent of Calhoun's learning philosophy.

Separation is handled gently on an individual basis: All children have a homeroom "cluster" area and a primary or "cluster" teacher; they travel from this cluster area to other rooms and specialists for certain subjects, depending on their grade level. Children in kindergarten and first grade have language arts, math, science, social studies, Spanish, block building, cooking, art, music, shop, library, computer, drama, physical education, theater and creative movement. Children take recess on the terrace or go to the park each day. Parents say, "Creativity and socialization and the three R's are all stressed in the Lower School." Discipline is recognized as an inner process that is developed with the aid of adults. Calhoun teachers are sensitive to the differing rates of social and emotional development in children. A parent said, "Many are creative kids who march to their own tune."

A broad based approach to teaching reading is employed, making use of Whole Language, phonics, and skill-based instruction techniques. In addition, an innovative program integrates children's creative writing and music. First graders, whose classrooms are on the top two floors of the Beir building, continue to gain spelling skills while given the freedom to use invented spelling. Throughout the school year, first through fourth graders proudly publish their own original books and research papers. First graders continue to follow a curriculum stressing hands-on learning, problem-solving and teamwork. Students begin a year-long study of Central Park. Weekly visits to the park provide experiences that are further developed back in the classroom, including detailed topographical maps of the park, observational drawings of its plants, animals, statues and structures, and classification of the various leaves and rocks that are collected.

Second through twelfth grades are located in the West End Avenue and 81st Street building, where each of the three divisions has its own floor. Second through fourth graders (the continuation of Lower School at 81st Street) are divided by grade level into groups or clusters of twelve to fifteen students, and assigned an advisor. They travel as a cluster to other classroom and activity areas within the school. (Calhoun's cluster advisory system changes somewhat in the Middle and Upper Schools, where clusters are formed across the grades and students follow increasingly individualized schedules.) In keeping with Calhoun's philosophy of learning as a shared, connected experience, there are few high walls or doors separating cluster areas. Table groupings replace the traditional desks in rows.

An eclectic approach is used to improve reading skills. Small reading groups are the norm. Students engage in creative and journal writing and learn the writing process. Research writing skills are introduced in first grade and developed further in successive grades. Each student chooses a topic and writes a formal thesis. By the end of the eighth grade, students are expected to have strong skills in research writing.

Math skills in mechanics and abstract thinking are taught in creative hands-on classes in which students participate fully, sometimes even writing their own math problems to share with other math students. Homework assignments reinforce skills as well as challenge students. Critical thinking and problem solving encourage divergent thinking.

The school recognizes the different talents, abilities and learning styles of individual children. The curriculum is flexible enough to address itself to varying developmental needs. Parents say there is always an appropriate level of challenge. A parent with a child whose reading level in kindergarten was at least three years above that of his classmates spoke of the expert and sensitive way in which that child was always challenged and excited by the work he was given while never having to be isolated from his peers.

Calhoun's interdisciplinary approach to learning is most clearly obvious, beginning at the Lower School level, when, for example, literature is integrated with social studies, science and other subjects. The artful interweaving of different subjects into a cohesive whole is the hallmark of the program, evident at each grade level.

Second graders spend a year studying New York City, beginning with Calhoun and extending to various neighborhoods, cultural and historical aspects of the city. Third graders study U.S. history and world geography, fourth graders delve more deeply into New York City's history, focusing on immigration, emigration, moving and settling, culminating in a research paper.

Kara Stern, Middle School Director and a Joseph F. Klingenstein Fellow, joined Calhoun after eight years at Little Red/Elisabeth Irwin. Ms. Stern, who was educated at progressive schools, is committed to a student-centered learning environment.

The Middle School at Calhoun is composed of grades five through eight. The integrated English and social studies curriculum for fifth and sixth graders was developed by two Calhoun teachers and won recognition from the National Conference of Teachers of English. "Ancient Civilizations" and "The Medieval World" represent the two-year cycle in which students examine the roots of Western civilization and read the literature of different ethnic groups, including Greek, Roman, Egyptian and Islamic. The course description says "Students discover similar motifs, plot devices and types of characters that reappear in old and new literature, no matter what its cultural origin." The academic curriculum is enhanced by related activities: art, music, drama, creative writing, or computer study. For instance, the art program, complementing the English and social studies curricula, might organize projects in stained glass and illumination (fifth/sixth grade medieval studies).

In computer class, sixth graders create a newspaper comparing and contrasting Islamic society with American society today. All fifth and sixth graders study music, drama, studio art and woodshop, in addition to their academic core courses. Seventh and eighth graders choose arts electives like oil painting, digital video, Shakespeare, directing, creative writing and graphic design.

Eighth graders write a formal term paper. Each part of the research process is graded, and after the finished product is presented, further revision may be done. An alumna who went on to Stanford University says that papers at college are easier than those at Calhoun. The Middle School math curriculum is viewed as a process that extends over the four years of the division. At the eighth grade level, students begin their study of algebra. Two math/science teachers at Calhoun have won recognition: In August, 2003, science teacher John Roeder, who has been at Calhoun for thirty-one years, won an Award For Excellence in pre-college physics teaching, from the American Association of Physics Teachers. Middle School math teacher Phil Bender earns praise for his innovative conceptual math program. One project in applied math involves baseball statistics; another uses a trip to the Bronx Zoo as an opportunity to collect and process data. Each year a number of Calhoun students are accepted to the specialized math and science public high schools (see pages 475–477, *infra*).

Students begin formal instruction in modern language, electing either French or Spanish in the fifth grade. Latin is an elective choice beginning in seventh grade. The program continues into the Upper School through advanced literature, and conversation courses.

Calhoun's computer program spans all grade levels. In the Lower School, students use graphics and word processing programs, in addition to educational games which reinforce math, language, and problem solving skills. Lower school students (grades 2–4) use the computer as a tool to enhance the curriculum in all subject areas. By the end of fourth grade all children complete a keyboarding program and use application software through group projects. Fifth graders are introduced to SketchUp, a computer program that enhances visualization and measurement skills, which dovetails with workworking class. Sixth grade projects include multimedia presentations that are integrated with social studies and English. Seventh and eighth graders choose from a variety of electives in advanced technology including video production and web design.

Basic Upper School computer courses include word processing, database, spreadsheet, desktop publishing and image scanning. Upper School students can also choose from advanced electives, including programming, web design and computer math. Several Calhoun Upper School students have parlayed their computer expertise into well-paying summer jobs.

The Upper School at Calhoun consists of grades nine through twelve. Parents describe the Upper School student body at Calhoun as diverse; students have different strengths and interests as well as different backgrounds.

Loretta Ryan, Upper School Director, has been at Calhoun for nineteen years. An anthropologist and formerly a member of the social studies department, she has promoted diversity of all kinds and introduced an inclusive two-year world history program in the Upper School. As Academic Dean for the school, she works to preserve the school's long-standing goal of offering students a strong academic program and support for personal and community growth.

Early Fall activities for all ninth graders include an orientation day prior to the official beginning of classes, and a two-day overnight with peer leaders and faculty in late September. Peer leaders, specially chosen and trained seniors, also lead weekly discussions with small groups of ninth graders throughout the year, in a course called Life Skills.

The cluster advisory system continues in the Upper School. Parents find that it is an excellent and easy way to keep communication open and consistent. Beginning in the Middle School and continuing through the senior year, students are scheduled once a week to meet individually with their cluster advisors. For graduation, 21 credits are required, including three in science, one-half in computer science and three in modern language. There are, in addition, the following noncredit requirements: four years of physical education and sixty hours of community service.

Classes are mostly discussion-based seminars. Parents say it is impossible for students to be lost in the shuffle because classes are small (a maximum of fifteen per class), and students are always active participants. Parents and graduates praise the exceptional preparation in interdisciplinary writing and research. Qualified students are invited to do Honors projects and participate in weekly Honors discussion groups. The school offers advanced English, Biology, Physics, Chemistry, and Spanish classes, and teachers assist students preparing to take AP Calculus, English, Biology, and Physics. But the school no longer offers AP courses as such.

A Senior Masterworks Program allows students to design their own projects for half or one credit in the subject of their choice, culminating in an oral or written presentation or performance before a Masterworks Committee. Sample projects have included play directing, a personal family history of the Holocaust, a collection of short stories, a sculpture, a dance demonstration/performance and vocal recital.

Calhoun participates in the Network of Complementary Schools, which offers a three-week exchange program for students as well as faculty at other innovative schools throughout the United States and Canada. For example, students may attend a school on a Navajo reservation in Arizona, an arts program in Interlochen, Michigan, an outdoor survival program in the Colorado mountains, or they can study architecture in a San Francisco school. Through Network, select students are also given the opportunity to attend a Multicultural Leadership Workshop in Toronto. In the past, Calhoun has been host to students from the Navajo reservation, from Seattle, Washington and from a small rural town in Kansas. While on an exchange visit at a school in San Francisco, an Upper School English teacher developed a curriculum in Latino literature, now used at Calhoun.

Upper School students, from ninth grade on, may leave school during a free period or during lunch. An active Student Government Executive Council is made up of class officers from each class along with an elected president, vice-president, secretary and treasurer. The student government has, among its many activities, sponsored students at the AIDS Dance-a-thon and raised money for UNICEF.

The MCC (Multicultural Committee) organizes assemblies and discussions on cross-cultural issues. Free the Children, SAC (a gay-straight alliance) and Students for Choice raise consciousness about social concerns. Other clubs reflect student interest in French, astronomy and Scrabble. Calhoun also has a Model UN team whose members have participated in various yearly events.

There are Middle and Upper School theater productions each year held in the new 200+ seat auditorium. Café Calhoun, sponsored by student government, is a showcase for Upper School student talent.

Students may work on the staffs of the school newspaper, literary magazine and yearbook.

Varsity sports include league-winning volleyball, basketball and soccer teams, in addition to track, cross-country, golf, softball, tennis and sailing. Calhoun also offers intramural swimming at Asphalt Green.

In their weekly College Seminar, second semester juniors begin discussing the process of choosing and applying to colleges. This seminar continues through the middle of the senior year, and individual consultation continues until acceptances are received and final choices must be made.

Calhoun is a charter member of the Cum Laude Society and annually elects outstanding seniors for membership. Numerous awards are presented at Class Day, Athletic Awards Assembly and Commencement. There are named memorial awards in many subject areas as well as athletic awards. Awards recognize academic strengths, character, integrity, maturity and service. Students can also graduate with distinction in given disciplines. Calhoun graduates go on to a variety of colleges, reflecting the diversity within the graduating class.

Popular College Choices   Brown University, Wesleyan University, Colgate, Kenyon, Skidmore, New York University, Oberlin College, Vassar College, University of Michigan, George Washington University, Bard College, and Pitzer College

Traditions   Harvest Festival (annual school Thanksgiving celebration with thematic activities organized around a community service project), Fall and Spring MS/US dramatic productions. Café Calhoun (Upper School talent show), Book Fair, Spring Carnival, Cluster and Grade Trip Days (special activities for grades 2–12), Intersession classes/activities, Wednesday evening volleyball for parents, artist-in-residence program, annual trustees' fund-raising event, Curriculum Expo (which includes an art show), Class Day, Athletic Awards Assembly, Commencement exercises

Community Service Requirement   60 hours

Publications   Newspapers: *The Issue, The Slice*
Literary magazine: *Antithesis*

Newsletter/alumnae/i publication: *Calhoun Chronicle*
Yearbook

Hangouts   Riverside Park, student lounge, the plaza on 81st Street
outside Calhoun, neighborhood coffee and pizza shops, Barnes &
Noble Bookstore

The Cathedral School

1047 Amsterdam Avenue
New York, NY 10025–1702
(212) 316-7500, FAX (212) 316-7558
website: www.cathedralnyc.org
e-mail: admission@cathedralnyc.org

Coed
Kindergarten–8th grade
Not accessible

Marsha Nelson, Headmaster
Linda Mathews, Director of Admissions

Uniform   Dress code: white or navy blouses/shirts, navy or khaki pants, shorts (in warm weather)

Birthday Cutoff   Children entering kindergarten must be 5 by September 30

Enrollment   Total enrollment: 248
Kindergarten places: 29–30
Graduating class 2004: 30

Grades   The Lower School (kindergarten–grade 4) is on a semester system
The Upper School (grades 5–8) is on a trimester system
Letter grades begin in 5th grade
Full departmentalization begins in 5th grade

Tuition Range 2004–2005 $21,750 to $22,700, K–8th grade
Fees and lunch are included in the tuition

Financial Aid/Scholarship   39% of the student body receives some form of aid based on financial need

Endowment $3.6 million

After-School Program   The school has an extended day enrichment program for Cathedral School students. In addition, the Cathedral of St. John the Divine's A.C.T. program offers after-school and holiday programs. A.C.T. is open to students from other schools but Cathedral students have priority when registering; an additional payment is required

Summer Program   A.C.T. uses the 13-acre Cathedral Close for the summer program; a variety of creative and athletic activities are offered for an additional payment

————

The Cathedral School was founded in 1901 to provide choristers for the Cathedral of St. John the Divine. Now a fully coeducational independent school, the tradition of providing the choristers for the Cathedral is still one of the school's unique features. When the strains of evensong float out of the gothic cathedral over the 13-acre close of flowering shrubs and herb gardens, shade trees and strolling peacocks, Cathedral School seems like a place out of time, yet this school is very much in sync with modern life and the latest educational practices. One of the best kept secrets on the Upper West side, Cathedral School is a vibrant community. Its growing popularity is due to not only its extraordinary location but also a strong academic program, an enthusiastic new head of school, and a diverse and talented pool of students.

Marsha Nelson, former Associate Head of Trinity School, became Head of School in 2003. It appears to be a good fit.

Getting in: Parents can attend information-gathering open houses in the fall. They have ample opportunity to observe classes, and special events and ask questions of school administrators and parents. The school retains an affiliation with the Episcopal Church but admits students of all faiths. The ERB is required for admission. Parents come for a tour and applicants are interviewed individually at the school. Cathedral School has always valued diversity and a full 39% of students receive financial aid. The school roster reads like a mellifluous mix of nationalities. Entering kindergarten and first grade students visit the school in late May. All new students attend a one-day orientation at school before opening day.

Parents: The parent body at Cathedral School represents a hip cross-section of city life and includes some prominent writer/editors, well-known actors, academics from Columbia University, professionals, musicians, and artists. Parents value the inclusiveness of the community and everyone is made to feel welcome. Though most parents work, the Parents Association is very active and sponsors fundraisers, book fairs, class dinners, workshops, and picnics.

Program: Classes throughout the school are small. The atmosphere is academic but nurturing and the curriculum celebrates the diversity of the school's community. The Lower School is composed of grades kindergarten through four, and the Upper School is composed of grades five through eight. Each division has its own Division Head, faculty, schedule and special facilities. Lower School students, working in a self-contained classroom setting, master basic skills in the three R's and science. French or Spanish is introduced in kindergarten.

Students enjoy music and art classes twice a week, library once a week, and physical education four times a week. Whenever possible, teachers in different departments join together to write and teach an interdisciplinary curriculum so that students learn the connections between subject areas. For example, when Lower School students study the history and culture of Native Americans in social studies, they visit Manitoga in Garrison, New York, a living archeological site replicating an Indian village. They read Native American myths and folk tales and create their own, make Indian artifacts in art, write and perform original plays in music class.

The use of technology at Cathedral is curriculum driven. All classrooms have at least one computer and printer with access to the school's network and the Internet. The computer lab has eighteen computers, the library has seven and the science lab and art room share seven iBooks.

The Director of Technology and the librarian work with teachers to integrate a sequence of technologically appropriate skills including keyboarding, word-processing, telecommunications, graphing, on-line research, spreadsheet, and multimedia design. Recent projects include a volcano project in third grade, an animal research project in fourth grade, an African folktale project in fifth grade, an Ancient Roman project in sixth grade, and eighth grade French and Spanish projects. New technology units are developed through brainstorming sessions with the Director of Technology, librarian, teachers and learning specialists.

Art is integrated into the curriculum wherever possible and student artwork is prominently displayed throughout the school. Students work in traditional media as well as nontraditional art forms like mosaic, architecture, and book-making. For good reason, the

Medieval Studies curriculum at Cathedral School is the best in the city. Students tour every inch of the Cathedral and seventh graders celebrate the period's art, music, English and Latin in a Medieval Evensong, held in the Great Choir of the Cathedral of St. John the Divine. They carry personal coats-of-arms, banners, and cardboard gargoyles, wear period costumes, recite original sonnets of courtly love, and sing and perform a regal dance that they choreograph themselves.

The interdisciplinary music curriculum is skills based and emphasizes fun and appreciation. Through the study of musical concepts of melody, harmony, and rhythm, students learn to read music and experience song and dance from different cultures. Violin instruction begins in first grade. Approximately 25 fourth through eighth grade students are choristers. All third graders are auditioned for the choir, a very selective process; however, joining the choir is optional. Choristers receive superior musical training, a stipend towards tuition and a wealth of performing experience. Student choristers have performed at Shea Stadium for the opening game, at Harvard University, at the lighting of the Christmas tree at Rockefeller Center, and at the memorial services for Jim Henson, creator of the Muppets, and jazz-great Louis Armstrong.

The physical education department uses Cathedral School's two gymnasiums and two outdoor playgrounds, as well as the adjacent playing fields in Morningside Park. Major playground and library renovations were recently completed. Intramural and varsity sports, both single-sex and coed, include basketball, soccer, softball and volleyball.

Hot lunch (a salad bar and sandwiches are also available) is served family style with mixed age groupings at tables; grace is led by student volunteers, including kindergartners, and sung by all. Older students take turns as waiters and servers, helping the younger students. On specific days throughout the year lunch features traditional ethnic cuisines such as African-American, Caribbean, Chinese, and Greek.

Every Friday morning Lower School assembly is held in the common room. One parent said assembly reminds him of why he chose Cathedral School in the first place: "The spirit, the mix of interests, the obvious involvement of the teachers." The assembly room overflows with parents who act as both audience and participants.

The Upper School at Cathedral (grades 5–8) is departmentalized.

147

Each student carries a full program in English, social studies, math, science, French or Spanish and Latin. Latin is required in the seventh and eighth grades in addition to French or Spanish. For the last few years, Cathedral School's top Latin students have won first place in a New York City public and private school competition. Latin teacher Dr. John Vitale makes a compelling case for the relevance of studying classical Latin today (and not just as a vocabulary booster for the SAT's).

Students visit the cathedral twice each week for services led by the chaplain. While the services concentrate on stories, feasts and values derived from the Judaeo-Christian tradition in the West, students are also exposed to the world's great religious traditions. For example, the entire Lower School celebrated a multiethnic Passover seder. Students at the school represent a variety of religious traditions, including Buddhist and Muslim. "The goal is to affirm the religious tradition of every child." Parents praise the spirituality which infuses learning at Cathedral School. Each fifth grade student works with the chaplain in an experiential course called "World Religions" which is intentionally non-denominational.

The Secondary School Placement Director works individually with each student and their parents beginning in seventh grade to develop an appropriate list of high school options. Placement Counseling emphasizes self-awareness and a search for a school that would be appropriate for each individual's talents and interests.

Popular Secondary School Choices Trevor Day, Dalton, Columbia Grammar and Prep, Fieldston, Friends Seminary, Trinity School, Riverdale Country Day School, Horace Mann School, Marymount, Stuyvesant High School, LaGuardia High School of Music and Art and the Performing Arts Boarding: Milton Academy, Emma Willard, Exeter, Kent, St. Andrew's, Miss Hall's

Community Service Requirement Students develop projects to support Cathedral outreach and environmental programs, care for Cathedral Close, or raise funds for outside organizations; Lower School Evensong in Action is a new initiative.

Traditions New parent dinners, all-school picnic on the grounds, class dinners, an annual fundraising auction, theater parties, Arts

Festival, Earth Day, Alumni Day, Grandparents Day, Class Reps, Spring Fair, Field Day, Upper School Camp Trip, Chorister Tours, Peace Tree Ceremony, Passover Seder, Kwaanza Assembly, Eighth Grade Musical, Eighth Grade Class Day, Chorister Divestiture and graduation

The Chapin School

100 East End Avenue
New York, NY 10028
(212) 744-2335
website: www.chapin.edu

All girls
Kindergarten–12th grade
Accessible

Dr. Patricia Hayot, Head of School
Tina Herman, Director of Upper School Admissions
Elizabeth Ferenzi, Director of Lower School Admissions

Uniform   Lower School: light green or dark green jumper, white blouse or polo shirt
Middle School: dark green pleated skirt with white collared shirt, khaki pants
Upper School: dress Gordon or dark green kilt or skirt, collared shirt or blouse, khaki pants
Uniforms can be purchased from the Corey Uniform Company

Birthday Cutoff   Children entering kindergarten must be 5 by September 1

Enrollment   Total enrollment: 650
Kindergarten places: 50
Graduating class 2004: 39

Grades   Semester system in the Lower and Middle School
Trimester system in the Upper School
Kindergarten–3rd grade: detailed progress reports
Classes 4–12: letter grades and comments
Departmentalization begins in 4th grade
First final exam in 7th grade

Tuition Range 2005–2006 $25,600, Kindergarten–12th grade
Additional fees: approximately $950 to $2,300
School bus available for K–6; cost depends on type of service

Financial Aid/Scholarship $2,129,000 in tuition aid for 16% of the student body in school year 2004–2005

Endowment $49 million

Diversity 27% according to NAIS; the school works closely with Early Steps, A Better Chance, Albert G. Oliver Program, TEAK and Prep for Prep; the school has a diversity coordinator who oversees programs and clubs including the Cultural Awareness Program, the Gay Straight Alliance, and P.O.C.C. (Parents of Children of Color)

Homework Class 1: reading
Class 2: 20–30 minutes
Class 3: 30–40 minutes
Class 4: 20 minutes per subject (average 3 subjects)
Classes 5–8: approximately 2–3 hours spent on an average of 4 subjects, depending on grade level
Classes 9–12: 3 hours

After-School Program The Clubhouse is an after-school program at the Brearley and Chapin Schools that provides a variety of classes for students in kindergarten through fifth grade, Monday through Friday. There is a play period before class when the girls are given a snack or, on Friday, lunch.
The school oversees the organization of various activities in fine arts, computer science and physical education for Middle and Upper School students
Middle School intramural program
Green and Gold team competition (girls in classes 4–12 at Chapin are either Green or Gold)
AAIS League interscholastic competition
Elective offerings in both the Middle and Upper Schools
Night Owl Study Hall

Summer Program June Jamboree, 2 week summer camp

The Chapin School was founded by Maria Bowen Chapin in 1901 as an elementary school called "Miss Chapin's School for Girls." After the death of Miss Chapin, in 1934, it became The Chapin School, Ltd. Throughout the years Chapin has had strong leadership: Miss Ethel Grey Stringfellow, headmistress for twenty-four years, was succeeded in 1959 by Mildred J. Berendsen, who, after leading Chapin into the nineties, retired after thirty-four years in 1993. Dr. Patricia Hayot was named head in 2003.

In the 1920s and 30s, Miss Chapin's School groomed New York's young women to take their place in Society. At that time, there were no afternoon classes. Some girls had great academic potential, and some less; classes were designated "general" or "college," depending on the aspirations of the individual.

Chapin in the new millennium, as in the nineties, has an excellent academic reputation and sends its graduates on to the very top colleges throughout the country, but the tone of the school remains decidedly traditional. A parent told us "We wanted a place where our daughter would feel valued and loved. They care about keeping our girls sweet." And she added, "They highlight what she does well."

A major building program was recently completed. Improvements to the school included an additional gym, new science labs, more classroom space and new dance, art and computer facilities. Additional construction completed in 1998 includes: a two-floor library/multimedia center, a new gymnasium, a drama classroom/black box theatre and a foreign language lab. The greenhouse, outdoor play yard, art studios and dining room were also renovated and a third kindergarten space was added.

Pat Hayot, current head of School, became the sixth Head in the school's 103-year history. A former Klingenstein Fellow at Columbia University's Teachers College, she arrived at Chapin on the heels of serving as Head of The International School in Paris and the Columbus School for Girls. Unlike some of her predecessors, and more like Miss Chapin, a suffragette, Dr. Hayot is open and inspired. "Where's your center?" she asks.

Planning ahead is first on Dr. Hoyt's agenda, as Chapin undergoes a massive strategic planning process. Some key issues are building a more global curriculum that is reflective of today's world, electives for ninth graders, more AP classes, and even more personalized scheduling.

Spring 1998 marked the official opening of the new library, The Annenberg Center for Learning and Research. An outdoor playroof was converted to create this "Titanic" space which features porthole windows and a grand staircase. The library has a multi-media center with capabilities for video-conferencing, private study rooms and in one section—plush purple armchairs! On previous tours The Chapin School felt like a renovated mansion; the effect of the current renovation is like taking down the heavy drapery and letting in the light.

Modernization is underway in other areas of the school as well: In 1998 the Upper School at Chapin voted to add khaki pants to the school uniform, supplanting the Gordon Plaid kilt. The traditional Friday Morning Assembly, also known as Prayers, has been updated to include celebrations of a range of faiths. The girls now have a part in designing the program on Fridays which reflects the diversity within the school community.

The Life Skills Committee which began several years ago, reshaped life at the school. Two outgrowths of this committee are 1) Appointment of a full time coordinator of counseling services and life skills education who oversees the social and emotional growth and health of the school. 2) The introduction of a Peer Leadership program which prepares a select group of twelfth graders to counsel ninth graders.

Getting in: Parents tour Chapin after applying. Prospective kindergarten parents meet in a group with the Lower School head in the Reception Room for a short talk. Each family is given the tour individually by a parent tour guide and interviewed by a member of the admissions office staff. Parents return with their child for a play group interview during which Dr. Hayot and an Upper School student answer questions. Every applicant receives a plant from Chapin's greenhouse. After admissions decisions have been made, a wait list is maintained. The wait-list letter informs parents how to notify the admissions office of their continued interest in The Chapin School.

Parents: The Chapin parent body is very involved and supportive of the school. The school, in turn, is supportive of parents: "There is total emphasis on the whole child; kindness and warmth pervade the Lower School. They are sensitive to individual needs and are concerned when there is a divorce or sickness in a family," parents say. "They are interested in making life easier for parents."

Chapin is also social in the traditional sense. "You would never dress informally for a school event," although khakis and hair clips have replaced suits and headbands at drop-off and pick-up. The school now hosts a reception in the fall for parents in each division with faculty attending.

Parent involvement is welcomed. Parents with a particular skill or interest are invited to share it with the class. In one kindergarten class, for instance, parents were invited to celebrate the Japanese holiday "Girls Day" with rice cookies and tea.

Program: The Lower School consists of kindergarten through Class 3. Separation is handled gradually. By the second week the whole kindergarten group is staying until 2 P.M. Monday through Thursday and until 12:45 on Friday. Parents had praise for the kindergarten teachers' warmth and skill. The days have a predictable structure, which gives the girls a sense of security: They know what to expect. Attention is paid to students' different learning styles. Although traditional in tone, there is a lot of creativity in the classroom. Art projects are used to enhance units of study. For example, a kindergarten group built its own solar system with tinfoil stars and plaster of Paris planets. As one parent said, "These are sophisticated projects; there's no macaroni and glue here." Another commented, "It's very well rounded. Activities are transformed; the doll corner or blocks might be changed into a restaurant or doctor's office for dramatic play." The Macmillian/McGraw Hill Program (with workbooks) focuses on both expressive and receptive language as well as reading and writing readiness. Each letter sound is reinforced in other activities: art, cooking, literature. Independent decision making is fostered.

Manipulative materials (Cuisinaire rods, blocks, etc.) and everyday experiences are used to teach math concepts. Girls go out of their homerooms for music, dance, science, computer and library, as well as physical education including gymnastics.

Classes 1 through 3 stay until 3:00 P.M. each day except Friday when dismissal is at 1:00. The curriculum is a continuum, each year building upon previous experiences. In Class 1 reading, writing, spelling and oral expression are emphasized using both phonetic and sight word instruction. Work is published, bound and illustrated. Classes 1 through 3 girls participate in a strong writing program emphasizing creativity and clarity of expression as well as reading with an emphasis on critical inferential thinking and critical analysis called Writers Workshop.

Where possible, social studies is integrated with language and performing arts. Social studies in Class 1 focuses on neighborhood and school study. Second graders learn about Native Americans, New Amsterdam, Slavery and the Underground Railroad, and Westward expansion. Another unit in Class 2 focuses on China, integrating many disciplines. The girls read Chinese folk tales and try their hand at writing in a similar style. A visit to The China Institute corresponded with Chinese New Year. A Chinese watercolorist and calligrapher taught her skills to the class. Symmetry was studied in mathematics using Chinese paper cut-outs. In Class 3 the girls construct a geographical 'compare and contrast' three culture project. In 2003–2004, the countries were China, Kenya, and Mexico. Class 3 girls also work under the guidance of members of the staff of the Metropolitan Opera to write, compose and perform an original opera.

Throughout classes in the Lower School, mathematics continues to be taught using an array of manipulatives and concrete objects, and focusing on basic operations and problem solving. The students practice many life skills such as measurement, time-telling and understanding money. Homework begins in Class 1. Multiplication, division and fractions are studied in Class 3. Use of the computer lab is an integral component of the curriculum with lessons in a new computer lab as well as the computers in each classroom. The students learn keyboarding in Class 3, to create a database, to word-process, to program, and to illustrate/animate.

Traditions that persist in the Lower School are Teddy Bear Day, Field Day, Pumpkin Day, Holiday concert, Hat Day and Sock Day: You bring your own from home or make one.

Middle School at Chapin includes Class 4 through Class 7, where children are taught organization and study skills including how to read a text book, take notes, study for a test, and related skills. Again, the English and history/geography curricula are coordinated where possible, and studio art is integrated with other subject areas. Clear and expressive writing is stressed, and writing skills are reinforced. Classes 4 through 7 meet weekly to put out one annual edition of the Middle School literary magazine, which is called *The Cog*. Class 7 is introduced to Shakespeare with *A Midsummer Night's Dream*. The study of foreign language begins in Class 5 with French or Spanish. Latin is introduced and required in Classes 7 and 8. Chinese is offered in ninth grade. Social studies units in Middle School cover U.S. geography and Native Americans, a study of ancient and medieval civilizations and American history. In Class 7 there is an immigration project in which each student does individual research on a specific country.

Science highlights: Several classes at Chapin work in the greenhouse and in Class 4 students begin lab sciences. Class 4 does a project on weather using Chapin's weather station. Formal health education begins in Class 1 with a unit on nutrition. Class 6 offers an introduction to biology that covers all the systems of the body, including reproductive, and the effects of drugs, alcohol and tobacco on the human body. Class 6's program revolves around the Laptop Immersion Program

(L. I. P.). Students lean to use technology as part of their daily classes in all subjects, including homework. At the end of Class 6 students go on "an intensive three-day field trip, an experience that focuses on environmental science."

Beginning in Class 5 girls go to nearby Asphalt Green (across the street) for outdoor sports once a week. Field hockey, soccer, softball, track and swimming are offered. Afternoon electives in physical education are available for Classes 5–7 including fencing and gymnastics. Chapin girls are separated into the Green and Gold teams for intramural competition culminating in an entire day of competition at Bear Mountain in May known as Field Day. Interscholastic competition, which boasts 26 teams in 13 sports, begins in Class 5 with gymnastics, in Class 6 with soccer, track and swimming, and broadens in Class 7 to include basketball, fencing and volleyball. The number of different sports offered and access to outdoor playing fields increases in the Upper School, and Chapin has several strong interscholastic teams.

Extracurricular activities in the Middle School include chess club, computer club, intramural and interscholastic sports teams, model rocketry, the literary magazine, readers' club, puppetry, art, drama, dance, music, debating and science. In addition, self-government begins in the Middle School.

The Upper School at Chapin consists of Classes 8–12. Chapin's Upper School remains a caring, close-knit community with a shift in ninth and tenth grades as some girls leave for boarding schools or coed schools. Sixteen academic credits are required for graduation. Most students complete more than twenty-two. There are sixteen AP's offered, including art history, French literature, calculus I and II and physics. For Upper School students the Individual Study Option, Interschool courses and a residential term away (abroad, Vermont, or Maine) add breadth as well as depth to Chapin's curriculum.

Multicultural perspectives are explored in the Class 8 Asian and African History course which covers the cultures of Japan, China, India and Africa and the Americas. English students contrast and compare a Japanese novel to Shakespeare's *Romeo and Juliet*. An elective called The African-American Experience is offered.

Tenth graders are required to take an English course called "Self Discovery: a Thematic Approach to Literature and Writing" in which students read literature from many different cultures. Juniors and seniors can choose from a variety of English electives including "Southern Voices" (Toni Morrison, Josephine Humphreys, *et al.*),

"The Urban Scene" and "The Lost Eden." History electives include "Women of the World," an introduction to comparative religion. and "European History."

The Upper School curriculum includes a Class 9 unit that entails a three-day workshop on New York City, entitled "Urban Study." Class 10 attends an Interschool conference on environmental issues. Class 11 travels to Washington, D.C., where they visit the Holocaust Museum in addition to the usual sites.

Physics, chemistry and biology are offered in the Upper School, with AP courses available for juniors and seniors. Students in the Upper School take algebra, geometry and trigonometry with calculus A and B offered to juniors and seniors.

In the Upper School, Chapin students continue active participation in studio art, dance, drama and music with opportunity for advanced work along with a wide variety of electives. For serious artists there is a portfolio course in preparation for the AP Studio Art Program, and there are courses in photography and multimedia studies as well. For drama students there is a playwright's workshop for Classes 10–12, and a course called "The Uses of Enchantment." The Drama Club involves all areas of theatre production. A Choral Club performs at holiday time as well as throughout the year. Dance Club members choreograph and perform their works in an annual performance. Club Night is a unique tradition in the Upper School. The Halloween Club gives a party for the Lower School girls; Dance and Drama Clubs put on student performances at night; and Holiday Club in December provides an evening for students, faculty and parents to join in singing together.

Upper School girls can participate in the student Self-Government (established in 1909), Science Club, S.A.V.E., an environmental organization, Amnesty International, Volunteer Community Activities, the Cultural Awareness Project, Model U.N., French, Latin, Spanish/Latin American Club, Literary Magazine, Yearbook, and *Limelight*, the school newspaper.

One parent says, "The curriculum is geared for the above-average girl." A former teacher says that "honor, achievement and academic rigor are valued at Chapin and that adds up to competition." But nobody describes Chapin as a "pressure cooker." "Chapin never gives up on a child," one former teacher said. "People seem to hop out of the woodwork to help each other, there's lots of cooperation and teamwork." Individual attention and concern for the development of the individual are hallmarks of a Chapin education. One parent described

Chapin as "the most well-rounded girls' school." Another parent said that although "nastiness is discouraged, cliques form early." One parent described a common scenario (seen in one form or another at all schools): "Cliques form between third and seventh grades. Seventh- and eighth-grade cliques form around physical development and looks and competition for clubs and boys." The parent of an alumna said that the girls "individualize their uniforms and can frequently be heard chatting away about the latest party." The net result of all this sociability is a boon for the school. Chapin's alumnae remain connected to the school long after they have left. The alumnae bulletin is bulging with notes and snapshots as if this were the largest extended family on the East Coast, and perhaps it is. It's no wonder that Chapin has had great success in fund-raising.

Chapin is working had to overcome the White Glove image. (The school used to emphasize "good form" in everything from dress to term papers, an alumna recalls.) Today, the rigor of the curriculum and the variety of cultural perspectives cater to the interests of a more diverse student body. One parent said, "People don't know what a jewel Chapin is, except for the Chapin parent."

The day before commencement for the Middle and Upper Schools there is a final assembly at which awards are given for achievement in athletics, fine arts and academics. Chapin commencement is held at the school. The girls graduate as a class with no special recognition for any individual student.

Popular College Choices   Barnard, Brown, Cornell, Dartmouth, Duke, Emory, Harvard, Middlebury, Princeton, Stanford, University of Pennsylvania, Yale

Traditions   Fall Book Fair, Club Nights, Grandparents' Day, Lower School Halloween party, Holiday Program, Field Day, Chapin Spring Benefit

Publications   Upper School literary magazine: *The Wheel* (since 1917)
Middle School literary magazine: *The Cog*
Newspaper: *Limelight*
Computer news publication: *The Chapin Chip*
Yearbook
Alumnae Bulletin

Community Service Requirement   Community service is encouraged but there is no specific requirement

Hangouts   The purple chairs in The Annenberg Center for Learning and Research, student lounge, coffee shop on 84th Street and Second Avenue

The Children's Storefront

70 East 129th Street
New York, NY 10035
(212) 427-7900
website: www.thechildren'sstorefront.org

Coed
Prekindergarten–8th grade
Accessible only at 70 East 129th Street

Kathy Egmont, Head of School

Birthday Cutoff   Children must be 2.9 years old by September 1st

Enrollment   Total enrollment: approximately 168
Preschool places: approximately 15
Graduating class size: approximately 10–15

Tuition Range   Tuition free

Financial Aid   100% of the student body

Endowment $3.5 million

After-School Program   After-school programs in music from 3:30
P.M. to 5:00 P.M.; free of charge

Summer Program   For Lower and Upper School students, a six-
week academic summer program
Summer Camp, end of June for six weeks for children in grades 1
through 8

———

In 1966, The Children's Storefront was founded as a "grass-roots
school" in a storefront on Madison Avenue. The school subsequently
moved into four converted brownstones. The Children's Storefront is
one of a few private schools that are tuition free. The Storefront
receives the bulk of its funding from foundations, corporations and
individuals. The Children's Storefront's annual fundraiser, A Night for
Changing Lives, attracts many of New York's "A-list" partygoers. The
school is accredited by The New York State Association of Indepen-

160

dent Schools. There is a broad range of ability within the student body. Tracking students since graduation shows that 80 percent of Storefront students go on to graduate from high school, compared to 33 percent in the community at large. Average class size is fifteen, providing students with the attention they need to succeed. There is a waiting list of approximately five hundred students.

City & Country School

146 West 13th Street
New York, NY 10011
(212) 242-7802, FAX (212) 242-7996
website: www.cityandcountry.org

Coed
Nursery–8th grade (ages 2–13)
Not accessible

Ms. Kate Turley, Principal
Ms. Lisa Horner, Director of Admissions

Birthday Cutoff Nursery 2's must be 2 by September 1; October 1st is the cutoff for 3 through 12 year olds.

Enrollment Total enrollment: 250
   Nursery 2's places: 29
   Nursery 3's places: 12
   Kindergarten (5's) places: 8–10
   6th grade places: 2
   Graduating class 2004: 14

Grades No grades; detailed narrative reports, at mid and end-of-year; parent/teacher conferences, in October and March

Tuition Range 2005–2006 $11,800 to $22,200, nursery 2's, 4 days–8th grade
   Additional fees: $400 enrollment fee. II's and III's pay $900 building fee; IV's to XIII's pay a $1400 building fee; $25 Parent Association dues

Financial Aid/Scholarship 20% of the student body receives partial financial aid

Endowment None

After-School Program Open only to City & Country students; an elective program that offers a variety of creative and recreational activities, a technology program, and homework help, from 3:00 P.M. until 4:30 P.M. for 8–13 year olds

Additional specialty classes for 4–7 year olds, with an early drop off at 8 A.M. option until 5:45; additional fee required. Sixth through eighth graders can participate in an intramural sports program.

Summer Program   A six-week summer camp for 3–7 year olds from
mid-June until the end of July
These programs require an additional payment

———

City & Country School, founded in 1914, is one of the oldest progressive elementary schools in the United States. Located on a historic block in Greenwich Village, the school occupies three adjoining brownstones on 13th Street and three floors in a brownstone on 12th Street; the brownstones are connected by courtyards that are used in the school's outdoor yard program.

Getting in: Parents may tour the school and attend the open house before submitting an application. The ERB is not required for prekindergarten, kindergarten, or first grade admission but a screening is done of each applicant for kindergarten. Older applicants are academically screened and spend a day with a group of their peers, and are observed by a group teacher, and specialists. Younger children come for a group visit (about an hour) and are observed at work and play in a classroom by teachers and the director of admissions.

Parents: The parent body runs the gamut from "corporate lawyers, bankers and doctors to writers and illustrators." What they have in common is that they want their children in "a quintessential progressive school."

Program: Visionary educator and founder Caroline Pratt believed children learn best through practical and meaningful experiences. The process of education and the tools of learning are important here. The kindergarten usually consists of two groups of sixteen to twenty students each. From the earliest years, students work with open-ended materials: blocks, water, paint, clay, and wood. Vs through VIIs plan their work as groups, which they sustain for a week or longer, creating cities with building blocks, wooden people, handmade signs, fabric and plasticine items and even electricity and running water. Frequent trips to observe the community at work are an important part of the program. In the outdoor yards, students create their own play environment each day with large boxes, blocks, boards, ladders and sawhorses. Older groups use the yard for running and ball games and team sports. Students bring their own lunch, and milk is provided as is midmorning juice and snack.

Reading and writing begin with frequent exposure to literature, experience charts, language arts games and activities, and early story-writing. Spanish is taught, beginning with the X's or fifth grade until 8th grade (or XII's). From grades VII to XIII, all students have half an hour of independent reading in the library every day.

As a practical application of their academic skills and to develop social awareness, self-esteem and responsibility, older children participate in the Jobs Program—running the school post office or store, operating printing presses, working with younger children, writing and publishing the school newspaper. Group and individual research using primary and secondary sources, literature, and trips rather than textbooks to study a civilization, time period, or major issue forms the core of the Middle and Upper School curriculum. This curriculum is integrated with the Special Subjects and Jobs Program for the VIIIs through XIIIs. For instance, a study of "living documents" of the Revolutionary period in American history is coordinated with the older children's job of running the school newspaper. The annual IX's week-long country trip to Connecticut is a highlight. After completing a unit on the Oregon Trail, the students reenact everything they have learned. For example, they maneuver a covered wagon through the countryside, construct trailside rock-heated "ovens" and cook and eat real buffalo meat. Parents say the trip "really bonds the group; they come back changed."

All students participate in Rhythms (the music and movement program), and older children use the fully equipped woodshop, the art room, the science lab and the technology center. The music program includes singing and instruction in recorder and stringed instruments. Chorus and orchestra are required in the upper grades.

Parents whose children have been in the school for several years note several changes which indicate that City & Country is not the bastion of progressive education it once was: "Traditionally each class has a job in the school but because the school has nearly doubled in size in the last 10 years there is less opportunity for children to actually take part in running the school."

Popular Secondary School Choices Berkeley Carroll, Fiorello LaGuardia High School of Music and Art and Performing Arts, Trevor Day School, Fieldston School, Friends Seminary, Packer Collegiate Institute, Bronx Science, Marymount, Dalton, Calhoun, Elisabeth Irwin, Horace Mann, Loyola, Marymount, Poly Prep, Regis

Collegiate School

260 West 78th Street
New York, NY 10024
Tel (212) 812-8500 Admissions x552
FAX (212) 812-8547
website: www.collegiateschool.org

All boys
K–12th grade
Accessible

Mr. Bruce Breimer, Principal
Mrs. Joanne P. Heyman, Director of Admissions and Financial Aid

Uniform   Kindergarten and Lower School: long pants and a shirt with a collar
Middle and Upper School: grades 5–12, collared shirt and tie, long pants, shoes or sneakers,

Birthday Cutoff   It is recommended that boys be 5 by the start of Kindergarten

Enrollment   Total enrollment: approximately 625
Kindergarten places: approximately 45
5th grade places: approximately 2–3
6th grade places: approximately 4
7th grade places: approximately 4–6
9th grade places: approximately 6–10
Graduating class size: approximately 50

Grades   Trimester system (Lower and Middle School), Semester system (Upper School)
Grades Kindergarten–4: detailed anecdotal reports and conferences
Letter grades begin in 6th grade
Departmentalization begins in 5th grade
First final exam is given in 7th grade

Tuition Range 2005–2006 $25,500 to $25,650, K–12th grade
Tuition at Collegiate includes lunch, books, fees overnight trips, and most additional costs, but not athletic equipment or special functions

There is an alternative payment plan through Academic Management Services

Financial Aid/Scholarship   Approximately 20% of the student body receive financial assistance

Endowment   Approximately $52 million

Diversity   Approximately 25% children of color
36 Prep for Prep students enrolled as of Fall 2004
Collegiate enrolls students from Early Steps, A Better Chance (ABC), The Albert G. Oliver Program, and TEAK Fellowship
JAMAA: an organization for students families, alumni and faculty of color founded in the 1960s
Collegiate Teaching Institute for prospective teachers of color

Homework   Classes I and II: 1/2 hour reading every night
Classes III and IV: approximately 45 minutes plus reading
Classes V and VI: approximately 2 hours
Classes VII and VIII: approximately 2 1/2 hours
Classes IX–XII: 2–3 hours

After-School Program   In-house after-school activities program available for Kindergarten–6. Collegiate boys participate in various sports programs; Athletic teams practice after school

Summer Program   Two-week June basketball clinic for Lower and Middle School boys
For older boys there are exchange programs in Europe, China and Latin America

———

Collegiate is the oldest independent school in the United States. It marked its 375th year in 2003. The school maintains a continuing relationship with the Dutch Reformed Church. Collegiate's strength is an emphasis on classical education combined with modern innovations. Collegiate is a well-rounded, academically rigorous school with a superior college placement record.

Collegiate has had a long-standing relationship with the West End Collegiate Church. In 1940 the church and school separated but they still share some facilities. The "Moving Up" ceremonies for the Lower and Middle School are held at the West End Collegiate Church, as is graduation. There is a school chaplain who is also an Upper School advisor. The Holiday program, held in the church, includes various religious traditions. Seventh grade students study world religions. In the Upper School, students must choose two three-credit religion courses.

All Collegiate students benefit from a recently completed series of renovation and building projects. In 1990, the school added a fabulous new gym and weight room, two new art rooms, a black box theater, a photography lab and a music room. In September 1997, Collegiate opened a kindergarten in the West End Plaza building of the school. Two spacious classrooms with an adjoining block/project room provide room for academic centers, computers, creative movement, music, blocks and art projects. In the same year, the new science laboratories were installed for Lower and Middle School students. In 1998, a rooftop play area opened on top of the school's new six-story structure. The school's dining facilities were expanded, a two-story Middle School center was completed and state-of-the-art biology, chemistry and physics laboratories were built for Upper School students.

Getting in: The application fee is $50. Parents are encouraged to tour when their sons are eligible for kindergarten. Once parents have applied, they bring their son to the school. Kindergarten applicants visit in small groups with members of the faculty. Middle and Upper School applicants have interviews and guided tours of the school. Parents of applicants are interviewed on an individual family basis. There is a policy favoring siblings and legacies but admission is not automatic. Is there a typical Collegiate Boy? An alumni said, "He is self-confident, slightly preppie, a social, smart kid."

Parents: The parent body at Collegiate runs the gamut: Academics, artists, writers, professionals, musicians, and some Wall Street types mingle comfortably in what most say is an intellectual atmosphere. About half come from the East side and half from the West side. "It is a fun loving group, easy to connect with," said one parent. Another told us, "The parent body at Collegiate is tremendously diverse and not stuffy; cocktail parties might be held in an apartment in the Village with people eating cross-legged on a futon or in a Park or Fifth Avenue apartment." Jewish parents have long been comfortable at Collegiate. There are many Jewish legacies attending Collegiate and school is closed on the major Jewish holidays. Parents Association meetings are scheduled on the school calendar and all parents are invited to attend.

Program: Academically, the early years at Collegiate are "challenging, yet comfortable." Learning is developmental and low-key. A former Lower School teacher said the style of the school "is not extreme, not too traditional or informal, but they've borrowed what's best and held onto the things that have worked." Throughout the kindergarten and Lower School there is the understanding that boys develop at different rates. Table groupings in classrooms are informal; no rows. The heterogeneous classrooms (approximately 20 boys in each with one teacher and a full-time assistant) often break into small groups for activities. There is an eclectic approach to reading instruction: some boys come in reading and some don't, it's not an admissions requirement. There is recognition of different learning styles.

First grade homework is approached with the attitude that parents are partners. Parents are encouraged to come in to the classroom to share their skills and talents, or to simply read to the boys during library time.

Lower School boys leave their homerooms to go to specialists in art, music, physical education and science. Kindergarten boys usually have science in their project room while all Lower School students go to a specially designed Lower School science lab. Through second grade there is a teacher and an assistant for each class. All Lower School students have access to computers in the classrooms. The boys have regularly scheduled classes in the Lower School technology lab. The full-time Lower School technology coordinator works closely with teachers to support computer-related activities. In the Lower School, boys learn keyboarding, basic computer skills and begin to use computers as tools to create documents and multimedia presentations.

In the early grades reading and math are "geared to the individual." The Fisher Landau department consisting of learning specialists provides support and enrichment.

In memory of the founders, third graders celebrate Dutch Day. In social studies, third graders study immigration and learn about the Dutch settlers of New Amsterdam. One year, third graders doing a unit on Japan studied haiku, learned calligraphy and made kimonos in art, read Japanese fables, and went to a tea ceremony. They clipped articles about modern Japan and read them aloud to the class.

The music program at Collegiate is very strong; renowned pianist Emanuel Ax is a former trustee and parent of an alumnus. Lower School boys have music twice a week. In fourth grade recorder is introduced; in fifth and sixth grades students study a stringed instrument; in seventh grade guitar is required. Each year students are given an instrument for use at school or practice at home. On our tour we saw eight boys playing their violins in a practice room. Private and semi-private instruction is available and music theory is taught. Third and fourth graders have a string ensemble and chorus. One year, the fifth and sixth grade chorus sang at Carnegie Hall as part of the Canterbury Choral Society's Fortieth Anniversary Celebration. Eighth graders are introduced to music technology and composition. The boys explore music and creativity through the use of computers and synthesizers.

In fourth grade the work load is stepped up and letter grades begin in sixth grade. Parents stressed, however, that "Nobody is pressured at Collegiate, the boys are encouraged to do their best."

The Middle School at Collegiate consists of grades five through eight. According to parents, Middle School demands a greater amount of independence. In fifth grade, departmentalization has begun. Fifth graders get lockers; desks are still organized in groups, not rows. There are regular forty minute periods. The Middle School technology lab is easily accessible and often used. Technology skills are put to use as boys write papers, examine data and learn to use digital information sources for research. Students use computer-generated graphic materials in oral presentations in many of their classes. Fifth graders select either French or Spanish which they can take through high school. They can also begin Latin in eighth grade.

Beginning in fifth grade, students are given long term assignments. Students learn to plan their weeks and organize their time. At Collegiate, students really know how to think. "My fifth grader was asked to write a paper about one of Robert Louis Stevenson's books from the point of view of a minor character," a parent said. Another fifth grade assignment was to write a piece of historical fiction. One student wrote a piece on a Vietnamese teenager and the assignment was graded by both the history and English teachers.

Fifth through eighth graders take regular tests during the school year. At the end of seventh and eighth grades there is a formal exam period.

The social studies curriculum begins in the Lower School with the study of families and communities, and expands in the upper grades to include the wider world. Fifth graders study ancient civilizations and read Greek myths and English folktales. Sixth graders study the Middle Ages, the exploration of the New World and the Cultures of the Americas and American colonial history. Seventh graders focus on American history from George Washington to the present. Eighth graders study World History (Asia, Africa, Islam and Europe). Research papers and projects are completed in all Middle School grades.

There is a non-academic elective and activities program for Middle Schoolers "to broaden and enrich the boys' experience." Course offerings include: community service projects, computer, photography, drama, architecture, student government, Middle School newspaper, literary magazine, and excursions away from school to take advantage of the urban setting.

Experience in public speaking is gained through weekly assemblies, morning meetings and many opportunities to perform in dramatic and musical productions. One trimester of drama is required in seventh and eighth grades. Arts for grades seven and eight includes the opportunity for the boys to play in a chamber music group, study photography, produce two dramatic pieces and learn musical composition using computerized synthesizers during the year.

Middle School boys can participate in coed afternoon activities that are occasionally held with girls schools.

Summer reading is required for grades five through ten. Most boys purchase their books at the Paperback Book Fair held in the Spring. They also gather books at the Annual Book Festival organized by the Parents Association in the fall. Guest authors often include Collegiate parents. Sixth graders produce their own anthology of original literature. Grades six through eight take a three-day trip to locations of interest. Sixth graders visit an environmental study center, and seventh graders begin the school year with a three day trip to Frost Valley. The eighth graders end their year with a trip to Washington, D.C.

Prep for Prep students usually enter in either sixth, seventh or eighth grades.

Interscholastic sports begin in seventh grade; participation is stressed over competition. After spring break, eighth graders can sign out for lunch and join their older peers at "Big Nick's Pizza." After school the courtyard handball court is the social gathering spot.

Upper School at Collegiate consists of grades nine through twelve. The Upper School curriculum, according to a trustee and former PA president, is both "traditional and innovative." The school is not rigid in its approach to education, though the backbone of the curriculum is classical. There is an academic core program with electives offered in eleventh and twelfth grades. Some readings focus on the classics. Other perspectives are explored in courses such as:

Contemporary American Poetry, African and Caribbean Writers, and Women in Literature. In history, Civil Liberties, Civil Rights and Human Rights in a Wider Perspective, Modern China and Japan, The Middle East, History of Psychological Thought, and African History are offered in addition to the normal selection of required courses. In math and science, AB and BC Calculus, Statistical Modeling, Environmental Issues and Astronomy are among the courses offered.

Parents say there is an emphasis in all grades on good writing and research skills. A former PA President told us that Verbal SAT scores are consistently high because of the emphasis on language arts and the academic core program. There is no summer reading list for grades ten through twelve. Summer reading is encouraged for pleasure at all grade levels.

The Technology Department offers an expanding program in computer and technology education and there are numerous opportunities for students to use computers in conjunction with course work in all disciplines. An academic local area network connects computers in the computer labs, the library, the science department and classrooms throughout the school. Access to the network allows students to "plug-in" to the many resources available through the system, including the Internet, the library catalog and reference materials on CD-ROM.

In addition to the yearly course offerings, Collegiate students can design an Independent Study course in an area of interest, taken in addition to the minimum course load. A senior project in an area of the student's choice (often some form of internship) can be undertaken in the last semester of the senior year if all other requirements are completed.

"The faculty at Collegiate is extraordinary," says an alumnus. A parent said, "They are a very senior faculty. Teachers average ten to twelve years of experience and three-quarters have advanced degrees." There is an assistant teaching program in the Lower School in which less experienced teachers work with a mentor, eventually becoming head teachers. A big incentive to keep faculty is housing provided in a building connected to the school. A former PA President said, "Collegiate has one of the lowest tuitions yet offers the highest remuneration for independent school teachers which is why it keeps and attract good teachers." The faculty is part of the larger Collegiate community: there is a parent/faculty chorus which performs yearly at a "Celebration of Music" event.

Student government at Collegiate consists of three representatives from each grade. The Middle School student government meets regularly and plans student programs and special events. Upper School student government has tackled furnishing the student center, finding summer jobs for students and relaxing the dress code.

Theater continues to be a strength in the Upper School at Collegiate. Upper School students put on two to three plays per semester, both in the school's two hundred and sixty-seven seat theater auditorium and in the recently enlarged "black box" theater.

Clubs at Collegiate are popular. The Model U.N. Club, the Science Olympiad Team, the Debate Team, and JAMAA, an organization for students, families, alumni and faculty of color are among the more active ones.

There is a community service requirement at Collegiate of one hundred credit hours, twenty of which must be done outside of school. Programs include opportunities such as tutoring at IS 44 at 77th Street or the East Harlem School at Exodus House on East 103rd Street, working at the West End Avenue Collegiate Church soup kitchen, The Yorkville Common Pantry, or volunteering at various museums or hospitals throughout the city. There are special food drives each year and the proceeds are donated to various community programs. In-house tutoring performed at Collegiate is also a way to fulfill the requirement.

The atmosphere at Collegiate is shaped by the interaction of the student body and a sense of community within the school. In the Upper School, as far as contact between grades, one alumnus said, "There's sports, the drama program, clubs and chorus. It's too small a school for hazing." "Of course, you can only get a Collegiate varsity jacket if you play on a varsity team," an alum mentioned. The Dutchmen's colors are orange and blue, the same as the the Knicks and the Mets. Collegiate's biggest rivals are Trinity, Poly Prep, Riverdale and Fieldston. The traditional Friday night basketball games are popular. Collegiate also has a championship cross-country team that runs in Riverside Park as well as championship teams in soccer, basketball, track and wrestling.

A recent alumnus told us that more important than the traditions themselves is the sense of success you get at Collegiate: "When you've been there a long time, you begin to think 'I can do anything.' If anything, Collegiate boys spread themselves too thin." Another alumnus said, "Athletes are also actors or musicians too."

The school stresses values, particularly integrity. "They are sticklers for honor and principle; competition is stressed in a healthy way. But it's tough and demanding," according to an alumnus. Collegiate is structured but students may choose from a growing number of electives from ninth grade on.

Collegiate enjoys great success at college placement. Mr. Bruce Breimer, Class of 1963, is now the school's principal and has been Director of College Guidance for many years. He is known in independent school circles as one of the most powerful figures in college admissions. Since the graduating class usually numbers about fifty, it not difficult for him to know each boy. Parents and alumni say Briemer is a strength of the school, with his over thirty years experience. It's a highly personalized process. Each senior takes control of his own college search in an independent fashion and is encouraged to go beyond the obvious in the quest for the best match. A 1991 graduate told us, "Breimer makes or breaks your career; he's the guy you want on your side."

There are no academic prizes at Collegiate. Seniors with outstanding grades are inducted into the Cum Laude Society (the secondary school equivalent of Phi Beta Kappa). The Collegiate faculty and graduating class vote for the Head Boy each year, a senior who shows a combination of leadership, sportsmanship and citizenship.

There is a genuine school spirit at Collegiate demonstrated at class dinners, the holiday assembly and at Moving Up Day. One parent said, "They all sing the school song and you cry no matter how many times you've seen it." A traditional graduation ceremony is held in the West End Collegiate Church. Cap and gown are worn and the alma mater is sung.

Popular College Choices   Yale, Harvard, Brown, Dartmouth, Princeton, University of Pennsylvania, Columbia, Wesleyan, Williams

Traditions   Library Week, Parents Association Book Festival, Paperback Book Fair, 2nd grade trip to Manhattan Country School Farm, 3rd grade trip to an outdoor environmental education center, 7th grade trip to Frost Valley, 8th grade trip to Washington, DC, Middle School Special Days, 10th grade Interschool trip to Frost Valley, Lower and Middle School Field Day, 5th and 6th grade music evenings, Grandparents Day, Moving Up Days for Lower and Middle Schools, Athletic Banquet, graduation at Collegiate Church, alumni reception

Publications   Newspaper: *The Collegiate Journal* (monthly) Yearbook: *The Dutchman*

French publication: *Charabia*
Spanish publication: *La Herencia*
Literary magazine: *Prufrock*
Science and Technology publication: *Technically Speaking*
Opinion publication: *Issues*
Lower School: *Lower School News*
Middle School literary magazine: *Jabberwock*
Collegiate publication: *News From Collegiate, The Collegiate Review*
Parents Association: *Newsletter*

Community Service Requirement   Grades 9–12: 100 credits by graduation (40 minutes–1 hour = 1 credit)

Hangouts   Collegiate cafeteria (the menu is in French, Spanish and English), the courtyard, library, Upper School student center, and technology labs

Columbia Grammar and Preparatory School

5 West 93rd Street
New York, NY 10025
(212) 749-6200
website: www.cgps.org

Coed
Pre-kindergarten–12th grade
Grades 5–12 accessible

Dr. Richard J. Soghoian, Headmaster
Ms. Simone Hristidis, Director of Admissions
(Pre-K–12)

Uniform   No torn jeans, sweatpants, T-shirts with inappropriate messages, tank tops, cutoffs, boxers, gym shorts or bicycle pants

Birthday Cutoff   Children entering Kindergarten must be 5 by August 1

Enrollment   Total enrollment: 1020
   Pre-kindergarten places: 22
   Kindergarten places: 30–40
   7th grade places: 10
   9th grade places: approximately 10–15
   Graduating class size: approximately 60

Grades   Semester system
   Letter grades begin in 7th grade
   Departmentalization begins in 5th grade
   First final exam is given at the end of 7th grade

Tuition Range 2005–2006 $25,250 to $27,200, pre-kindergarten–12th grade
   There are no additional fees
   A revolving loan policy requires that each family make an interest-free loan ($1,500 for grades K–8, $1,000 for grades 9–12) to the school for each child enrolled
   A Tuition Refund Plan and a Student Accident Reimbursement Plan are available

Financial Aid/Scholarship   In 2003–2004, 21.3% of the students received aid totaling $2.6 million

Endowment $12 million

Diversity   12.7% students of color PreK–12,
72% of the families of color received aid in 2003–2004
MECA, Multi-Ethnic Cultural Awareness Club
18 Prep for Prep students enrolled as of Fall 2004
Parent Diversity Committee

Homework   Kindergarten: none
1st: 20 minutes
2nd: 30–45 minutes
3rd, 4th: approximately 1 hour
5th–8th: $1^{1}/_{2}$–$2^{1}/_{2}$ hours
9th–12th: approximately 3 hours

After-School Program   CGPS After-School Program for grades K–6 offers a variety of creative and recreational activities until 4:30 P.M., Monday–Friday

Summer Program   CGS Summer Camp: for Pre-kindergarten–2 from the end of school until the end of July, staffed by CGS teachers, an additional payment is required

Columbia Grammar School was founded in 1764 and functioned as a feeder school for King's College (later, Columbia University). Now CGPS graduates go on to a much wider range of universities and colleges. CGPS became a nonprofit school in 1941 and merged with a nearby girls' school. Since 1981 CGPS has been guided by Richard J. Soghoian, who holds a Ph.D. in philosophy from Columbia University and is also an International Fellow at the School for International Affairs. His expertise is manifested in the innovative social studies, history and geography programs throughout CGPS. Dr. Soghoian guided the school through major construction projects and opened two new buildings that serve the entire school community that include a state-of-the-art 200+ seat theater, computer and science labs, five art studios with photography and filmmaking equipment, a third library, a gym, and additional academic areas. Moreover, the school purchased another brownstone down the block to house admissions, administrative offices and pre-kindergarten. Yet individual class sizes will stay small, with twelve to fifteen students per class.

Columbia Grammar offers a well-rounded but structured program for able students. The Grammar School is now composed of pre-kindergarten through sixth grade. The Prep School consists of seventh through twelfth grades.

The Director of the Lower School, Stanley Seidman, was formerly head of Dalton's Lower School. Parents say Seidman is well-liked, knows all the children's names and is very accessible. Parents say they feel free to call the teachers at any time, and their calls will be taken even during classroom hours using the school's new voice mail system.

Getting in: The application is very straightforward. There are one or two essay questions. The ERB/ISEE is required. Please note that all applications for kindergarten and first grade must be filed by mid-November. There is one Open House where prospective parents meet grammar school teachers and admissions staff. Once an application has been filed, parents are taken on a more extensive tour of the school while their child is being interviewed (a small group interview of four children at a time, which lasts about one hour during which the child is observed by the Director of Admissions as well as admissions personnel). After the tour, parents meet with Mr. Seidman and Mrs. Hristidis over coffee. Parents say that the admissions process at CGPS is low-key and comfortable. "They are really interested in the child, not scrutinizing the parents," we heard. CGPS has not gone to their wait list in three years. What are they looking for? Hristidis told us, "A bright child who can handle an enriched curriculum, eager to learn; nice, well adjusted children; we're not looking for a type, a range of children would do well here but they must be academically inclined."

Prospective applicants to the Preparatory School attend one of several afternoon meetings or morning coffee chats in which the program is described followed by a tour. Tours are given by current Prep students. The application deadline is also usually mid-November.

For ninth grade, the primary goal according to Hristidis, "is to enroll kids from schools that end in eighth grade like Town, Rodelph, Grace Church, Allen-Stevenson and Bank Street." She warns parents seeking to move kids from rigorous schools like Dalton, Horace Mann or Riverdale, to a school with softer academic expectations, that CGPS isn't the place. "Kids must be exemplary candidates in every way," she asserts.

The typical CGPS student? "This is not a jock school," said one parent. "The typical student usually has some artistic bent." "The *atypical* student," one parent said, "is pushy, snotty or overly competitive."

But, now that CGPS is growing, there are students who are getting more involved in a wide range of athletics.

Parents: The parent body at CGPS consists of many professionals. There is an equal division between West Siders and East Siders. Social competition is negligible. According to one mother, the parent body is "unpretentious, no limos or jewels, and if they have it, they leave it at home." "CGPS has a lot of generally liberal parents who might otherwise have sent their children to public school," said another. There are a number of Parents Association events such as the Skating Party, Theatre Party and Spring Benefit (held at Cipriani's in 2004). They are fun, low-key events. At the annual holiday concert "First Noel" as well as "O Chanukah" are sung. "What you see is what you get," says one parent with two children at CGPS. "There are absolutely no surprises."

Program: The pre-kindergarten and kindergarten year begins with a fall picnic in Central Park, held before the beginning of school. The school provides a very informative handbook for each division (Lower and Upper). Parents say CGPS is supportive about separation when school actually begins.

All students have a well-rounded schedule, which includes a strong swimming program (required for grades kindergarten through fourth grade and optional for fifth grade.) Kindergartners swim twice a week for forty minutes, once a week in the middle grades) plus art, music and academics.

Presently, the Grammar School (composed of pre-kindergarten through fourth grades) is housed in five interconnected brownstones on West 94rd Street connected to the original school building on West 93rd Street (now housing grade four). Children and adults develop strong legs because of the many stairways in the school. The classroom space is long, with windows at either end, but well laid out and bright. There is a courtyard play area for recess. Parents say that the kindergarten teachers are warm, and make learning fun, although by third grade they get more serious. "The children respect the teachers," a parent commented.

Throughout the Grammar School learning is viewed as a progression, especially in math and reading. The brochure says: "Each grade's work builds on the work of previous years." Individual rates of learning in math and reading are accommodated. Wherever possible, art is coordinated with work in other subjects in the Grammar School. Pre-kindergarten and kindergarten have two teachers and one assistant. For first through third grades there are two teachers for approximately twenty to twenty-two children. Although it is considered a "structured school," the teaching at CGPS is flexible, "using a variety of approaches and techniques." Parents praise the well-paced reading program. In kindergarten reading readiness is the focus; in first grade "a phonics sequence is the basic method used for the teaching of reading." Whole Language literature based books are used. Math instruction in kindergarten stresses experiential learning through the use of manipulatives and games. There are at least three computers in all of the classrooms and LOGO and word processing are taught in the Grammar School. Third graders go out to the computer lab.

The extensive music program begins with the Kodaly and Orff methods, which are used for ear training. Second graders learn to play the recorder. Instrumental instruction begins in fourth grade and students are given an instrument to take home. Opportunities to perform include the third- and fourth-grade choir, a recorder ensemble for second and third graders, a string ensemble and a chamber music ensemble for more advanced students. In fourth grade students pick one instrument for further study.

The social studies curriculum for pre-kindergarten through fourth grade begins with families and community and broadens to include a study of ethnicity and immigration in second grade (including a trip to Ellis Island with students dressed as their immigrant forebears). Native Americans are the subject in third grade, explorers and Colonial America in fourth.

Fifth graders study the Revolutionary War and slavery. They use primary sources and read Early American folklore. Sixth graders study ancient civilizations and the Middle Ages and write a research paper. The Writing Workshop is a standard part of the curriculum in which students practice the steps of good writing (see Glossary, p. 48, *supra*). Fifth and sixth graders also take public speaking, engage in debates and practice speech writing.

The approach to science in the Grammar School "is firmly experimental and based on the scientific method." Environmental awareness begins as early as first grade with a discussion about how waste leaves Manhattan island. First graders study endangered animals; second graders learn about water pollution and testing; third graders study air pollution; fourth graders examine wind and solar energy and travel to Nature's Classroom, an environmental study center in Connecticut. Sixth graders take a unit on environmental issues.

Parents say that by third grade the academic pace picks up and the work gets much more serious. Extra help is readily available. One

179

mother said her daughter received extra help with reading during recess time.

Foreign language study is offered after school.

In mathematics, the focus is on problem-solving skills. There are enrichment topics in each grade. In fifth grade these are palindromic numbers, tangrams and hieroglyphics. Other enrichment projects include curve stitching and M.C. Escher's tessellations and participation in the Math Olympiad.

Reports and grades come home twice a year. The anecdotal reports in the Lower School are extensive and detailed. In addition, there is a checklist in each subject area showing that the student is either "progressing well," "developing" or "needs strengthening."

If a child has a learning deficiency, CGPS will "provide some degree of professional skills remediation on a temporary basis." CGPS also has a highly specific and intensive in-school treatment of learning disabilities called the Learning Resource Center, staffed by ten highly trained professionals. The program is limited to forty students, grades kindergarten through twelfth, who are otherwise fully mainstreamed students. There is an *additional* cost of approximately $15,000 per year. This program is an in-house program only. No outside applicants are admitted.

For physical exercise students play in the courtyard, on the roof turf playground or go to Central Park, which is located only a block from the school, weather permitting. A play yard is being constructed for fifth and sixth graders. Physical education is required in all grades. Intramural and interschool sports begin in fifth grade. After-school sports are available. A Field Day with games is held at the end of the year for each division.

The Prep School (grades seven through twelve) is on a semester system. Grades are issued quarterly, there are two parent conferences and two narrative report cards. The school day begins with a ten minute homeroom period and is divided into forty minute periods, ending at 2:55 P.M.

The building at 36 West houses grades five and six as well as seven through twelve. It is bright and spacious, with special space for the arts: photo lab, filmmaking, jewelry-making and so on. The "underground" theatre holds 150 but is mainly used by Grammar School students. Stagecraft models (made by students) on display in the lobby are wonderful.

In seventh and eighth grades students are required to take English, science, social studies and math as well as art, music, computer and

PE. Foreign language study begins with a two month sequence in each of four languages: French, Spanish, Latin and Japanese. In eighth grade students choose one of these languages for continued study.

Seventh graders are ready to think critically and express themselves clearly and sensitively on issues of social relevance. In history the horizons have broadened to include examination of the effect of historical policies such as apartheid and colonialism on emerging nations and current events. Seventh grade English is coordinated with the seventh grade history curriculum and covers the themes of prejudice, tolerance and freedom. Readings include *The Crucible* and *To Kill a Mockingbird*.

Latin America and African history, culture and geography are the focus of the history curriculum in eighth grade and students make African masks, symbolic flags and maps and graphs. The study of geography at CGPS is considered "essential to the appreciation of today's international interdependency." A unit on "the origins of the U.N. and the vital role it plays in the international environment" is included in the eighth grade year.

In grades nine through twelve students are required to complete four years of English, math and social studies, as well as three years of science. A foreign language must be studied through the end of eleventh grade. Other requirements include a course in computer literacy (there are two computer labs, one with Macs and the other with PC's) two of three offerings in the history of art, theater or music, and a community service requirement of one hundred hours to be completed by the end of the senior year. Electives are available in all the major subject areas. Six courses are the normal course load, except during the senior year when five are required. Students can arrange independent study projects in their final semester.

Ninth and tenth grades are assigned to full year English classes. In ninth grade, the class addresses the fundamental human theme of coming of age and exposes the students to a wide range of literature. In tenth grade the course focuses on the fundamentals of good writing, as well as a selection of British and American literature. Eleventh and twelfth graders choose from a variety of electives but they must take at least one course in each of the following: British literature, American literature, and pre-twentieth century literature.

When asked about a multicultural curriculum at CGPS, Dr. Soghoian responded that "CGPS has always emphasized Africa, China, Japan and South America on nearly an equal footing with the study of Europe in the preparatory school program." CGPS also uses its extensive assembly program to emphasize multicultural performers and themes.

The history sequence reads like a description of an advanced college history program. Students in ninth and tenth grades study Western Civilization, including European history from Greek and Roman times to the French Revolution and continuing through the Reactionary Era, Imperialism, World Wars I and II, and the Cold War. Eleventh graders study U.S. History, and juniors and seniors can choose from electives such as economics, philosophy, the Holocaust, and a course taught in conjunction with Tufts University, as well as AP courses in comparative government, modern European history, and U.S. government.

Calculus BC and AB (college calculus and preparation for the AP exams) are offered by the math department, and graphing calculators are used in the calculus classes. At the annual Math/Science Fair, student teams present the results of their research on a variety of topics such as the mathematics of sound or an analysis of hurricane paths. The science department offers AP biology, chemistry and physics as well as electives in astronomy, consumer chemistry, human evolution, and a three year research course.

There is a great range of choice in the arts at CGPS. Photography, drama and filmmaking are popular. The ceramics room is full of inspired and beautiful work ready to be fired in the kiln. Wood shop and jewelry-making areas are busy places too.

The Prep School has its own Winter and Spring Concerts, (choral and instrumental) and a three day Arts Festival. There are several major theatre productions each year and at least one musical.

The student government, with elected representatives from each grade, helps coordinate activities such as the annual Field Day and fundraising for various causes. Clubs include MECA (the multicultural awareness group), Model U.N., Model SADD Congress, (Students Against Destructive Decisions) and Environmental Awareness.

At the Annual Social Issues Day a topic of importance is examined in depth through seminars and small group discussions. One year Gay Men's Health Crisis was invited to participate in small group question-and-answer sessions.

About 60 percent of the high school students participate in a varsity sport. The new spectator gym is large and cheerful with wooden bleachers. At the end-of-the-year Sports Award Banquet the year's outstanding teams and coaches are recognized and individual achievement is honored. CP has strong teams in soccer, cross-country and varsity basketball. There are trophy cases in the school lobby.

Moving Up Day at CGPS reinforces the feeling of a warm community. It is a special day when all the students from pre-kindergarten through twelfth grade, faculty and staff gather together in the gym to share awards for academic excellence, citizenship and character, success in sports and so on. Songs are sung and class banners are handed down from one class to another to signify graduation.

Alumni speak about fond memories of CGPS: "Reunions hold good memories," "CGPS was a little more laid-back and less pretentious than some of the other schools but we all did well there."

Popular College Choices   University of Wisconsin, Boston University, Brown, University of Michigan, Tufts, Cornell, Columbia, Vassar, University of Pennsylvania

Traditions   Grammar School Science Fair, Earth Fest, Field Day, Prep School Math/Science Fair, class dinners, kindergarten Grandparents' Day, Holiday Concert, Skating Party, theatre benefit, Winter Concert, Spring Concert, Instrumental Concert, 4th-grade trip to Nature's Classroom, Gymnastics Week, Spirit Week, Spring Benefit, The Reading Club, Operation Santa Claus, Social Issues Day, Sports Award Banquet, Moving Up Ceremony, Young Alumni Reunion

Publications   Alumni magazine: *Columbiana Today*
Literary, news and art magazine: *CPJ* (Columbia Prep Journal)
Yearbook
Newspaper

Community Service Requirement   Grades 9–12: one hundred hours, cumulative

Hangouts   McDonald's, deli around the corner

Convent Of The Sacred Heart

1 East 91st Street
New York, NY 10128
(212) 722-4745
website: www.cshnyc.org

All girls
Pre-kindergarten–12th grade
Accessible

Mary Blake, Ed.D., Head of School
Mrs. Barbara S. Root, Director of Admissions

Uniform   Pre-kindergarten: gray smock jumper. Regulation sneakers and shoes must be purchased at East Side Kids (15% discount on sneakers when buying SH shoes *and* sneakers)

Grades K–4: gray jumper, white blouse with McMullen collar, white anklets (warm weather), red long-sleeved mock turtleneck shirt and medium gray knee highs (cool weather); red-and-white-check pinafore worn every day, navy stretch shorts worn every day under gray jumper

Grades 5–7: gray kilt, medium gray knee socks or white anklet socks, white long-sleeved blouse, oxford-collar or white polo shirt with collar or white turtleneck; tights must be white, black or beige and can be worn under knee socks; seventh-grade privilege: crew neck or cardigan sweater with detail or pattern may be worn except for formal occasions

Grades 8–12: blue pinstripe cotton kilt; solid blue or white blouse with collar or turtleneck (spring and fall); solid color tights, no long underwear or leggings; Coburn plaid kilt; white, red, yellow, or navy blouse or turtleneck; no oversized clothing; white, yellow, red, green, navy or black socks or tights; no sweat pants, long underwear or leggings

Birthday Cutoff   Pre-kindergarten 3's applicants must be 3 by May before entering

Pre-kindergarten 4's applicants must be 4 by September 1 before entering

Children entering kindergarten must be 5 by September 1

Enrollment   Total enrollment: 635
Pre-kindergarten 3's places: 14
Kindergarten places: approximately 35
Graduating class size 2004: 48

Grades   Trimester system
Letter grades begin in 5th grade
Departmentalization begins in 5th grade
First final exam is given in 8th grade

Tuition Range 2004–2005 $12,950 to $25,400, pre-kindergarten
3's –12th grade

Financial Aid/Scholarship $1,743,000 (13% of the operating
budget)

Endowment $17 million

Diversity   26% students of color; 17 Early Steps students, 2 TEAK
Fellowship students, 7 DeLaSalle students, 7 Prep for Prep students
enrolled as of 2004
Women of Proud Heritage (founded 1991)
Women's History Assembly

Homework   1st: 15–20 minutes
2nd: 30 minutes
3rd and 4th: 45 minutes
5th–7th: 1–2 hours
8th–12th: 2–4 hours

After-School Program   All Lower School (K–4) after-school programs require an additional payment; ballet, ceramics, cooking, dramatics, gymnastics, photography, violin, arts and crafts, recorder, dance, tennis, sewing, puppets, computer, music, team sports, stichery, math for fun, swimming, ice-skating, typing. Private instruction in piano is available for students in kindergarten and up
Middle School: required Middle School electives are offered from 3:40–5:00 P.M. (the elective fee is included in the tuition); choices include a variety of recreational and creative activities, gallery and museum visits; sports activities and teams include: soccer,

swimming, volleyball, basketball, softball, track, running club, tennis and gymnastics according to the season

Upper School: Junior Varsity and Varsity interscholastic athletic competition in the Athletic Association of Independent Schools of New York City and the Ivy League

Summer Program Creative Arts Summer Program: a multi-arts summer program for boys and girls ages 6–15 (junior program for ages 6 and 7) offering instruction in art, drama, film, computer, science and athletics; all-day arts festival at conclusion of the program; an additional payment is required (limited financial aid is available)

Chartered by the International Society of the Sacred Heart in 1881, Convent of the Sacred Heart is the oldest independent girls' school in Manhattan. Sacred Heart is housed in two magnificent land-marked buildings—the former Otto Kahn and James Burden mansions. The winding marble staircase leads from the vaulted lobby to bright and spacious classrooms as well as banquet hall and ballroom in the manner of Versailles, complete with tapestry and marble. The ballroom was a wedding gift to Adele Burden née Sloane (great-granddaughter of Commodore Cornelius Vanderbilt) and the scene of many splendid parties and dances in the 1890s. Today the ballroom is used for Sacred Heart commencement, dance classes and assemblies, and is rented out on the weekends for corporate and charitable events and weddings, providing the school with additional income.

Sacred Heart, although a Catholic girls' school, is neither cloistered nor parochial in its outlook. Sacred Heart is governed by a lay board of trustees and Dr. Blake is the first lay head of the school; the nuns are elegantly dressed (habits are not worn) and approximately one-third of the students have a mixed religious background. As one parent said, "It's a Christian school because Sacred Heart stresses how you lead your life—there is an emphasis on ethics."

The idea of social service is built into a Sacred Heart education. The catalog states: "A primary aim of a Sacred Heart education is the development in each individual of a personal faith that impels to action." All schools claim to care about every student as an individual; at Sacred Heart, parents say, "They really mean it." Service begins with age appropriate projects in the lowest grades and continues through the Upper School where Sacred Heart has led other city students in the Conference on Homelessness and intensive summer service programs.

Sacred Heart has enjoyed a decade of enrollment growth. Additional sections have been added in most Lower School grades, facilities have been upgraded, technology has been integrated into the curriculum; amenities have been added including a lunch program and cafeteria/dining room, weight-training room and exercise studio, automated library accessible via Internet, new science labs, upgraded libraries, a new theater, and renovated classrooms.

Off campus, Sacred Heart is experiencing a historic expansion of its recreational and athletic facilities. The school has joined the Black Rock Forest Consortium providing access to a forest and an environmental sciences center shared with several other independent schools. Sacred Heart has also endowed lanes at the Asphalt Green Aqua Center and it is one of the seven schools pioneering the renovation of sports fields on Randalls Island. Sacred Heart has committed to an extensive athletics rentals program to supplement its capabilities and 80% of the students participate in one or more JV or Varsity teams, often bringing home the championship trophies.

Getting in: Parents can request a tour of the school or attend one of the open houses before applying. Largest points of entry are Pre-K, kindergarten and ninth grade. The application fee is $65 and the application asks for parents' education and employment. After applying, parents come for their tour and interview on the same day. Brick Church, Park Avenue Christian, Episcopal, West Side Montessori, International Pre-school, and St. Thomas More Nursery School are all considered "feeders" to Sacred Heart. The admissions office is sensitive to the needs of parents: "They are very courteous," one parent said, "and particularly accommodating to families from abroad." "When you're accepted at Sacred Heart you're accepted as part of a large international family," said a parent. Another parent said she found Sacred Heart's geographical and ethnic diversity "with a lot of families from Europe and Latin America," refreshing after her daughter's homogeneous nursery school.

Parents: Sacred Heart parents say that social competition is negligible. They don't need to dress up to pick up their daughters at school. Parents are considered partners in their daughters' education. Newsletters are sent home three times a year. Communication from teachers, the PA, and administration is frequent. There is a new parents' cocktail party and family dinner held in May for incoming families, as well as a welcoming party in September. The Parents

Association consists of officers, school representatives and class representatives and hosts an annual spring meeting and cocktail party and the annual auction or benefit fund-raiser and family events. There are two or three dinner dances held each year including the bi-annual Spring Ball (held at the American Crafts Museum one year) and the Hatter's Ball featuring custom or homemade hats, "ostrich plumes à la *My Fair Lady*," which benefits the Creative Arts Summer Program Scholarship Fund. Other Parents Association functions include Christmas caroling, tree lighting and sale (neighbors are welcome) at which you can buy your tree as well as the ornaments and have a picture taken with Santa Claus by the Otto Kahn fireplace outside the former dining room where Enrico Caruso once sang.

Program: At a recent Upper School open house, five elements of a Sacred Heart education were delineated: 1) faith: You will learn "what you are going to be and give in this world"; 2) academic challenge: Sacred Heart's rigorous academic program will impart a love of learning and enable each girl to become an independent thinker and grow in her own particular gifts; 3) social awareness: Everyone does service at Sacred Heart, and "we do not count hours" and the school has regular all-school service days, during which the entire community, including alumnae, get involved in a service project; 4) growth as a community: There is a strong relationship between faculty and students, and a diverse student community; 5) personal growth: To recognize your strengths, gifts and limitations, "you come as you are and are loved into being the very best that you can be." A Lower School parent said that what she likes best about Sacred Heart is that the headmistress and the heads of the divisions "have a real concern for each and every family—people are what matters."

Religion and social service go hand in hand at Sacred Heart. According to the brochure, the "basic intent of the Lower School religious program is to build in each student a positive sense of herself in relation to God and to her community." Ethics and spirituality are stressed—the basic premise is "you have a friend in God." There is Mass once a week in the beautifully appointed chapel and parents are always welcome. In Middle School "the link between faith and action is forged by social action activities that reach out to communities beyond the school." Middle School service projects include working in a day care center and participation in walkathons, God's Love We Deliver (meals delivered to AIDS patients) and Amnesty International. In the Upper School community service is coordinated through the campus ministry and the Student Activities and Service Program.

Students are expected to volunteer on a regular basis in a social service agency outside of school, keep a journal and share their experiences in a weekly meeting. Students in Class ten must complete a final project in which they examine a social issue in depth through academic research and field experience.

Recently, Sacred Heart started an Institute for Peace and Justice, a school-wide event attended by over 600 people. Born out of a desire to respond to 9/11, the institute is a community think tank of ideas, education and service with teach-ins, workshops, forums and lectures.

The Lower School at Sacred Heart is composed of grades pre-kindergarten through grade 4. In Lower School, the girls wear the signature Sacred Heart uniform: a gray jumper with a red-checked pinafore (both machine washable). Each Lower School girl has an "Angel" or "Big Sister" to guide her. The fourth graders are partners with seniors in the Upper School and Middle School girls read weekly to Lower School children. There are three kindergarten classes of approximately seventeen children each and two teachers in each classroom (plus a rabbit). Beginning in kindergarten the following subjects are taught: language arts, math, science, social studies and, in third grade onward, French. Students meet weekly for religion, art, music, library, gym and drama/movement. There are formal as well as informal assembly presentations. Exercise is taken on the two play terraces, which have views of the reservoir, or in Central Park across the street.

Parents say academics in the Lower School consists of "good old-fashioned teaching combined with some of the newer methods" and "there's a lot of structure." Conferences are held twice a year but parents say you can schedule one any time if necessary. A tone of "warmth and acceptance" prevails along with academic rigor. Director of Admissions Barbara Root describes Sacred Heart as "not overly pressured, but everyone is expected to do serious work." The mother of a third grader concurs: "Sacred Heart is competitive but each girl is encouraged to do her best." Collaborative learning is emphasized in the early years, and there are no individual desks until third grade.

The reading program begins in kindergarten and becomes more formal in Class one. Phonics is taught as an essential reading skill along with creative writing, Writers' Workshop, whatever works. If a student is not progressing well she will begin working with a reading specialist. There is individual as well as small group instruction and basal texts are used. Girls are taught to experience mathematics "as an integral part of everyday life" through cooking, manipulatives and

189

math games. For example, to learn the value of a million, one class is collecting and counting tea bag tags. The project is on display in the classroom.

Lower School science makes frequent use of technology, emphasizes the skills of observation and investigation. There is a two-day field trip to an environmental center in fourth grade. The social studies curriculum begins with a study of the students' own families, then extends to a study of the community. Students in Class three research topics such as the rain forest or deserts. Class four studies Early Explorers and American History.

Art is integrated into the science and social studies curriculum in many ways. Students in Class two pick an animal to study and model it in clay, then the entire class works together to create a Calderesque circus from wood, wire, foam and fabric. Students in Class three made "incredible" papier-mâché vegetables in art and studied the growth of plants from seed through maturation in science. Fifth graders studying antiquity create a museum of ancient cultures.

Drama and movement activities are "designed to enhance the students' understanding of dance as a means of communication and expression." By Class four the girls create and perform their own original dance/drama pieces.

George Orio, Convent's Director of Technology, is credited with seamlessly integrating technology into the classrooms and curriculum. Formal computer instruction begins in first grade. The classes are team taught by a computer specialist and the classroom teacher and use multimedia CD-ROMS and related software. Fifth graders work with LEGO LOGO, a robotics application, and by sixth grade students and teachers use *Hyperstudio* to create multimedia research projects.

Study of the French language begins in Class three through songs and games to teach vocabulary and pronunciation.

A team of Lower School psychologists and learning specialists give additional help where necessary. Project Charlie, an anti-drug program that focuses on self-esteem, is taught in the Lower School. A comprehensive health program which focuses on nutrition begins in Class 2.

Birthdays in Lower School are special because the birthday girl can wear a party dress, bring in cupcakes or another sweet and can donate a book to the library in her name. Another fun event in Lower School is the Halloween costume party. The Lower School Christmas Pageant "can make you weep" it is so beautifully produced, parents say.

Middle School at Sacred Heart consists of Classes five through seven. All six Middle School homerooms are located on the fourth floor. Each new Middle School student has an "angel" for the first weeks of school. New students and their angels are invited to school for a luncheon and orientation day the week before school begins. Flexible ability grouping in mathematics begins in Class six. French ability groups begin in Class seven. The first half of French I or Spanish I is offered to all seventh graders. The second half of this course is given in eighth grade. In Middle School, a study skills and research course and Latin (Class seven) and Spanish (Class seven) are added to the core curriculum of English, math, science, social studies, and religion. Students say there is an increased workload in Class six and the development of good study skills is emphasized.

By Class five, computer work is integrated into the English, math, social studies and science curricula. Fifth grade students explore the physical concepts of simple machines through LEGO LOGO. A unit in Class six on computer database filing uses *ClarisWorks*. Seventh grade students create multimedia presentations on the American Colonies using the Powerpoint application.

Art continues to be integrated with the curriculum at many levels. Students in Class six studying Medieval and Renaissance Europe create family crests and banners, work on tapestry projects and make stained-glass windows. The study of South America in Class seven is supplemented by the creation of relief sculptures and the study of pre-Columbian art.

The Middle School elective program is a required weekly enrichment elective. Among the choices are sports, drama, literary magazine, photography, ice skating, swimming and ceramics.

There is a Middle School musical production in the fall as well as smaller productions in the winter and spring. Other highlights include the Class seven father/daughter volleyball game, the pancake breakfast and the mother/daughter liturgy.

The Middle School has its own student government, a Committee of Games, that oversees the sports competition between the Green and Buff teams. There is also a Big Sister Program. Each class takes an overnight trip, which is coordinated with the curriculum. Class five travels to Mystic, Connecticut, sixth graders to a Pennsylvania Renaissance Faire and seventh graders to Plymouth, Massachusetts.

Beginning in Middle School and continuing through Upper School, academic achievement awards are given to students who maintain an A average for the year in four or more academic subjects.

At the end of the year there is a Sports Banquet to honor athletic achievement.

The Upper School at Sacred Heart consists of Classes eight through twelve. Class eight is a transition year at Sacred Heart. In Class nine there is an influx of new students from parochial and independent schools in the New York City area while some of the students who have been at Sacred Heart since pre-kindergarten or kindergarten opt to leave for a coed or boarding school. Incoming ninth graders have an overnight immersion program and each new student in the Upper School has an "angel" for the first weeks. Upper School students at Sacred Heart say they feel they have more opportunity to take risks and to be more articulate in an all-girls school. (But the school continues to be strict about skirt length.)

Students say that the academic expectations are high—Sacred Heart was recognized by the U.S. Department of Education as a National School of Excellence. "The teachers work you hard, and honors courses are pushed," they say. The sense of community continues in the Upper School: "It's not so competitive because we're all friends and we help each other." There has been an enormous change in the emphasis on the sciences in the past four years—now 90 percent of the students take an advanced science course during their senior year. Students take six or seven academic subjects in Classes eight through ten and add electives in Classes eleven and twelve. A former Parents Association president told us, "The Upper School is rigorous but there is a lot of support." The study of religion includes textual study, literary exegesis, historical background, comparative religions, ethics and philosophy. In the eleventh grade the interdisciplinary approach culminates in a thirty-page baccalaureate level thesis and oral presentation of a topic combining Christology and the Arts. Recent topics have included examinations of the films of Fellini, the music of J.S. Bach, and Beguin lace makers.

Because the Upper School is small, the teachers know each girl very well. Teachers are approachable and there are peer tutors.

There is an intensive five-year writing program in the Upper School and students become familiar with all literary genres. Students are expected to write well in all disciplines. In Class nine there is an interdisciplinary social studies and English project that produces *Medieval Magazine* and culminates in a banquet. Juniors and seniors can choose from courses in Asian and African-American literature. The "Memoirs" course examines feminist thinking through the stories of women in a variety of cultures. For "New York City in Literature," students read the work of an author (such as Edith Wharton, who lived in New York City) and visit his or her home and/or sites in the novel.

Students who excel in mathematics can take calculus AB and BC. Members of the Mathematics Club compete with other Catholic high schoolers in the tristate area.

The school has a standing research internship program at Rockefeller University where several girls study each year. Students have also interned at the Museum of Natural History, the New York Academy of Sciences, the Cooper Union Engineering School, the Columbia Science Honors Program and the U.N. A lab science research internship is available to students in eleventh and twelfth grades. Interns spend six hours a week in a laboratory and write a research paper.

The art department has been expanded in recent years.

In May there is a three-week Festival of the Arts when students celebrate their accomplishments in many areas. Artwork is on display throughout the school, and there are dance recitals, as well as performances by the handbell choir and the Speech and Drama Clubs.

Many of the extracurricular activities in the Upper School are coed. There are Upper School dances in September and at Christmas each year, and Sacred Heart students can audition for roles in the Collegiate, Regis and Browning Schools' plays and musicals. At Sacred Heart the drama department produces one-act plays or Shakespeare in the fall and a musical in the spring in which boys play some parts. There are also Service Days together with neighboring boys' schools.

Students can also join the Interschool Orchestra or the Sacred Heart Handbell Choir.

Other extracurricular opportunities include student government, Peer Support, Archeology Club, Drama Club, Environmental Club, yearbook, literary magazine, newspaper and Women of Proud Heritage. Sports are popular and plentiful: There are eighth grade teams, intramural clubs and eight varsity sports. Two of Sacred Heart's chief competitors are Trinity School and Brearley.

Sacred Heart students in Classes nine through twelve can participate in the exchange program at other Sacred Heart Schools either here or abroad. Students have studied in France, Belgium, Spain, California and Louisiana.

College guidance begins in Class nine, and there are assemblies with alumnae. Students say that because the teachers know and remember them so well it is easy to get recommendations. A young woman, a senior, who came to Sacred Heart from a public school, says she "holds school dear, it has molded me into what I am."

Popular College Choices   Columbia, Georgetown, Harvard, Kenyon, Middlebury, Princeton, University of Pennsylvania, Vassar, Yale, Boston University

Traditions   Big Sister/Little Sister Cookout, used uniform sale, class coffees, Middle School Mother/Daughter Liturgy, Upper School Mother/Daughter Tea, Senior Mother/Daughter Breakfast and induction into the Alumnae Association, tree sale and caroling party, Christmas Pageant, Sacred Heart Antiques Show, Father/Daughter Dinner Dance, Dad/Daughter boat cruise, Black History Month (February), Women's History Month (March), Ring Day, Sacred Heart Feast Days, First Communion, Confirmation, May Festival of the Arts, Spring Book Fair, Grandparents' Day, archeology trip, class nine Blairstown trip, class eleven retreat, Upper School service trip in March, Sports Banquets, Hatter's Ball, Senior Dinner Dance, alumnae mothers lunch, Senior cut day, Spring Street Fair, Prize Day, Homecoming

Publications   Newspaper: *Spirit*
Upper School Literary magazine: *Zenith*
Yearbook: *Cornerstone*
Women's issues: *Women of Proud Heritage*
French Literary Magazine: *Sous Presse*
Middle School Literary Magazine: *Millenium*
Annual report
Parent/Alumnae Newsletter
Alumae Magazine: *Les Amies*
Visual Arts Magazine: *Iris*
Spanish Literary Magazine: *A Toda Vela*
Science Magazine: *Catalyst*

Community Service Requirement   Each student is expected to give of herself to the school community and to the community at large—hours are not counted

Hangouts   Jackson Hole (hamburger restaurant), Pintaile's Pizza

Corlears School

324 West 15th Street
New York, NY 10011
(212) 741-2800
FAX **(212) 807-1550**
website: www.corlearsschool.org

Coed
Nursery–4th grade
Not accessible

Ms. Thya Merz, Head of School
Ms. Rorry Romeo, Director of Admissions

Birthday Cutoff   Children entering kindergarten should be 5 in September

Enrollment   Total enrollment: 130
Largest point of entry is 2.5/3s
Kindergarten places: varies from year to year
Graduating class 2004: 16

Grades   Anecdotal reports and checklists

Tuition Range 2005–2006 $13,200 to $19,200, 2½'s–4th grade
Additional fees: $600 building fee; reduced to $360 for a second child in the school

Financial Aid/Scholarship   30% of the student body receive some form of aid

Endowment   None
Each family makes a non-interest-bearing loan of $1,000 per child
There is a 3-year staggered payment system for this loan

After-School Program   Child care available after school Monday–Friday until 5:45 P.M.
Corlears After-School Specialty Program: open to Corlears students only; weekdays from 3:15 P.M. to 4:15 P.M.; an additional fee required; activities include music, drama, sports, chess, gymnastics, chorus, Spanish, art and cooking

Summer Program   Summer Science Camp: four weeks from mid-June to the end of July for children ages 3 through 8; children explore scientific themes such as energy, animals, dirt and water as well as taking part in recreational and creative activities, swimming and trips; an additional payment is required

---

Corlears was founded in 1968 on the Lower East Side and moved to West 15th Street in 1971. Corlears has well-equipped classrooms, an art room, wood shop, library, two gyms and a lovely play yard. Children bring their own lunches. Admission is based on a personal interview and available school records. Corlears is small and nurturing and parents describe it as a neighborhood school. Corlears goes to fourth grade, specializing in the education of children in the early years. There are interage classroom groupings throughout. There is a supervised early-morning drop-off for children age four and older.

Corlears' program is designed to be suportive and fosters a genuine love of learning, teaching students how to solve problems, think creatively and how to become competent in basic skills. Spanish, art, music, movement, physical education and library supplement the program. Developmental stages and individual learning styles are respected. Classroom computers are available for children six to nine years of age. Use of the computers is integrated into classwork. An extensive counseling placement program assists fourth grade graduates with entrance to ongoing schools.

The Dalton School

108 East 89th Street
New York, NY 10128-1599
(212) 423-5200, FAX (212) 423-5259
website: www.dalton.org

Coed
Kindergarten–12th grade
Accessible (4th through 12th grades)

Ms. Ellen Stein, Head of School
Dr. Elisabeth Krents, Director of Admissions, Kindergarten–12
Ms. Eva Rado, Director of Middle School/High School Admissions
Dr. Lisa Waller, Associate Director of Admissions, Kindergarten–12

Birthday Cutoff   August 31st; Children must be 5 for kindergarten

Enrollment   Total enrollment: 1294
   Kindergarten places: approximately 90
   Graduating class size: approximately 100–115

Grades   Semester system
   Letter grades begin in 8th grade
   Full departmentalization by 6th grade
   First midterm and final in 9th grade

Tuition Range 2004–2005 $24,560 to $25,910, K–12th grade
   No additional fees other than minimal PTA and activities fees

Financial Aid/Scholarship   Approximately 20% of families receive
   some form of financial aid
   $4.2 million available

Endowment   Approximately $25 million

Diversity   Approximately 25% children of color
   35 Prep for Prep students enrolled as of fall 2004
   Affiliated with Early Steps Program, TEAK, A Better Chance,
   Albert G. Oliver Scholarship Program for children of color, Faculty Diversity Committee, PTA Diversity Committee; Full Time

Diversity Coordinator, Affinity Groups, Mentoring Program for students, S.E.E.D. Program

Homework   Kindergarten: none
1st: none
2nd: ½ hour nightly (15 minutes of work, 15 minutes of reading, except for weekends or vacations) building to ½ hour of homework and minimum of 15 minutes of reading
3rd: 45 minutes plus reading (not on weekends)
4th–6th: 1–1½ hours
7th–9th: 2–3 hours
10th–12th: approximately 3 to 4 hours a night

After-School Program   The Dalton Serendipity Program: a variety of creative and recreational activities including computer, foreign language instruction (including French, Spanish, Chinese, and Japanese), newspaper, opera, ballet, cooking, cartooning, sports and games; an additional payment is required; Kids Club: after-school care daily on premises until 5:45 P.M.; Middle School After School Program; an additional payment is required
The Dalton Chess Academy for all age students
Interscholastic athletic competition, clubs and committees for Middle and High School students

Summer Program   Summer camp for Lower School students, open to children from other schools; an additional payment is required

Since its founding in 1919 by visionary educator Helen Parkhurst, The Dalton School's mission has been the improvement of education. Dalton is often described as having "one foot in traditional education and one foot firmly planted in the progressive movement." Known for inculcating independence of thought combined with intellectual rigor and for having a plethora of innovative programs with an emphasis on the use of technology to enhance education, The Dalton School serves as a model for other schools around the world and Dalton clones can be found in England, the Netherlands, Australia, The Czech Republic, Chile, China and Japan. Dalton is a famous school well known for its philosophy and is historically rich in people and programs.

The foundation of a Dalton education is still the Dalton Plan which is not as complicated in actuality as it appears in writing. It consists of

House (the home base for each student); *The Assignment* (the work: a type of contract between student and teacher); the *Laboratory* (one-to-one or small group sessions between student and teacher that augment classroom work). Dalton is unique in that Lab time is built into each teacher's schedule and students say that teachers are very accommodating and Labs often take place on the same day they are requested. Throughout the First Program and the early years of Middle School, the House Advisor is also the classroom teacher. House groups change each year and are comprised of students of the same age until high school. Then there are mixed grade levels in each group and these students remain with the same House Advisor for four years. The role of the House Advisor is to act as an advocate for each child and as the key contact person for parents with the school. The Assignment is a document created by the individual teachers that covers a period of time and details the academic expectations in a unit of study. It is introduced at the First Program (Lower School) and increases through Middle and High School.

Getting in: Dr. Elisabeth Krents, a Dalton alumna with a doctorate in Education, is the Director of Admissions for kindergarten through twelfth grade. Parents describe her as "knowledgeable, enthusiastic and warm." She brings a welcome professionalism to the process. Parents interested in learning more about the school can attend spring tours conducted by Elisabeth Krents or attend open houses at both the First Program and Middle and High School in the fall before applying. Dalton takes a close look at parents to make sure they have a clear understanding of the school's philosophy and to see if they have solid values. For First Program applicants, Dalton requires both a parent tour and a meeting with Elisabeth Krents or another senior admissions staff member. Children are either interviewed at Dalton in small groups or observed in their nursery schools. Letters of recommendation from those who really know the applicant are optional. Don't waste time with letters from every celebrity or politician you ever met unless they really know your child. This is true of admission to Middle and High School too.

In the two upper divisions, Dalton is looking to admit students who seek an extremely challenging academic environment that also stresses a deep appreciation for the visual and performing arts. Once an application is received, prospective students and their parents are invited for an individual family tour given by a member of the faculty or a senior. The tour is followed by a class visit for the student and a meeting with Eva Rado for the parents. Applicant families get a chance to meet Dalton students, teachers and administrators at each visit.

Dalton doesn't merely pay lip service to diversity. The school follows through with respect and support, providing an afterschool program for children whose parents work, diversity literacy training, parent and student support groups and a superb mentoring program that pairs high school students of color with successful professionals of color. These high school students, in turn, mentor younger students coming up through the Middle School and in First Program. High school students join with the PTA Diversity Committee to organize the First Program, Multicultural Festival featuring, art, food, music and storytelling.

What are they looking for? Elisabeth Krents told us "We are trying to get away from the myth that there is a 'Dalton type' of child. We look for *all* kinds of children. Helen Parkhurst's goal was to have a community of different individuals and to educate every type of child, preparing each for the real world. We want to admit students (and families) who reflect the diversity of the real world and that means geographic, socioeconomic, racial and religious diversity." Parents say that eccentricity and ethnicity are valued. The 2004 First Program is composed of 32% children of color and of children from all over the city. One does not have to be a genius to be accepted to Dalton; a former admissions director told us they look for "the child who is not just a sponge, but who will contribute." Dalton has a policy of preferring, but not automatically admitting, siblings and children of alumni. Dalton will accept an "at risk" child and does mainstream children with moderate disabilities provided they can keep up academically.

Parents: The school views parents as partners in the education of their children and they are invited to be involved in many different ways: There are committees that focus on ethics, gender, community service, the Book Fair, safety, and children's entertainment. Ongoing parent dialogues are conducted at the First Program. Kindergarten to grade 12 parents are invited to "Rap sessions", meetings for parents and administrators to discuss developmental and social issues.

Dalton's glamorous, materialistic image of the 1980's is no longer accurate. In the past, students had been labeled "spoiled." Years ago a student described the problem as particularly acute in Middle School "where students are not as considerate of one another as they could be" but this has changed over the years. Values education is at the top of the school's agenda and an Ethics Committee, made up of administrators, faculty and parents, works hard to integrate ethics into the curriculum and the life of the school in a meaningful way.

Dalton families have changed over the years. The Downtowners Committee meets regularly since Dalton has an ever increasing number of children who live throughout that area. A three division PTA Diversity Committee (made up of Uptowners Committee as well as the Bridge and Tunnel group) exists to support families of color. If there's any question as to how Dalton families align themselves politically, just peek into the Lower School library where, instead of the chiseled faces of Dalton's former headmasters, you'll see portraits of John and Robert Kennedy and Martin Luther King. Dalton no longer has the monopoly on glitz which is spread more uniformly among the private schools today including those which were traditionally more staid such as Trinity and Spence. And according to a parent who is also a trustee: "There's no fuss over famous families; it's old news." Still, with so many prominent families in the school, networking opportunities abound. For instance, a Dalton high schooler working on a journalism project was advised by a senior writer at *The New York Times* who has a child at the school. An alumna told us she landed her first fashion internship with Diana Vreeland at the Metropolitan Museum Costume Institute thanks to a Dalton connection.

Dalton parents have created an extensive internship program for students. Opportunities include working as an intern in the sciences, arts, publishing and politics. Recently, a senior developed a project through an internship that led to her winning the national Siemens/Westinghouse award.

Dalton parents are generous in their financial support of the school. A capital campaign funded major improvements in the school's facilities. A 32,000 square foot Physical Education Center was constructed at 200 East 87th Street with a spectator gym (the basketball team is a strong draw) and other amenities. A floor was added to the top of the 89th Street building that houses a visual arts center with seven skylit studios. An 8,000 square foot science center was built increasing the space allocated to the science program by 25%. Recent renovations include updating the Martin Theater as well as construction of the state-of-the-art Performing Arts Center which augments the other arts facilities.

Program: First Program (affectionately known as Little Dalton) consists of kindergarten through third grade. It is housed in three interconnected townhouses on East 91st Street. Recent renovations added 2,000 square feet of instructional space to the school which includes a science center plus a spacious commons area used by all the grades. The children still find Little Dalton "cozy" and move about the building freely.

Ellen Stein, a Dalton alumna, and former vice principal at Friends Seminary, was the Director of the First Program for six years and is now Head of School, after serving for two years as Associate Head of School. Parents speak highly of her commitment to ethics and the establishment of a strong sense of community in the school. "While Dalton is noted for its individualization, we also want to develop children's senses of their responsibility as members of the school and to the community at large." After Ms. Stein's arrival, parents noted that the First Program tightened the kindergarten through third grade curriculum to create a more even balance between rigorous skills and "process learning." Janet Shaw, a gifted administrator and well-respected educator, is the Director of the First Program.

Academics are approached in a structured but relaxed setting. In kindergarten the school becomes acquainted with a child's learning style. Instruction is individualized, some parents say "to a fault." While the day is highly organized, children are encouraged to proceed at their own pace within the context of curricular goals for the year that are consistent across the grade levels. "The children learn how to think, how to take risks and how to make mistakes," according to a parent. Children are not expected to read by the end of kindergarten but if they do, individualized work is planned for them. Careful attention is paid to the placement of each student with the right teacher and right class.

From the very beginning of the learning process at Dalton, young students are actively and creatively involved in what they study. Dalton is historically known for its strength in the arts which are integrated into the curriculum. Dalton's First Program is based upon a social studies "core" where language arts, math, science, music and art are directly related to the core study. Second graders focus on New York City. The children create a model city which reflects what they have learned about city needs and urban design. They write and revise written reports about landmark buildings on the computer. In music classes the children put their own city poems into song and in art they paint murals of city scenes. In science class while studying animals, specifically birds, they dissected owl pellets classifying the excreted bones and formed hypotheses about what type of prey the owl had consumed. In addition, second graders created their own multi-media magazine on the theme of "diversity in the city." One class photographed neighborhoods, buildings and faces, another class focused on jobs and workers, interviewing parents in their workplaces and analyzing the data they collected, creating graphs (and posting data on the Internet). Another class concentrated on schools, foods and neighborhoods.

Former art teacher Sheila Lamb, a Dalton institution and now its "Artist in Residence," has guided the creative work of First Program students for over thirty years. "I treat every child like an artist," she says. Her approach "is to be with the children with their imaginations . . . nurturers of their visual language." First Program art integrates all forms of arts and crafts. Creativity carries over to the sciences as well. One of our favorites is a third grade unit in which students study the unusual properties of planet "Oobleckia" (the name is based on a Dr. Seuss book, the planet is made of cornstarch, water and food coloring). Students must come up with solutions to problems such as "How would you land a spaceship on Oobleckia?" They work in groups and make a final report at a mock conference.

Dalton is at the forefront of independent schools for its commitment (both financial and philosophical) to technology and education. Under the Dalton Technology Plan, faculty have designed projects and curricula that utilize advanced multimedia technology. According to a former headmaster, technology does not replace traditional educational methods: "It allows us to deliver the Dalton Plan more powerfully than ever and is consistent with Dalton's individualized approach, sense of community and mission to prepare students for life after Dalton. Technology shifts education from adults giving answers to students seeking answers to their own meaningful questions."

Walking through the halls one can see kindergarten children making their own interactive counting slide shows, sixth grade students being introduced to history and scientific principles through simulated excavations of Assyria and Greece, high school students participating in advanced astronomy simulation, and English students exploring the ideas of Shakespeare's *Macbeth* through online resources, including digitized versions of scenes from the play by three different repertory companies.

Specialists enrich the Dalton experience. It's a school with an archeologist in residence who spends six weeks with each third grade class excavating a dig set up in the backyard. Sixth graders participate in the Archaeotype program, "a computer-based, integrated curriculum unit" developed by Dalton faculty in which they examine artifacts from ancient Greece and Assyria, conduct their own research and discuss their findings. It is also the only school in the city to have a special lecturer who teaches Dalton classes at the American Museum of Natural History. Chess is taught to kindergartners and first graders by an experienced chess master.

Don't worry if your child is fidgety—there's plenty of opportunity for the children to stretch their limbs as well as their minds here. In addition to daily play on the two play roofs and at the gym several times a week, beginning in second grade students use Dalton's impressive Physical Education Center located on east 87th Street. Children are bussed to and from the center.

At the end of third grade the children at Little Dalton pass through the arch during the traditional Arch Day Ceremony in June and move on to Big Dalton. Before they do, each makes his or her own colorful ceramic tile that is permanently mounted in a hallway of Little Dalton. The transition to Big Dalton seems to be an easy one since the children have frequently visited "Buddy Houses" and attended a variety of events at the ivy-covered 89th Street building.

In Middle School, fourth and fifth graders are taught in self-contained classrooms in which the House Advisor teaches most subjects. Departmentalization begins in sixth grade and all students in sixth through eighth grades are taught math, social studies and English by a core group of three teachers who work together. The core groups make Big Dalton seem small and provide a comfortable transition to the more demanding high school. Each core teacher is an advisor and each student has a sense of belonging to a particular core. Students are placed in different core and House groups every year. Individual differences in levels or skills are recognized by grouping within the classroom, by the individualized assignments and by the enrichment and support provided in the classes and in Labs.

Student life at Dalton's high school is informal. There are no bells and the dress code is relaxed. "There's a small grunge element," said a student. Starting in late spring ninth grade students can sign out and leave school during a Lab period. Students who serve as peer leaders or peer tutors are involved with faculty in programs for incoming freshmen. A parent told us, "They do a superb job to ensure that the transition is smooth."

There is no Dalton "type" per se; there are jocks and artists and techies, and cliques form around interests. There is a strong drama group, a newspaper group, and athletic teams. Dalton students embrace technology and communicate through Forum, an active e-mail message system. Amusing top ten lists are popular; students also discuss community and current events online. With a focus on ethics in place, students pay more attention to how they treat one another, including keeping the cafeteria clean.

Community Service is one avenue for teaching ethics and values and it is integrated into the curriculum at every grade level. A recent project brought senior citizens from a local center to Dalton for computer lessons. Paired together with individual Dalton children, seniors learned how to operate a mouse and access the Internet. The students, in turn, learned about life in the city before the advent of television. Other community service projects occur throughout the year: making bread for a homeless shelter to distribute, or First Program parents and children getting together to decorate bags for the God's Love We Deliver Program for homebound patients with AIDS.

Third grade students recently founded the Human Rights Club whose mission is to acknowledge and support human rights both locally and globally. Over thirty third graders are interested in being socially active and creating positive change For example, a former Dalton student, a son of a Kenyan activist and now a member of Parliament, maintains close contact with Club members about serious ecnomic and environmental problems in Kenya. The club is raising tuition money for Kenyan children so they may continue their education beyond elementary school.

In the High School, Community Service is required and viewed as an opportunity for students to learn through interaction with the world beyond the school. One of the longest standing among the city's private schools, the service program encourages students to assume an active civic role. Students must complete four projects during their high school years, each being a sustained, meaningful commitment to one agency or cause that provides a valuable service to those in need. Students work with such agencies as the Youth Service Opportunity Projects, the East Harlem Tutoring Program, where children are tutored both in and outside of school, the Borden Center for Aging, and Public Color, where students paint public schools and community centers.

Dalton students are politically savvy. During the war in Iraq, they held town meetings, and during the presidential election, students had an electoral college discussion and expressed their views through political videos, radio ads and cartoons. Dalton students have created their own video news program modeled on CNN and do not shy away from open and difficult discussions concerning race and gender. There are diversity groups such as: DAALAS (Dalton Alliance of African-American and Latino Students) and the more inclusive group,

Another Perspective. A discussion might be sponsored by Another Perspective, or Gender Issues or Human Rights or by the Exploration Committee and speakers such as Ralph Nader and Katie Roiphe are invited to address the students in groups both large and small. Environmental issues are important to the community and the student government instituted a recycling program and convinced the cafeteria to stop using styrofoam products.

In general, teachers are addressed formally (Mr. Smith, Mrs. Brown) but it depends on the teacher. Students describe the staff as "relaxed, intense, knowledgeable." And because of Lab time, students have the opportunity to develop close relationships with their teachers. Dalton nurtures its faculty providing some of the highest salary and fringe benefit programs offered by the independent schools. The school takes special pride in recruiting and retaining a talented, caring and charismatic faculty.

Faculty are encouraged to take advantage of sabbaticals, travel grants, workshops and funded summer curriculum grants. During one recent summer, teams of Dalton apostles were abroad in Taiwan, Turkey and Australia to spread the word about the Dalton Plan and the use of technology in education. Among members of the high school faculty are published historians, philosophers, writers and artists. They can be characterized as committed to creating a classroom environment that challenges students to pose compelling questions and to analyze and interpret texts and data. In addition, during Lab, when students work one on one with faculty, the faculty validates students' academic work and their creativity in a tutorial mode. Students emerge as independent and confident thinkers.

Dalton's requirements and course offerings in the high school seem quite traditional in scope. Freshmen, sophmores and juniors have to take at least five major courses. Core courses are English, history, languages, math and science. Students take elective courses as juniors and seniors. A junior can choose among five different courses in American literature, each with a different focus and reading list. A senior can choose among such humanities courses as "Asian Literature: East Meets West" and "Postmodern America," or "All the News That's Fit: The Press and the Public Interest." In 2003–04 AP courses were eliminated in favor of enriched courses created by Dalton's faculty, that provide students with in-depth study of all subject areas in a creative and analytical way so students can take, and do well on, AP exams.

Personal exploration is also provided in Lab throughout the

students' years and particularly in the high school as students become increasingly independent learners. "It's not an easy school to go to," said a junior, "because you can't squander your free time—you do have to go to Lab." The Assignment might be a month long project; for instance, students studying the pre-Civil War years might write a newspaper typical of the period.

In keeping with the emphasis on creative expression and intellectual pursuit, many students elect to produce senior projects in which they demonstrate their abilities to work as visual and performing artists, historians, scientists and writers. Recently, a senior initiative program, promoted through the student government, was established. During the final month of senior year, students focused on scholarly, creative and service work and presented their results to an audience of faculty, students and parents.

At Dalton, there is tremendous support and encouragement for students seeking their own personal vision in the arts. Whether developing an energetically choreographed piece set to hip hop, studying the complexities of a Schubert Mass, designing an original set for Stephen Sondheim's *Company*, or studying life drawing for three consecutive years, a Dalton student is guided by professional artists who are committed to teaching. One student described his experience this way, "If you're interested in a certain area, you are given a great deal of support and encouragement to pursue it in depth." According to a senior art teacher, "The skylit art center is a place where everyone uses every inch of space for the creation and consideration of art."

Dalton students display an array of musical gifts. There are two orchestras for the Middle and High School, a chamber music ensemble, a percussion ensemble, and a jazz-rock ensemble; and chorus. And all groups perform at the Annual Spring Concert.

While Dalton High School students are serious in their endeavors and ambitions, they also embrace opportunities for poking fun at themselves and the school community. A humor magazine, *"Liquid Smoke"* and Phase, a student cabaret replete with spoofs, give the students an avenue for expressions of irreverence.

Dalton's logo shows a child confidently leaving a mother's embrace. After thirteen years of self-discovery and academic adventure, Dalton's graduating seniors sing the words of the school motto: "Here we have learned to go forth unafraid."

Popular College Choices   Brown, Harvard, Cornell, Yale, University of Pennsylvania, Wesleyan, Amherst, Williams

Traditions   Greek Festival, Candlelighting, Arch Day, Dance Theater Workshop Performance, Spring Concert, parent discussion days, annual trips beginning in Little Dalton and throughout Middle School, First Program Multicultural Festival, school street fair on 91st Street, High School prom

Publications   Monthly student newspaper: *The Daltonian*
Literary Magazine: *The Blue Flag*
Middle School Literary Magazine: *Whispers*
Art, photography: *Fine Arts Magazine*
Public Affairs Journal: *Macrocosm*
Science publication: *Quantum Leaps*
Ethics publication: *Voices*
Yearbook

Community Service Requirement   Four approved projects during high school

Hangouts   Starbucks, Stargate, The Bagelry, the gym

The Dwight School

(admissions and mailing address for all grades)
291 Central Park West
New York, NY 10024
(212) 724-2146 ext. 1
website: www.dwight.edu
e-mail: admissions@dwight.edu

Nursery Division
Woodside Preschool
Trump Place
140 and 160 Riverside Boulevard
(West 67th Street)
New York, NY 10069
(212) 724-2146 ext 0
e-mail: admissions@woodsidepreschool.org

Coed
Pre-K–12th Grade
Not Accessible

Mr. Stephen H. Spahn, Chancellor
Ms. Emily Lyons, Director of Admissions, K–6
Ms. Marina Bernstein, Director of Admissions, 7–12
Mrs. Samantha Allen, Associate Director of Admissions, Pre-K

Uniform   K–8 boys: khaki or gray slacks, blue blazer or sweater with Dwight crest, collared shirts or turtlenecks
K–8 girls: jumpers, gray, khaki or dark blue skirts, white collared shirts and blazers or sweaters
9–12 boys: collared shirt with tie, no denim or turtlenecks
9–12 girls: skirt or slacks (not denim), collared shirt, or turtleneck

Birthday Cutoff   Children entering Kindergarten must be 5 by September 1; International applicants for kindergarten must be 5 by December 31

Enrollment   Total enrollment: 590
Nursery places: 60
Nursery enrollment: 150
Lower Division (Grades K–5): 109

Upper Division (Grades 6–12): 331
Ninth grade places: 35
K places: 20
Graduating class approximately 70

Grades Trimester system
Formal letter grades begin in 5th grade
Departmentalization begins in 5th grade
First final exam is offered in 5th grade

Tuition Range 2005–2006 $25,000 to $26,850, K–12th grade
Additional fees for registration, graduation and support activities
range from $900 to $1500
A tuition payment plan is available for families

Financial Aid/Scholarship $1,100,000 in financial aid is available
26% of students receive some form of financial assistance

Endowment $5 million

Diversity 15% students of color
30% of the students were born in a foreign country
The International Baccalaureate (IB) is offered
English as a Second Language (ESL) instruction is available
Dwight has an expanded language program offering French, Latin,
German, Spanish, Italian, Japanese, Hebrew and Chinese

Homework K: 15–20 minutes
1st and 2nd: 1/2 hour
3rd and 4th: 45 minutes
5th and 6th: 1 hour
7th and 8th: 1½–2 hours
9th–12th: 2–3 hours

After-School Program Dwight's After-School Program is not open
to students from other schools
Grades Pre-K–6: Spanish, creative and recreational activities for
an additional fee
Grades 7–12: there are approximately 37 clubs and activities
offered before and after school, including an after-school study
program; Middle School, junior varsity and varsity sports teams

and clubs including fencing, soccer, tennis, squash, volleyball, basketball, track, cross country, boxing, workout, dance, and yoga.

Summer Program   Woodside Summer Camp runs from mid-June through early August. The Dwight Intensive Review Program is an academic summer program for students who need extra support or wish to accelerate; the program runs from mid-June through the end of July; an additional payment is required
An intensive ESL summer program is offered to current and incoming students; there is an additional charge for this program; a Spanish environmental studies and community service program is available in July.

———

The Dwight School was founded in 1880 as an academy of classical studies, became coed in 1967 and added a London campus in 1972. The Woodside Preschool campus was opened in 2004–2005. Dwight merged with the Anglo-American International School in 1993 and offers three International Baccalaureate (IB) programs. This consortium works out very well because the Spahn family has had a long association with both schools. Stephen Spahn, the chancellor of The Dwight School, attended Anglo-American and his father headed that school for more than thirty years. The Dwight School retains its identity as "a small traditional school" while adding the international elements of the Anglo-American School. The Dwight School follows the International Baccalaureate Curriculum from pre-kindergarten through twelfth grade. The Dwight School also offers a fully mainstreamed program for children with mild learning differences (the Quest program).

The new nursery school has 10 large classrooms, two indoor play areas and an outdoor recreation area.

The main school occupies three buildings—a five story building on 89th Street, a brownstone on 88th Street and a space on Central Park West. In addition to classrooms, these buildings contain a photography darkroom, two computer centers, a theater space, and two gymnasiums.

With students and faculty from over thirty nations, the school has a unique social as well as academic environment. Internationalism has been a natural part of the curriculum for many years. Students learn that there are many ways to celebrate and observe holidays. One of the highlights of the primary school is the annual holiday show. Each grade selects a country (often the country of origin of a classmate) and celebrates the country's most important holiday. Middle and Upper School students attend and some are involved in production and musical elements.

The Dwight School is one of the few New York area schools to offer the International Baccalaureate diploma. As described in the brochure, "eleventh grade students may enroll in this challenging curriculum in six subjects requiring solid academic skills and the ability to think clearly and communicate effectively. The IB curriculum is a deliberate compromise between the specialization required in some national systems and the breadth preferred in others." Foreign students planning to return to their countries of origin are often required to have passed the "bac." The IB program is acknowledged as an excellent preparation for the more competitive U.S. colleges and can often represent a year's college credit.

Perhaps the most intriguing innovation is the school's creation of a non-profit organization based at Dwight, The Institute for Civic Leadership (ICL). The goal of ICL is to train all students to become leaders in social and community entrepreneurship. The school has successfully organized two student-run "Dare to Dream" conferences at the American Museum of Natural History on Martin Luther King Day. The keynote speakers always include the Mayor as well as other leaders who discuss how students can make a difference.

Presently, the ICL has expanded its program and works with student leaders from forty other schools. During the summer, ICL sponsors programs to build schools in Kenya and Thailand. In addition, it partners with a school in Costa Rica—that also offers an IB program—to educate orphans from all over Latin America, stresses practical ways to organize a community service project, for example, improving Costa Rica's rainforests through a buddy program that involves working with an orphan.

The school believes that everyone has the capacity to excel at some endeavor. The inquiry-based curriculum that Dwight has used in the Lower and Middle Schools for over twenty years, relates to Dr. Howard Gardner's theories of "Multiple Intelligence." (See *Glossary*). The Dwight School appreciates the differences in students' learning styles and interests.

In addition, the low student/teacher ratio (12:1) allows for small classes and individual attention. The faculty create many of the imaginative programs that prepare students to think critically while demonstrating common sense, the ability to work with others and manage time, people and information.

"Any child can succeed with a properly designed program," says Mr. Spahn. "We can take virtually any college preparatory youngster, motivate him, provide positive reinforcement and transform him into a serious and enthusiastic learner." There is constant communication between the school and the families. "We welcome input from parents," Mr. Spahn says. "We have an open door policy." Parents say the warm, dedicated faculty come in early and leave late—new challenges are there when needed. Student progress is monitored through standardized tests including the SATs. Grades are given on most work in the upper houses (grades). Parents meet with teachers two times a year, and in individual conferences when requested.

By focusing on a student's strengths, transfers to Dwight get better grades, and acquire improved self-esteem and develop their talents. A student who transferred into Dwight from Dalton said, "At Dwight teachers and peers give you lots of attention; everybody knows your name. Dwight has a traditional curriculum. They don't offer as many courses, but there is more structure." One mother said her daughter went from "just keeping up" at her old school to "doing very well at Dwight." The amount of homework was the same, about two to three hours, but she made honor roll. "She got so much out of it," says her mother, "real values and friendships." One parent whose child had a vision problem said it was handled so that her child never felt bad about herself.

Getting in: Upon request, parents can tour The Dwight School before filing an application. Once an application is filed the child's current transcripts are requested. The school will call the parents to arrange dates for their child's interview. Parents say the setting is relaxed. Applicants for grades 1 through 12 have a one-on-one interview. Applicants spend part of the day visiting classes. Pre-kindergarten and kindergarten applicants visit in groups.

Program: Dwight is described as "a family school" with many siblings in attendance. The preschool program utilizes the Primary Years Program (PYP) of the International Baccalaurate as well as other creative and developmentally appropriate early childhood programming. The Lower School is small; all of the primary school-children know each other and the teachers. However, some European formality prevails, as the teachers are addressed as "Mr. Jones" or "Miss Smith." In the after-school clubs a first grader can get to know a fourth grader. Because reading and math are taught on an individual basis, a child can advance at his or her own pace.

Perhaps the most distinctive feature of The Dwight School, in the words of a student, is that "there is no norm here." The student body is composed of children from diverse cultural, religious and geographic backgrounds. There is also a broad spectrum of academic ability at Dwight: a talented and superior group of international students who take advantage of a well-arranged ESL program and the opportunity to take the rigorous International Baccalaureate; average students taking the program, all of whom show significant improvement because of the baccalaureate's flexibility, and students with mild learning difficulties who are taking regular college prep with the support of the Quest program. There is a positive emphasis on differences. But all see themselves as part of the school.

The Quest program was started at Anglo-American in 1976 to provide additional support for children with minor learning differences (not behavior problems) so that they could participate in a challenging college preparatory curriculum without having to go to a tutor every day after school. All Dwight students are expected to develop a solid foundation of basic skills but the teachers at Dwight understand that children learn differently. Quest teachers provide extra support outside and within the classroom allowing students to be part of the group. Approximately 10 percent of the school is involved in the Quest program and parents must pay an additional fee for Quest program specialists. A parent said, "The teacher-student relationships are very personal and caring. The individuality of the students is stressed." Parents say that the program instills confidence: "My child thinks that he's a good learner now," said one parent. Parents with children enrolled in the Quest program say that reports are informative and elaborate with over thirty categories. Parents also learn the results of special testing in speech, reading and hearing.

The Quest program can serve students with mixed abilities; for instance, one student who is in the Quest program for science takes the International Baccalaureate course in history. Quest teachers also provide enrichment in English during the schoolday. Foreign students taking English as a second language often need assistance in certain subject areas.

The Timothy House students (grades K–4) play in Central Park or the gym every day. Reading is taught using an individualized eclectic approach. A combination of literature, phonetics and basal readers is used through third grade. First graders use invented spelling but the work we saw on display was corrected. French and Chinese language instruction begin in kindergarten. There are spelling tests every Friday in first grade. Lower School students have computers in their classrooms. Writing is incorporated into all areas of the curriculum: In addition to science and social studies reports, daily diaries are kept. Second through fourth graders use Writers Workshop, in which they learn the steps for effective essay writing: brainstorming, first draft, editing, final draft. Timothy House students study French.

Lower School students go to the art and music rooms twice a week. There is a darkroom, a music room and a painting annex.

Dwight's Middle and Upper Schools are divided into three houses. Each house has its own Dean. The first class period is a House Community or Advisory meeting. Advisors are selected by matching students and teachers.

Bentley House is composed of grades five through eight. Average class size is fourteen to seventeen students. Study skills are taught in all grades. Students learn how to prepare for tests and quizzes. In addition to the usual academic offerings, all students take art and music. Fifth graders study ancient Egypt and Greece. They read such classic children's literature as *Charlotte's Web* and *Treasure Island*. They are introduced to LOGO and word processing on the computer. (Spahn says that when handwriting is a problem, the student can write on a word processor and the ideas flow.) Either advanced or beginning Spanish and French conversation and culture are required.

Sixth graders study the history of Europe from ancient Rome until the early eighteenth century. Latin is introduced in this year. Hebrew is offered after school. Seventh graders read *Of Mice and Men* and *Animal Farm* among other books. In mathematics they study pre-algebra and algebra I. Native Americans and American history as well as geography are part of the curriculum. Life science and the environment are part of the science curriculum along with a health course. A range of foreign languages is available.

There is an honor roll. There are intramural and middle school teams. Extracurricular activities include Photography, Riding, Music, Drama, Chorus, Newspaper, Yearbook, and the Dwight Environmental Action Committee.

Franklin House is composed of grades nine and ten. Students learn computer applications—Hypercard and Pascal. A course is offered in world cultures, "a thematic study of global diversity: Latin America, Africa and Asia." All students write a weekly essay in English class and complete a research paper. There is an honors humanities course in which students do readings in historical and political classics. The study of foreign language in Franklin House expands to include Spanish, French, Italian for native speakers, Latin, Japanese, Hebrew and German.

In ninth grade, health and social education topics cover the issues of substance abuse and AIDS awareness. Counselors will not break a confidence if a student wishes to discuss a personal issue. Special course offerings include film-making, dance, music, art, and drama.

Anglo House is composed of grades eleven and twelve. Students are prepared for the SAT and achievement tests in English, mathematics, history, science and languages. In response to student interest Dwight has added courses in constitutional law, military history, environmental studies, physiology and filmmaking. There are AP and/or IB courses in computer science, chemistry, physics, biology, art, English, Drama, music, art, and foreign languages.

For students interested in science and the study of medicine, Dwight offers internships at the American Museum of Natural History and Rockefeller University. Recently, students worked in a cancer research laboratory. One student participated in the creation of the shark exhibit at the American Museum of Natural History.

The Adventure-Based Curriculum for grades five through twelve offers various outdoor experiences including orienteering, whitewater rafting, backpacking and caving. The Adventure-Based Curriculum has a three-part goal: 1. To develop the student's maturity and ability to interact with groups; 2. To impart key academic concepts in new and innovative ways; 3. To familiarize and acclimatize a primarily urban group of young people to the natural world.

The school considers building character an important part of its mission through community service, extracurricular activities, and sports. The Dwight athletic program works with students who have the talent and determination to become potential world class athletes and provides them with a flexible academic program combined with superior coaching. The fencing team has a healthy enrollment of eighty students and is among the nation's finest. A U.S. Women's Olympic representative graduated three years ago and is now attending Princeton. Self-esteem is bolstered through participation in athletics, and Dwight's trophy case is full. Dwight has championship boys' basketball and baseball teams as well as strong girls volleyball and basketball teams. The track and baseball programs are being expanded. Scholar-athletes at Dwight have included six ranked tennis players and a women's U.S. Sailing champion. Students can play on middle school, junior varsity or varsity teams.

Students are encouraged to participate in extracurricular activities including the Model U.N., Newspaper, yearbook, the literary magazine, social service, civic leadership training, drama and the contemporary arts society.

Popular College Choices   Brown, Columbia, Cornell, Dartmouth, Bowdoin, Boston University, Harvard, George Washington, Princeton, Georgetown, University of Michigan, MIT, Northwestern, NYU, Skidmore, Syracuse University

Traditions   History Research Paper Competition, Art Exhibition, Camerer Essay Writing Contest, Shakespeare Competition, Doris Post Oratory Competition, Annual Benefit Gala, assemblies with guest speakers, International Food Fair, Model U.N., Spring Arts Festival, Carnegie Hall performances, Peer Leaders

Publications   *Camerer Essays* (winning essays from the Camerer Essay Writing Contest)
Yearbook
Literary magazine: *Muse*
Dwight School newspaper: *Dwightonian*
Alumni magazine: *Dwight Today*

Community Service Requirement   All students are required to do community service; in addition to the Community Service Club and the Institute of Civic Leadership, Dwight students volunteer in soup kitchens, Dwight Environmental Action Committee, Make-A-Wish Foundation, tutoring, SAVE THE CHILDREN

Hangouts   Micro Grill, Columbus Star, McDonald's, Winston's Deli

The Ethical Culture Fieldston School

The Ethical Culture Fieldston School encompasses three divisions: Ethical Culture, Fieldston Lower, Fieldston Middle School, and Fieldston Upper School. Each division has its own principal; there is a central Administrative Council, consisting of the head of school, the principals and the heads of centralized administrative offices.

Ethical Culture

33 Central Park West
(at 63rd Street)
New York, NY 10023
(212) 712-6220 (main number)
(212) 712-8451 (admissions)
FAX (212) 712-8441
main website: www.ecfs.org

Fieldston Lower

Fieldston Road
Bronx, NY 10471
(718) 329-7310 (main number)
(718) 329-7313 (admissions)
FAX (718) 329-7337

Fieldston Middle and Upper School

Fieldston Road
Bronx, NY 10471
(718) 329-7300 (main number)
(718) 329-7306 (admissions)
FAX (718) 329-7302

Coed
Pre-kindergarten–12th Grade
Elevator at Ethical Culture
Fieldston Lower and Fieldston Middle and Upper, partially accessible

Dr. Joseph P. Healey, Head of School
Ms. Ellen Bell, Assistant Head of School for
Admissions and Financial Aid
Ms. Ann Vershbow, Principal Ethical Culture
Ms. Soraya Diaz, Admissions Ethical Culture
Mr. George Burns, Principal Fieldston Lower
Ms. Rita McRedmond, Admissions Fieldston Lower School
Dr. John Love, Principal Fieldston Upper School
Mr. Bill Bertsche, Principal Fieldston Middle School
Ms. Taisha Thompson, Admissions Fieldston

Birthday Cutoff   Children entering pre-kindergarten must be 4 before the day school starts

Enrollment   Combined enrollment: 1610
Total enrollment Ethical Culture: 512
Total enrollment Fieldston Lower: 317
Total enrollment Fieldston: 781
Kindergarten places: approximately 36 at Ethical Culture and 18 at Fieldston Lower
Size of graduating class: approximately 130

Grades   Semester system
Scheduled parent-teacher conferences pre-kindergarten through Form VI (12th grade)
Kindergarten–6: detailed anecdotal reports and checklists of skills
Letter grades begin in Form I (7th grade)
Forms I-VI (Grades 7–12): letter grades with teacher's comments; first final exam given in Form IV (10th grade)
Students taking accelerated science have a final exam in Form III (9th grade)

Tuition Range 2005–2006 $24,250 to $24,950, pre-kindergarten–Form VI (12th grade)
Additional Fees: books, supplies and other course-related expenses are approximately $250 for grades 7–12 only; lunch and yearbook are included in the tuition

Financial Aid/Scholarship   The Ethical Culture Fieldston School has one of the largest financial assistance programs of any independent day school in the country. $5.8 million was granted in 2004–2005

24% of the students schoolwide receive some form of financial aid in 2004–2005.

Monthly payment plan with no interest charges available to all enrolled families.

Endowment $50 million

Diversity   23% students of color throughout ECFS
26 Prep for Prep students enrolled at Fieldston School as of fall 2003
Fieldston enrolls students from the Early Steps, Albert G. Oliver, and A Better Chance, and Pan Asian Alliance programs among others.
Multicultural Committee for parents and faculty at all campuses, student clubs include: S.U.M.E. (Students United for Multicultural Efforts), Pan Asian Alliance, African-American Jewish Alliance, Gay/Straight Alliance, Interfaith, Social Justice Watch, Women's Issues, and Troubled Times.

Homework   Kindergarten and 1st: no homework
2nd: varies from 10 minutes to $1/2$ hour and 15 to 30 minutes reading
3rd and 4th: varies from 15 minutes–one hour plus additional $1/2$ hour of reading each night
5th, 6th: 1–2 hours
7th and 8th: no more than 3 hours
9th–12th: $3^{1}/_{2}$–$4^{1}/_{2}$ hours a night

After-School Program   At ECS and Fieldston Lower: after-school program for pre-kindergarten–6 with some mixed-age groups; selections include sports, dance, music, martial arts, shop, cooking, drama, arts and chess (for fun) for an additional payment; classes meet from 3:30–5 P.M., Monday through Thursday; Friday after-school programs begin and end earlier. Drop off and extended hours options at EC and Fieldston Lower. "Good Deeds Bandits" for grades 1–2, and "Cookies and Dreams," for grades 3–5 at EC introduce children to community service;

Before School Music at EC is small group instruction in instrumental music for grades 4–5;

7th and 8th: intramural sports, extracurricular clubs, Middle
School newspaper and musical

9th–12th: interscholastic sports, extracurricular clubs, newspapers, literary magazines and yearbook, two theatrical productions,
jazz, chorus, and orchestra and several student-written and produced plays

Summer Program   Weeks of Discovery: at EC, Winter vacation
and June Weeks: a variety of creative and recreational activities
pre-K–3 are offered for an additional payment

Compuart and Design Camp: a June weeks program at Ethical
Culture: Lego building programming and web design and animation are offered for grades 3–8, for an additional payment.

Sports Break: a June weeks program at the Riverdale campus: all
sports/learn to swim program for Kindergarten–grade 6, basketball camp for grades 3–9, for an additional payment

Fieldston Outdoors Day Camp: for ages 5–12, at Riverdale campus, full activities including swim instruction; focus on nature,
environment and Hudson River region; trips. Head counselors
are experienced teachers, an additional payment is required

Fieldston Summer Service Institute: The summer program of a
year-round academic enrichment program for public middle-
school students taught by Fieldston juniors and seniors under the
supervision of Fieldston faculty

Fieldston Enrichment Program (FEP): A four-week program on
the Fieldston campus for public school students in grades 7–8,
beginning in July, offering rigorous academic classes and team-
centered recreational activities; field trips, students who complete
the program are invited back for school year Saturday sessions

Young Dancemakers Company: a tuition-free project for public
high school students, performances are open to the public and the
schedule is posted on the school website

The Ethical Culture Fieldston School was started in 1878 by
Felix Adler, the founder of the Society for Ethical Culture. The school
was tuition free only until 1890, but continues to follow many aspects
of Adler's original vision of active learning. The school has always been

diverse ethnically, racially, and financially. In ECFS's recent strategic plan, the school restated its commitment to the original mission of the school: to ethical education as a foundation, to diversity in all its manifest aspects, and to being a "beacon for progressive education." A capital campaign in progress will address the school's plan for a new Middle School academic building, athletic complex, facility upgrades, and so on. In 1994–1995 an agreement was reached separating the schools from the Society, but ECFS continues to offer nonsectarian ethical training beginning in second grade. ECFS backs up its values with financial support and personal commitment. The school gives out more financial aid than most other independent day schools in the country.

Today many schools boast about "educating the whole child"; it is in vogue to have a child-centered curriculum. The Ethical Culture Fieldston school has been doing this from its inception, and is way out front in developing an integrated curriculum that emphasizes experiential learning. Children are active participants in their education here. Head of School, Dr. Joseph P. Healey writes, "Schools, such as ours, that nurture in their teachers and students a passion for questioning and inquiry coupled with a sense of balance between the given and the possible, produce dedicated life-long learners and strong analytic minds."

Getting in: Don't be intimidated by the imposing turn-of-the-century stone edifice on Central Park West; Ethical Culture (EC) is a warm and friendly place. One parent described the admissions process at ECS as "humane." Parents bring their child for a group interview. The interviewer asks, "Who's ready to come and play?" "Whose name begins with A?" and so on. After some leg hanging, all the children go off to play while the parents tour the school and ask questions of the admissions personnel and/or parent guides.

What are they looking for in a candidate? A child who feels good about him/herself, who is enthusiastic, who enjoys being part of a group (there's an emphasis on collaborative learning). The child should enjoy his visit. If your child was unusually cranky at the interview and you go home that night and he's got a full-blown ear infection, let them know. "We look at all the measures of a child to make sure we have an accurate picture of each applicant," say Director of Admissions Ellen Bell. After admissions decisions have been made, the wait list is active. There is no typical student, but one parent said the children are "bright, and laid-back yet outgoing."

Parents: The parents are "a low-key mix" of West and East Side professionals, artists and media people "but without the pretentiousness you find at other schools," parents say. Perhaps there is a larger percentage of working mothers. There is an acknowledged association between Ethical Culture, liberal thinking and progressive education.

There are many opportunities to socialize, and interesting lectures and discussion groups are offered for parents on child-related, topics such as learning styles and parenting issues. Class dinners are potluck, usually held at the school. Social competition is minimized and celebrity parents (there are a few) enjoy their anonymity. Parents get involved in the school in the early years and stay involved. Parent volunteers help with awards dinners, book sales and weekly lower school bulletins, for instance. Here, you can have lunch with your child (K–2). School events include plays. concerts, picnics in the park, carnivals and auctions. Birthday parties run the gamut.

Program: An awareness of ethics is implicit from the moment children begin their Ethical Culture Fieldston education. Formal ethics instruction begins in second grade with community responsibility and decision making. The emphasis is on ethics in action. The million-penny drive began as a math exercise at Fieldston Lower, then quickly expanded to include participation in the yearly Penny Harvest. Community service is part of the ECFS experience, from fifth grade editors assisting first grade authors to Fieldston high school students giving a party for a local community center.

One parent described her daughter's move from nursery school to Ethical as a "warm to warm transition." Pre-kindergarten and kindergarten separation is handled gradually; parents can stay for the first week if necessary. There is a staggered schedule. Under the guidance of two full-time teachers, children often work on group projects. For instance, the kindergarten creates a school-wide post office, each year, complete with student designed stamps and mailboxes, with daily pick up and delivery of internal mail.

In kindergarten, children begin going out to specialists in half groups but are not fully departmentalized until sixth grade. Most "specials" (library, movement, music, computer, science, social studies, workshop and so on) are taught by the specialist in half classes. The other half of the class either attends another special class or remains in the classroom, allowing the core teacher to work with small groups in math and writing.

Parents say there's a new emphasis on building a collaborative approach between child/faculty and parents, as well as a greater openness at EC. The most noticeable change is improved articulation of the curriculum through the grades. The emphasis is still on full mastery and competence with awareness that children work at different paces. "The focus is still on what's developmentally appropriate," with much "horizontal enrichment."

During the elementary years, students learn how to gather, organize, analyze, evaluate and communicate information. The work load increases appropriately as children are guided toward internalizing the learning process and becoming independent learners.

Ethical Culture has resisted pressure from high-powered parents to "hurry" the curriculum. Departmentalization doesn't begin until sixth grade, and no final exam is given until tenth grade. (Most schools start these in seventh grade.) Parents say, "Children at Ethical Culture develop a positive attitude about learning, which prepares them for the academically demanding high school." Proof that children with different learning styles can find success here is that more than 95 percent go on to the Fieldston School, which is considered a "very selective" high school. It is one of the three "hill" schools (along with Riverdale Country School and Horace Mann School) located in Riverdale, New York, just north of the city proper—a twenty minute drive that might take forty-five minutes at some hours.

Every activity in the Lower School is coed. No basal textbooks are used in the first years. Homework is given in appropriate amounts, not as busywork or evidence of academic rigor. Some parents, who grew up in schools that stressed rote memorization and drill, are a little perplexed by these methods and a commonly voiced concern is, "Is my child learning enough?" They can be reassured that in addition to early childhood readiness assessments, teachers' own assessments throughout the grades drive their instruction.

While there is a definite curriculum for each grade, Ethical's developmental approach to learning anticipates that not everyone will get to the same place at the same time. Children learn at their own pace. Emphasis is placed on conceptual development in tandem with building skills in reading, writing and math." Because the program is responsive to children's needs and interests, it varies from year to year. Most of the children will learn to read in the first grade. From pre-kindergarten on, you see words all over the classroom. There is mixed-ability grouping throughout the school and at various times throughout the week students break into half groups. Ethical Culture and Fieldston Lower each have math specialists who work in the classrooms and coordinate the programs. The math specialists hold workshops for parents throughout the year.

Ethical Culture has three science centers: one is a fully equipped laboratory with sinks, microscopes and computers. Wherever possible, science is hands-on and the scientific process is stressed: collect data, analyze it, construct a hypothesis, test it, reach a conclusion. In one classroom the students were studying the use of earthworms for indoor composting. In grades kindergarten through third, there is a deliberate effort to integrate science into the broader curriculum. Fifth and sixth grade students chart the constellations on the computer. ECFS has completed a four year plan to enhance the level of technology in the classrooms, establishing common areas for the use of technology, and creating "libraries without walls," i.e., information network accessibility to and from classrooms, homes, major universities, as well as the Library of Congress. The computer curriculum focus on computers as tools to expand thinking and problem solving skills. Each of the school's divisions has a computer coordinator who helps the teachers integrate technology into the curriculum. In grades 4–6 children are introduced to Ethics of the Computer, LOGO, use of spreadsheets, databases, word processing, graphics, web pages, and on-line and multimedia presentation tools.

The library at EC is equipped with laptops and a wireless network. Schoolwide, ECF has an extensive network that encompasses, libraries, classrooms, and computer labs. A new technology plan is being implemented that will, among other improvements, provide wireless access throughout the campus. The school's Web site is highly interactive and is an essential conduit of information between the school, its immediate community, and the world outside.

Ethical says it educates the "whole child," bringing out his or her natural creativity and encouraging its expression. The creative arts are considered intellectual disciplines; it follows that the arts at Ethical are strong. Four full-time art and workshop teachers are available at EC; there is an art studio with a pottery center equipped with a kiln. Art is integrated into the curriculum at many points. "Social Studies Workshop," a hands-on program relating to the social studies core, includes woodworking, sewing and cooking.

A hallmark of education at the ECS is an integrated curriculum, with subject areas overlapping in many different ways. Creativity and writing ability are also fostered. These elements combine in dramatic play. As part of the kindergarten curriculum, children learn that people live in communities, including the home, classroom, school, as well as the larger world. They interview people who work in the school about their jobs, from the principal to the head of facilities.

Critical thinking skills are emphasized from early on. A fifth grade class studying Greek myths switched the gender roles—Hercules became a she—and there was much discussion about the implications. There are many ways in which students are asked to examine the underlying assumptions about our culture. A parent told us that when a student brought in a Barbie doll for a model science fiction project the class got into a discussion about cultural artifacts: If Barbie were found by an advanced civilization, what conclusions would be drawn about our civilization? Students brought in other objects. A fifth grade class studying ancient Egypt and Rome had a discussion about heroes. "Malcolm X, Superman and Audrey Hepburn" were some of the names written on the board.

Ethical has two recently renovated full-size gyms: the sixth-floor gym, which is large enough to be subdivided, and a lower level gym with an overhead track. The gym program stresses individual skills development, games and sportsmanship. Ethical makes use of its location next to Central Park in many ways. The park is used as a laboratory and playing field, and of course, the children get to play in the snow and mark the change of seasons.

Manhattan parents should note that while Fieldston Lower, a second ECFS elementary division located in Riverdale, primarily serves families from Upper Manhattan, all sections of the Bronx, Northern New Jersey, Riverdale and Westchester, almost 15% of its students travel from Manhattan. Parents should tour its lovely campus and outdoor play areas, and observe the teaching of its "core" curriculum to see if they are interested in this unique program. Following are some examples of the subjects Fieldston Lower uses in constructing the core curriculum. First graders become experts in North American bird life. Third graders enact the lives of the Northern Woodland Indians who once inhabited the school's site. Fifth graders have a medieval fair; one class built a model cathedral and played roles in the social hierarchy of the time.

Like its hilltop competitors, Riverdale Country and Horace Mann, Fieldston is building a new middle school building, adding new athletic facilities and making renovations that will include more space for the performing arts as well as various other areas.

Fieldston is "a big school that seems small." In good weather, the grassy quad surrounded by fieldstone buildings is full of students. But the "Senior Grass" is not to be trod upon by underclassmen/women. The Tate Library is an award-winning facility (students say it's the best of the three "hill" school libraries) with over 40,000 volumes, an on-line catalog, multiple databases, media center and classrooms. Unique to Fieldston is a state-of-the-art print shop where everything from invitations to personal notepads are printed. In the spirit of founder Felix Adler, who believed in learning by doing, Fieldston is the only school that produces its own school publications from composition to final product. There are no bells, dress is casual and students seem relaxed. Sophomores can leave school grounds during "frees" and lunch. But by first form (seventh grade), college preparation has begun in earnest.

Fieldston's course guide is clear, descriptive and informative. The curriculum is broad, with electives that reflect a diversity of interests in the student body. Requirements are similar to those of the other independent high schools: a minimum of five academic courses per semester, with more elective choices as the students progress. Students do make choices about their academic careers; ninth graders have electives in language, arts and science. By junior year students can choose electives in English, math, history, language, science, visual arts, performing arts or computer. Six year sequences are offered in French, Spanish, and Latin, beginning in seventh grade. Conversational Spanish is part of the EC and Fieldston Lower experience. Courses are offered in Modern and Ancient Greek as well as Mandarin Chinese and Spanish for native speakers. An ethics course is required each year in Forms I through IV (grades 7–10); juniors and seniors must take a one semester course in Ethics. Advanced electives are offered in all disciplines, and are so strong that Fieldston has discontinued the standard AP curriculum, a decision encouraged by colleges, parents, and faculty.

Two programs that typify Fieldston's unique approach to learning are "the summer reading book" and "awareness days." The summer reading book is tied into a theme, such as "global studies," "science and math," or "social justice." In the Fall, a student/faculty group plans an entire day of activities related to the author's visit to the school. Recent books were Kurt Vonnegut's *Slaughterhouse-Five*, and Jose Saramago's *Blindness*.

"Awareness Days" address relevant political or social themes—Presidential elections, or the Middle Eastern countries—through a day-long line-up of speakers and workshops.

Although independence is fostered in the high school, support is always available. Fieldston has a well-developed advisors system. Each grade has a dean who stays with the form until graduation. A tenth grader said that she could talk to her advisor about anything and that students feel "the administration is on your side." Respect for individual learning styles continues at Fieldston, and the Learning Center helps students with individual learning differences. There are centers for writing, history and math, where English and history teachers and peer instructors are always available. Students can also meet with teachers during free periods. Outside tutors are recommended if necessary but in the words of one student, "Most people don't hire a tutor unless it's a desperate situation." Students say that although a lot is expected of them and they work hard, homework is not oppressive. One student said she has friends who are "drowning in work" at other schools.

Elective choices in English include, "Film and Literature," "Social and Political Issues in Literature," "African-American Literature," "Russian Literature" "Women and Literature" "Dramatic Literature and Theatre" and "Shakespeare." Course offerings change annually.

All seventh graders ("firsties") are required to take "Patterns of Human Behavior," an anthropology course. History survey courses in eighth through tenth grades provide a solid footing for later electives, which include: "The U.S. since 1940," "African Studies," "History and Science," "China" and "Russian Civilization," and "History of the Working Class."

There is a six-year unified mathematics sequence culminating in an advanced calculus course. There are many offerings in computer science.

At Fieldston there is a continued commitment to the artistic development of the students. As at Ethical and Fieldston Lower, the arts at Fieldston are considered an essential part of the curriculum and the offerings are extensive. Seventh graders begin with a visual arts sampler. In tenth, eleventh and twelfth grades a visual arts major is available. Elective offerings include "Ceramics," "Life Drawing" (with live models), "Creating from the Keyboard," "Architecture" and "Photography." Fieldston's Graphic Communications Department, based in its print shop, offers electives and a major for grades 10–12.

Dance at Fieldston is considered a key part of the performing arts program. In addition to modern, jazz and ballet, electives include "Multicultural Dance." There are numerous opportunities to perform: The dance company tours and there is an annual dance concert with student choreography.

Students who like drama can take advantage of a well-developed theatre program. There is a theatre minor or major for juniors and seniors. There are six student-directed shows every year, plus one major drama (*The Laramie Project* one year) and a musical (*Hair* one year). Students can take a course in stagecraft and practice their skills in the Alex Cohen Memorial Theatre. The drama and dance groups tour elementary schools. All "firsties" (seventh graders) must study a musical instrument or sing in an ensemble. Small group and ensemble instruction is available.

In addition to arts there is a full athletic program. Fieldston has a three season interscholastic sports program for eighth graders. Ninth through twelfth graders have a full interscholastic sports schedule, including strong teams in girls' field hockey, tennis and volleyball; coed cross-country, boys' basketball, baseball, football, lacrosse, and soccer. Fieldston has two large gyms, four tennis courts, a weight room and a renovated pool. There is a healthy competitive spirit. One student said, "At Fieldston team sports are for fun; at Riverdale and Horace Mann they're out for blood." That doesn't mean Fieldston doesn't play to win. In recent years, the girls volleyball team were the Independent School Athletic League champions, girls tennis was Prep League champion. The baseball team won the Ivy Prep League Championship. Basketball games always draw good crowds. During football season the school mascot, the Eagle, walks around campus. Homecoming is a major event at Fieldston. First there is a pep rally the day before big games, which besides football include soccer, volleyball and field hockey.

Student government is the PAC or Principal's Advisory Committee, a longstanding organization that meets regularly to discuss academic and social affairs. One year students initiated a program to get teachers to bring a mug from home instead of using Styrofoam cups. The money saved was donated to a charity to benefit the environment. PAC also deals with social aspects of life at Fieldston and the bolstering of school spirit. PAC organizes the annual fall barbecue and Fieldston Awareness Days that raise community awareness of the school's mission and goals. In addition to PAC there is STS, a student-to-student counseling program. In the high school there are electives in ethics including an advanced course in peer leadership and peer mentoring.

Tolerance and respect for difference are at the heart of Fieldston, and by and large relations between different groups are harmonious. One student said, "Fieldston is a lot more politically correct than other schools; I've become a lot more aware here."

There are over forty clubs at Fieldston that vary from year to year, depending on the interests of the student body. An activity period is built into the school day so that students can participate in a club and perform in a school play or compete in interscholastic sports. Some clubs are the ever-popular Amnesty International, Social Justice Watch, Environmental Club, and S.U.M.E. (Students United for Multicultural Education).

John Love, Fieldston principal, said, "The ECFS mission to provide a humanistic, ethical and progressive education really is present in the day-to-day life of the school. ECF attracts and nurtures people who question, think and aren't afraid to act."

Parents say that ECFS is not merely a college preparatory school, but that Fieldston prepares students to be citizens who are analytical thinkers, creative problem solvers, lifelong learners and agents of positive change in the world. Apparently the colleges agree; Fieldston students are accepted at a range of colleges and universities including the big Ivies—one recent year ten students went off to Yale.

Popular College Choices Brown, Carleton College, Columbia, Cornell, Dartmouth, George Washington, Harvard, Oberlin, NYU, Northwestern, Skidmore, Stanford, University of Chicago, Washington University, University of Wisconsin-Madison, Vassar, Wesleyan, Yale

Publications Yearbook: *Fieldglass* (since 1929)
Newspaper: *The Fieldston News* (since 1929)
Monthly parent newsletter: *Field Notes*
Literary magazine: *Litmag*
Alumni magazine: *The ECF Reporter*
Student community service magazine: *Community Server*
Student visual arts magazine: *Eagle Eye*
Alternative student literary magazine: *Maverick*
Student history magazine: *The Fieldston Historical Review*
Student on-line young women's magazine: *Roxine*
Faculty newsletter: *Fieldston performing Arts Newsletter*
Note: Most of ECFS's publications are printed at Fieldston's own printing press.

Community Service Requirement 60 school hours or 120 summer hours beginning in 9th grade; Academic community service courses are offered

Hangouts The Quad, Student-Faculty Center, Form Dean's offices, Riverdale Diner (if you have a car), the cafeteria for breakfast

The Family School

Dag Hammarskjold Plaza
323 East 47th Street
New York, NY 10017
(212) 688-5950, FAX (212) 980-2475
website: www.famshq.org
e-mail: famschool@aol.com

The Family School West

308 West 46th Street
New York, NY 10036
(212) 582-1240

Coed
Nursery (18 mos) through 6th grade
Not accessible

Mrs. Lesley Nan Haberman, Headmistress
Mrs. Ann Baker Reed, Director of Admissions

Birthday Cutoff   Children entering nursery school must be 18 mos
by September 1
Children entering kindergarten must be 5 by September 1

Enrollment   Total enrollment: 220
Toddler places: 60 (18 mos–3 years)
Family School West places: 40 (2.6–6 years)
Kindergarten places: 21
Elementary places: 30 (6–12 years)
Graduating class size: 8–10

Tuition Range 2005–2006 $5,990 to $13,500 (5 full days—Toddler
Program)–Elementary, 6–12 yrs)
Additional payment is required for children with special needs
who require additional support

Financial Aid/Scholarship   On a individual basis

Endowment   None

After-School Program Monday through Friday, 3:00–6:00 P.M., supervised homework time and a variety of recreational and creative activities for an additional payment; winter and spring recess programs are also available

Summer Program Weekly camp program from mid-June through the end of August, 8:30 A.M.–6:00 P.M.; a variety of recreational and creative activities and academic maintenance, weekly field trips, older campers swim three times a week; if families enroll for the entire summer, they receive one week free

———

Founded in 1975 by the current headmistress, Lesley Nan Haberman, The Family Schools are members of the American Montessori Society. "We call ourselves eclectic Montessori," explained the admissions director, a comfort to those who think of pure Montessori as too rigid. All of the teachers are certified Montessori teachers and traditional Montessori materials are used in the classrooms. Children are placed in heterogeneous mixed age groupings, also characteristic of the Montessori approach.

Getting in: All candidates are informally interviewed and invited to spend time in a classroom. Applicants to kindergarten and above are required to take the ERB.

The Family School was founded as a nursery school, added a toddler and elementary school program, and now serves children through twelve years of age. The Family School is housed in a bright, up-to-date (and meticulously clean) building adjacent to the Church of the Holy Family, and the Japan Society. Although the school rents space from the church there is no religious affiliation, and it is nondenominational. The school has a state-of-the-art auditorium/gym but children also play outdoors in McArthur Park next to the United Nations building. Children bring their own bag lunch and parents take turns providing snacks and flowers. The Family School West serves twenty-eight children (ages 2½ through 6) in a one room school house, the former gym of a Lutheran Church with its own backyard.

As its name suggests, The Family School is an inclusive, warm community. The students come from all parts of the city. Some parents commute to work in the neighborhood. The school also has a limited program for children with special needs, some of whom receive additional support services.

In a pre-primary classroom (ages three to six) each day begins

232

with the morning circle. Children then choose materials and work either independently or in small groups with their teachers. Areas of study include sensorial, geography, language, math and practical life. Children experiment in all art media, and the school has a kiln and pottery wheel. Music, foreign languages, guitar, chess and Tae-kwon-Do classes enrich the curriculum, and creativity is encouraged. Examples of the children's work adorn the walls of the school. In the primary school children continue learning in a practical context (for example using math manipulatives) and begin to move toward the understanding of abstract concepts. Reading is taught using several methods with a phonetic base.

Parents receive written narratives twice a year and the ERB is offered each spring. The school-parent partnership is an essential component of the Family Schools' experience and parent-teacher conferences are held three times a year. Parent classroom observations are mandatory. And, families are encouraged to share special talents and interests with students.

Traditions   Grandparent's Day, holiday programs and Family Field Day in Central Park's Sheep Meadow.

Popular School Choices   Browning, Dalton, Columbia Grammar and Prep, Sacred Heart, Friends, Hewitt, Marymount, Nightingale-Bamford, Riverdale, St. Davids, Spence, Town, UNIS, and various public school programs.

Friends Seminary

222 East 16th Street
New York, NY 10003-3703
(212) 979-5030, FAX (212) 979-5034
website: www.friendsseminary.org

Coed
Kindergarten–12th grade
Partially accessible

Robert Lauder, Principal
Harriet Burnett, Director of Admissions

Birthday Cutoff   Children entering kindergarten must be 5 by September 1
Children entering Grade 1 must be 6 by September 1

Enrollment   Total enrollment: 650
Kindergarten places: 42
Grade 6 places: 18
Grade 9 places: 25
Graduating class size: approximately 65

Grades   Semester system
Lower, Middle and Upper Schools: conferences and written reports
Letter grades begin in Grade 9
Departmentalization begins in Grade 5
Final exams begin in Grade 7

Tuition Range 2005–2006 $24,250 to $24,950, Kindergarten–Grade 12
Additional fees: Building Improvement Fund, PTA dues, accident insurance, beverage plan, lunch, approximately $2,000
Lunch is required in kindergarten and optional in Grades 1–12

Financial Aid/Scholarship   26% of students receive some form of financial aid

Endowment $4.5 million

Diversity   27% students of color
17 Prep for Prep students enrolled as of Fall 2004
Friends participates actively in Early Steps, Prep for Prep, The
TEAK Fellowship Program, Albert G. Oliver, and ABC (A Better
Chance) programs
Friends receives foundation grants to support diversity
CARE (Cultural Awareness Reaching Everyone) is a student-run
organization that "takes an active role in discussing and educating
the community about cultural diversity"
Office of Multicultural Affairs: liaison for both students and par-
ents; PTA Diversity Committee, Faculty Diversity Committee,
and the Board Diversity Sub-Committee; all provide a forum for
issues of concern
Student-led "Day of Concern" (recent topics: Gender Issues,
Political Issues, Race in America)
Student committee on gender issues
Alumni Peer Mentoring Program

Homework   Begins gently in Grade 1
Grades 2–3: 20–30 minutes per night
Grade 4: $1/2$–1 hour per night
Grades 5–6: up to 1–$1^{1}/2$ hours per night
Grades 7–8: up to 2–$2^{1}/2$ hours per night
Grades 9–12: 3–4 hours per night

After-School Program   Early Bird Program: (Lower School)
8:00 A.M. to 8:45 A.M.
Friends After Three Program: 5 days a week for Lower and
Middle School; creative and athletic activities from 3:00 P.M.–
4:30 P.M., Monday–Friday; the library is open until 4:30
Extended coverage available until 5:30 P.M. each day
Vacation program during school breaks
All of the above programs require additional payment
Athletics: Team Sports, Grades 7–12

Summer Program   Summer Friends: A seven-week program in
June and July, open to 4–11 year olds from all over the city,
offering a variety of recreational and creative activities; The
Friends Summer Institute, open to students in Grades 5–12 offers
courses in academic enrichment and creative arts

Friends Seminary, the oldest continuing coeducational day school in New York City, is hardly the most traditional. Friends is distinguished by its Quaker heritage. Founded in 1786, Friends is under the care of the New York Quarterly Meeting of the Religious Society of Friends. The brochure says: "Administering the School is viewed as a team effort." There is a Principal rather than a Headmaster. Friends provides a value-based, academically distinguished, program centered on the tenets of Quakerism shaping the school's philosophy: the belief in each person's unique strengths and possibilities; the value of community and the individual's role within the community; decision-making by consensus; and the peaceful resolution of conflict.

In 2003, Robert "Bo" Lauder became the thirty-fourth Principal of Friends Seminary after several years at Sidwell Friends in Washington, D.C.. With a handshake and a smile, Bo greets students and parents in the morning setting the tone for community and accessibility.

Academically, Friends begins gently and becomes increasingly rigorous as students progress. A former Parents-Teacher Alliance president told us: "Friends is not a socially competitive school but Friends does create competitive students."

Getting in: Parents are invited to tour Friends before making application to the school. For kindergarten and Grade 1, a group of six students meet with two teachers for one hour during which time each family has a twenty to thirty minute interview. Friends is a very popular choice not only for those who live downtown, but also for families throughout the city. Admissions are competitive. It is the school's policy to give priority consideration to qualified children of members of Quaker Meetings. Qualified siblings and children of alumni are given priority as well. Admission, however, is not automatic; one parent told us her daughter was deferred a year even though she had an older sibling at Friends. There is a wait list.

Parents: Parents talk about the family feeling at Friends. One mother described the school as "a community of shared values. Everyone is on a first-name basis." There is a buddy system called Parent Connection to help new parents get involved in the school. Parents say there are definitely more working mothers than not. Fathers are very involved in the school; in fact, several fathers serve as class representatives and pick up their children at day's end. In response to the changing needs of two-career families, Friends provides programs before and after school and during vacations.

Socially the parents are very low-key; there is a form of reverse snobbery: "Downtowners don't flaunt," says a parent.

The Friends Spring Fair is an annual event made possible through the efforts of hundreds of parents and students. In addition, there is an annual benefit and potluck suppers. Many Friends parents remain involved long after their children have graduated. Because it is a Quaker school, raffles and games of chance are prohibited.

Friends parents feel they have a voice. Throughout the year the PTA sponsors dialogue meetings for each division of the school. Examples of topics discussed include "Seventh graders and their need for independence," "The role of the advisor," "Substance abuse" and "Conflict resolution." The PTA has organized a PTA-community service partnership in which parents and students work together in support of a specific community service project.

Program: "Quaker philosophy permeates the school and after you've been there a while you recognize it," said one parent. Service to the community is important at Friends. It begins in kindergarten and extends through Grade 12. Walking through the hallways you might see tenth graders working with first graders; fifth graders helping in the library, and parents working with students of all ages in workshops to decorate bags for God's Love We Deliver. At night, a common room at Friends is used to shelter and feed the homeless. A few years ago, when some parents expressed fears about tuberculosis, alterations were made to the building to provide adequate ventilation rather than do away with the program.

Quaker Meeting is the heart and soul of the school. Meeting is a time for students and teachers to come together in silent reflection, and if moved to do so, share thoughts and feelings with their community. In Lower School, a few moments of silence takes place in the classroom during the beginning of circle time. Once a week, Lower School students go to the landmarked meetinghouse, for silent Meeting. Both Middle and Upper School have Meeting four times a week. In Middle School, Meeting always begins with ten minutes of silence, followed by announcements, assemblies and so on. In Upper School, students have silent Meeting twice a week for twenty minutes, while the two other weekly Meetings focus on relevant issues and school business. The mother of a fifth grader says, "Everybody thinks that because Friends is a Quaker school there are hours of silence, but that's not so; Meeting is a quiet time to come together, discuss the day, and to hear announcements." A former PTA president said that "even the shy child will speak out and feel comfortable at Meeting." Parents are invited to attend Meeting whenever they can.

The Lower School focuses on academics as well as children's emotional and developmental needs. Friends recognizes that young children learn at their own pace and that the development of self-esteem early on will lead to future success. Lower School placement is considered carefully at Friends. Teachers know their students well and consider a variety of factors before making placement decisions. A father told us that his children's reports were "wonderfully detailed with a huge space for comments."

Parents say the emphasis at Friends is on learning how to learn. "Students don't just memorize the date of a battle but rather what really happened at the battle," said one. "Learning is an ongoing process," said another. "My daughter's teacher said, 'Just because you turn it in doesn't mean it's over.' " Some parents whose own educations stressed rote memorization have asked, "Are they getting enough facts?" But while the students may not realize that when they are measuring and baking they are using mathematics, this integrated approach to education in the Lower School is becoming the norm among most independent schools.

The Lower School classroom is a "combination of teacher-directed instruction and self-directed exploration and learning." Children spend much of their time working in groups toward a common goal (collaborative learning), and learning is hands-on whenever possible. No one approach to teaching reading is used because teachers consider the approach that is best for each child. Students use math manipulatives as well as workbooks, and computers are in every classroom to support the curriculum. Spanish begins in Grade 2. In social studies students begin by looking at themselves and their families, widening their perspective to include the city, the country, and the world of other cultures. Lower School children at Friends leave their classrooms for science, art, music, library, gym, dance, and multi-media workshop.

Middle School consists of Grades 5 through 8. Middle Schoolers hang out in the courtyard, cafeteria or library, not in the hallways. The head of the Middle School, Pam Wood, is well-liked and students feel they can talk to her about almost anything. Students and parents say that the workload increases in fifth grade and again in seventh and ninth grades. In fifth grade departmentalization begins. Concrete work (including plenty of homework) is given "and the kids crave it," one mother said. A parent said, "The kids are more comfortable and really show progress quickly and early in the year." Math for fifth and sixth graders is grouped by homerooms with subgroups based on ability. One mother said her daughter started to slack off and wasn't keeping up with her math work. The teacher discussed the problem with the student before it became a pattern, and she got back on track without her parents having to exert pressure. Students who need enrichment can get it. One mother said her son needed more work, so creative homework, not just busywork, was given.

Beginning in Grade 5, students have increasing opportunity to make choices for themselves in the areas of foreign language and performing arts. French or Spanish begins in fifth grade. In Grades 7 and 8, students are required to add two years of Latin.

Literature, grammar, and good writing are emphasized in English. Eighth graders have weekly writing assignments using creative and analytical skills. Topics in social studies begin with the study of ancient civilizations in fifth grade and progress through Medieval and Renaissance History in sixth grade, including the history of civilization in Africa or the Americas. Seventh graders study the American Constitution and government, African-American history and "The Immigrant Experience." Eighth graders focus on world history.

The Middle School science program is comprehensive, beginning with a hands-on general curriculum for Grades 5 and 6 encompassing areas of life, earth, and physical sciences. In Grade 7, students concentrate on earth science and ecology with some chemistry added. In Grade 8, biology is introduced. Middle Schoolers also take a human relations course that examines the physical changes and social issues of adolescence.

The visual arts program at Friends includes both two- and three-dimensional offerings as well as many performing arts electives. In addition to two art studios, the Seegers Arts Center houses a photography lab and art gallery. Seventh and eighth graders can take art electives. Under the direction of Jennifer Fell Hayes, an award-winning playwright, the Friends Seminary drama program features three major theatrical productions annually. Recent productions include: *A Winter's Tale, Into the Woods, You Can't Take It With You*, and *On the Town*. In addition, drama electives are available to students in seventh through twelfth grades. Theatre is performed in both the Meetinghouse and in the new "black box" theatre.

In Middle School, each day begins with Meeting, and Quaker values continue to play a central role in school life, particularly regarding discipline. Each student from seventh through twelfth grade has an advisor who offers curricular guidance and who is an advocate in matters of discipline.

The Middle and Upper School music program at Friends is focused in two areas: classical and jazz. Students can also choose from a range of electives including chamber music, instrumental music and vocal jazz ensemble, wind ensemble and instrumental instruction. Students can learn an instrument in fifth grade; jazz instruction begins in seventh grade. Bob Rosen, Friends' jazz impresario, exemplifies the private school teacher who not only teaches but *does*. Mr. Rosen is a clarinetist, saxophonist, composer and conductor. He arranges for Friends students to jam with noted jazz musicians: Each year, students perform in concert.

Remarkably, Friends fields 26 sports teams in Grades 7–12. Accomplishments include league tournament championships and state invitationals and the spirit in which teams conduct themselves in competition is particularly valued.

Athletics at Friends is competitive. In Grades 9–12, there are varsity and junior varsity teams in soccer, basketball, softball, baseball, volleyball and tennis as well as coed teams in squash, track/cross-country and swimming. (One seventh grade boy said he longed for football.)

President Theodore Roosevelt, an alumnus, would be pleased to note the schoolwide emphasis on experiential education. The wilderness and outdoor adventure programs at Friends begin in kindergarten with apple picking and become more sophisticated in the Middle and Upper Schools. First and second graders make their own maps of their routes from home to school and go to a nature study workshop. Third and fourth graders go to a nature center for outdoor education programs. Middle Schoolers also travel outside the city to learn mountain climbing and rappelling. Upper School students take backpacking trips, go sea-kayaking and master rock-climbing skills.

A large number of new students enter Friends at sixth grade. "Friends is an easy school to start," says the mother of two. "There are many new kids and there's an enormous effort to be welcoming." Current Upper School students mentor ninth graders. Ninth graders and above can leave school for lunch or relaxation in adjacent Rutherford Place (but have to sign out first).

The Upper School, Grades 9–12, is a a rigorous program. Minimum requirements for graduation include four years of English, three years of history and math, two years of a modern foreign language, a minimum of two years of laboratory science, and twenty-seven hours of community service per year. Advanced Placement courses are given in all major disciplines. If a student is interested in pursuing an AP course and if there are not enough students to form a full class, a teacher will mentor that student so he or she can sit for the AP exam. In addition, Friends has a relationship with New York University, enabling qualified juniors and seniors to take courses for high school credit free of charge.

One Upper School parent commented that the Upper School course offerings looked like a mini-college catalog. For example, English electives include "Tragedy and the Limits of Language," "Fiction, Fact and Film," and "The Empire Writes Back: Literary Visions & Revisions of Empire." Choices in history include "Great Ideas" "Ethnically NY: Historical and Contemporary Perspectives," "African Studies" and "International Relations: Latin America."

Friends has made a serious commitment to technology. There are two computer labs plus a foreign language lab in addition to classroom computers. The entire school is networked. Students interested in media can take advantage of the outstanding Chapman Media Center which houses a screening room with editing capability.

Upper School students participate in several international and national study programs including School Year Abroad, a semester at St. Stephen's School in Rome, The Mountain School, Maine Coast Semester, and The Network of Complementary Schools.

The Social Action Committee "informs the Upper School on issues and activities of community and global concern." Friends students volunteer to help the less privileged or donate time to Amnesty International, "Children of War" or to an environmental group. Friends students are not afraid to speak up and speak out. They are socially aware and committed to service. A father of two children at Friends told us, "The philosophy of the school prepares children to deal with the outside world. They become independent and self-assured."

The centerpiece of the Friends graduation is Quaker Meeting. One parent said that out of the silence of the Meeting "the students speak with remarkable self-possession; some of their speeches are political and some are nostalgic." There are no caps and gowns.

Popular College Choices Brown, Oberlin, Georgetown, Wesleyan, University of Chicago and Cornell

Traditions Quaker Meeting, nature and wilderness trips, Friends Spring Fair, Book Fair, potluck suppers, concerts, God's Love We

Deliver bag decoration workshops, Lower and Middle School Field Days, Halloween Party, drama, concerts, and musical theater productions

Publications Literary magazine: *The Magpie*
Yearbook
Middle School newspaper
Upper School newspaper: *The Quaker Shaker*
Photography journal: *Exposures*

Community Service Requirement Kindergarten–Grade 8: performed within the school; Grades 9–12: performed within and outside of school
Grades 7–8: minimum of 15 hours, within the school
Grades 9–12: minimum of 20 hours, outside of school, 7 hours in school service
Grade wide service projects for ninth and tenth graders are included in the requirements

Hangouts Mariella's Pizza, Joe Jr.'s Coffee Shop, Gramercy Coffee Shop, Stuyvesant Square Park

The Geneva School of Manhattan

583 Park Avenue
New York, NY 10021
(212) 754-9988
FAX (212) 754-9987
e-mail: Admin@genevaschool.net
website: www.genevaschool.net

Coed
Preschool–8th Grade
Not accessible

Mr. Scott Parson, Director

Uniform Girls wear a plaid jumper or navy skirt, a white blouse, and a navy cardigan sweater with the school logo. Boys wear khaki pants, white shirt, and a navy cardigan sweater with the school logo.

Birthday Cutoff Children entering preschool must be 3 by October 31
Children entering kindergarten must be 5 by October 31

Enrollment Total enrollment: 115
3 year old places: 8
Pre-K places: 12
Kindergarten places: 16
Approximately half of the admissions occur after Kindergarten

Grades Parent conferences and progress reports six times a year. Progress reports are issued three times per year. Letter grades begin in 4th grade. The CTP4 and WRAP tests are given each year in the Spring.

Tuition Range 2005–2006 $7,500 to $14,000, Preschool 3's through 8th grade
Additional fees are approximately $200

Financial Aid/Scholarship Available upon request

Diversity Approximately 50% students of color

After-School Program A recreational and a music program are available

Summer Program In development

The Geneva School of Manhattan was founded by a small group of Christian parents and educators who wanted to provide a classical education based on Christian tenets. Funded by private individuals and foundations, the school opened in 1996–97 with pre-kindergarten through first grades.

A Christian-based independent school, the first in Manhattan, is likely to appeal to many parents who now home-school their children and to others who want a correlation between their faith and their children's schooling.

The founders were inspired by Dorothy Sayer's essay "The Lost Tools of Learning." The school name refers to Geneva, Switzerland, a center of the Protestant Reformation in the 1500's. "Geneva was a training ground for missionaries who went out all over Europe to spread the Gospel," explained one of the former Directors.

Getting in: A personal interview and a screening test, administered by the school, are required. The school has a non-discriminatory policy but parents must sign a statement of faith and a statement of cooperation. (The school will discipline children but corporal punishment is not permitted.) The registration form asks parents to describe their children and also to "Please give a short explanation of who you understand Jesus Christ to be and what His death and resurrection means to you," as well as to "Describe briefly your relationship with Jesus Christ."

Parents: All parents are required to volunteer at the school. Parents are also involved and participate in the school-wide prayer ministry, plan field trips, and other extracurricular activities and special events.

Program: The school "teaches the truth from the Bible," including creationism. But according to a staff member, "Our school doctrine is not specifically in support of the fundamentalist movement." According to the school's literature, the educational program is founded on the principles and values set forth in Scripture. The Geneva School will revive the educational style that uses the classical "trivium," a three phase model that corresponds to the different phases in child development.

The Geneva School's distinctive characteristics include: 1) curriculum based upon the Bible as God's Word; 2) Classics taught as enduring works of excellence; 3) rigorous academics and small classes; 4) emphasis upon languages with foreign language instruction beginning in pre-school; 5) disciplined and nurturing Christian faculty; 6) involved parents who volunteer time and talents; 7) affordable tuition based on financial need.

The preschool program provides three- and four-year olds with cognitive, language, motor and social skills. Children learn English and conversational French, math, science, art, bible and music.

The Lower School offers students in kindergarten through fifth grade a deeper understanding of God, along with basic academic skills in a literature-based program. Subjects are taught in a traditional way, the focus is on phonics, penmanship and formal grammar.

Students in Upper School, grades six through eight, take language, math, science, history, Bible, Latin, and fine arts. Readings stress the Classics, all students must read Homer, Virgil, and Dante.

Grace Church School

86 Fourth Avenue
New York, NY 10003
(212) 475-5609, FAX (212) 475-5015
e-mail: mhirschman@gcschool.org
website: www.gcschool.org

Coed
Junior Kindergarten–8th grade
Accessible

Mr. George Davison, Head
Ms. Martha Hirschman, Director of Admissions

Birthday Cutoff   Children entering junior kindergarten should be 4 by September 1
Children entering kindergarten should be 5 by September 1

Enrollment   Total enrollment: 394
Junior kindergarten places: 30
Kindergarten places: 12
Graduating class size: approximately 40

Grades   Semester system
Letter grades begin in 5th grade
Departmentalization begins in 5th grade

Tuition Range 2005–2006 $22,650 to $25,150, junior kindergarten–8th grade
Additional fees: Lower School approximately $50; Upper School approximately $450
Families with more than one child enrolled receive a discount on the additional tuition

Financial Aid/Scholarship   22% of the student body receive some form of aid

Endowment $8.2 million

After-School Program   The Grace After-School Program (GASP) is scheduled Monday–Friday until 5:30 P.M., students participate in a variety of age appropriate activities; both a structured play-group, and homework supervision are available.

Summer Program June School from the close of school until the end of June; a variety of creative and recreational activities for an additional payment

———————

Grace Church was founded in 1894 as the first Choir Boarding School for Boys in North America. Coeducation at Grace Church began in 1947. The school occupies nine adjoining buildings and is a popular choice for many downtown and even some uptown families. The school is traditional and follows a structured curriculum. There is a dress code and teachers are addressed formally ("Mr. Smith," "Miss Jones"). The school has a greatly enlarged library with state-of-the-art computer catalog, a reading room, and research facilities. There are two computer labs. The computer center, all classrooms, and the library are connected via a local network with Internet access; e-mail links the entire community.

The arts center has a sculpture studio, a music room, dance and drama studio, and digital technology lab integrating computers with the arts. There is a separate play roof for the younger children in addition to a gymnasium, outdoor play yard and dance studio. Park facilities, Chelsea Piers, and a neighborhood indoor swimming pool are used to augment the physical education program. A hot lunch, included in the tuition, is served family-style in the dining room.

Getting in: After submitting an application, parents must call to schedule a tour and interview. ERBs are required for admissions as well as an interview. (Junior Kindergartners, Kindergartners and first graders are interviewed in small groups.) Grace Church School has three divisions: The Early Childhood Division: junior kindergarten and kindergarten; Lower School: grades one through four; Upper School: grades five through eight. A choice of French or Spanish is offered in third grade. Latin is offered in seventh and eighth grades. The arts play a vital part in the curriculum. Instrumental music is offered beginning in third grade. Children may sing in the school chorus or audition for the church choir. Two major drama productions are staged each year in the Upper School. Recent productions have been *You're A Good Man, Charlie Brown*, *Fiddler on the Roof*, and *Ozma of Oz*. Children perform at music and dance assemblies and in class plays throughout the year.

There is weekly chapel and students study the Bible in lower grades and comparative religions. Grace Church School families observe a wide variety of faiths. Grace Church enrolls students from Early Steps and Prep for Prep.

Graduates attend independent day schools, boarding schools and the specialized New York City high schools.

The Hewitt School

Middle and Upper School (Grades 4–12)
45 East 75th Street
New York, NY 10021
(212) 288-1919
Admissions: (212) 994-2600
Not accessible

Andrew J. McKelvey, Lower School
(Grades K–3)
3 East 76th Street
New York, NY 10021
Accessible
website: www.hewittschool.org

All girls
Kindergarten–12th grade

Ms. Linda MacMurray Gibbs, Head of School
Ms. Anita S. Edwards, Director of Admissions
Carrie B. Wessel, Assistant Director of Admissions

Uniform   Lower School: Hunter green and navy plaid jumper; a white blouse, tights or socks and sensible, non-skid shoes
Middle School: a Hunter green plaid kilt, a white blouse, tights or socks and closed low-heeled shoes with non-skid soles. Casual options for both Lower and Middle School include uniform slacks, skirt, and a variety of uniform shirts, blouses, and sweaters. Sneakers can be worn
Upper School: Navy or khaki cotton or corduroy pants; navy, khaki or plaid A-line skirt; polo shirts and turtlenecks. Seniors have a dress code that specifies appropriateness

Birthday Cutoff   Children entering kindergarten must be 5 by mid- to late October but readiness is the most important factor

Enrollment   Total enrollment: 460
Kindergarten places: 42
Average graduating class: 28

Grades   Semester system

249

Letter grades begin in 5th grade
Semester exams begin in 7th grade
Narrative reports and checklists twice a year for all grades

Tuition Range 2005–2006 $25,900 to $27,500, K–12th grade, all inclusive

Financial Aid/Scholarship $1,100,000

Endowment   Approximately $4 million

Diversity   18%; 6 Early Steps, 12 Prep for Prep students
Diversity Task Force; Multicultural Club

Homework   Kindergarten: reading with parent/caregiver 20 minutes
Grade 1: 15 minutes, 15 minutes reading
Grade 2: 30 minutes, 15 minutes reading
Grade 3: 45 minutes, 15 minutes reading
Grades 4 and 5: 45–90 minutes including reading
Grades 6 and 7: 1½–2 hours per night
Grades 8 and 9: 35 minutes per subject per night
Grades 10–12: 45 minutes per subject per night
In Middle and Upper school, no more than two tests are scheduled per day.

After-School Program   Hewitt AfterNoon: (primarily a service for grades K–3) 3:00 to 4:45 P.M., supervision available until 6:00 P.M. Monday–Friday; chorus, sports, music lessons, cooking, arts and crafts, French club, chess, an additional payment is required
Clubs that meet after school include gymnastics club, crafts club, computer club, French club, and chess club
After-school study hall: a supervised study period Monday–Thursday 3:15–4:00 P.M., for grades V–XII

Summer Program   Summer Magic: two week camp in late June; Summer Academy: Open to Middle school students during the last week of August. Taught by Hewitt faculty. English, math, and study skills

The winding staircase and floral wallpaper lined with class pictures of girls in white dresses holding bouquets harks back to the 1920s, when the school was known as "Miss Hewitt's Classes" and educated the daughters of the city's socially prominent families. In the eighty-plus years since then, Hewitt has evolved to meet the needs of modern young women. When Ms. Linda Gibbs became head of school, she said that Hewitt, as the smallest of the girls' schools in Manhattan, "offers an academic environment that meets the strengths and challenges of each girl, all within a safe atmosphere." Ms. Gibbs' goal for Hewitt includes "rebranding and long range strategic planning to reexamine and reaffirm everything about the school and to give us clarity about the future. We've formed a steering committee and we've had a Board retreat, and a community retreat with parents and students. Out of this patterns emerged—what drives us is what's best for the students." The school now offers, "A rigorous academic program as well as a supportive environment."

Today, each division of Hewitt is housed in its own renovated townhouse. Hewitt's facilities include technology labs and stations, a dining room, performing arts center, administrative offices, and a newly renovated library media center. A connecting wing through the buildings provides space for music rooms, a counseling office, science labs and a darkroom. The new McKelvey Lower School building provides developmentally appropriate libraries on each floor, science exploration, a music room, art studio, a dining/multipurpose room, and wireless access points for technology.

Getting in: The application fee is $50. Parents visit Hewitt with their daughter for a tour and interview. They are interviewed by the director of admissions in her office. Kindergarten and grade 1 candidates take a brief screening test before visiting classes. The director of admissions and the early childhood specialist also observe every kindergarten candidate at her own nursery school. One parent told us "Hewitt spent one and a half hours with the family and demonstrated a real appreciation of who my daughter was. Not only did they remember us but they were able to describe her whole personality." She felt the other girls' schools were much more aloof. Applicant parents are also invited to a morning "Conversation with the Head of School." At this breakfast meeting applicant parents have an opportunity to hear from Ms. Gibbs, as well as other members of the administration and students. Questions are encouraged at this meeting. In recent years Hewitt has set record levels in kindergarten enrollment.

For middle and upper school, applicants and their families tour the school with a student tour guide and have individual interviews with the Assistant Director of Admissions, Division Heads and the Associate Head of School.

A parent said, "Hewitt lacks some of the social crustiness of the other girls' schools"; Hewitt is "definitely nurturing and traditional, with a less aggressive atmosphere than some other places." There are achievement assemblies for the Lower, Middle and Upper Schools that recognize accomplishment in academics, athletics, art and community service. "They play down competition but there are prizes and awards." One mother said her "tomboy/nonconformist child fits in just fine at Hewitt." The brochure says that Hewitt provides "an environment of understanding, trust and affection." Many parents describe Hewitt as "a very comfortable environment."

Parents: Although most mothers and fathers work outside the home, parental involvement is encouraged. One parent describes the Hewitt atmosphere as "small, cozy and inviting; you never feel out of place. You can be there as much as you want." The Parents Association meets four times a year; there are many social and fund-raising events throughout the year. Some highlights are the annual Skating party at Wollman Rink, Annual Book Fair, a Parent Book Club, the Spring Benefit, and lower school party. The Parents Association provides summer study and travel grants for faculty members through an application process that is peer driven.

The recently formed Dad's Committee hosts the annual Family Picnic at Randall's Island and other events like a dinner at the Stock Exchange for fathers and daughters and a golf outing. There's also an evening education program for parents called Hewitt Parents on the Move: Back to School: Parents are invited to attend a variety of courses taught by Hewitt teachers including Digital Photography, PowerPoint, Ceramics, French for Travelers, and the History of Presidential Elections. Parents may accompany their daughters to breakfast at Hewitt, from 7:30 A.M. until 8:15 A.M.; parents say it's a nice way to spend some quiet time together each day.

Program: The Lower School at Hewitt consists of kindergarten through third grade. The kindergarten is a full-day program. A parent said that Hewitt girls are very busy after school; she has to book play dates at least three weeks in advance because girls are enrolled in ballet, swimming or religious classes.

Hewitt has an integrated curriculum including reading, writing, literature, math, science, social studies, art, music, dance, foreign language and physical education. Academic subjects are introduced in kindergarten and are built upon in developmentally appropriate ways in the succeeding years. French and Spanish are introduced in kindergarten through songs, games and activities that foster conversational language skills. There are computers in the kindergarten classrooms and computer instruction in the computer lab. Hewitt has laptops in its High School, training for teachers, and all of the classrooms are wired for LCD's. The computer labs were recently renovated with help from a $50,000 Edward Ford Foundation Grant.

Individualized attention is a hallmark of instruction at Hewitt. The teacher-student ratio at Hewitt is high. The majority of the faculty hold advanced degrees. Students learn at their own pace and teachers pay careful attention to different learning styles. There is individual as well as small-group instruction in writing and reading.

Math is taught with manipulatives like unifix cubes and games that develop a strong number sense. There's no one way to do something. "There are a lot of creative children here," says the director of admissions. One mother said that her daughter, who has musical ability, takes private lessons at school and was encouraged to write a song that she'll sing with her class.

In the first grade classrooms are furnished with tables in clusters. By second grade there are weekly spelling tests. Lower School parents receive narrative reports and checklists twice a year; there are individual conferences in fall and spring. Assemblies begin with the pledge of allegiance. In special assemblies the author of a children's book might speak, or a dance or musical group might perform.

Parents say at Hewitt, which is committed to single-sex education, "there is an implicit validation of female values." One mother praised the emphasis on women in society.

Middle School at Hewitt is composed of grades four through seven and occupies the 75th Street building. The girls have advisors they meet with for morning announcements, who monitor each student's program. Departmentalization begins in fifth grade and is completed by seventh grade. Girls continue to study a full schedule of subjects including English, history, math, science, computer, French or Spanish (with the addition of Latin in grade 8), studio art, drama, music and gym.

The focus of the integrated curriculum is on humanities and American History. Strong emphasis is placed on the spoken and written word. Sixth and seventh grade programs also add courses in Life Skills, leadership, drama and public speaking. There is a new emphasis on math and science in the Middle and Upper Schools.

The Middle School has its own student council, clubs and its own literary magazine, *Enterprise*.

Overnight trips begin in Middle School. Students in eighth grade go on an overnight to Camp Mariah, and ninth graders spend an overnight at Soundwaters in Stamford, Connecticut. Tenth grade girls travel to Washington, D.C. and Virginia as part of their course in American History.

The Outdoor Educational initiative provides an opportunity to explore environmental education and build community. Fourth grade girls take part in programs at Prospect Park and Alley Pond Park. The fifth grade travels to Frost Valley for a two-day overnight to study recycling and the raptor recovery program. And, sixth and seventh graders focus on marine biology on their three-day overnight trip to Greenkill.

The High School at Hewitt is composed of grades eight through twelve. Students have faculty advisors. A minimum of five to six academic subjects per year is required but most girls take five major subjects and choose from numerous electives, like, Film, the New York Art World, astronomy, genetics, Women in Literature, Comparative religion and the Holocaust. Eighth grade students take algebra I or II and conduct experiments and write lab reports in eighth grade earth science. Three lab sciences are required as are four years of English and three years of math, history and foreign language. There are ten AP classes offered, significant since Hewitt is so small. In addition, the school offers an Upper School laptop computer program that gives students universal access to a completely wirless network that accesses the Internet and many other resources. Every eighth grader gets her own Dell laptop; relevant online links, and homework assignments are posted online.

There are several dramatic productions a year, at least one of which is performed in conjunction with boys from other independent schools. Many students participate in the production, either as cast or crew. Recent musicals were *Footloose* and *Oliver*.

Clubs at Hewitt include: Video Club, Photo Club, Worldbeat Music, Students Against Destructive Decisions (SADD), Student Council, Amnesty International, Book Club, Earth Committee, and Model U.N. There are also junior and varsity sports teams.

Senior privileges include using the front staircase, the "Senior Stairs," instead of the back stairs and a four-week, year-end independent project with an individual faculty advisor. Eleventh and twelfth graders can leave school with parental permission.

Community service is required at Hewitt. Beginning in Lower School, there are many opportunities for students to volunteer. Hewitt families participate as a team in the Breast Cancer Walk for the Cure in Central Park, collect cans of food for the Yorkville Common Pantry, coats for New York Cares, and books for the Cicero Book Drive. The school also has a Community Service Day in which the entire community perform "good works" where Hewitt volunteers can be found working for a wide variety of organizations including Habitat for Humanity, Coler-Goldwater Hospital, Graham-Windham Services for Families, Jewish Home and Hospital, the Lower East Side Girl's Club, and Head Start.

Hewitt has teams in volleyball, basketball, soccer, cross country, gymnastics, badminton, swim, track and field and tennis.

Commencement exercises at Hewitt are traditional. The seniors wear white dresses, gather onstage and are joined in the processional by their kindergarten little sisters. Faculty members and trustees who have daughters graduating are allowed to present the diploma.

Popular College Choices   Barnard College, Brown, Connecticut College, Duke, Skidmore, Vassar, Trinity, Harvard, University of Michigan, Stanford, NYU, Tufts, Princeton, Georgetown, Boston University

Traditions   Arts Festival, Book Fair, New Parents' Reception, Grandparents' Day, Parents' Visiting Day, Thanksgiving Concert, All School Holiday Concert, Model UN trip to Washington, Sports Banquet, Achievement Assemblies, senior projects, Old Girl-New Girl Assembly, Hewitt-Browning Exchange Day, Literary Week, Ms. Hewitt's Birthday Celebration, Senior Project Trip to Italy and Switzerland, Holiday Sing Along, Big Sister-Little Sister Program, Senior Prom, Senior Staircase, Lower School Valentine's Day Breakfast

Publications   Upper School newspaper: *The Hewitt Times*
Middle School literary magazine: *Enterprise*
Art and literary magazine: *The Venturer*
Photography magazine: *Perspicacity*
Yearbook: *Argosy*
School magazine: *The Hewitt Anchor*
School newsletters: *Hewitt Happenings*

Hangouts   La Viande Coffee Shop, 3 Guys Coffee Shop (both on Madison Avenue)

Horace Mann School

Horace Mann Nursery Division
55 East 90th Street
New York, NY 10128
(212) 369-4600

Horace Mann Lower Division
4440 Tibbett Avenue
Riverdale, NY 10471
(718) 432-3300

Horace Mann Middle/Upper Division
231 West 246th Street
Riverdale, NY 10471
(718) 432-4000
e-mail: admissions@horacemann.org
website: www.horacemann.org

Coed
Nursery–12th grade
Accessible for Nursery Division and Middle/Upper Division
Not accessible for Lower Division

Dr. Thomas M. Kelly, Head of School until July, 2005
Dr. Barbara Tischler, Head of Upper Division
Ms. Marian Linden, Head of Middle Division
Dr. Steven Tobolsky, Head of Lower Division
Ms. Lisa Moreira, Director of Admissions
Ms. Wendy Steinthal, Director of Admissions, Lower School
Mrs. Patricia Yuan Zuroski, Director, Nursery Division
Mrs. Lydia Hechter, Director of Admissions, Nursery Division

Birthday Cutoff   Children entering nursery 3's must be 3 by September 1
Children entering kindergarten must be 5 by September 1

Enrollment   Total enrollment nursery–12: 1,740
Total enrollment nursery division: 165
Kindergarten places: 35

Total enrollment lower division, grades kindergarten–5: 440
Total enrollment upper division, grades 6–12: 1,135
Graduating class size: varies, from 150–170
Horace Mann also has a kindergarten with one class of up to 21 children located in Riverdale, serving families from Riverdale, Westchester, the Bronx and New Jersey
The sixth grade admits 50–55 new students and is the largest point of entry each year

Grades   Trimester system
Kindergarten–3: detailed anecdotal reports, conferences and checklists; check, check-plus or minus grades; weekly quizzes
Letter grades begin in 4th grade, and anecdotal reports continue
Departmentalization begins in 4th grade, is completed by 5th grade
First final exam is given in 7th grade

Tuition Range 2005–2006 $19,600 to $27,350, nursery 3's–12th grade
Additional fees for books, transportation and lunch, approximately $1,100 to $3,000

Financial Aid/Scholarship   Over 5 million is awarded annually for financial aid
There are 12 named scholarship funds in the Upper Division

Endowment   Approximately $68.5 million

Diversity   56 Prep for Prep students as of Fall 2003
The Union is an organization of students of color at Horace Mann
There is a parent support group

Homework   1st grade: Worksheets, always due on Fridays
2nd: 4 times a week, 10–15 minutes in the beginning of the year going up to 20 minutes, 2 worksheets per night
3rd and 4th: 30–45 minutes a night
5th: 1 and ½ hours a night
9th: 2–2½ hours per night
10th–12th: 50 minutes per subject per night, approximately 3 to 4 hours; more time is required for studying for exams and long-term projects

After-School Program For grades K–5 in Riverdale: a variety of recreational and creative activities; an additional payment is required

Upper Division: 40–70 clubs, which vary from year to year depending on the interests of the student body

Competitive sports in the Ivy Prep League

Summary Program Six weeks of courses for credit or review for Horace Mann students and new students; many summer camp programs available.

———

"Harvard man" is what many parents are wishing for when they enroll their three and four-year-olds at this very selective school. If you have a vision of your youngster in a crimson uniform cavorting on a grassy field with the best and the brightest, then this might be the right place. (HM's colors are crimson and white.) And as at an Ivy League campus, most of the old stone buildings at Horace Mann High School are named after former headmasters and founders: Tillinghast Hall, Van Alstyne Auditorium, Pforzheimer Hall, the Loeb Reading Room, the Prettyman Gymnasium.

The school opened two new buildings in 1999: a new Middle School building for grades 6 through 8 and an Arts and Dining Center serving grades 6 through 12. These buildings highlight the Middle Division programs, increase student and public spaces, focus on art and music offerings, and make the existing T1 Internet and WAN accessible from every classroom.

In September 2002, Tillinghast Hall re-opened after undergoing a sizable renovation that included the addition of three computer labs, a foreign language technology lab, thirty-two classrooms with wireless internet access, and a new addition that houses the Katz Library and the Loeb Reading Room, the 650-seat Alfred Gross theater, dance studio, black box theater, and state-of-the-art theater scenery shop with a hydraulic lift that serves both as an orchestra pit and as an elevator to convey sets and equipment to the stage.

It is somewhat ironic that this prestigious private school is named after a man known as the father of public schools. Horace Mann actually had nothing to do with this namesake. According to HM's history *The First Hundred Years*, it was founder Nicholas Murray Butler who chose the name because "at the time it was the only household name in American education." Blessed with strong leadership through the years, HM has served as a model for both public and private schools, combining the traditional and the innovative, and has always encouraged physical hardiness as well as academic rigor. Originally coed, except for a forty-year hiatus when the campuses were separate (under Inslee "Ink" Clark), Horace Mann readmitted women in 1974. Along with Clark, Dr. Mitchell Gratwick, HM's head for seventeen years, left an indelible stamp on HM: "High standards, conservative values and innovative methods." Gratwick was a founder of the AP program and acquired the John Dorr Nature Laboratory, two strong components of the HM experience.

HM uses the building-block approach to learning: "Each step leads to the next." This philosophy is carried all the way through HM, ultimately leading to preparation for advanced college study. HM's bottom line: With superior preparation, a good measure of ability and the willingness to work like an ox, a student can achieve excellence here.

Horace Mann Nursery Division was originally established as a service for the children of alumni "who wanted to start their offspring in a Horace Mann system." It is located in a tight but tidy converted coach house on 90th Street between Madison and Park. There is no indoor gym but children use a rooftop playground or a yard for at least an hour a day and go to Asphalt Green once a week. Classrooms are colorful and well ordered—if crowded—reflecting a structured but stimulating "hands-on" curriculum. The staff psychologist is available to parents for consultation. All the head teachers have a Masters in Education.

Getting in: You must apply to the Nursery Division (HMND) when your child is two and a half years old. Getting in at the nursery level is far easier on the parents because the ERB is not required for admission at that time. However, there is a caveat. At the age of three there is really no way of knowing if your child will be able (or willing) to keep up with the high expectations and the work required later on. Also, potential learning differences that might be picked up by the ERB are not apparent. We know too many parents who boasted about their children getting into HM Nursery only to have to tutor them after school or (like one parent we know) over the summer. Parents may have to consider a change of school by third grade because a child is falling behind. It is not that HM weeds out children. The school is prepared to give as much support as is needed but there is a process of self-selection.

Applicants to Lower, Middle and Upper divisions come to campus for a student and parent interview. Tours are led by student "ambassadors." Applications should be filed by December 1st and must be completed by January 15th. Families who request an application are invited to Fall open houses. The ratio of applicants to places at the kindergarten and nursery levels is about ten to one. It's easier to get into HM at sixth or ninth grade.

The relocation of the sixth grade to the Middle School campus has led to a significant change in Middle School Division admissions. At present HM enrolls approximately 50–55 new sixth graders and 15 or fewer seventh graders. Lisa Moreira, Director of Admissions, says the transition resulted in four applications for every place in sixth grade and more than six applications for every seventh grade opening.

The Upper Division enrolls approximately 35 new students each year in ninth grade with eight applications for every place and receives 30–40 applications for 5 tenth grade places. Few openings are available at eighth and eleventh grades.

Kindergarten applicants may be observed at their nursery schools if there are many children applying from those schools, but all children are observed in a group interview at HM in the afternoon (1:30 or 3:30). "By kindergarten," one interviewer said, "it doesn't bode well if a child doesn't separate well in the interview."

Some entering students don't know how to write their names while some come in reading. But by the end of kindergarten most kids have "cracked the code." Formal instruction begins in first grade, and reading is expected to be well under way by second grade. "The curriculum in the early years is geared to the readiness of the children," says the brochure. There is a strong emphasis on basic skills balanced with new techniques and tools. Experiential learning is stressed, and computer, chess and other learning games are introduced. There is a resource room with six computers for kindergarten. One parent praised the fact that here children "capture the enthusiasm for learning young." During the second half of the year kindergartners travel up to Riverdale to get acquainted with the elementary school campus. (We suggest that parents applying to the Nursery Division take a tour of the Elementary Division, because before you know it your child will be up in Riverdale.)

Parents: The Nursery Division is homogeneous. Parents describe it as predominantly Jewish and financially mixed. One said, "I thought the parents would be a lot hipper." There is a very active Parents Association. One mother recalls attending her first parents' meeting thoroughly underdressed. Where do many families go on weekends and vacations? "You know," said one parent, "it's the triangle: the

Hamptons, Boca, Vail." But parents report that once they reach Riverdale the school community is more mixed. Communication with the parents is frequent, and there is a Parents Association newsletter. Nursery Division parents can be class representatives and they may also serve as elected members on the Horace Mann Board of Trustees.

Since the Elementary Division, located in Riverdale, is "no one's neighborhood school," communication between home and school is very important. Teachers often call and chat with parents. There are many student-teacher conferences.

Program: Horace Mann is very honest in acknowledging that this school is not for everyone. Director of the Lower School, Wendy Steinthal says, "There is a quick pace with lots of enrichment." Most children thrive on the stimulation—the classrooms are buzzing with activity and the students are clearly engaged. The PA president said that the school "breeds independence." At the beginning of third grade a letter is sent to parents urging them not to help their children with their homework, and parents must sign it. Parents may only suggest, "Try this or that." Wendy Steinthal stresses that Horace Mann is supportive and committed to each child. "Yes, there is a lot to do but the children meet the challenge," she says. "This is a school for children who really like to learn." There is a real emphasis on teaching study skills and on learning how to be a student. One parent summed up the issue of competitiveness at HM astutely: "It's not that the school or the kids are necessarily so competitive; it's the high-powered parents behind them." The same can be said for all the top tier schools in New York City.

The Elementary Division has large open areas, although there are no "open classrooms." Some of these large areas are shared by four classes, with cubbies in the center. Some classes have two sections, one for reading lab or language arts, one for math. Formal reading instruction begins in first grade with an eclectic approach. There are three reading specialists and a communication skills specialist. Emphasis is placed on the writing process. HM children are tested for reading each year and there is a full reading lab.

HM is known for having strong math students. There are many classroom projects: The computer program begins in kindergarten. Elementary students have computer lab (Macintosh) at least once a week for forty-five minutes. Beginning in fourth grade, they learn word processing and keyboarding; in fifth grade, graphics and programming. By fifth grade nearly 90 percent of the students use a computer at home.

The new Middle Division facility prompted a re-evaluation of the Middle School curriculum. There is increased emphasis on interdisciplinary works and team teaching at the sixth, seventh, and eight grade levels. Students have more choices to make and more accountability, including the introduction of "free periods." Lower School PA president Pam Stuchin says: "It's wonderful for the sixth graders to experience the independence and increased responsibility that comes with the Middle School environment. Until my older daughter started seventh grade I didn't realize how much they crave that sense of freedom."

There are three art teachers on staff. The Art Enrichment Program is an enhancement to the Lower School curriculum. Using a variety of media (painting, collage, papier-mâché, ceramics, metal tooling and felt appliqué) students create two and three dimensional forms to go with a topic being studied in English, reading, social studies or science. Students from first grade through fifth work to create individual as well as large group projects. The completed work is often used as a learning tool or teaching aid in the classroom.

Foreign language study begins in first grade. First graders take *both* French and Spanish. In second grade students choose French or Spanish for the remainder of the Lower School. In eighth grade students can elect Latin, German, Spanish, French, or Japanese.

Parents of active children will be glad to know that there is time for physical exercise: In first through fourth grades gym meets four times a week in a huge gymnasium. Fifth graders have gym four times a week. Students use a playground and the AstroTurf field year-round, and can use the tennis courts and pool at the upper division.

Special trips: Fifth graders take a three-day trip to Washington, D.C.; all second, third, fourth and fifth graders spend time at the John Dorr Nature Lab.

Programs are held at the John Dorr Nature Lab for incoming sixth and incoming seventh, eighth, ninth, and tenth graders for orientation and exploration, which includes the Searchers program, an adapted Outward Bound program.

The Upper Division: Now the group is larger and more diverse (26 percent are children of color), "large enough to be happy as they grow and change." In general "students respect the school" and enjoy the freedom of an open campus. There are no bells, and teachers are addressed formally. In 1995, Dr. Eileen Mullady became the first woman to head the school. Her background is in higher education (Columbia and Princeton). Parents say she has "cleaned house" and has successfully run two capital campaigns. One of Dr. Mullady's realized goals was to "build an exemplary Middle School." She notes that while HMHS is known to be hard and rigorous; it is also "a school that celebrates intellectualism; a joyful, adventurous place." Dr. Mullady's last year at HM will be the 2004–2005 academic year. Dr. Thomas Kelly is HM's ninth Head of School. Dr. Kelly, 39, had been superintendent of the Valhalla Union Free School District in Westchester. Colleagues feel Dr. Kelly's experience in the public sector will bring a fresh perspective to the post. They admire his energy and enthusiasm for the job.

In preparation for the challenge of the upper grades, students who need review attend the six-week summer session. Seventh and eighth graders also take mandatory life skills courses. Readings include *Inherit the Wind, Things Fall Apart* and *Ishi: Last of His Tribe*. Students gain experience in creative and critical writing. Eighth graders celebrate "Pi Day" (on 3/14 of course) and build solar houses which are tested for temperature and heat retention on the football field on a cold day.

Historically HM has been strong in English and history, and now HM's science labs are state of the art. Four out of ten faculty members hold Ph.D.'s and the chemistry department has three research-quality lab instruments. The science library and resource room has six microcomputers and is often open for independent study. Science teachers are very accessible to students with an interest in advanced study.

The course catalog says that most of the eighth grade courses are equivalent to ninth grade courses at many high schools. And even the introductory courses move along at quite a clip. One alumnus said, "It was like going to college before college." In keeping with Dr. Gratwick's legacy, HM was a pilot school for the AP program, and HMHS offers more AP courses than any other school, including "AP Psychology," "AP Latin: Epic Poetry" and "AP Economics." The math department offers AP Calculus AB, AP Calculus BC Honors, and Probability, Statistics and Social Science. English courses stress the classics but there are interesting electives in Memory and Identity, Heros and Heroines, and the works of Toni Morrison.

One Horace Mann (class of 1990) and Cornell (class of 1994) alumna says, "Academically there's lots of freedom and choices but there are no gut courses at HM; no course can be blown off." The average grade is a B, which, one student boasts, "would be a B+ anywhere else." One HMHS student says, "Some people work hard for grades, and some people work harder for excellent grades." "It's as hard to get an F as it is to get an A" is also heard. Testing is so frequent (quizzes every week, exams every other), "you always know how you're doing." What is not listed in the catalog is the advanced level of maturity and independence required of students at HMHS, qualities already ingrained in students who came up through the HM system. The pressure is real, but one student said, "It's mainly self-inflicted." Yet another student told us that "teachers go to extremes to make the homework challenging." All homework requires a lot of time and thought, and one student said that he might blow off homework in one subject to study for an exam in another but if he missed two nights of homework assignments, he would fall behind.

Some students thrive under pressure and rise to the challenge of the competitive atmosphere, like the young woman (a HM "lifer" who has been at HM for twelve years) who takes three AP courses, does four hours of homework a night and still manages to watch her favorite TV shows. The minimum amount of homework is three to four hours each night, more on weekends. "This school makes you hungry," a student told us. "You get used to working hard and getting what you want, and you take that with you." One private school advisor tells families who are considering a most demanding school like Horace Mann to consider their family lifestyles. Some students will be able to accompany the family on weekend ski trips and still get their work done (one student trains for competitive ski racing). Others will be hitting the books in the chalet.

Contrary to popular belief, students at HM do support one another. There is a peer leadership training program and a student tutorial program, and most evenings HM students spend lots of time on the phone or on-line discussing homework or exams.

Does this leave time for extracurricular activities? One student put it this way, "If you want to be in a play or a sport and you don't mind sacrificing that time, then you do your work when you get home." Still, extracurricular activities are encouraged even for kids who aren't excelling academically. Lisa Moreira says, "Because the academics are so challenging, it's even more important for students to pursue their other interests. We want every student to experience successes, to explore abilities in and out of the classroom."

The community service requirement also contributes to personal growth. One alumna told us that HM helped her find a job as a counselor at a summer camp for homeless children and she then returned for four consecutive summers and found it an invaluable experience.

HM students are far from one-dimensional math nerds, as evidenced by the variety and number of their extracurricular activities. Every year there is a huge musical, and three smaller plays are put on annually. HM produces more than a dozen publications. Students can choose from up to seventy clubs in any given year. Popular ones include The Union (formerly the Joint Minority Coalition), which is open to everyone, political clubs (there is a Young Republicans of HM Club), the East Wind, West Wind Asian Club, Glee Club, Model U.N., Junior Statesman Club (debating) and a Shakespeare Club. The Glee Club and Chamber Chorus are very popular; they have made their own CD and traveled to Europe and the Middle East.

Students do have a voice in setting policy affecting student life at HM through the governing council, comprised of twenty-four students and fifteen faculty members who are elected annually. There is an annual tenth grade health survey (anonymous), and students are required to take health courses. In 1997 the Governing Council passed the "Teacher and Course Evaluation Bill." The Council spent three meetings debating the document, which called for written evaluations by the students twice a year. The bill compelled the school faculty and administration to pass a similar resolution, making teacher and course evaluations a reality.

They say that Harvard is tough to get into, but easy to stay in; HM is tough to get into and tougher to remain in, but there is no question that the child who stays the course at HM will receive a superior, accelerated education. One alumna told us, "Horace Mann's great strength is it instills good work habits and is superior in college placement: HM goes above and beyond to get you into one of the colleges of your choice." It's prep for success. If your child makes it through, maybe you'll get to the Harvard-Yale tailgate picnic after all.

Popular College Choices   University of Pennsylvania, Cornell, Yale/Columbia, Brown/University of Wisconsin, Harvard

Traditions   The Buzzell basketball game (vs. Riverdale), Senior Absurdity Day, Holocaust Remembrance Assembly and Martin Luther King Assembly, East Wind–West Wind Dinner (Asia Night), Lower School Family Picnic, Lower School Caring in Action Day

Publications   Yearbook: *The Mannikin*
   Newspapers: *The Record*
   Literary magazine: *Manuscript*
   Prose literature: *Legal Fiction*
   Science magazine: *Spectrum*
   Math magazine: *Mantissa*

Sports: *The Lion's Den*
Journal of opinion: *Outlook*
Multicultural paper: *The Drum*
Photography: *Insight*
Movie/Theater Review: *The Cinemann*
Alumni publication: *Alumni Bulletin*
Student Opinion Journal: *The Horace Mann Review*

Community Service Requirement 80 hours in grades 9–12; special activities in grades 6–8
Student Voluntary Service Organization

Hangouts Riverdale diner, the library or cafeteria, The BBQ or the field outside on nice days

La Scuola D'Italia G. Marconi

12 East 96th Street
New York, NY 10128

Middle School
406 East 67th Street
New York, NY 10021
(212) 369-3290, FAX (212) 369-1164
e-mail: secretary@lascuoladitalia.org
website: www.LaScuolaDItalia.org

Coed
Pre-kindergarten–12th grade
Not accessible

Ms. Bianca Maria Padolecchia Goodrich, Head of School
Ms. Pia Pedicini, Vice Principal and Director of Admissions
Ms. Augusta Fleischer, Middle School Coordinator
Ms. Marisa Laroca Riccioli, High School Coordinator

Birthday Cutoff   Children entering at the nursery level must be 3 and toilet-trained by December 31
Children entering kindergarten must be 5 by December 31
Children entering first grade must be 6 by April 30

Enrollment   Total enrollment: 190
Pre-Kindergarten 3/4's places: 34
Kindergarten places: 20
Graduating class size: 7–10

Tuition Range 2005–2006 $15,000 to $17,000, pre-kindergarten–12th grade
Additional fees: for application, registration and activities supplemental fees are approximately $1,100 for all grades

After-School Program   For children in grades Pre-K through 8th grade, from September through May; Monday–Thursday; 3:15 P.M. until 5:00 P.M.; for an additional charge activities include: English and Italian homework, Italian Language, Arts & Crafts, Singing, Creative Movement and Computer

La Scuola D'Italia G. Marconi, of New York was founded in 1977 by the Italian Ministry of Foreign Affairs and is dedicated to Guglielmo Marconi, the inventor of the wireless. The school is a co-ed English/Italian bilingual institution that offers an international education. The bilingual curriculum is rooted in the European classical tradition. La Scuola is now housed in a historic building, once a private mansion, on East 96th Street.

La Scuola's Middle School (grades six through eight) is located at 406 East 67th Street, and offers a challenging liberal arts curriculum that includes math, science and in-depth study and appreciation of American, European, and Italian civilizations and cultures. The program, with English as the language of instruction, allows students to acquire strong language skills along with a classic academic curriculum.

Students must become fluent in at least two languages. There is total immersion in Italian from the outset, but fluency in Italian is not a prerequisite for admission. Bilingual instruction in English and Italian begins in pre-kindergarten. There is a four-year requirement in Latin for the ninth through twelfth grades and in French for the seventh through ninth grades. High School students graduate after passing the end-of-the-course State Exam, with the equivalent of the International Baccalaureate. Students must bring their own lunches.

La Scuola is legally recognized by the Italian Ministry of Education and chartered by the Regents of the University of the State of New York as a private, independent American school.

Graduates attend European universities and major American colleges.

Little Red School House and Elisabeth Irwin High School

Lower and Middle Divisions
292 Sixth Avenue
New York, NY 10014
FAX (212) 677-9159

Upper Division
40 Charlton Street
New York, NY 10014
(212) 477-5316 (main number), FAX (212) 675-3595
website: www.lrei.org

Coed
Pre-kindergarten–12th grade
Accessible

Phil Kassen, Director
Samantha Caruth, Director of Admissions

Birthday Cutoff   Children entering pre-kindergarten must be 4 by October 1
Children entering kindergarten must be 5 by October 1

Enrollment   Total enrollment: 540
Pre-kindergarten places: 30
Kindergarten places: 50
Graduating class size: approximately 40

Grades   Semester system in Middle and High School
Letter grades begin in 6th grade
Departmentalization begins in Middle School

Tuition Range 2005–2006 $22,800 to $25,905, Pre-K–12th grade

Financial Aid/Scholarship   33% of the student body receives some form of aid

Endowment $128,000

After-School Program   All programs are for LREI students as well as for students outside the community.

The Early Bird Program: for 4–13 year olds, 7:45 A.M. to 8:30 A.M. The general after-school program is divided into three age groups: four-year olds–1st graders, 2nd–4th graders, and the Middle School group. The program runs from 3–6 P.M., Monday through Friday, and includes a structured variety of creative and recreational activities.

The Enrichment Program also runs from 3–6 P.M. Monday through Friday, includes weekly classes such as Art in Motion, Hip Hop Dance, woodworking, ceramics, Mandarin Chinese, karate, dance, theater, tennis, super sports, chess and parent/child yoga.

The Instrumental Program includes private instruction in such instruments as flute, saxophone, piano, guitar, voice and drums.

Summer Camp Program   Open to children from other schools, the traditional Day Camp is offered for age 3.5 through 14. The camp includes age-appropriate activities including arts & crafts, drama, recreational sports, swimming and field trips. Also offered are specialty camps such as, Musical Theater and Mandarin Chinese Language and Culture. Camps run from mid-June through July. An additional payment is required.

———

Little Red School House and Elisabeth Irwin High School (LREI) was founded in 1921 by Elisabeth Irwin. Working closely with such luminaries of the progressive movement as John Dewey, William Heard Kilpatrick and Lucy Sprague Mitchell, Ms. Irwin set up a "model school" within New York City's public school system with an emphasis on experiential (or active) learning. She eventually moved the program out of the public schools. Ms. Irwin selected students she thought reflected the diversity of New York City and aimed for a school with an exceptionally involved parent body. Today, faculty, parents and students remain active in the school.

In the early 1930s Ms. Irwin moved the school to Bleecker Street and Sixth Avenue, where it has grown. A second site was acquired on Charlton Street, a few blocks away, when the high school grades were added in 1941. The facilities include a cafeteria, a library and technology center, and Middle School classrooms, including a sky-lit art studio. The high school's extensive renovations include a library, a performing arts center, a media lab, classrooms and a lobby.

Getting in: The ERB is required for admission to grades four through twelve. All applicants and their families tour the school and are interviewed. The school is composed of three divisions. Lower School: four year olds through fourth grade; Middle School: fifth through eighth grades; High School: ninth through twelfth. A hot lunch is provided for all grades. Formal foreign language instruction begins in the fours with Spanish; in sixth grade students may choose between beginning French or continuing Spanish.

Parents: LREI parents are active in the school. The PA sponsors a Book Fair, a Literary Evening, and an art auction at a gallery in Chelsea in the spring. The parent body includes many notable area artists.

Program: Little Red and Elisabeth Irwin recently celebrated its seventy-fifth anniversary and maintains a progressive approach which nurtures both intellectual rigor and a genuine joy of learning. The school retains its original emphasis on experiential and collaborative learning, and a commitment to diversity—both in the student population and curriculum. During the 1960s the "Red" in the school name supposedly implied sympathy for the leftist viewpoints. Today, LREI remains an activist school, with many students impassioned about human rights, but as an institution the concern is with critical thinking.

True to its mission as a model school, LREI provides an atmosphere in which innovative teaching thrives. The faculty create exciting curricula which can then be replicated in other schools. Frequent field trips provide experiential learning opportunities. Third and fourth grade students spend four days on a working farm. Social Studies in the Lower School begins with the neighborhood and extends beyond to Harlem and Chinatown. Specialists in science, math, visual arts, music, woodworking, Spanish, library and technology also work with students through project-based activities.

At LREI the classes are small and the student teacher ratio is approximately seven to one. Classes are structured but informal; most everyone is on a first name basis. Formal reading instruction begins in first grade. A student's progress is constantly being assessed, and teachers are able to address each child's progress in kindergarten and first grade by working in very small groups. There is always a reading teacher along with the classroom teacher in every Lower

School classroom during reading time. There are rigorous academic expectations while allowing for plenty of creative expression. Community service is a requirement beginning in the Middle School. LREI enrolls Prep for Prep students.

Parents say that LREI has always been in the forefront of innovative education. "Elisabeth Irwin has taught my son to solve problems and think through issues. Yet at the same time it has encouraged him to take risks regardless of the outcome," said a parent. Essentially it provides a very comfortable learning environment with a solid academic foundation: "The day is tightly structured without being constraining; one subject flows into the next"; "The Gestalt at a school has to be right for learning and at Little Red, it is." A teacher at LREI told us "Their first priority is to really love and care about the kids . . . they feel it is their responsibility to find a way so that each child can grow and be challenged."

The High School and Middle School each perform one musical and one drama production every year. Drama in the Lower School is usually something that grows out of the classroom curriculum. At LREI the classroom meeting is a long-standing tradition, as is the assembly program. Guest speakers address a range of topics. Student representatives organize and run Middle and High School assemblies. Every class in the school is paired with a buddy class in another division. They meet informally during the year to read together, as well as for special days, such as Poem in Your Pocket Day, Founders Day and Field Day.

The Lower School Thanksgiving Assembly is a tradition that reflects the sense of community at LREI. The room is decorated with a beautiful display of autumn cornucopia and corn stalks. The children and teachers sit in chairs and on the floor and there is a big basket in the middle. Representatives from each class get up and read a poem and put something they've made—cornbread, for example—into the Thanksgiving basket (the gifts are donated to the needy.) One of the faculty talks about the origin of the Thanksgiving tradition and they sing a Native American song. "It was not a spectacle for the parents, it had real meaning and was very moving," said a participant.

In Middle School, science and technology projects include robotics using microprocessors, sensors and programming software to create original simulations. Visual, musical and performing arts are integrated with the core social studies curriculum. Fifth and sixth graders study ancient and medieval societies and create Egyptian sarcophagi and artifacts for the Ancient Art and Artifacts museum, and stained glass windows, personal coats of arms and scenery for the annual Medieval Pageant.

Seventh graders combine their reading of *The Crucible* and their study of colonial American history with an investigation of McCarthyism that culminates in a week-long trip to Colonial Williamsburg; eighth graders go to Washington, D.C. for a combined study of art, history and government.

High School classes are one-hour long and are combined with frequent field trips. Courses are interdisciplinary and organized around real-world themes, issues and problems. Ninth and tenth grade science classes integrate biology, chemistry and physics, and the development of international human rights is a central theme of ninth grade history. Tenth grade students read the literature of social justice, and all eleventh graders study the history of New York City. Juniors and seniors are eligible to take courses at NYU. The Senior Project includes extensive research and an internship; assessments include exams, written assignments, exhibits, portfolios, and research projects.

Lower School students have physical education three times a week in a new physical and performing arts room. Younger children play on the school's rooftop playground. Older students use the Houston Street playground down the block for recess. Competitive sports begin in Middle School. Fifth and sixth graders have intramural sports and seventh and eighth graders compete against other schools. The High School offers track and field, cross-country volleyball, soccer, basketball, softball and golf teams. The PE program offers yoga, dance, aerobics, karate and personal training.

Popular College Choices   Bard, Barnard, Bennington Brown, Columbia, Cornell, Hampshire NYU, University of Pennsylvania, Vassar, Wesleyan, Yale

Traditions   Weekly Assembly Program, Buddy classes, Division and class trips, Book Fair, Halloween Fair, Arts Auction Literary Evening, Poetry Slam, Poem in Your Pocket Day, Founders Day, Lower, The Coffehouse, German Exchange Program, High School Jazz Ensemble Community Service Round Table

Publications   Yearbook: *Expression*
Literary Magazine: *i.e.*
Newspaper: *The School Times*
Lower School yearbook: *Really Red*

LREI newsletter (five times a year)
Monthly: *Monthly Mailings*
LREI *Bulletin* (three times a year)
Weekly emails

Community Service   Community service is a requirement in all three divisions of the school. Lower School students hold food and clothing drives to help support families in need. Middle and high students work in local soup kitchens, clean up the neighborhood and participate in such events as the AIDS Walk. LREI is also the headquarters of the city wide Urban Citizen Project, which involves students in issues of urban life and governance

Hangouts   Student lounge, Pizza Box, In the Black Coffee Shop

Loyola School

980 Park Avenue
New York, NY 10028
(212) 288-3522
website: www.loyola-nyc.org

Coed
9th–12th grade
Not accessible

Rev. Stephen Katsouros, S.J., President
Mr. James Lyness, Headmaster
Ms. Lillian Imbelli, Director of Admissions

Uniform   Dress code consists of blue blazer with Loyola patch for all students. Boys: collared shirt, tie, slacks. Girls: collared blouse, skirt or slacks. No jeans, T-shirts or sneakers

Birthday Cutoff   None

Enrollment   Total enrollment: approximately 200
Graduating class size: approximately 50

Grades   Semester system
Numerical grades for exams and report cards; letter grades for progress reports

Tuition 2005–2006   Approximately $20,000; additional fees $650

Financial Aid/Scholarship   Approximately $400,000
Approximately 30% of the student body receives some form of financial assistance

Endowment $5.4 million

Diversity   As one student said: "Loyola has a very diverse group of students from different walks of life. When the student body comes together a very special atmosphere is created."

Homework   Approximately 2½–3 hours per night

After-School Program   Extracurricular activities and clubs meet after school and during a mid-day period set aside for this purpose. Varsity and Junior varsity teams compete in the Independent School Athletic League, the Girls Independent School Athletic League, and the Independent Baseball Association.

Summer Program   None

––––––

Loyola School was founded in 1900 by Jesuits at the request of parents who wanted a Catholic alternative to non-sectarian prep schools. At that time the school was "up in the country" but featured the most up-to-date classrooms in the city. It became coed in 1973. Loyola School is the only independent coed Jesuit high school in the New York tri-state area. Loyola combines Jesuit traditions with a strong college preparatory program. The school's motto, *Ex Fide Fortis,* means "From Faith, Strength." The school is governed by a lay board of trustees and has been named a School of Excellence by the U.S. Department of Education.

The school is housed in an imposing stone building at Eighty-third Street and Park Avenue. In September 1996, Loyola completed a half-million dollar renovation of the fourth floor. This expansion allowed the school to enlarge its science and computer labs. In September 2000 a 2.8 million dollar renovation of the cafeteria, student life office and locker rooms was completed. The gym is now air-conditioned.

Getting in: Applicants and their families are invited to an open house in the Fall. Applicants are evaluated on the basis of their academic and personal qualifications. Admissions requirements include: a transcript from the current school, a personal interview, two letters of recommendation, and Loyola's entrance exam, or the ISEE. In addition, applicants are encouraged to spend a day visiting classes.

Parents: A "New Parents" evening is held in the Fall of the freshman year, an opportunity for parents to socialize and to familiarize themselves with their child's daily life. Parent-teacher conferences are held four times a year and either a written report or a report card is sent home approximately every six weeks. There is an active Parents Association and the Headmaster distributes a newsletter to parents regularly.

Program: There is a warm and friendly family atmosphere at Loyola. As one student said: "At Loyola, they care about us as students and as teenagers getting through today's world." Every student has a faculty mentor who assists with student's academic, spiritual and extracurricular options.

Loyola's goals are to promote religious, intellectual, cultural, social and physical growth in every student as well as a concern for social justice. "Jesuits are known for being very independent," we were told. While the majority of students are Roman Catholic, a wide variety of faiths are represented. According to the school, Loyola's philosophy is: "Strong faith must be founded on a solid understanding which extends to theology classes, where knowledge rather than belief is stressed." The curriculum in religious studies is complemented with a program of retreats, and each morning, before classes begin, optional Mass is available in the chapel.

The core curriculum consists of four years of theology, English and physical education; three years of history, math and foreign language; three years of science, one year of speech, composition skills, art history, computer, health and music history. Writing skills are stressed; freshmen are required to take seven periods a week in English and composition skills.

Students may take elective courses in art history, art studio, computer science, writing fiction, poetry, discrete mathematics, Latin, modern drama, modern American fiction, film study, chorus, ensemble, modern British and American poetry, philosophy in literature, global perspectives, political science and economics. French, Spanish, Italian and Latin are offered. Advanced placement courses are offered in American history, European history, biology, physics, calculus, computer science, English, French and Spanish. Advanced Italian is offered in conjunction with Fordham University as a college credit course.

Loyola students excel in speech and debating, and there is a trophy case filled with the forensic and debate clubs' winnings. Loyola often places first in the small school division for State Championships. The school competes successfully in many local, regional and national competitions.

There is a large art studio and students work in many media including drawing, pastels, prints, watercolors, and oil painting. Students' musical activities include solo, ensemble instrumental and choral performances. "The Loyola Players" produce two professional level drama productions each year; one is usually a major musical major musical. Recent productions: *A Midsummer Night's Dream* and *Oliver*.

The elected student government is an integral part of school life at Loyola. Representatives help plan school dances as well as address student's issues. The volunteer service program, whose motto reflects the Jesuit motto, "Men and Women for Others," provides opportunities for students to help others.

During Spring Break, fifteen to twenty seniors and some faculty spend two weeks traveling through Italy from Milan to Rome, with Easter at the Vatican. The school also sponsors several overnight ski trips a year. Loyola also offers a spring vacation trip to another country, open to all students. One year the trip was to France; another year there were trips either to Austria and Germany or to Spain.

The athletic teams at Loyola are competitive. For boys, sports teams include junior and varsity soccer, basketball and baseball. Girls teams include volleyball, basketball, softball and coed varsity track and cross country. In a recent year the girls were finalists in the GISAL volleyball championship. The girls varsity softball team was season champions in GISAL. In recent years the boys' varsity basketball, soccer and baseball teams won championships. A professional quality gym, paddle tennis courts, and a fully equipped fitness room are also available to students.

The school has a cafeteria that serves a hot lunch daily. Beginning in ninth grade with parents' permission, students may leave for lunch.

Popular College Choices   Amherst, Brown, Boston College, Columbia, Georgetown, Holy Cross, Loyola College, New York University, Princeton, Wesleyan, Williams

Traditions   Freshman/Senior Night, Junior Talent Night, Family Day, Fall/Spring Drama Productions, Christmas Concert, Awards Convocation, Sports Night, Sophomore/Junior Semi-Formal, Senior Prom, Senior Trip to Italy

Publications   Newspaper: *Blazer*
Literary Magazine: *Knight*
Yearbook

Community Service Requirement   There is a four year Christian service requirement. Choices include: annual school-wide service projects at Thanksgiving, Christmas, and during Lent, which provide food, clothing, toys and monetary donations. Students also tutor underprivileged children, visit shut-ins, prepare and deliver meals to an SRO and to the homeless, work in metropolitan area hospitals, and help senior citizens. In addition to community service, students also volunteer in the weekend homeless shelter at St. Ignatius Loyola Church.

Hangouts   The Commons, Ray Bono Pizzeria, the steps of the Metropolitan Museum of Art, Loyola Cafe and Senior Section

Lycée Français de New York

The French Baccalaureate School

505 East 75th Street
New York, N.Y. 10021
(212) 369-1400 FAX (212) 439-4200
website: www.lfny.org
e-mail: admissions@lfny.org

Coed
Nursery–12th grade
Accessible

Mr. Yves Thézé, Head of School
Boualem Maizia, Deputy Head and Director of Secondary School
Joël Guignolet, Director of Primary School
Martine Lala, Admissions Director

Uniform   All students have a dress code: white blouse and grey skirt or trousers

Birthday Cutoff   Children entering at the pre-nursery level must be 3 by December 31; at the nursery level they must be 4 by December 31
Children entering kindergarten must be 5 by December 31

Enrollment   Total enrollment: 1,075
Nursery places: 75
Pre-kindergarten places: 79
Kindergarten places: 82
Graduating class size: approximately 50

Tuition Range 2005–2006 $14,000 to $19,000, Nursery–12th grade; additional fees for registration enrollment and for new students, $2,150; tuition payment plans are available

Financial Aid   Approximately 20% of the student body receives some form of aid

After-School Program   After-school program for nursery and elementary only; activities such as painting, sculpture, dance, ballet, theater, chorus, soccer, yoga, fencing, rollerblading, ice-skating, gymnastics, flute, piano, guitar, violin, saxophone, chess club and supervised homework study time are offered; an additional payment is required

Summer Program   Weekly sessions from June 28–July 30; Full and half day sessions available; all activities are conducted in both French and English; each group participates in a daily French course. There are trips to museums, parks, and the zoo; an additional payment is required

———————

Founded in 1936 by a group of French and American individuals, the Lycée Français de New York offers a classical Franco-European education as well as an English/American Social Studies program. At least forty nationalities are represented in the student body. The dual approach produces bilingual students, proficient in both English and French who have a deep understanding of both cultures. "Here we are not just French students," wrote one student in the *Memory Book.* "We are part of an international community. We live together and we share our experiences, our cultures."

The firm that planned the Clinton Library designed the school's new spacious facility which has central offices, a cafeteria, a gym, and many new classrooms and labs, an atrium, computers, and state-of-the art technology. The 150-square-foot buildings rise above a beautifully landscaped courtyard in two separate five-story towers, one for the Lower School, the other, for older students. Three full-lot floors connect these towers and act as the *coeur,* or heart of the Lycée. The entire school uses the two libraries—both have wireless Internet access—the cafeteria and gyms, one that will soon have the only rock climbing wall in a NYC private school, which unite the school's community. A 350-seat auditorium is presently under construction, and there's a roof-top play area for younger students.

Upper School students have their own spacious art studio, science labs, and "smart classrooms" with video screens, Internet access points for laptops.

Getting in: Applicants to nursery through fifth grade are admitted on a rolling basis that includes interviews and school records. Applicants to the secondary school (sixth grade through *terminale*— thirteenth year) must take an entrance examination unless they are transferring from an accredited French School (in France or elsewhere). The admissions office recommends that applications be submitted early in the Fall.

Program: The Lycée is accredited by the French Ministry of National Education and by NYSAIS. No knowledge of the French language is required for nursery through kindergarten, (though recommended for kindergarten). Students in grades two and above should have a working knowledge of the French language. Bilingual instruction is given in nursery and kindergarten. By first grade, French is the main language of instruction except for English, American literature, civics, and history, and other foreign languages. English as a Second Language (ESL) classes are available for non-English speaking students. Specialized teachers work with non-French speaking students in small group settings for at least one year.

Middle School consists of grades six, seven, eight and nine. Students take classes in math, science, geography, French, English, art, music, computer science, and physical education. Each subject is taught in French by specialists. In sixth grade, students choose a third language; choices include German, Italian, and Spanish. An introduction to Latin and Greek is optional in seventh and ninth grades.

Throughout Middle and Upper School the program is literature-based. By the end of ninth grade, students are expected to take a French national exam called the *Brevet des colleges*, which measures and evaluates a student's knowledge of French, math, history and geography.

By the last two years of Upper School, grades ten, eleven and twelve, students must choose a "major," in either Literature and Languages, Economics and Social Sciences, or Mathematics and the Sciences." Because of an accelerated curriculum, a high school diploma may be awarded to students after eleventh grade. All students are required to continue to the end of *terminale* and take the French Baccalaureate. The Lycée also offers students the option of taking the International Option of the French Baccalaurate (OIB) which allows for more writing, English and Social Sciences. Advanced Placement (AP) exams are offered in French (many ninth graders qualify), English, and Geography.

Graduates: Brown, Bryn Mawr, Cornell, Dartmouth, Duke, Harvard, MIT, Princeton, Smith, University of Chicago, University of Virginia, Yale, University of Quebec. Graduates also enroll in the "cours preparatoire" system before attending the "grandes écoles" of France, including Ecole des Hautes Etudes Commerciales, Ecole Polytechnique, Ecole Normale Superieure, Institut d'Etudes Politiques; European Universities include Université de Paris La Sorbonne and the American Business School in Paris.

Lyceum Kennedy

225 East 43rd Street
New York, NY 10017
(212) 681-1877 FAX (212) 681-1922
website: www.lyceumkennedy.com
e-mail: Info1@lyceumkennedy.com

Westchester Campus:
Cross Road
Ardsley, NY
Tel (914) 479-0722
Nursery–5th grade
e-mail: Info2@lyceumekennedy.com
LYKennedy2@aol.com

Co-ed
Nursery–12th grade
Partially accessible

Mr. Yves Rivaud, Head of School
e-mail: Head@lyceumkennedy.com
Ms. Voahangy Siraisi, Admissions Coordinator
e-mail: Adm@lyceumkennedy.com

Birthday Cutoff   Children entering preschool must be 3 by the start of school

Enrollment   Total enrollment: approximately 150

Tuition Range 2005–2006   Approximately $14,000 to $18,200; additional fees approximately $800

After-School Program   A daily program for children in grades nursery through 6th, from 3:30–5:30 P.M.; extracurricular activities are taught by specialist teachers in French and English, art, computers, theater, dance, martial, arts, photography, cooking and other activities

Summer Program   A bilingual summer camp programs offers a myriad of recreational and academic activities for 5 weeks from the end of June through the end of July; a 2-week minimum enrollment is required

———

Founded in 1964 as a French-American International School that offers a French immersion program, Lyceum Kennedy boasts a diverse, multicultural, international community. According to the Head of School, Yves Rivaud, "We have 150 students representing 25 nationalities and more than 20 languages spoken." The school enrolls both French and non-French speaking students from around the world.

The school is small with only one classroom per grade, and the student-teacher ratio is low. All students take American and French tests and exams at both the elementary and secondary levels.

All subjects are taught with a dual approach to learning that combine the flexibility and creativity of the American system with the more rigorous French method.

The Ardsley campus also offers the same bilingual program and educational philosophy for younger students, 3 to 11-years of age.

Manhattan Country School

7 East 96th Street
New York, NY 10128
(212) 348-0952, FAX (212) 348-1621
website: www.mcs.pvt.K12.ny.us
e-mail: mcs@mcs.pvt.K12.ny.us

Coed
Pre-Kindergarten–8th grade
Not accessible

Dr. Michèle Solá, Director
Ms. Elizabeth Jarvis, Director of Admissions

Uniform   None

Birthday Cutoff   Children entering the 4/5's must be 4 by October 31 of the year for which they are applying

Enrollment   Total enrollment: 180–190
4/5's places: 18
Graduating class size: approximately 20

Grades   Detailed anecdotal reports
Three parent conferences required per year
No letter or number grades in the Lower School (through 4th grade); Effort is graded in the Upper School
Departmentalization begins in 5th grade and is completed by 8th grade

Tuition Range 2005–2006 $19,600 to $24,500, 4/5's–8th grade
All parents pay according to family income on a sliding scale. The maximum compares to full tuition at other schools
Fees are included in the tuition
Parents can pay tuition on a monthly basis
There is a 25% deposit required when contracts are signed

Financial Aid/Scholarship   Approximately 76% of the student body receive some financial aid

Diversity   50% students of color

285

Endowment $8 million

After-School Program   A variety of creative, academic, and recreational activities. MCS After-School Program meets Mondays–Thursdays from 3:00 P.M. until 5:30 P.M. for 4 year olds to 5th graders, an additional payment is required

Homework   Nursery and K—None
    1st grade: Once a week, 30 minutes
    2nd: 30 minutes, 3 times a week
    3rd and 4th: 45 minutes, 4–5 times a week
    5th and 6th: 1–1½ hrs per night
    7th and 8th: 2–3 hrs per night

Summer Program   Three-week summer farm camp program in the Catskills; for 20 children age 9 and up; open to students from other schools; an additional payment is required

----

In 1966, Manhattan Country School was founded by Augustus and Martha Trowbridge, on Manhattan's Upper East Side, in an elegant private landmark building designed by Ogden Codman. Manhattan Country School's origins are deeply rooted in the social and ideological principles of the Civil Rights Movement. Its commitment to equality, social justice and cultural diversity are at the center of its curriculum. MCS has achieved what many independent schools with far greater endowments and financial aid claim is their goal: a truly diverse school. Fifty percent of the student body and faculty are people of color. There is a unique tuition/scholarship program at MCS. The school is a recipient of a private family foundation grant to develop a gender-equity curriculum.

Getting in: All parents applying to MCS should visit the school as a first step in the admissions process. From mid-September until mid-December, tours are held during the school day. Additional tours are available in May. Parents of children applying to Pre-K through first grade should attend a tour before December. In the Fall, an evening open house is held at the school. Parents who have requested admissions materials prior to October will automatically receive an invitation.

For applicants from pre-kindergarten through first grade, MCS does not require the ERB test. However, if the test is administered MCS should receive a copy of the test results. Children are observed and asked to play games, draw or do a puzzle at the group interviews. For applicants for second grade and above, ERB test results are required, as well as the applicant's school report and an interview. "Most importantly, we're looking for a good match, families that are comfortable with a diverse community." says Michèle Solá, Director of MCS.

Parents: Parents at MCS, as well as parents of alumni, are active fund-raisers for the school. They help organize many events throughout the school year. The parents of each class are responsible for one event, a total of ten in any given year. These include: Farm Festival, Grandparents' Day, Kwanzaa Festival, Spring Benefit, Dr. Martin Luther King, Jr. Commemorative Walk, and Farm Outing Day. There are many opportunities for parents to come together with the faculty and administration, to discuss common issues relating to education and child development. Parents Association Meetings are well attended and committees meet regularly.

Parents are an integral part of the social studies curriculum. The 4/5's class take "home visits"; the 7/8's study their families in depth for one semester; the sixth grade invites parents and other relatives to share their histories as part of their study of the Civil Rights Movement. Teachers at MCS welcome the opportunity for parents to share stories and talents and accompany students on class trips. Parent-teacher conferences are held three times a year, and parents may meet more often if there's a need.

Program: The Lower School at MCS is composed of six mixed-age groupings from 4/5's through 9/10's. The Lower School groups span two overlapping age levels. These mixed-age groupings offer flexible academic and social placements for children and enable the school to meet the developmental needs of each child. Within this framework, a grade level for each student is designated by the school. The average class is eighteen, but many classes are taught in smaller groups of eight to ten students. Each of the four youngest classes has a head teacher and an assistant, as well as student teachers, in most classrooms throughout the school. One parent told us, "To me the most important characteristic of MCS is the deep respect shown to students and their individuality. In this school community, students learn to value themselves along with their peers. The artificial barriers that schools routinely set regarding the teaching experts and the learners are less visible in the MCS environment. Everyone is learning and everyone is teaching."

The core curriculum at MCS is its social studies program. It allows the school to apply its multicultural perspectives and fosters positive social values. In the Lower School, social studies is integrated into all areas of the classroom through graphs, geography and mapping, creative writing, literature, drama and art. In the Upper School, social studies and history follow a chronological organization. Students refine research skills, and learn how to write formal research papers, as well as point-of-view essays.

Formal reading instruction begins in the 5/6's class. In small groups, (approximately half the class), students have reading and writing times. MCS takes into account that children learn to read in a variety of ways, and the teachers use many materials, including basal readers, structured phonics materials and literature. For students who need reinforcement, a reading specialist works in the classroom with small groups of students. If additional support is needed, a student will work with the specialist in another room. If a tutor is recommended, the school will work together with the student's tutor to help meet the student's needs.

The school considers Spanish to be an essential component to the multicultural experience at MCS. Beginning with the four-year-olds, Spanish is taught at every level in mixed-age groupings. Signs throughout the school are written in Spanish. The Lower School Spanish program is culture-based and integrated into the classrooms. The Upper School Spanish program is textbook based and prepares students for the New York State Proficiency Exam in Spanish.

The Upper School at MCS is composed of grades five through eight. Departmentalization begins in fifth grade. Fifth and sixth graders study English, social studies and math with their group teacher. Specialists teach Spanish, science, art, music, shop and physical education. In seventh and eighth grades, students are divided into two mixed-age homerooms, and each student is assigned a faculty advisor. Classes for seventh and eighth grades are fully departmentalized.

The math program follows four fundamental themes: making sense of data, patterns and predictions, numbers and number sense, and geometry and spatial sense. In the Lower School, math is integrated into the children's daily activities and manipulative materials are used. Upper School students follow a common text.

MCS has taken a hands-on approach for the science curriculum. Teachers and science consultants make use of Central Park as a nature laboratory. Students learn to use the scientific techniques necessary for accurate observation, problem-solving and recording. Classrooms have work areas for experimentation, science displays, and science libraries. A goal of the science program is to instill a critical understanding of the ethical questions surrounding scientific issues.

MCS is wired for Internet access and classrooms are networked. Beginning in the second grade, students have computer and Internet access available in their classrooms. Fifth through eighth graders must complete a four-year computer literacy course and older children are offered electives in computer graphics and design. An after-school computer class is offered to the 4/5's through fifth grades.

Computer use is directly related to the curriculum. For example, the seven- and eight-year-olds host their own website on Mammal Study; the eight- and nine-year-olds communicate via e-mail with the Zuni nation in New Mexico; shop students use AutoCAD to design woodworking projects, and the seventh graders produce a literary magazine, *Lit Mag.*, using desktop publishing.

Art, music and drama enhance the curriculum. Art is required of all students through sixth grade; seventh and eighth graders must meet a combination requirement in the arts, with additional electives available in each subject.

All students have weekly library classes. The library hosts presentations by visiting authors, such as Jamaica Kincaid, Milton Meltzer, Brian Pinkney and Vera B. Williams. It is also where class plays and family story-telling gatherings are held.

Children in the 4/5's through 7/8's have daily outdoor activities at a nearby playground or in the meadow at Central Park. There are structured group activities with a physical education teacher once a week either in the school's music room or in the park. The 8/9's through eighth grade have outdoor time in Central Park three times a week and a structured physical education class twice a week at the 92nd Street Y. There are elective classes in track, basketball and tennis for older students.

MCS owns a small working farm, located on 177 acres in the Catskill Mountains in Roxbury, New York. Students with their teachers, begin going to the farm in the spring of their 7/8's year. By fifth grade, they have three week-long trips a year. The farm acquaints students with a self-reliant way of life. "One of my favorite times was at the farm. My farm education gave me an appreciation for a completely different lifestyle, as well as teaching me various things like milking cows, tapping trees, creating textiles," says an alumna. The farm program leads to six graduation requirements: to milk a cow; to plan and cook an evening meal for the entire class and to bake bread or another yeast dough product without adult assistance; to identify birds, plants, animals and their tracks, to describe the life cycle of one animal; to produce an original textile from fleece to a finished garment, artifact or material; and to participate in a "town meeting" on an environmental issue. A recent graduate told us, "Looking back at my years at MCS, I realize that I loved everything about it. At the time I remember feeling that the school was so small and undeveloped. However, MCS had everything I needed. The diverse community and the close relationships with my teachers were experiences that I would not have gotten anywhere else."

Graduates: About half go on to the specialized public high schools; half go on to the independent schools including Riverdale, Fieldston, Friends, Dalton, Calhoun, Trevor Day; one or two students attend boarding schools such as Andover and Suffield

Marymount School of New York

1026 Fifth Avenue
New York, NY 10028
(212) 744-4486, FAX (212) 744-0163
website: www.marymount.K12.ny.us

All girls
Nursery–12th grade
Accessible

Ms. Concepcion R. Alvar, Headmistress

Uniform Lower School—Fall/Spring: blue cord jumper, white short-sleeved blouse, navy blue blazer or sweater. Winter: navy blue jumper, white or red turtleneck, navy blue sweater or blazer; pants option
Middle School—Fall/Spring: blue cord skirt, white short-sleeved shirt or blouse, navy blue blazer or seater Winter: plaid or gray skirt, white turtleneck blouse, navy blue blazer or green sweater
Upper School—Fall/Spring: blue cord skirt, white, pale yellow, pale pink, pale blue, or navy blue short-sleeved shirt and sweater, navy blue blazer. Winter: plaid or gray skirt, white, black, grey, navy blue, forest green, white, or pale yellow, pale pink or pale blue turtleneck/blouse and sweater or navy blue blazer; pants option

Birthday Cutoff Children entering at the nursery level should be 3 years old by August 31
Children entering kindergarten should be 5 by August 31st

Enrollment Total enrollment: 520
Nursery places: 16
Kindergarten places: approximately 25
Graduating class sizes: approximately 48

Grades Semester system
Letter grades begin in Class V. Grades are distributed each semester, interim reports are given in November and April at parent-teacher-student conferences twice a year
Departmentalization begins in Class VI

Tuition Range 2005–2006 $15,850 to $25,850, Nursery–Class XII
Additional fees for books and activities approximately $950
$1,050 lunch fee for kindergarten through Class VII

Financial Aid/Scholarship   Approximately $1.2 million dollars is
available in financial aid/scholarships to those who qualify
Approximately 27% of students receive some aid

Endowment   N/A

Diversity   Approximately 23% students of color
6 Prep for Prep students enrolled as of Fall 2004
32 nationalities are represented
Cultural Awareness Club, Diversity Committee, Bias Awareness
Training, Jazz Festival, Harambee Night, International Week,
Monthly Culture Celebrations, Senior Class trip to the U.S. Holo-
caust Memorial Museum, Native American Exchange Program;
Japan Exchange Program; China 2000 Program, Exchange pro-
grams with other Marymount schools in London, Los Angeles,
Paris and Rome; variety of conferences including: Asia Pacific
Americans Youth Association, Diversity Awareness Initiative for
Students, NYSAIS Diversity, NAIS-People of Color/Student
Diversity Leadership

After-School Program   Marymount's after-school program for K–III
requires an additional payment
After-School Activities Program: for grades kindergarten through
Class III, Monday–Thursday until 4:30 P.M., Fridays until 3:30 P.M.;
a variety of creative and recreational activities
Classes IV through VII offer a variety of sports and clubs
throughout the year including a musical dramatic production,
spring concert, Lessons and Carols, and instrumental recitals
Supervised Study Program, Monday–Thursday until 6:00 P.M. for
Kindergarten through Class VII

Summer Program   Marymount Summer Program: coed, ages 8–12,
open to students from other schools; five weeks, mid-June
through July; a variety of creative and recreational activities; *Performing Arts Camp:* acting, improvisation, dancing, singing, and
set design; the program culminates in the production of a full-
scale musical; *Science/Technology Camp:* exploration in laboratory

and technology centers, field trips; team sports and swimming are part of both programs

————

The Marymount School of New York was founded in 1926 as part of an international network of schools directed by the Religious of the Sacred Heart of Mary. The founder, Mother Butler, believed that women should be leaders in society and that, "the world never needed women's intelligence and sympathy more than it does today." The school became independently incorporated in 1969.

The Marymount School is housed in three adjoining Beaux Arts mansions on Fifth Avenue, part of the Metropolitan Museum of Art landmark district. The breathtaking ballroom on an upper floor serves as an auditorium, lunchroom and gymnastics/movement room. The Middle School is located at 2 East 82nd Street, a completely renovated six-story turn-of-the-century townhouse. Sixty-five percent of the student body is Catholic and thirty-two different nationalities are represented. Headmistress Concepcion Alvar attests, "Spiritual values, community service and liturgy are the moral thread that binds the school." Chapel service, held once a week, may be conducted by students of any faith. Students attend Mass at least six times a year. Students can participate in an exchange program with other Marymount Schools in Los Angeles, London, Paris or Rome.

Getting in: Parents applying for Middle and Upper School are invited to attend a Fall open house. Call for an application in September. Parents may schedule a tour before applying. Parents meet with the director of admissions and tour the school. On a separate date, applicants are interviewed individually at the school. Beginning in pre-kindergarten, ERB testing is required for admission. The school says it "thoroughly considers the unique qualities of each applicant including academic curiosity, humor, diligence, and sensitivity."

Parents: The parent body includes business people, artists, academicians, engineers, doctors, lawyers, researchers, educators, bankers, socio-civic leaders and government officials. Parents are an active and integral part of the school. They give tours as parent ambassadors, volunteer to read to children, accompany classes on field trips, etc. Activities sponsored by the Parents Association include parent meetings, spring benefit, Christmas Fair, Book Fairs, the Skating Party, the Mother/Daughter Book Club and others that strengthen school-family ties. Parents and alumnae give career seminars and offer their places of work for senior internships.

Program: The Lower School is composed of nursery through third grade. Each Lower School classroom has a head teacher and an assistant. The program is structured and traditional, but aims to be creative and dynamic. Organized learning centers are equipped with hands-on, interactive materials that encourage experimentation and collaboration.

Beginning in nursery school, Lower School students learn in the state-of-the-art science and technology laboratory with its child-size tables and stools.

Students are grouped according to skill levels in reading and math. Science and technology education begins at the nursery level in the state of the art science and technology laboratories. The children are taught by specialists in art, music, science, foreign language, computers and physical education.

Marymount has a unique relationship with the Metropolitan Museum of Art, ranking first among all city schools in the use of the museum as a learning resource. Other city resources that the school uses include the United Nations, Ellis Island, the Stock Exchange, the Central Park Zoo, the Metropolitan Opera, Lincoln Center, Sloan-Kettering Research Labs, the Staten Island Observatory and various galleries and museums as classroom extensions.

Each Lower School student has a big sister in the Middle or Upper School. This bond is strengthened throughout the year by trips, special events and collaborative academic projects. The recent project on water has been installed at the United Nations as part of their "decade of water" celebration.

According to the brochure, in Middle School, grades four through seven, "Each student is encouraged to develop and pursue areas of interest, to think honestly and critically about the world around her and to acquire a sense of social responsibility in school, at home and in her community." The integrated core curriculum gradually increases in the degree of departmentalization at each grade level. Research and study skills, with a focus on time management and organization, are emphasized.

French and Latin are introduced in Middle School, and there is a Class VII study tour in France. A leadership training program begins in seventh grade. Speech, debate and drama are incorporated into the program and students participate in weekly assemblies, chapel services and an annual drama production.

Marymount School integrates technology into the curriculum creatively, and appropriately. Technology provides multiple tools for gathering data, sharing information and completing assignments. The school has over 300 computers and numerous servers that are all networked—wired and wireless—on a dual platform system. All computers have direct access to the Internet via a T-1 connection. Through technology, students collaborate on curricular-based projects, master software, learn to use the Web for information, research, communication and publishing, and master a variety of computer-related materials such as scanners, digital cameras and digital probing equipment.

All staff and Upper School students have their own e-mail accounts; on-line courses are offered to Upper School students. Lower and Middle School students have class accounts that are under a teacher's supervision. There's a laptop program in art, library and science, and computer clusters are available for independent work, as well as "smart" classrooms for group work, a computer center for one-on-one computer work, and "one computer" classrooms for demonstrations and introducing new topics.

Upper School students take three years of laboratory science and ninety-five percent elect a fourth year of science. AP courses are offered in chemistry, biology, physics B and C, statistics, calculus AB and BC, English, French, Latin, Latin Literature, Spanish, Spanish Literature, American History, European History, Studio Art and Art History.

The Upper School consists of grades eight through twelve. In addition to French, Latin or Spanish students may choose to take Greek as a second language. Graphing calculators, computers, and other technological tools are used frequently in math, science and computer courses. The ninth grade team-taught Integrated Humanities Program links interdisciplinary themes in English, history, art history, religious studies, and studio art. Students visit the Metropolitan Museum of Art at least once a week. In the spring, seniors begin a five-week internship program, sponsored by the city, alumnae, parents, and friends, during which they are exposed to a wide range of careers. Students take four years of religious studies including World Religions, Social Justice, Hebrew and Christian Scriptures and Ethics. With the Director of College Counseling, seniors take part in a weekly senior career seminar hosted by alumnae who discuss their lives and work, as well as college placement.

All Marymount students are encouraged to participate in a variety of extracurricular activities, and they can select from a wide range of sports and clubs. Clubs include three publications, the Finance Club,

Simply Shakespeare, Philosophy Club, Set Design and Tech Crew, Forensics, Model UN, Mock Trial, Art Club, Student Government and more. Fourteen team sports are offered, including swimming, field hockey, tennis, golf, and fencing. In addition to varsity sports there are six junior varsity teams and Class VII/VIII teams.

At weekly assemblies, students make presentations and gather to hear various speakers address the school community. The alumnae sponsored Vincent A. Lisanti Speaker Series has brought in well-known speakers such as Pulitzer Prize winning author Jhumpa Lahiri, *Washington Post* foreign correspondent Robin Wright, the HIV/AIDs Prevention Organization's founder Sr. Tribebemaco, and many more.

Each year students from classes nine through twelve spend time at retreats. Ninth grade students travel to Frost Valley to bond as a class, sophomores focus on community service, juniors on leadership and seniors on ethical values/transition into colleges and careers. All students participate in community and school service. Students in tenth grade are required to contribute forty hours of volunteer service at hospitals, schools or agencies in New York City as part of their Social Justice class. Lower and Middle School students visit senior citizens and participate in holiday food drives. Students volunteer as student ambassadors, office assistants and peer tutors.

Federal Judge Katharine Sweeney Hayden, Class of 1959, described her experience at Marymount: "We were always encouraged to express ourselves! We read and read and learned to absorb, synthesize and digest large amounts of material. As a lawyer and judge, I draw upon the benefits of my Marymount training every day."

Popular College Choices   Barnard, Boston College, Boston University, Brown, Columbia, Cornell, Harvard, University of Virginia, New York University, Duke, Tufts, University of Pennsylvania, Vassar, Georgetown, Holy Cross, Wellesley, Loyola College, Princeton, Wesleyan, Villanova

Traditions   Founder's Day, Father-Daughter Square Dance, Vespers, Christmas Fair, Christmas Pageant, Lessons and Carols, Family Ice-Skating Party, Grandparents and Special Friends Day, the Book Fair, New Parents Reception, Field Days, Upper School retreats, Family Picnics, Athletic Awards Ceremony, Spring Benefit, Junior Ring Day, Alumnae Reunion, 100 Nights Senior/Faculty Dinner, Parent/Daughter Book Club, RSHM theme of the year, Senior Appreciation Week, Pre-season sports camp

Publications   Student Newspaper: *Chez Novs* (Middle School), *The Joritan* (Upper School)
Student Literary Magazine: *The Muse*
Yearbook: *The Marifia*

Community Service   Community Service is required of all students. Opportunities include participating in New York Cares Day and the Achilles Club; visiting the elderly at the Mary Manning Walsh Nursing Home and the Kateri Residence; and sponsoring food and toy drives for the families of New York's Incarcerated Mothers Program and fund raising for sister schools in Zimbabwe. Community service activities are coordinated through Campus Ministry, one of the largest student clubs at the school; students volunteer as student ambassadors, office assistants, and peer tutors; Class X contributes 40 hours of service as part of a social justice course; proceeds from dances, and local coffee houses support causes

Hangouts   Amity Coffee Shop, Metropolitan Museum of Art steps, Marymount teahouse

Metropolitan Montessori School
325 West 85th Street
New York, NY 10024
(212) 579-5525, FAX (212) 579-5526
website: mmsny.org

Coed
Pre-kindergarten through 6th grade
Accessible

Ms. Mary Gaines, Head of School
Ms. Jeanette Mall, Admissions Director

Birthday Cutoff   Children entering Pre-kindergarten must be 2.9 years old by September 1st

Enrollment   Total enrollment: 200
Pre-K and Kindergarten places: 30–40
Kindergarten places only: as available
Graduating 6th grade class size: 10–15

Tuition Range 2004–2005 $16,500 (primary half-day)–$20,300 (upper elementary)
New students registration fee: $1,500 paid upon enrollment

Financial Aid/Scholarship   12% of the annual budget is allocated to financial aid

Endowment $2.5 million reserve fund
A capital campaign was begun in 1996 to replenish this fund which had been used for the renovation of the new building

Homework   1st grade: 20 minutes three times a week
2nd grade: 30 minutes three times a week
3rd grade: 45 minutes three times a week
4–6th grades: 1½–2 hours four times a week

After-School Program   A variety of offerings including cooking, dance, and music enrichment; a before school program from 8 A.M. to 9 A.M. offers physical education, art, and chess classes

Summer Program   Weekly sessions from the first week after the
end of regular school year until Mid-July; for 3 to 6 year old children; activities include field trips, arts and crafts, outdoor games,
and wading pool activities

————

Metropolitan Montessori School, formerly St. Michael's Montessori, was founded in 1964 and took its name from its previous location
in St. Michael's Church on West 95th Street. In 1996, this popular
nursery and elementary school moved 14 blocks south into a stately
red brick building in the heart of the gentrified West Side. The new
building, an extensively renovated 1865 carriage house which once
belonged to William Randolph Hearst, provided the growing school
with an additional 5,000 square feet of space. Characteristic of this
nurturing school, when digging the foundation for the new building
they took great care to preserve two one-hundred-year-old London
plane trees at the building site.

Getting in: After submitting an application, parents tour the
school. Tours are given twice a week in the mornings, followed by a
question and answer period. Children are invited back with their parents for a small group visit with a primary teacher to "see if they are
developmentally ready to start." ERB testing is required for applicants
to first through third grades. Students of color constitute approximately 20% of the school.

Program: The brochure states that "While educational method
and classroom materials are firmly rooted in the philosophy of Dr.
Maria Montessori, the school addresses the unique issues and concerns of today's children." There are Montessori materials in carefully
planned classrooms, and parents are pleased with the way the school
imparts the academic groundwork necessary for later learning.

Mixed-age groups of children remain in the same classroom for
three years. Children in grades one through six keep journals for all
subjects and continue working in them as they move up through the
school producing a visible record of their academic progress. All students learn the fundamentals: math, grammar, spelling, and other disciplines. Grammar is taught through the use of symbols; it looks
difficult but most children have achieved mastery by third grade.
Attention is paid to individual development within a group setting and
students are ability-grouped for every subject. For instance, a first
grader might be reading at a fourth grade level, a sixth grader might

be doing seventh grade level math. There are clear curriculum guides for each grade level, and a syllabus, that is supplemented with guest speakers and field trips around the city and region.

Children leave their classrooms for music, art, French or Spanish, library and physical education. Quizzes and tests begin in fourth grade and students receive letter grades in all subjects. A checklist and narratives are sent home once a year and there are two parent/teacher conferences.

Community service and respect is an important component of a Metropolitan Montessori education. The school has a new Environmental Stewardship program featuring an intensive sixth grade study of the Hudson River with weekly outings on the school's boat, an organic lunch program, and a heightened awareness of environmental concerns.

Graduates: Metropolitan Montessori graduates attend various public and private schools including Allen-Stevenson, Brearley, Bronx Science, Browning, Buckley, Calhoun, Chapin, Collegiate, Columbia Grammar, Dalton, The Delta Program, Fieldston, Friends, Horace Mann, Hunter, Nightingale-Bamford, Riverdale Country, Sacred Heart, Spence, Stuyvesant, Hunter, Town and Trinity

The Nightingale-Bamford School

20 East 92nd Street
New York, NY 10128
(212) 289-5020 (main number), Admissions: (212) 933-6515
FAX (212) 876-1045
website: www.nightingale.org
e-mail: bscott@nightingale.org
info@nightingale.org

All girls
Kindergarten–12th grade
Accessible

Ms. Dorothy A. Hutcheson, Head of School
Ms. Barbara H. Scott, Director of Admissions

Uniform Lower School: navy or houndstooth jumper with white collared shirt

Middle School and Upper School: navy skirt, gray or light blue lightweight kilt, white blouse or turtleneck, navy knee socks or navy or white tights

Upper School: navy, light blue or gray skirt, solid-color collared shirt, solid-color ankle or knee socks or tights. Middle and Upper School: navy corduroy pants, Thanksgiving to Spring Break. Seniors can be out of uniform on Fridays and after Spring Break

No boots, clogs, or sandals

Birthday Cutoff "No strict birthday cutoff" but most girls are 5 by the start of school

Enrollment Total enrollment: 550
Kindergarten places: 40–42
Graduating class: approximately 40–45

Grades Semester system, K–IV detailed narrative reports and checklists. Comments continue through upper grades
Letter grades begin in 5th grade
Departmentalization begins in 5th grade
First final exam in 7th grade

Tuition Range 2005–2006 $25,810 to $27,665 all inclusive, kindergarten–12th grade. Optional fees include Parents Asssociation dues and a yearbook fee. A Tuition Refund Plan is available

301

Financial Aid/Scholarship   19% of students receive some form of aid
$1,890,000 was budgeted for financial aid in 1999–2000
Average grant per student is $18,694

Endowment $45 million
$54,545 per student

Diversity   24% students of color, NBS enrolls students from Prep for
Prep, TEAK, Albert G. Oliver and ABC (A Better Chance) among
other programs; C.A.F.E.: Cultural Awareness For Everyone
(school multicultural club that meets biweekly) sponsors assemblies, dinners, evenings with faculty advisors playing an integral role
Parents of C.A.F.E. (meets once a month) to plan meetings and
discussions; oversees a series of multi-cultural events throughout
the school year
Nightingale students participate in the Interschool Multicultural
Coalition which meets monthly

Homework   Lower School families are expected to read aloud with
their children from kindergarten on, a half hour a night reading or
being read to by the child.
Kindergarten: none
1st and 2nd: 1/2 hour
3rd and 4th: 45 minutes
5th and 6th: 1 1/2–2 hours with built-in study hall during the
school day
7th and 8th: 2 1/2 hours
9th–12th: approximately 45 minutes per subject a night (with one
homework-free subject per night) Weekly assignments are given
to encourage long-term planning

After-School Program   Hobbyhorse: coed, a variety of recreational and creative activities for kindergarten–Class 4 until 6 P.M.
Boys from Allen-Stevenson and St. Bernard's Schools also participate. 12–15 courses are offered including gymnastics, drama,
dance, chess, fencing, tennis, swimming, cooking, magic, knitting,
photography, computer; an additional payment is required.
Junior varsity and varsity sports for Middle and Upper School
girls, NBS participates in interscholastic athletic competition and
also the 12-team Athletic Association of Independent Schools.
The NBS gymnasium is usually open every Saturday for "pick-up"

games and practices and Nightingale girls can participate in Saturday sports at St. Bernard's School.

Some special interest clubs, Glee Club, drama and dance rehearsals, literary magazine and newspaper also meet after school. There is also music instruction available.

Summer Program   Sunny Days Program: coed, a June program for children ages 5–12 from 8:30 A.M. to 3:00 P.M.; trips, arts and crafts, swimming, computer, cooking and so on; open to children from the community; an additional payment is required

———————

The Nightingale-Bamford School began with classes held by Miss Nightingale in 1906. In 1919 Miss Nightingale was joined by Maya Stevens Bamford and together they founded The Nightingale-Bamford School in 1920. In 1989 the school began a $15 million renovation and expansion, completed in 1991. The school now has central air-conditioning, state-of-the-art science labs and a hi-tech theatre/ auditorium, a photo lab, three computer labs and a new cafeteria. "Formal, but not rigid, for very bright girls who know where they stand; not overly competitive," is the way one mother describes the school.

Traditional in the early years, Nightingale offers more choices later on. There is a conscious attempt to avoid gender stereotyping, while still instilling the social graces. They've struck a nice balance— keeping the best of the old while incorporating the new. "Academic rigor with a soul," says one parent.

Only the sixth head in the history of the school, Dorothy Hutcheson was preceded by the formidable Mrs. Edward McMenamin, who reigned for twenty-one years. "Ms. Hutcheson, now the senior head amongst the girls' schools, can be warm, accessible and fun and also strict and firm. She listens to and also takes action for the students," a senior said. Ms. Hutcheson knows each student by name and often greets them and shakes their hand as they enter the blue doors in the morning. A ninth grader told us, "Ms. Hutcheson cares and is very open to new ideas and suggestions. It's good to be able to tell her the way we feel." A full-time working mother, Ms. Hutcheson has already made her refreshing presence known in other ways too. She accepted the Student Government's proposal to add pants to the dress code (after allowing female faculty members to wear pants). She re-established the Senior Independent Study project which allows qualified seniors to drop some of their required courses and pursue in-depth a topic of their choosing. There is great emphasis on integrating technology into the classroom. One parent remarked after her tour, "At Nightingale there was a sign that said 'Have you checked your e-mail today?' " Nightingale's time to gather by division, a time to reflect, to make announcements, and to discuss issues of moral and ethical concern, was formerly known as "Prayers." By renaming it "Morning Meeting," which more accurately describes it, Ms. Hutcheson has shown that she is not afraid to break with tradition.

Getting in: One parent described NBS's application process as "warm and welcoming." Parents can arrange for a tour before applying. When the application is received, parents are given an appointment for a tour and an interview with a member of the admissions staff. On another date kindergarten applicants will have a group interview with Lower School teachers while their parents meet with Ms. Hutcheson or Mrs. Blanche Mansfield, the head of the Lower School. Middle and Upper School girls take their tours with student tour guides. (Significant points of entry in addtion to kindergarten are seventh and ninth grades.)

Individual interviews with a member of the admissions team or a division head are required. Girls do placement work during a separate testing visit held after school or on a Saturday morning. If admitted, girls and parents are invited to re-visit and spend time in the school. There are welcome parties for all new students and parents in the spring and early fall. A great deal of care is given to having families make a smooth transition to Nightingale. Preference is given to siblings and legacies, but they are not automatically accepted, and an active wait list is maintained after admissions decisions have been made. No letters of recommendation are required or desired as part of the process. Admission is based on the right academic match, not the correct social connections, they say. Nightingale has made a major commitment to diversity, and enrolls girls from a range of socioeconomic, ethnic and geographic backgrounds.

A mother who eventually chose NBS said that she "couldn't sit up straight enough at some of the other schools," and while she noticed "a lot of scarves on the parents at other girls' schools," she was impressed by "the sensible shoes" she saw at NBS.

Is there a typical student? It depends on whom you ask. According to one parent, "She has blond straight hair, uses little or no makeup and carries an L. L. Bean bookbag." Yet another parent told us the typical student is "earnest, engaging, vibrant and aware," referring to an Upper School student she felt exemplified NBS qualities. A tenth grader said "We are smart, involved in the life of the school and have learned to speak with confidence." Obviously!

A parent told us that NBS delivers "a ton of nurturing." She felt her daughter walked the line between "funny and fresh." Since it sometimes seems that outgoing girls receive the most attention, it was refreshing to see that Nightingale awards the Molly Hemmerdinger Scholarship Fund, in memory of Molly Hemmerdinger, "for support of a shy student with hidden potential." An NBS mother with two daughters at the school said she feels the school "is making little Eleanor Roosevelts out of the girls: self reliant, inner-directed and well versed." A father said, "They learn to be independent, to do for themselves." He also believes there is a hidden agenda, to teach the girls the social graces. He also said he thought "Nightingale makes feminists of the fathers."

Parents: The parent body is diverse and varies from class to class. "There are lots of mixed [religion] marriages," said one parent. Jewish and Christian holidays are observed. "When you give at Nightingale, you receive," said one parent. "It's good to be an involved parent and make yourself known." One father who admits he always shaves before attending a school event or dropping off his daughter, yet describes himself as "one of the youngest and loosest" parents there, said he enjoys serving on "Daddy Patrol" (safety patrol) and walking his daughter to school with other Nightingale fathers and daughters.

A mother remarked, "As a parent of color in the school, I wanted to be vigilant, vocal and visible. Nightingale has welcomed me and my daughter fully and made us feel comfortable and I've loved the C.A.F.E. dinners and volunteering for various committees."

The Parents Association plays an integral role in the life of the Nightingale community by providing communication among parents, staff, administration and faculty and by supporting the school. Many parents volunteer their time and talents for school activities and events such as Grandparents' Day, Father-Daughter breakfast, programs on parenting, Safety Patrol and the Book Fair. Other ways that parents are involved include speaking to classes and assemblies, asking friends with special areas of expertise to share them at school, inviting students to visit them on the job, singing at an all-School concert, performing in or helping with costumes and make-up for an all-School play, chaperoning class trips, volunteering in the library and cooking or baking for class get-togethers. In addition, the Parents Association sponsors the fair, a "Fathers Who Cook" dinner, and other major fundraising events to benefit the scholarship fund. There are other outings, including family picnics and skating parties. Courses are also offered for parents in the evening. One of the most beloved English teachers, Christine Schutt, who has just had her book of short stories, *Nightwork*, published by Knopf, has a parent reading/discussion group. Various faculty members will also teach classes in computers.

The Parents Association meets monthly to discuss issues of general interest; meetings are scheduled at convenient times for working parents, there is childcare provided and meetings are well attended. Mothers are listed by their first names with their husbands' names in parenthesis. Nightingale's Speaker Series is one of the best in the city. The series is sponsored by the Parents Association and seeks to address issues concerning girls' intellectual, social, and emotional development. Recent participants include Joan Jacobs Blumberg, author of *The Body Project*; JoAnne Deak, a specialist on "cliques" and girls' social development and author of *How Girls Thrive* (a NAIS publication, see *infra* page 481); and Catherine Steiner Adair, author of *How to Counter the Culture: the Challenge of Raising Healthy Girls*. The public is invited to attend these lectures, an example of the N-B sense of community extending beyond the schoolhouse. Parents also publish a very helpful monthly newsletter, *The Nighthawk,* which includes calendars, updates on what is going on throughout the School, and thoughts from Dorothy Hutcheson, the Head.

"Socially the school is low-key," said a parent. The kindergarten new parents' dinner is usually potluck. The fundraising functions are "a lot of fun," said another. Class coffees to discuss parent concerns at each grade level are held at the school throughout the year. A parent who summers in the Hamptons told us that there is an annual August picnic there for about seventy-five NBS families hosted by a member of the NBS board.

Program: A great deal of care and intelligent planning went into the physical renovation and updated curriculum at Nightingale, taking into account the latest research into how girls learn. Carol Gilligan, author of *In a Different Voice*, which examines the differences in girls' and boys' approaches to life and learning, was invited to speak to the Nightingale parents. Based upon some of this research, furniture in the math teaching rooms was changed. Even the rooftop playground is completely modernized with an emphasis on play that strengthens the upper body, an area where girls are traditionally weak. Math and science are taught by hands-on methods. Girls use math manipulatives and play math games such as chip trading. Extra math periods have been added at the Lower School level to permit special attention to spatial relations, another area where girls tend to need reinforcement.

According to the brochure, in the Lower School homeroom teachers in each grade teach reading, English, math, history, and geography, and all of them incorporate use of computers. Other Lower School faculty, specialists in their fields, teach science, music, art, library and physical education. Collaborative learning, an interdisciplinary approach and other innovative educational techniques are used in the Lower School. "Girls at Nightingale are not allowed to talk their way through understanding. When they study machines, they create an invention; they build castles in conjunction with the Class III study of the Middle Ages. This helps them with their spatial relationships and understanding of three dimensions." We saw a group of first grade girls on the floor doing a lesson with the Cuisenaire rods. Differences among teachers are also respected. Each classroom is set up differently, most with desks in groups, depending on the teacher's preference.

Kindergarten at Nightingale is described as "nurturing," and we would add "busy." Each kindergarten girl is paired with a senior "big sister" who shows her to her room. There are four full-time teachers with master's degrees. Basic number concepts and reading readiness are stressed. The structured reading program emphasizes phonics, but is eclectic, employing a Whole Language approach as needed. Girls keep journals, and practice their D'Nealian handwriting. They study communities, cultures, traditions and occupations and endangered animals. Kindergartners use the computer in their classroom, however, formal computer instruction begins in Class I.

Art and music are integrated into the curriculum. Girls go out for library (cozy and carpeted) and cooking (a recipe each week for each letter of the alphabet). There are museum trips and visits to other local points of interest, as well as talks by parents. Independence is valued, cooperation not competition encouraged.

The Lower School curriculum is integrated where possible. Kindergartners studying communities make clay houses; second graders studying Native Americans make kachina dolls, clay animals and learn techniques of weaving. Third graders studying the Middle Ages make unicorns, swords, stained-glass windows and prepare a medieval feast; fourth graders studying colonial America examine early American crafts including quilting, and make traditional toys like dried apple-head dolls with currant eyes and cotton hair.

The Lower School science lab houses a live snake and rabbit. In a lovely example of how the Lower School science curriculum is integrated, fourth graders studying skeletons in science also study the use of gesture in dance and art. Fifth graders construct papier-mâché whales in coordination with a unit on marine life in science.

Classes I through IV learn to read using an eclectic approach which stresses phonics but also employs elements of Whole Language and other programs. "Whatever will break the code," one teacher told us. Girls are expected to read every night. There is "daily practice in oral and written communication." A parent told us that her third grader has reading and writing homework every night. We saw work with corrected spelling hanging up on the walls; attention is paid to grammar and vocabulary too. By Class IV girls are writing book reports and short essays. Public speaking is reinforced through recitation in class, at assemblies and dramatic productions and on Class III's traditional Famous Women's Day. Older girls are required to take a public speaking course in Class XI.

History and geography in the Lower School "draw upon materials from the Boston Children's Museum, which provides authentic artifacts and activities." The curriculum guide says, "An interdisciplinary approach incorporates trips, projects, novels and discussions of current events." For instance: in Class III girls create a persona and deliver a "famous woman monologue" while dressed in costume; Class IV girls create a Plasticine terrain model to learn about features of landscape. Projects are researched in the state-of-the-art computerized library and on the Internet.

The school gathers together twice a week, once for Morning Meeting and once for assembly. Assembly is for discussion of current events or curriculum issues (environmental, cultural, political), with student participation.

In a music program, girls sing folk songs and songs from different cultures in various languages. They start with Orff instruments and the Kodaly system of sight-singing. They are introduced to opera and perform their own opera in Class IV. Girls learn to play the recorder in the Lower School. Music appreciation classes are offered at many levels. Each class presents musical performances integrated with other studies. Instrumental instruction after school is available.

There is always academic support available at NBS. In the Lower School, tutoring in-house is a way of fulfilling the students' community service requirement, and a learning specialist is assigned to the Lower

School. After school, "labs" in math, languages and science are available four days a week with Nightingale faculty for girls who would like enrichment or extra help. In class, if there are two teachers, one will offer individual help. A third grader told us there is an "I did it" board in her classroom to mark achievements large and small. A parent said, "They feel it's really important for every child to have one special thing to be an expert at." Exams preceded by one week of review begin in seventh grade. "Some girls fall apart and some sail through," a parent said.

In the Upper School there are built-in study halls during the school day and after-school lab time when teachers are available for extra help. While many describe Nightingale as rigorous, no parent or student described it as a sweatshop either.

The Lower School library was located on part of the Upper School floor to facilitate interaction between divisions. "Younger girls see what is ahead of them and the Upper School girls are reminded of where they came from," said an administrator. The girls consider it a real rite of passage to change from their Lower School tunics to the skirts and blouses of Middle and Upper School. Few girls seem to object to the dress code, saying that it removes competition in clothing. Girls do accessorize with jewelry and hair items.

Middle School at NBS is composed of Classes V through VIII. The Middle School homeroom teacher is the anchor. She says hello and goodbye each day and follows each girl's progress offering guidance along the way. The academic program includes English, history, math, science, Latin (beginning in Class VI), a choice of French or Spanish (beginning in Class V), visual arts, music, physical education, ethics and health. A parent said "They are building study skills all the way through." There is also a Middle School advisory program.

An extensive offering of extracurricular activities begins in Middle School. Choices include: A select chorus for Class VIII; the Middle School newspaper, *Bytes from the Bird*; the Middle School literary magazine, *Out of Uniform*; dance club, recycling, student government and drama. There is an annual Gilbert and Sullivan production and a musical performed with boys from Allen-Stevenson. Class VIII performs a Shakespeare play. Team sports begin and there is a no-cut policy.

Part of the Middle School art program is the photography requirement for fifth through eighth graders. The photo lab has fourteen processing stations. The high quality of the photography program is evident from the results published in the *Philomel*, the Upper

School literary magazine, it's some of the best photography in terms of selection, subject matter and quality of the printing. For five out of the past six years, *Philomel* won the Gold Crown, the highest award given by the Columbia University Scholastic Press Association for excellence in writing and production. The ceramics studio is open to fifth through twelfth graders.

The Upper School at NBS consists of Classes IX through XII. Tenth through twelfth graders have the privilege of being able to sign in and out of school during the day at the front desk, a privilege that can be revoked. The Nightingale school jacket cannot be purchased until tenth grade, and the entire class must raise enough money for every member of the class to purchase one.

Peer group counseling, in which a group of eight or nine freshmen meet with two seniors to talk about topical issues, such as dating or eating disorders, is a feature. Students pick their own faculty advisors in the Upper School, and interaction among the grades is encouraged.

Most seventh through ninth graders carry six courses per semester. NBS's commitment to math and science is evident in the four-year Upper School math requirement (algebra starts in eighth grade); three years of lab science are required. Eighteen credits are required for graduation, but most students complete more.

Grades are compared but not posted. The average grade is a C, one student said. Many teachers seem to go at the pace of the smartest students. Teachers notify students of forthcoming tests on a "test board" so that a balance can be maintained in students' workloads and schedules. Ninth grade is a big jump in difficulty from eighth grade. A new interdisciplinary unit in Class IX on Humanism continues the collaborative learning of earlier years. English, history, science, Latin, French, Spanish, art, music and drama teachers team-teach this unit.

"The Diversity and Richness of World Literature" is explored in tenth grade with a focus on the classics. There is a single semester requirement of public speaking. Eleventh and twelfth grade English electives include "Exiles: The Lost Generation in Paris" and "The New Woman in Shaw and Ibsen." After a solid grounding in modern history and non-Western history, eleventh and twelfth graders can take electives that include "Social Movements in the Twentieth Century," which examines reform movements, and "The Advent of Feminism, Black History and Civil Rights." Students can take advanced study in English, languages, history, math and science. A parent said: "The girls are intelligent about current events; they have common sense. There are articles in the school newspaper about how much the students know about government, for example."

The science department offers a course in Applied Chemistry, "ChemCom" ("Chemistry in the Community") as well as Environmental Science and Marine Biology and Genetics. The new science labs (separate biology, physics and chemistry labs) are state of the art, complete with an air vent for working with hazardous fumes, emergency eyewash and shower, and a laser disc player. NBS has three computer labs with both IBMs and Macs. Josh Feder, Director of Technology at N-B, facilitates the seamless integration of technology into the curriculum. "At Nightingale our goal is to have every teacher in every subject be fully capable of using technology to augment the best methods of instruction." Feder, author of *Teaching With the Web*, designs and conducts workshops on multimedia, the Internet, and Website design for teachers at N-B as well as other independent schools. The school is fully networked and all Middle and Upper School students have e-mail addresses.

NBS students can enroll in Interschool courses, design an independent course of study, or take courses at Barnard, Columbia or other New York universities with school approval. There are some intriguing opportunities for travel and study abroad: The Japan trip and the Latin study trip to Italy are offered over spring vacation. For those who want to spend a semester or full year abroad Nightingale has sister schools in Australia, France, Switzerland and Spain. Two juniors and a faculty member visit St. Paul's Girls School in London. For those who love the outdoors there is The Mountain School option, a Maine coast semester, and the Island School.

Socially, one student noted, there was a definite "in" group, and because the school is so small, it can be quite obvious. But a ninth grader said she had made "friendships that will last for life" at NBS and the "family-like environment makes learning more bearable and enjoyable." On the subject of single-sex education, one ninth grader told us, "You won't get distracted by a guy you like, it's easier to focus on schoolwork. On the other hand, it can be very hard to feel comfortable around boys because you don't get to spend much time with them." There are ample opportunities, however, for coed experiences through Interschool activities. At a recent open house an eleventh grader commented: "I came to NBS from a downtown coed school in ninth grade and I thought I'd really miss boys. Instead, I feel liberated. I don't have to worry about distractions during classes and I've kept my old friends who are boys and made new ones through Interschool activities."

Community service is a requirement and in the Upper School; twenty hours in school and twenty hours outside of school are mandatory, plus twenty hours in an activity of choice. The Nielsen Service Prize "endows an award to a student who makes a genuine commitment and important contribution in the area of social service." A student said, "Community service is stressed." NBS girls are very concerned about their community and participate in park cleanups, Special Olympics and AIDS walks and tutor at a nearby public school or volunteer at hospitals. In-house service includes library work, assisting the school nurse, stuffing envelopes, tutoring, helping in art studios or the science labs.

Popular clubs in the Upper School include C.A.F.E: Cultural Awareness for Everyone, and the Gender Issues group. Other choices include the Drama, Dance and Glee Clubs, Interschool plays and musicals, student government, yearbook, newspaper, literary magazine, Model U.N, Photo and Film Clubs, Debate Club and Environmental Club. The Glee Club had toured Italy where, among other events, they sang for the Pope, and in a recent year went to London. Students can work on stage crew or perform in the Interschool drama or musical. There is an Interschool drama production as well as an Upper School musical in alternate years. A recent production was *The King and I*, with NBS students playing both male and female roles. Faculty, staff and parents join the students in producing the Upper School musical. Those who have an interest in the visual arts can take a full year of studio art: design, painting, photography, video, ceramics, or sculpture.

The new gym has bolstered school spirit in the area of athletics. Teamwork is stressed. The Nightingale Nighthawks field strong teams in soccer, basketball, tennis, gymnastics, badminton and swimming.

During "Senior Weeks" girls take courses in everyday living including: "How to Manage Your Money," "How to Change a Tire," "Date Rape on Campus" and "Let's Experience New York's Cultural Life" with trips to the opera, ballet, Philharmonic or a play.

Seniors at NBS have the use of a senior lounge (all others hang out on the sunny back terrace), and can ride the school's elevators. There is an Honors and Awards Assembly the day before graduation: Achievements in academic areas are rewarded as well as effort and improvement.

Director of Admissions, Barbara Scott, describes NBS girls as "good-natured, hardworking, self-confident and well-prepared for life after NBS."

Nightingale alumnae feel a strong connection to the school. "During a recent visit last spring I was pleased by the friendliness, the familiarity of the uniforms, and the sense that Nightingale is still a superior learning environment and a safe haven in a frenetic city," said an alumna. According to a mother, "Nightingale is a traditional community where people really care about each other, the girls are well mannered and well behaved . . . there are high expectations and they measure up from day one."

Popular College Choices   Harvard, Brown, Cornell, Vassar, Wesleyan, Yale, Dartmouth, University of Pennsylvania

Traditions   All-School Fair (proceeds support the Scholarship Fund), Big Sisters/Little Sisters, singing holiday songs before winter break; the Daisy Ceremony for Class IV; Honors Assembly; Athletic Awards dinner; Class VII Gilbert and Sullivan production; Class VIII Shakespeare play with Allen-Stevenson; Festival of the Written Word assembly; Famous Women's Day; Field Day; Cum Laude and other weekly assemblies with a mix of prominent speakers and student-led discussions; Winter Concert; Homecoming, an annual soccer and volleyball game against Brearley on a Saturday in the fall; C.A.F.E. (Cultural Awareness for Everyone) dinners for students and their parents each year; The Father/Daughter breakfast; Grandparents Day; Book Fair

Publications   Middle School newspaper: *Bytes From the Bird*
Upper School newspaper: *Spectator*
Middle School literary magazine: *Out of Uniform*
Upper School literary magazine: *Philomel*
French Journal
Alumnae magazine
Yearbook
Monthly parents newsletter: *Nighthawk*

Community Service Requirement   20 hours in school, 20 hours of service in the community, and 20 hours in an activity of choice

Hangouts   The Upper School terrace, Jackson Hole Burger Restaurant, Ciao Bella, Yura's, Timothy's, senior lounge, Student Center

313

The Packer Collegiate Institute

170 Joralemon Street
Brooklyn, New York, NY 11201
(718) 875-6644, FAX (718) 875-1363
website: www.packer.edu

Coed
Nursery–12th grade
Not accessible

Dr. Bruce Dennis, Head of School
Ms. Valorie Iason, Director of Admissions,
Preschool and Lower School
Mr. Noah Reinhardt, Director of Admissions,
Middle and Upper School

Birthday Cutoff   Children entering at kindergarten must turn 5 in December
Children entering first grade must be 6 by August 31

Enrollment   Total enrollment: approximately 940
Kindergarten places: 25
First grade places: 10
Ninth grade places; 25
Graduating class size: approximately 75

Grades   Semester system:
K–4, detailed anecdotal reports and checklists
Letter grades begin in 5th grade; in addition, detailed anecdotal reports are sent twice a year

Tuition Range 2005–2006 $12,150 to $22,700, Nursery 3's–12th grade
Additional fees: under $300 for books (5th–12th grades only)

Financial Aid   30% of students receive some form of tuition assistance

Endowment $11 million

Diversity   25% children of color; Packer enrolls students from Prep for Prep, Albert G. Oliver and other diversity programs
Packer Collegiate has a Diversity Committee

Homework   Kindergarten and 1st grade: none
2nd grade: formal homework begins
3rd and 4th grades: 1 hour, each school night
5th and 6th grades: 1–2 hours
7th and 8th grades: 2–3 hours
9th–12th grades: 3–4 hours

After-School Program   Packer Plus is open to Packer Collegiate students only in kindergarten through 8th grade; a variety of creative and educational activities from 3:15 P.M. until 6:00 P.M.; for an additional charge
Packer Plus Courses are offered on a trimester basis and meet from 3:30–4:30 P.M. for eight weeks. Vacation Packer Plus Playgroups are available during Winter Break, Spring Break and between the close of school and the beginning of the summer day camp.
Extracurricular clubs and activities
Junior varsity and varsity athletic competition

Summer Program   Summer Camp: open to children from other schools; mid-June through the end of July; an additional payment is required

———

Founded in 1845 as the Brooklyn Female Academy, and endowed by Harriet Packer, The Packer Collegiate Institute is the oldest independent school in Brooklyn and was the first to offer higher education to young women. It became coed in the early seventies. Packer's architecturally unique landmark building boasts many beautifully renovated and connected new spaces that include a new Middle School, an Atrium, Commons, Arts Center, music rooms, theater, with retractable seating and tons of classrooms and more. In addition there is an elegant chapel with a 1906 Austin organ and nine Tiffany stained-glass windows. Chapel attendance is required once a week at which social, political, environmental and ethical issues are discussed. Packer also has an outdoor play area known as "The Garden." The style of the school is informal and there is no dress code. Hot lunch is available for grades three through twelve only.

Packer's diverse student body represents the five boroughs of New York City and the outlying metropolitan areas. Approximately 55% of Packer's Upper School students live in Brooklyn and 40% live in Manhattan. Parents say a distinct feeling of community exists among children of all ages and backgrounds and the faculty.

Getting in: Open houses are offered throughout the fall so prospective parents can tour the facilities and talk with students, faculty and administration. For pre-kindergarten through fourth grade applicants, Packer requires a completed application and fee with school and teacher evaluations when appropriate. Pre-school candidates, ages 3, 4 and 5, meet individually and in small groups. Applicants to kindergarten and first grade are interviewed and evaluated at the school to assess their aptitude and learning style. Candidates for grades 2 through 4 are interviewed at the school and tested at the ERB. Applicants for grades 2 through 4 also spend a day visiting a Packer class. Applicants to grades 5 through 12 have a personal interview and must submit previous school records, two teacher evaluations and results of the ISEE or the SSAT. There is a sibling and legacy policy for qualified candidates, but admission is not automatic. The main points of entry to the school are in kindergarten and ninth grades.

Program: The Lower School at Packer emphasizes an interactive, individualized, developmentally appropriate approach. The junior first grade program is a transition program for children who will turn six in the fall of the year. The transition program is like a kindergarten program in the fall semester and evolves into a beginning first grade program soon after the children return from winter break. The following year children move to first grade. Reading is taught using eclectic methods. "We use a wealth of materials to accommodate the variety of learning styles so characteristic of young children."

The Middle School at Packer begins in fifth grade. Students have one extended core class in English and history and another in mathematics and science. Computer, music, dance, theatre, chorus, gym and health round out the curriculum. All fifth graders must take a course called Frameworks which reinforces good study habits and skills such as note-taking, test-taking, research and so on. In sixth grade, some students, upon recommendation by their teacher, continue to build skills in a course called Language Extensions, with the expectation that they will begin foreign language in seventh grade. All other sixth graders begin study of a foreign language in French, Latin, or Spanish.

In seventh and eighth grades, the program is fully departmentalized. There are competitive sports teams and a variety of extracurricular activities from which to choose. Throughout Middle School homeroom teachers and advisors stay in close contact with both students and their families.

The laptop program provides all students in grades 5 through 12 with a varied grasp of techology and it's use. Packer has a wireless network and "Smart" classrooms.

Each Middle and Upper School student has an advisor who is a teacher in the school. The Peer Support program involves juniors and seniors who are selected to attend a leadership training seminar preparing them to meet with freshmen in small groups throughout the year to discuss their transition to high school.

In the Upper School, the freshman year is built around a study of major literary works. A collaborative program that involves faculty from the English, History, and Arts departments integrates the study of ancient civilizations through the Middle Ages. Freshmen also take a rigorous year of conceptual or computational physics, foreign language and mathematics. The interdisciplinary approach continues in the sophomore year as students study "The American Experience" from historical, literary and artistic perspectives. Chemistry, foreign language and mathematics complete the academic program. Students in their junior and senior years have many electives from which to choose, including AP courses in 17 areas. A junior year English course, biology, and Modern European History are requirements. The average class size in the High School is fifteen; the student-teacher ratio is 8 to 1 and the advisee to advisor ratio is 10 to 1.

Graduation requirements include four years of English and physical education; three years each of foreign language, mathematics, history, and sciences; two years of electives; two years of arts; one year of Health; and 45 hours of school and community service. Older students can participate in independent study, Senior Emphasis Program, Maine Coast Semester, High Mountain Institute, or a Cultural Exchange Program. Most seniors also use the second semester to work on a senior thesis.

Offerings in the arts are broad and include visual arts, photography, computer graphics, modern dance, orchestra, brass, choir, woodwind ensemble, jazz band and women's ensemble.

Clubs and organizations available to students include Amnesty International; Brothers and Sisters; Chorus (the Packer Chorus has been on two European Tours during the past four years.); Debate; Mock Trial; Model Congress; Multicultural Student Association; Drama Club, SAFE (feminist club); Packer Civil Liberties Union and the Social Action Committee; Student Government; and various school publications. There are numerous athletic teams in Middle and Upper School, including a Middle School coed soccer team, girls' volleyball, gymnastics, basketball, and softball, and boys' soccer, basketball, baseball, volleyball, tennis and squash.

Popular college choices   Brown, Harvard, Yale, Cornell, Wesleyan, Vassar, Dartmouth, Columbia, Connecticut College, Oberlin

Publications   Art and literary publication: *Packer Current Items*
Yearbook: *The Pelican*
Newspaper: *The Prism*

Community Service Requirement   45 hours in the Upper School (9th–12th), tenth grade service project at a day care center, senior center, or soup kitchen

Hangout   The B, McDonald's around the corner

Poly Prep Country Day School
Coed
Nursery–12th Grade
Not accessible

Poly Prep Lower School
50 Prospect Park West
Brooklyn, NY 11215
(718) 768-1103
website: www.polyprep.org
(Nursery–4th Grade)
Laura A. Schweizer, Head of Lower School
Pat Montero, Director of Lower School Admissions

Poly Prep Country Day School
9216 Seventh Avenue
Brooklyn, NY 11228
(718) 836-9800
website: www.Polyprep.Brooklyn.ny.us
(5th–12th Grade)
David B. Harmon, Headmaster
Lori W. Redell, Director of Admissions

Birthday Cutoff   Children entering nursery school must be 2.3 years old by September 1st;
Children entering kindergarten must be 5 years old by September 1st

Enrollment   Total enrollment: 960
Nursery–4th grade: 192
Nursery places: 25
K–4th grade places: 15
5th grade places: 35–40
6th grade places: 30
9th grade places: 35–45
Graduating class size: Approximately 115
45 Prep for Prep students enrolled as of Fall 2004

Tuition Range 2005–2006 $6,880 to $22,600, ½ day Nursery–12th grade
Additional fees: for lunch and graduation for grades 5th–12th approximately $850
No additional fees for grade N–4th

For grades 5 through 12, transportation for students from Manhattan, Staten Island, Brooklyn and Queens is provided at no extra charge.

After-School Program   Lower School, arts, sports, languages, electives program, Monday–Friday for K–4th grades, an additional payment is required; for grades 5th–12th, instrumental music, debate, dance, extracurricular activities and clubs, Varsity and Junior Varsity athletic competition.

Summer Program   For grades 5th–12th, Day Camp, Performing Arts Camp, Sports Camp, Science Camp and Computer Camp; from the end of June until the beginning of August; open to students from other schools; an additional payment is required

———

Founded in 1854, as part of the Country Day School Movement, Poly Prep has been located on a twenty-five acre campus in the Dyker Heights area of Brooklyn since 1917. The Lower School building or "castle" is located in a Park Slope mansion that's cozy and intimate. Children visit neighborhood shops, bakeries and do mapping exercises and enjoy playtime in nearby Prospect Park. The campus has a new science building, playing fields, a theatre, swimming pool, tennis courts, squash courts and a new fitness center and a dance center. ERB testing or the SSAT is required for admissions. The school is becoming increasingly popular and admissions are competitive.

Approximately 30 percent of students in grades five through twelve come from Manhattan and approximately 12 percent come from Staten Island. There is a dress code for fifth through twelfth grades. Hot lunch is provided.

The school's motto, *Virtus Vitrix Fortunae,* or "Hard Work Conquers the Vagaries of Fortune" is as relevant now as it ever was. It's one of our favorite school mottos. Poly Prep is diverse—children of color represent almost a third of the student body.

Getting in: Parents may tour the school, meet faculty and ask questions before applying, but call early as tours fill fast. All tours start at 9 A.M. and are for parents only. For children applying for nursery, pre-kindergarten and kindergarten, parents are asked to send a copy of the child's birth certificate. Separate appointments for interviews will be scheduled for parents and children after applications are received.

The Poly Prep Lower School is located in an historic 12,000 square foot mansion overlooking Brooklyn's Prospect Park. The Lower School is planning to build an extension which will house additional classrooms and a large, multipurpose space for dance, performance, physical education classes, and assemblies and also serve as a cafeteria. Weekly chapel meetings for the entire school are held in the Memorial Chapel on the Bay Ridge campus that was built in the early 1900's.

The Lower School curriculum draws on both traditional and progressive teaching methods. For example, second graders learn about symmetry by playing symmetry games, and studying symmetry and symbolism in Native American art and constructing Kachina dolls.

Writer's Workshop starts in third grade and by fourth grade students are analyzing chapter books and strengthening vocabulary by studying common Greek and Latin roots. Math starts with an exploration of patterns and shapes in kindergarten and extends to finding perimeter, volume and area by fourth grade.

Middle School at Poly, grades five through eight, is structured and traditional. Students take English courses that stress reading and writing, math is taught through algebra I as well as science, geography, American history, "Kingdoms and Cultures," and "Journeys." French, Spanish and Latin are offered. Art, computers and technology are thoughtfully integrated into the curriculum.

The High School program offers support, structure and rigor. There's an advisory/dean program that starts in Middle School and extends through High School where every student has hat least one and sometimes two advisors or deans. Poly is a proponent of the AP program and offers AP courses in almost every discipline. Last year, Poly boasted six Merit Scholar semifinalists. Poly has relationships with foundations that subsidize travel and require students to act as ambassadors, not just tourists. Students have traveled to Japan, India, Argentina, France, Turkey, Greece, Cuba and Italy.

Popular college choices Wesleyan, NYU, Columbia, Cornell, Amherst, University of Pennsylvania, Boston College, Johns Hopkins, Lehigh, Smith, New York University

Professional Children's School

132 West 60th Street
New York, NY 10023
(212) 582-3116, x135 Admissions answer line,
x112 Admission Director
website: www.pcs-nyc.org

Coed
4th–12th grade
Partially accessible

Dr. James Dawson, Head of School
Sherrie Hinkle, Director of Admissions

Birthday Cutoff   None; applications are accepted at various times during the year

Enrollment   Total enrollment: 190
4th grade places: 10
Graduating class size: variable, from 45–60

Tuition Range 2004–2005 $21,500 to $24,000, 4th grade–12th grade
Additional fees for books and supplies total approximately $500

After-School Program   Extracurricular activity groups are formed if there is enough interest in the student body

Summary Program   None

Professional Children's School was founded in 1914 as an academic program for children appearing in vaudeville or on the Broadway stage. Today, Professional Children's School is the only fully accredited independent school providing a college preparatory curriculum for children actively involved in the performing and visual arts as well as competitive sports. (It is to be distinguished from LaGuardia High School for the Performing Arts, one of the New York City specialized public high schools, depicted in the movie *Fame*.)

Applicants must have a serious interest in the arts/sports and academic ability—no auditions are required for acceptance. A transcript, personal interview, standardized testing, teacher references, and a visit complete the application process. About 40 percent of the student body receives partial financial aid.

Students follow a regular school day but the periods are slightly shorter. The school day ends at 2 P.M. so that students can go on to professional activities.

A Guided Study Program is available for students whose professional commitments keep them away from the classroom for an extended period.

Approximately 75% of Professional Children's School graduates attend college immediately after graduation on a full or part-time basis; another 15% go on to college after a professional career.

Popular College Choices: Barnard, Bowdoin, Brown, California Institute of the Arts, Carnegie Mellon, Columbia, Dartmouth, Johns Hopkins, Middlebury, NYU, Princeton, Sarah Lawrence, Skidmore, SUNY, Vassar, Wesleyan, Yale

Rabbi Arthur Schneier Park East Day School
164 East 68th Street
New York, NY 10021
(212) 737-6900
FAX **(212) 570-6348**

Coed
2's–8th grade
Accessible

Rabbi Edward Abramson, Head of School
Mrs. Toby Einsidler, Administrator

Birthday Cutoff   Children entering at the nursery level must be 2 by August 31
Children entering kindergarten must be 5 by December 31

Enrollment   Total enrollment: 300
2's places: 35
Kindergarten places: 10
Graduating class size: approximately 12

Tuition Range 2005–2006 $3,350 to $18,650, Nursery 2's (two half days)—8th grade, additional fees: $300 for 2's to $1,800 for 8th grade
There is a discount for synagogue members and siblings
A contribution of $500 is requested
Financial Aid is available for those who qualify

After-School Program   For Park East students only; a variety of creative and recreational activities Monday–Thursday from 3:30 P.M. to 4:30 P.M., 1:30 to 3:00 P.M. on Fridays; an additional payment is required

---

The Park East Day School was founded by Rabbi Arthur Schneier.

Park East's newly renovated eight-story school building includes classrooms, a science laboratory, computer center, art studio, library, auditorium, cafeteria, gym and outdoor playground. The program combines Jewish traditional religious values with a demanding secular curriculum.

Getting in: Students come from diverse Jewish backgrounds. ERB testing is required for admission to kindergarten and above. Admissions decisions are based on observation of the children, an interview with the parents and ERB test results.

Program: There are two teachers in each kindergarten classroom. The program is geared to the individual child's readiness and includes beginning reading and personal writing. A hot kosher lunch is served beginning in kindergarten. Kindergarten students eat lunch with their teachers in their classrooms. First through eighth grades eat together in the school cafeteria.

Class size from first grade through eighth grade averages 15 students. Beginning in first grade, students have a dual curriculum, with part of the day devoted to secular studies and part of the day devoted to Hebrew/Judaic studies. Formal Hebrew instruction begins in this year. Students are introduced to Hebrew grammar and vocabulary, Jewish culture, Torah, prayer and holidays. Both boys and girls participate equally in prayers. Thematic studies (Holocaust, immigration and the history of modern Israel) are integrated throughout. The curriculum is supplemented by trips to museums, Jewish theatre productions, and the study of Jewish authors. There is weekly instruction taught by specialists in science, computer, library, art, chess, gym and music.

Students who show proficiency in math receive enrichment several times a week. Park East students have the opportunity to participate in city, state and national math and chess competitions throughout the year. Students with a special interest or proficiency in English are enriched with in-depth assignments. Beginning in third grade students can attend a weekly book discussion club moderated by one of the teachers. There is a learning center staffed by a specialist for students who need strengthening in Hebrew, reading and mathematics.

The artist-in-residence program exposes students to various facets of the arts. Guests have included a classical pianist, a songwriter, a radio announcer, an actor, a stamp collector, an opera singer, a cellist and a designer. Literary Week, in November, is a school-wide celebration of books. Lecturers have included publishers, book designers, authors and illustrators.

A spirit of community is reinforced through various school assemblies such as the Biography Fair for grades 3 through 5, the first grade Siddur play, the second grade Chumash play and the Science, Math and Technology Fair presented by students in grades 1 through 8.

Extracurricular activities include: Chess, science, computer, painting, museum club, basketball, creative writing, cooking, costume design, team sports, softball and mathematics.

Graduates attend a variety of NYC private and specialized public high schools. Recent choices include Ramaz, Dalton, Columbia Grammar and Prep, UNIS, Solomon Schecter High School, Yeshiva of Flatbush, Elisabeth Irwin High School, Bronx Science, Stuyvesant, LaGuardia School for the Performing Arts, and Frisch High School.

Traditions Annual Purim Carnival, Chanukah party, Literary Week, Sukkoth dinner celebration, participation in the Salute to Israel Day Parade, Student Art Exhibit

Community Service Requirement Park East students are encouraged to participate in a wide-range of community service activities such as visiting nursing homes, helping to support synagogues on the Lower East Side, organizing coat drives, collecting Passover foods for Project Dorot, and entertaining the elderly during holidays

Ramaz

Lower School
125 East 85th Street
New York, NY 10028
(212) 774-8010

The Rabbi Haskel Lookstein Middle School
114 East 85th Street
New York, NY 10028
(212) 774-8040

The Rabbi Joseph H. Lookstein Upper School
60 East 78th Street
New York, NY 10021
(212) 774-8070
website: www.ramaz.org

Coed
Nursery–12th Grade
Accessible

Rabbi Haskel Lookstein, Principal
Mrs. Daniele Gorlin Lassner, Dean of Admissions

Birthday Cutoff   Children entering at the nursery level must be 3 by August 31
Children entering kindergarten must be 5 by August 31

Enrollment   Total enrollment: 1,133
3's places: 30
Kindergarten places: 25
9th grade places: 60
Graduating class size: approximately 100–110

Tuition Range 2005–2006 $12,100 to $14,100, nursery 3's–12th grade
Ramaz has a foundation fund for financial aid: nursery, $1,500; K–12, $2,500; suggested contribution to the Ramaz Foundation for each child is from $2,000 to $3,000; additional fees: for registration, lunch, student activities and overnight trips approximately $3,725

After-School Program   Lower School: a variety of creative and recreational activities until 5:00 P.M.; an additional payment is required

327

Upper School: a variety of creative and recreational activities until 6:00 P.M.; there is no additional charge

Summer Program   None

Ramaz is an Orthodox Jewish day school founded in 1937 by the late Rabbi Joseph H. Lookstein. The initials (in Hebrew) of the rabbi's name make up the acronym that is the school's name. Ramaz is committed to modern or centrist Orthodox Judaism. Applicant families may also be "conservative and committed" but all families keep kosher homes. The school just added a fully renovated top-of-the-line Middle School on East 85th Street to its facilities. Formal Hebrew language instruction begins in first grade. Half of the school day is devoted to Judaic studies and half the day is devoted to the general studies curriculum. Although all classes are coed, the sexes are separated during morning and afternoon prayers. Ramaz has a dress code and a kosher hot lunch is served.

Popular College Choices   Barnard College, Columbia University, Harvard University, New York University, University of Pennsylvania, Yale, and Yeshiva and Stern Colleges of Yeshiva University

Regis High School

55 East 84th Street
New York, NY 10028
(212) 288-1100, FAX (212) 794-1221
website: www.regis-nyc.org

All boys
9th–12th grade
Not accessible

Rev. Vincent Biagi, S.J., Principal
Mr. Eric P. DiMichele, Director of Admissions

Birthday Cutoff   None

Enrollment   Total enrollment: 520
9th grade places: 135
Graduating class size: approximately 125–130

Tuition   None: all students receive tuition-free scholarships and pay only laboratory and activity fees of approximately $300 to $400

After-School Program   A variety of extracurricular activities until 5:30 P.M.
Varsity sports competition in the Catholic High School Athletic Association

Summer Program   None

———

Regis High School was founded in 1914 by the Society of Jesus as a tuition-free school for Catholic boys. Regis High School is sustained through the original bequest of a generous parishioner of the Church of St. Ignatius Loyola as well as contributions from alumni.

Regis High School is highly selective. Only baptized Catholic eighth grade boys may apply. Regis does not accept transfers. The admissions process is rigorous: Applicants must score in the ninetieth percentile and above on standardized tests and have an outstanding elementary school record. In addition, students must sit for the Regis scholarship examination. Semifinalists are interviewed by faculty and alumni, and approximately half of this group is selected for admission to Regis. Financial need is one factor in the admissions process.

Regis offers a traditional liberal arts curriculum. The pace is accelerated, and the work load and expectations are most demanding. Four years of theology are required as well as participation in community service projects, liturgies and religious retreats. Catholic holidays are observed.

The average combined SAT score for the Class of 2004 was 1410.

Popular College Choices   Harvard, Columbia, Cornell, Fordham, Georgetown, Yale, New York University, Johns Hopkins, Williams, Princeton, Holy Cross, Boston College

The Riverdale Country School

Upper School or Hill Campus
5250 Fieldston Road
(at West 253rd Street)
Riverdale, NY 10471-2999
(718) 549-8810, FAX (718) 519-2795
website:www.riverdale.edu

Lower School or River Campus,
Spaulding Lane (between Independence and Palisades
Avenues)
Riverdale, NY 10471
main number (718) 549-7780, FAX (718) 432-4793
admissions (718) 432-4782 FAX (718) 432-4794

Coed
Pre-kindergarten–12th grade
Not accessible

Dr. John R. Johnson, Headmaster
Mr. Kent Kildahl, Head of the Upper School
Mr. Sandy Shaller, Head of the Lower School
Ms. Ridie Markenson, Director of Admissions
Ms. Sarah Lafferty, Director of Lower School Admissions

Uniform   Lower School: casual and neat, turtleneck, shirts with collars, no logos, no white T-shirts
Upper School: appropriate attire

Birthday Cutoff   Children entering pre-kindergarten must be 4 by September 1
Kindergarten: children entering kindergarten must be 5 by September 1

Enrollment   Total enrollment: 1,080
Lower School: 375
Middle School: 230
Upper School: 475
Kindergarten places: 44
6th grade places: 30–35

9th grade places: approximately 45
Graduating class size: approximately 110–115

Grades   Semester system
Kindergarten–6th: detailed anecdotal reports and checklists
Letter grades begin at the end of 6th grade
7th–12th: grades with comments twice a year; grades alone twice a year
Modified departmentalization in 5th–6th grade
Full departmentalization by 7th grade
First midterms and finals begin in 7th grade

Tuition Range 2005–2006 $24,500 to $29,500, pre-kindergarten–12th grade
Riverdale has a monthly payment option and a quarterly payment option running from June to March
Extended repayment plan (educational loan)
Tuition refund plan (insurance)
Busing from Manhattan is approximately $2,000 for Lower School students, approximately $1,000 for Upper School students

Financial Aid/Scholarship   20% of students receive some form of tuition assistance
$2.8 million available

Endowment   Approximately $22 million

Diversity   20% children of color
Riverdale enrolls students from the Albert G. Oliver program, and Prep for Prep as well as other diversity programs
Lower School multicultural literature program at all grade levels
School-wide diversity committee meets 3 times a year and is chaired by two parents and co-chaired by the school's diversity coordinator

Homework   1st: 15 minutes, Monday through Thursday
2nd and 3rd: 30–40 minutes, Monday through Thursday
4th: 45 minutes–1–1½ hour, Monday through Friday
5th and 6th: 1–2 hours a night
7th and 8th: 2–2½ hours a night

9th–12th: average of 3½ hours per night; more for those taking many APs
Assume 40 minutes per subject per night
In addition, parents of young children in Lower School are encouraged to read to their children every night; there is a Lower School recommended reading list

After-School Program   Riverclub: For grades Pre-k through 6th; 3:30–5:00pm; a variety of creative and recreational activities for an additional payment; transportation home is available
Grades 7–8: intramural and interscholastic sports
Grades 9–12: interscholastic sports, theatrical productions

Summer Program   The Summerbridge Program: a privately funded 6-week-long program (established in 1992) that prepares 90 talented Middle School students from the inner city for competitive high schools; it is tuition-free and taught by Riverdale High School students as well as college students under the guidance of two directors and several other teachers.
Summer camp: 7 weeks, for ages 6–11; sports, nature and creative activities; for an additional payment

———

After coming upon an intoxicated schoolboy in the street in New York City, Riverdale Country School's founder, Frank Hackett, decided to found a school in the countryside, far from the degrading influences of city life and offering abundant opportunity to play in the open air. Hackett coined the term "independent school" to distinguish his school from the "hoity-toity private schools." From the outset, Hackett had a vision of a "world school" with an "international curriculum."[*]
Today RCS offers a strong community with a diverse population. The curriculum is grounded in liberal arts basics. Parents say academic expectations are high and many types of students can find success here, but they must be committed to doing the work that is expected of them. Moreover, gaining admission to RCS has become increasingly competitive. "It happened because we've worked hard, and continue to work hard, to balance our strong academic program

[*]*The Quickened Spirit,* by Allen Hackett (The Riverdale Country School, New York City, 1957), p. 51.

with a genuine understanding of developmental issues. We have a well articulated academic program and an integrated ethics and values program called C.A.R.E. (Children Aware of Riverdale Ethics) package and we're fortunate to have a beautiful campus which we use both recreationally and as part of our academic program. We're a school that never stops refining itself," says Sandy Shaller, Head of RCS's Lower School.

The Lower School consists of grades pre-kindergarten through-fifth. At RCS's Lower School "There really is no typical student. Sixty per cent of our students come from Manhattan. The others come from The Bronx, Westchester or Northern New Jersey." One parental concern is that a car is necessary if you send your child here. Not true. Parents can easily find a ride to Riverdale for Parents' Night, two conferences, one music program, three parenting evenings and one play (in each grade), the Academic Fair, Book Fair and the carnival.

Getting in: Respect and consideration for the individual is a hallmark of RCS, beginning with the admissions process. RCS is one of very few schools to grant each Lower School applicant a one-on-one interview with either the Director of Admissions or one of her assistants. Continued interest in the Lower School by an ever-increasing number of qualified applicants has made it more difficult than ever to be accepted at RCS. Children who are shy in a group of strangers have nothing to fear here. "We don't have a mold that children must fit into," says a member of the admissions staff. The mother of a girl who transferred from a single-sex school said, "My child has never been negatively typecast here."

Cake, cookies and hot coffee greet you on the morning of your tour. Leave the Chanel suit at home, and it will not count against you if your husband cannot make it to Riverdale for the tour. Please don't brag about *your* many accomplishments; RCS is not scrutinizing the parents.

Admission to the Upper School is also very competitive. The RCS Upper School admissions staff are personable and friendly and offer students and parents a one-on-one interview with either Ridie Markenson, Director of Admissions, or one of her associates. "Careful attention is paid to making sure that RCS is the right personal and academic fit for each applicant," says Ms. Markenson. Once admissions decisions have been made, RCS maintains a small selective wait list.

Riverdale's pre-kindergarten program, at the River Campus, is helpful for parents of children with borderline birthdays and parents who know from the start that they want to send their children to Riverdale.

Parents: There isn't a typical student, nor is there a typical parent at RCS. All types can feel comfortable here. The class cocktail party might be held in an apartment on Park Avenue or on Riverside Drive. "There are as many Gucci loafers as there are Birkenstocks," one parent said after attending several school functions. Parent involvement is welcomed and parents can volunteer to go on class trips, work in the library or help teach computer. Communication between teachers and parents is just a phone call away, and one parent said her children's backpacks are always full of correspondence from Riverdale. One mother said, "A note came home the first day homework wasn't done." The school's bus service says they will drop off homework at your door "every day if necessary" if your child misses school (Lower School only).

Program: The Upper, or Hill Campus, serves grades seven through twelve, and the Lower School, or River Campus, serves pre-kindergarten through six. At the Lower School learning is more experiential; the Upper School is more traditional and structured.

Each morning as the younger children arrive at the River Campus, Sandy Shaller, Head of the Lower School, is there to greet them. He knows every child (and nearly every parent) by name, and is involved in almost every aspect of the Lower School. Parents say, "Mr. Shaller *is* the Lower School." Almost all prospective parents have a chance to ask Mr. Shaller questions about RCS, either when they tour or certainly after acceptance. Mr. Shaller and Mr. John Matthews (assistant head of the Lower School) each teach a class a day. At the 1998 Spring Carnival, with booths operated by each class relating to the theme "Broadway Theatrical Productions," Mr. Shaller roamed the campus as The Phantom of the Opera, "complete with mask, black costume, hat and cape," said one parent.

An architecturally eclectic group of buildings make up the River Campus. The latest addition is a three-story, twelve-classroom building with a 6,000-square foot gymnasium (designed by an alumna whose sons and daughter attend RCS). The Perkins Building houses an auditorium, library, classrooms, administrative offices and science resource room. The Junior Building contains admissions, the cafeteria, a computer complex and music classrooms. The Senior Building (Arts Building) houses two art studios, special music classes and support services. In addition, there are four newly resurfaced tennis courts, a soccer/football field, an environmental education area, patios and a well-designed play area. The River Campus is large enough to accommodate all these facilities in one place, and intimate enough to feel like a community. Children have the freedom to jump rope, build a snowman, enjoy the playground or throw a football at recess, depending on the season. Students are not allowed to wander around the River Campus alone; they are always well supervised, particularly at busing time.

Like a traditional elementary school, RCS has recess (formal recess ends after third grade), three gym periods each week and a health class. "It's an intense day and at recess there is an explosion of energy. It's a country campus and we use it." says Mr. Shaller. Each grade puts on a music and drama performance and there are bi-monthly assemblies where folk songs are occasionally sung. Pre-kindergarten and kindergarten at Riverdale stress readiness and provide individualized attention. Classes in pre-kindergarten through first grade all have a head teacher and an assistant teacher. There is traditional circle time, along with job charts and journal writing with invented spelling. Since the school is in a country setting, much attention is paid to the study of nature and environmental issues. For example, every Lower School student gets three seed pots and plants them in the wetlands area and will have a hands-on opportunity to work on the grounds. Pre-kindergarten and kindergarten children have garden plots where they plant flowers and vegetables as part of the Spring science program. Nearly every kindergarten and first grade class has a pet: guinea pigs, turtles or fish. Math instruction is hands-on in the early years. One kindergarten mother came in to make pizza for a math project that included grating the cheese and measuring the circumference of the pizza (she brought her own homemade sauce).

By first grade, formal academics are introduced and the teachers have serious expectations. For those who need strengthening there is the Small Group Reading Program. By first grade there are daily homework assignments four times a week. The Lower School administers the CTP III (a standardized test that measures academic skills and compares the test scores to other independent schools' test scores).

In second grade there is one teacher, and reading and math skills continue to develop and expand. There is ability grouping for reading in grades 1–5, and ability grouping for math in grades 2–6. Foreign language is introduced in third grade; those who need strengthening in language arts take "Fundamentals of Writing," in fifth grade. Writing is stressed in all subject areas, and creative expression is encouraged. The Lower School has its own publication called the

Rivulet. In sixth grade, students pick topics and learn how to research and write term papers. The first final exam is given in sixth grade.

Many class trips are scheduled, including a train trip for kindergartners up the Hudson for a picnic lunch and an annual three-day/two night overnight for sixth grade. All grades make use of the city's resources, museums, and art opportunities. Art, music, foreign language or science teachers accompany trips to integrate their areas of expertise with the classroom teachers'.

Sixth graders are introduced to independent research through an inquiry-based research project. Students are taught how to refine their topic, take notes, isolate facts on index cards with titles, write outlines, and produce a final documented paper. Modified departmentalization begins in fourth grade but is not complete until seventh.

Computer study at Riverdale is strong. The school has a fiber optic cable that connects all of the buildings and allows the RCS community to gain access to the Internet in all of the classrooms. The use of the Internet is curriculum driven and is primarily for educational purposes. An "Acceptable Use Policy for Technology and Computer Networks" is sent to all Riverdale families to inform parents of possible issues concerning the use of this technology. For parents who aren't as computer savvy as their children, RCS provides parents with on-line (Internet) and off-line (books, videos, etc.) materials, a Parents Association course on computers and technology, and a list of books that offer guidance to new users. Almost all members of the administration, teachers and Upper School students have e-mail addresses. Lower School students do not presently have e-mail accounts, but e-mail can be sent through their teachers. A publicly viewable list of e-mail names at RCS is in the works. General queries can be sent to admin@riverdale.edu or postmaster@riverdale.edu.

There is a beautiful new computer lab and several mini-labs on both campuses. In addition, there is an updated computer room with twenty laptops and twenty IMACs for all students. RCS also has a Computer Coordinator (at the Lower School), a Director of Technology (at the Upper School), and a support staff of at least four trained professionals who run the computer science department and provide information on the use of computers. "Technology is a powerful tool. At Riverdale our curriculum drives technology, not the reverse," says Mr. Shaller in describing the Lower School's integration of computers and academics. From kindergarten through second grade, parent volunteers (who are trained) work with students on games and problem solving. In third grade formal instruction starts, in fourth grade LOGO is introduced. Fifth grade students collect science data and set up a data base to coordinate, record and graph information. For students in grades seven through twelve RCS offers four computer science courses—Introduction to Technology is a required course for all seventh and tenth graders—including two AP courses and Programming in Java. "The computer and the Internet are helpful tools, but they should be used sparingly. Children have a great deal of exploration to do away from the illuminated screen," says Mr. Shaller.

Although RCS is a coed school, there is concern about gender issues. In a recent year, the parents were invited to attend a Gender Issues Forum where the latest theories about gender and intellectual development were discussed. Mr. Shaller says RCS is sensitized to gender issues (and at least one kindergarten parent has seen him roll up his sleeves and invite girls into the block corner).

When asked what values are stressed at RCS, many parents and students said "teamwork," both on and off the field. One student described Riverdale as "a healthy environment that promotes community feeling." In 1989 the RCS Lower School Student Council created C.A.R.E. (Children Aware of Riverdale Ethics), a program that emphasizes problem-solving strategies, respect for differences and consideration for the feelings of others. The official C.A.R.E. song was written by a Lower School drama teacher, January Akselrad, and it evokes the spirit of the program in an entertaining way. This sense of consideration and caring extends to the larger community as well. Recently, Lower School students held a walk-a-thon that benefited the Cystic Fibrosis Foundation. Another year, Lower School students held a penny drive for Juvenile Diabetes.

There is positive interaction between the grades at Riverdale. Friendships between children in different grades begin on the bus ride to school, and also through various planned activities. All upper grades are buddied with younger grades. Fifth graders prepare the Holiday Feast with pre-kindergartners, second and fifth graders work together on a butterfly project, and second graders and kindergartners work together sewing an alphabet with each pair of children working together on a letter square. Fifth graders interact with younger children during lunch or recess. This community of students extends all the way up to the alumni. One student said, "The alumni are not just donors, they are people you know because you've worked and connected with them." Every three years, former Riverdalians return to conduct workshops and talk to the students about their professions.

Riverdale's new Middle School, serves grade six, seven and eight, and will officially open in Fall 2005. It will be housed in a completely renovated and restored Hackett Hall and will be connected it to Mow Hall via a second floor bridge to the new Student Center that features a new dining hall, multipurpose rooms and more. Beloved history teacher and Riverdale veteran, Milton Sipp, will head the new middle division and will work with faculty, many of whom teach across a wide range of ages. There will be student deans, home base teachers, and grade-level coordinators.

Middle School students gather most mornings for an all-school meeting, which can sometimes be a full length assembly. Sixth and seventh grade students have home base teachers who meet with them at the beginning and end of each day and accompany them to lunch. There's an emphasis on interdisciplinary work, study habits and in-depth topical studies and a full range of arts courses, intramural sports for sixth graders, and interschoolastic sports for seventh and eighth graders.

The Upper School consists of grades ninth through twelfth; the two largest points of entry are sixth and ninth. The Upper School is structured but not rigid. There are many required courses, but by eleventh and twelfth grades over forty electives are available, including: "Masterpieces of Western Literature," "American Government," "Non-Western Religions," "African-American Literature," "Native American Literature," "Molecular Biology" and "Race and Class in New York City." Math is "ability grouped" in the Upper School: Students with aptitude in this area move at an accelerated pace and those who need more reinforcement get it. There are twenty AP courses, and there are honors sections in math and language. Juniors and seniors take approximately 300 AP tests each May; 90–95% percent receive scores that qualify for college credit. No class ranking is made. The curriculum is challenging and rigorous, however, students are supportive of each other and there is no cut-throat competition. "It doesn't matter what anybody else gets as long as you did your best" is the message. And one student talked about "growth in grades": As the work got harder, her grades improved.

In October 1997, Riverdale underwent a NYSAIS (New York State Association of Independent Schools) evaluation. RCS was reaccreditated, and in its official report the NYSAIS Visiting Committee stated that many aspects of the school impressed them. "The vitality of RCS's academic program; outstanding, dynamic, creative teaching; diversity; and the balance of academics, arts, activities, and athletics.

Students are friendly and confident and display a strong sense of community. Riverdale students are outstanding examples of civility, which is a reflection of the care offered by the faculty and staff," states the NYSAIS report.

It's very difficult to fall through the cracks at RCS because there is a strong support network of people and programs. Advisors (for groups of ten or twelve) meet regularly. There is easy access to faculty, whose schedules are posted and who stay for the entire long day even if they finish early.

Seniors are required to take a year-long interdisciplinary course called I.L.S. or Integrated Liberal Studies. Introduced into the curriculum in 1980, I.L.S. surveys the cultural history of the West from the perspectives of four disciplines: literature, philosophy, the history of science and the history of music and art. The course culminates in a final oral examination.

Students help students in several ways. Eleventh and twelfth graders are selected, as an honor, and trained to act as peer counselors to seventh graders, dealing with academic and social issues under the Peer Advisory Leadership (PAL) program.

RCS welcomed Dr. John R. Johnson as the school's Headmaster in 1997. Dr. Johnson previously served as the President of The Mary Institute and St. Louis Country Day School in St. Louis, Missouri where he is credited with orchestrating the merger of the two single sex schools. He also taught classes in European History, including AP European History (which he also teaches at Riverdale) during his twelve years at the school. Dr. Johnson was also the Director of Studies at the Harvard-Westlake School in Los Angeles where he was responsible for the school's academic program. He is a warm and supportive leader and he attends many school events. Recently, he attended the Annual Fund committee's end-of-the-year bowling event held at Chelsea Piers where he fostered a feeling of support and appreciation among the attendees. When asked what Dr. Johnson's vision for Riverdale includes, he says "Riverdale has a balanced approach to education. It is a school that values first-rate training across the board, in academics, the arts and athletics. We attend to the whole child. Our faculty really know their students and their concern extends beyond the classroom."

RCS recently developed seven adjacent acres and several buildings that were purchased from Manhattan College. The property and buildings have been fully integrated with the Hill campus. Renovations were made to existing buildings on campus as well as those newly purchased including the gym, pool, locker rooms, physical fitness equipment, expansion of the 300-seat theater, a new arts center, offices, a day-care center, an admissions/administration center, two state-of-the-art science labs, a twenty-station digital language lab and many classrooms. A full-sized playing field, and the expansion of an existing practice field to a full-sized playing field were also added.

Mr. Satish Joshi, Director of Community Arts and Artist in Residence, has been inspiring students for many years. Graduating seniors leave farewell messages to him painted on the walls of the art room: "Satish, you know me. That in itself is a great thing. I ❤ you." and "Thanks for the best homeroom ever." Riverdale's art and literary magazine *Impressions* repeatedly won the award of the National Council of Teachers of English, the highest award for excellence in student literary magazines.

Seniors have a recently remodeled lounge, and the beautifully landscaped courtyard garden. Backpacks are dropped casually in the halls. Seniors can leave the campus when they are not scheduled for classes or other obligations. (These are privileges, not rights, and can be revoked for bad behavior.) Each year a Senior Leadership Conference is held at a camp or conference center at which seniors explore their own leadership role in school; teachers conduct workshops on the college application process and on coping with senior-year demands. Class officers are elected, and seniors get a sense of solidarity as a class. The weekend launches them in their role as leaders of the Upper School. The student government has three representatives from each grade.

The junior class is pushing for more privileges: RCS juniors can't leave campus until April of junior year. (At Horace Mann and Fieldston students can leave in ninth grade.) But one student maintained that having to stick around campus contributes to the feeling of community. Each year the senior class parents give a gift to the school.

Though sequestered from many of the ills of urban life, RCS students are concerned about the wider world. At the recent One World Day, students explored a wide range of cultural and world issues in a series of workshops on such topics as women's rights in developing countries, hip-hop culture, and the crisis in Sudan.

Frank Hackett's "spirit of internationalism" is translated into respect for differences between people. Relationships between groups at RCS are good. A tenth grader told us: "It's not too cliquey; everyone knows what they like to do and no one gets in anyone else's way." In athletics, "Everyone works together on the field."

There are over thirty-eight clubs, and new ones are added each year. They include the successful Mock Trial Club, S.C.C. (Students of Color Committee), Film Club, Environmental Club, Amnesty International, Model Congress and Community Service. An activity period for clubs is scheduled during the school day, so that students can find time to engage in extracurricular interests.

School spirit at RCS is manifested through athletic competition in the Ivy Prep League. Riverdale's athletic center was completely renovated in 1998. The athletic center houses an Olympic-size pool, where many trophies are on display. There are sixteen junior varsity and varsity sports teams including a swim team and a strong fencing team. Riverdale's football team achieved sports fame in the sixties when Frank Bertino coached Riverdale to seventeen undefeated seasons. Horace Mann alumni wince when they remember how future pro player Calvin Hill led RCS to a winning streak of fifty-one games. Today, the annual "Buzzell" basketball game in February against archrival Horace Mann draws a crowd of over one thousand people. The game was named for a Horace Mann student who died and the proceeds are donated to charity.

A Riverdale junior who plans to be a litigator describes RCS as "a healthy, fun environment that promotes community feeling. If you work hard and apply yourself, you'll really succeed and help is always there if you need it."

Popular College Choices   Brown, University of Pennsylvania, University of Michigan, Harvard, Duke, Yale, Vanderbilt, Washington University, Boston University, Tufts, Cornell, Columbia, Barnard, Williams, Dartmouth, NYU, Wesleyan. Although RCS students apply and gain admission to the top Ivy League colleges, they select a variety of colleges, which is consistent with RCS's emphasis on perceiving students as individuals, rather than types

Traditions   Grandparents' Day, Spring Carnival, Winter and Spring Concerts, Book Fair, Academic Fair, Parents' Association Dinner/ Dance and Auction, Buzzell games, Talent Show, Children Helping Children (charity outreach program), C.A.R.E. program (Children Aware of Riverdale Ethics), Homecoming Day, Career Day, One World Day, Shakespeare Recitation Contest, Friends of the Arts evening, Sixth and Twelfth Grade Graduation Ceremonies, Reunion and cocktail parties by decade for Alumni

Publications   Lower School literary publication: *The Rivulet*
Lower School newspaper: *The Riverdalian*
The Flying Falcon
Middle School literary magazine: *Crossroads*
Upper School newspaper: *The Riverdale Review* (since 1916)
Literary magazine: *Impressions* (winner of several national awards for excellence)
Alumni magazine: *Quad*
Yearbook: *The Riverdalian*
Photography journal: *Exposures*

Community Service Requirement   14 hours on the River Campus for grade 5
20 hours for grades 7 and 8
72 hours for grades 9–12

Hangouts   Dino's Pizza, Riverdale Diner, Bagel Corner, RCS cafeteria (with a view of trees and fields) and library

Rodeph Sholom School

Nursery Division
(2 and 3 year olds)
7 West 83rd Street
New York, NY 10024
(212) 362-8800
website: www.rodephsholomschool.org

Lower Elementary Division
(Grades Pre-Kindergarten–1st)
10 West 84th Street
New York, NY 10024
(212) 362-8769

Upper Elementary Division
(Grades 2–4)
168 West 79th Street
New York, NY 10024
(212) 362-0037

Middle School
(Grades 5–8)
168 West 79th Street
New York, NY 10024
(212) 362-0037

Coed
Nursery–8th grade
Accessible at 7 West 83rd Street and 168 West 79th Street
Not accessible at 10 West 84th Street

Mr. Irwin Shlachter, Headmaster
Mrs. Alice Barzilay, Director of Admissions and Placement

Birthday Cutoff Children entering kindergarten must be 5 by
September 5
Children entering at the nursery level must be 2.6 by September

Enrollment Total enrollment: 650
Nursery enrollment: 140
Lower and Upper elementary enrollment: 360

Middle School enrollment: 150
Average graduating class size: 30–35

Tuition Range 2005–2006 $8,900 to $26,950, nursery 2 1/2's–6th
grade
Temple membership, materials, insurance, and lunch fees of
under $650 for grades 2–8 are included
There is a tuition reduction of $500 per sibling for each enrolled
child beyond the first
Financial aid available for Kindergarten on

After-School Program   for Nursery through 6th graders; weekdays
until 5:00 P.M.; a variety of creative, recreational and educational
activities for an additional charge

Summer Program   Rodeph Sholom Summer Camp from late June
through mid-August; an additional payment is required

Founded in 1958 as a nursery school; the elementary level was
added in 1970 and the Middle School in 2000. The Rodeph Sholom
School is a Reform Jewish day school affiliated with the reform synagogue, Congregation Rodeph Sholom. It is the only Reform Jewish
day school in New York City. The Nursery Division is housed in the
temple building on West 83rd Street. Pre-kindergarten through first
grade are housed in a modern building on West 84th Street, connected via a courtyard to the 83rd Street building. Second through
eighth grades (Upper Elementary and Middle School Divisions) meet
in fully renovated brownstones on West 78th and 79th Streets which
house two gyms, three libraries (two are fully computerized and linked
to the Internet), two computer labs, four science labs, two art studios,
four "Smart" classrooms, and a cafeteria.

Getting in: Parents should call in the Fall for an application and
to reserve a place in a group tour. ERB or ISEE testing results,
(depending on the entry level), a school report, and individual or group
interviews with the child are required for admission to kindergarten
and above. "We are looking for students who can meet the demands of
our challenging and enriched academic environment," says the Admissions Director. Students come from a variety of backgrounds; most live
in Manhattan but some come from Riverdale and Brooklyn.

Parents: It's an eclectic mix of executives, artists, academics, physicians and so on. A parent who has been at the school for several years points out that as the school has expanded, the parent body has evolved from a fuzzy West Side school to a school with more polish and considerably more money: "Formerly the parents were psychologists, painters, a social worker—your basic West Side shleppers. Now they're media executives, managing directors, executive editors; people who golf." One parent said, "We have kept our child in Rodeph Sholom from nursery through the grades because it provides top-notch academic preparation without the personal competitiveness we see at many other schools. It's a warm community and the administration welcomes parental involvement. The sports and visual arts programs are great and the kids place into the top private high schools."

An active PTA organizes several annual fund-raisers including the book fair (open to the neighborhood), and the Spring Benefit. The PTA also sponsors dialogue meetings throughout the year; recent topics include: computers, Jewish studies, and neighborhood safety. The PTA frequently purchases blocks of tickets to sporting events and Broadway shows.

Program: The Rodeph Sholom School provides a combination of rigorous academics and a supportive environment. The school believes "the higher you place the bar, the higher the children will reach." Although there are four divisions (Nursery, Lower Elementary, Middle School, and Upper Elementary) there is interaction between older and younger students. For example, first graders read to nursery students, sixth graders perform Shakespeare for fourth graders, and the entire school visits the Science Week exhibit created by the fifth grade.

The Lower Elementary division is comprised of pre-kindergarten through first grade. All classrooms have computers and are filled with children's artwork, creative writing, poems and graphs. Younger children play outdoors in the courtyard daily, children in kindergarten go to Central Park every day. Jewish Studies are woven into the curriculum and each Shabbat (Friday) a different child's parent/guest is invited to participate in nursery and Pre-K classes.

The school's approach to teaching is a balance of traditional/ instructional and discovery-based methods. Literary instruction begins in Pre-K. By first grade students write, edit and publish their own books. Math, social studies, handwriting, writer's workshop, Hebrew and Jewish studies are taught in the classroom. Students leave their classrooms for special instruction in Jewish Studies and Hebrew, science, computer, library, art, music and physical education.

346

Beginning in Pre-K, computers equipped with Internet access are used in all classrooms at RS. The technology curriculum includes: keyboarding, graphics, spreadsheets, database management, telecommunications, Internet, e-mail and desktop publishing. At 79th Street, four classrooms have "Smart" boards.

The science curriculum focuses on problem solving skills in Life, Physical or Earth Sciences. Fourth graders focus on the earth, compare states of matter, analyze weather patterns, find earthquake foci, and hone mapping skills. Fifth graders study ecology and evolution, and seventh graders cover in-depth units on the human body.

The integrated curriculum is driven by social studies. Pre-kindergartners focus on "Me and My Family." Kindergartners study citizenship and their community. In first grade, the social studies curriculum expands to "The Neighborhood and the Market." First graders learn how fruit is grown, transported and sold; they take field trips to various neighborhood and open-air Greenmarkets in the city; they create their own market in the school lobby and sell produce to students, faculty, and parents; and they donate their profits to a charity of their choice. Second graders study New York City. Third graders cover core themes of social studies including history, geography, economics and government. Fourth graders survey the four regions of the United States in depth.

In the Middle School, fifth grade focuses on the leadership and sacrifices required to turn the colonies into an independent nation with a democratic government. The year ends with an in-depth study of the Civil War. In sixth grade, students begin a two-year study of world history beginning with the ancient world and ending with Asia and the Americas. Eight graders return to a study of the United States including units on Industrialization, and other watershed events with a special emphasis on the World Wars and the Holocaust.

The Jewish Studies curriculum includes music, art, dance and theatre projects in the Hebrew language, Shabbat, teaching of the Torah portion, holidays and festivals, charitable deeds, Israel, and Jewish history, life and traditions. Beginning in first grade, Hebrew is taught using a combination of phonics and whole language techniques, including reading, writing, conversation and music. A yearly musical Midrash Hour, with music and lyrics written by students and music teachers features a central Jewish theme.

Music is taught by two full-time instructors utilizing Orff instruments, Dalcroze Eurhythmy for movement and Kodaly Training for singing. All second through eighth graders have the opportunity to further their private instrumental studies. This after-school mini-conservatory features faculty made up of New York City's finest professional musicians and offers lessons on nearly all band and orchestral instruments. Students in this program also play in one or more of the school's eight performing ensembles; the program culminates with an annual spring concert.

As you walk the halls you notice that art is an important part of the Rodeph experience. The school has two fully equipped art studios. Three full-time art instructors give formal instruction, as well as helping classroom teachers integrate art projects into the regular curriculum. Students use the resources of nearby museums, including the Metropolitan, Natural History and Children's Museums. Starting in seventh grade, students choose an area of the arts as their major. If they choose to major in the visual arts, they have art classes twice a week. Students who are especially talented in the visual arts and who are focusing on attending an art school may take a portfolio class.

Upper and Middle School students have physical education three times a one of the school's two modern gymnasiums. There are four full-time coaches on staff. Students participate in a wide range of sports including, soccer, basketball, baseball, gymnastics, hockey, softball, and track and field.

There is a "no-cut" policy for athletes. The Middle School has its own teams. Many extracurricular activities take place during the school day and play an important role in the life of the school. The RS team, the "Future Problem Solvers," takes part in an international academic competition in which students brainstorm, research, and write solutions to current world issues. It has been recognized as New York State Champions for over a decade. Both Middle School and the Upper Division have student councils.

Parents say that Rodeph Sholom provides a well-rounded education. One father told us, "They do a great job of combining Jewish identity with a solid academic grounding. It's a first rate education without any pretensions, the kids work hard because the school makes it fun."

Popular on-going school choices Brearley, Bronx Science, Chapin, Riverdale, Horace Mann, Collegiate, Nightingale, Columbia Prep, Spence, Fieldston, Dalton, Abraham, Joshua Heschel, Trevor Day, LaGuardia High School, Stuyvesant, Trinity

Traditions   Jewish Holiday Celebrations (Purim Carnival, lunch in the Sukkah, Passover Seders, etc.), Science Week, 1st Grade Fruit Market, 2nd Grade Model Neighborhoods of NY, Midrash Hour, Teva Environmental trip

Publications   *The Rodeph Sholom Sun*
The Rodeph Sholom PTA Newsletter: *Worth Menschoning*
Graduation Yearbook

The Rudolf Steiner School

Lower School
15 East 79th Street
New York, NY 10021
(212) 535-2130 (main number)
(212) 327-1457 (admissions), FAX (212) 744-4497

Upper School
15 East 78th Street
New York, NY 10021
(212) 879-1101 (main number)
website: www.steiner.edu

Coed
Nursery–12th grade
Not accessible

Ms. Lucy Schneider, Faculty Chair
Ms. Marisha Plotnik, College Chair
Ms. Irene Mantel, Director of Admissions, 2's–6th grade
Ms. Miranda Litt, Director of Admissions, 7th–12th grades

Birthday Cutoff   September 1

Enrollment   Total enrollment: 350
  2's places: 24
  3's places: 25
  4's and 5's places: 20
  Graduating class size: approximately 20–25

Grades   Semester system
  Letter grades begin in 7th grade
  Departmentalization begins in 7th grade

Tuition Range 2005–2006 $15,900 to $24,600, nursery 2's–12th
  grade
  Additional fees under $200
  Lunch is included through 2nd grade and is optional thereafter
  for an additional payment; organic produce and milk and vege-
  tarian alternatives served daily

Financial Aid/Scholarship A fair portion of the student body receive some form of aid

Endowment $1 million

After-School Program Grades 1–5, Monday–Friday, 3–4:30/5:00
A variety of activities for an additional payment, availability depends on enrollment

Summer Program A 2-week June Days Camp is offered for children in preschool through grade 3 for an additional charge
A 3-week June Music Program is offered for children in grades 4 through 8 for an additional charge
Both summer programs are open to students from outside the Rudolf Steiner community

---

The Rudolf Steiner School in New York City (established 1928) is part of an international community of schools (160 in the U.S., 700 worldwide) that integrate intellectual and artistic development. Rudolf Steiner (1861–1925), was an Austrian scientist, philosopher, artist and educator. The school is housed in a beautiful Stanford White mansion just off Fifth Avenue; a sweeping marble staircase graces the foyer. At the heart of Steiner's Waldorf philosophy is the belief that education is an artistic process. There is a holistic approach to learning. "Innovative teaching methods work to develop clarity in thought, balance in feeling, and conscience and initiative in action." Steiner provides an education that balances individual development with a sense of social responsibility. There is even an emphasis on the "spiritual" side of children's growth—not religious, but focused on developing imagination, compassion, and ethical principles.

Getting in: "The Rudolf Steiner School isn't looking for any one type of child," we were told. In fact, ERB testing is not required for admission to the Lower School, but ISEE scores are required in grades six and above, along with two years of recent class records. The school's philosophy dictates that they teach to a broad spectrum of styles and abilities within each class and students come from varied economic and cultural backgrounds. Because of increased interest in Waldorf education and the competitive private school admissions climate, Rudolf Steiner maintains a wait list for admission.

Parents should call in early September for dates of Fall open

351

houses and to receive an admissions packet. Parents may tour the school without applying but must reserve space in advance. Children applying for pre-school, kindergarten, and first grade are interviewed in small groups. Students applying to second grade and up might be interviewed in a small group or individually. A parent interview is scheduled separately.

Parents: Parents are very involved in the life of the school and the Waldorf method depends on a certain level of parent support. An eclectic group of parents—business types and artists—animates the lobby at drop-off and pick-up times. Parents run the annual Fall Fair, worth attending if you're interested in the school, as it showcases Waldorf education. The Parent Association has two co-presidents, and there is a six-member Parent Council elected by the parent body, which meets monthly. There are evening parent study groups, and parent education forums throughout the year.

Program: the Waldorf method is based on the belief that children pass through three basic stages of cognitive development, and the curriculum is designed to engage the abilities of the growing child at each of these stages. In preschool this is accomplished through creative guided play; in elementary school through the imaginative and artistic presentation of material by the class teacher; and in high school through challenging the student's awakening capacity for independent thought. What's different about the Waldorf method is not so much the content—there is an in-depth curriculum—as in how and when they are taught. Parents say once you see it in action you will "fall in love with the school."

The preschool is a gem for those who like natural materials and loathe plastic primary colored toys. It has a timeless feeling: there are wooden blocks and toys; shells and stones; colorful cloths and soft dolls. The children model beeswax (a favorite Waldorf material), paint with watercolors, bake bread and make soup every week. They also play in Central Park every day, weather permitting, and end every morning with a story.

Don't think it is not academic—there's lots of learning going on: songs, stories and nursery rhymes expose children to the world of words; watching marionette shows and participating in dramatic play strengthen the power of memory and the imagination. Counting games and rhythmic activities build a foundation for arithmetic and number skills, and so on.

Beginning in first grade, reading and math are taught with the aim of developing each child's pictorial imagination. Foreign languages—

Spanish and German—are introduced. Each morning includes a "main lesson block" in one subject area, which is studied in-depth for approximately four weeks. Instead of textbooks, all students write and illustrate their own "main lesson books." (These are beautiful and impressive.) "The curriculum is designed as a unity and its subjects are introduced and developed in a sequence that mirrors the inner development of the growing child." Academic subjects such as English, math and foreign languages are scheduled for several weekly periods. Afternoons are reserved for additional academic work and for drama/movement, gym, music, or crafts.

In accordance with the Waldorf method, teachers stay with their class for several grades; a teacher might stay with her students from first all the way though eighth grade! Needless to say, students develop lasting relationships with their teachers. One parent said, "The Waldorf teachers are intellectual as well as artistic and they have amazing respect for the children."

The high school academic program prepares students for college; it cultivates artistic expression, promotes academic excellence and develops practical skills. At this point new students join those who have come up from the elementary school. Each class has its own faculty advisor who coordinates class activities, monitors the students' academic and personal progress, and serves as a liaison between the school and home. Students say that the social life is lively and warm.

Many students participate in sports; there are teams in soccer, volleyball, basketball, softball and track. Teams are open to all students and compete in the Independent School Athletic League, and also against other Waldorf Schools.

For close to twenty years, Steiner has maintained a very active exhange program with European Waldorf Schools. Tenth grade students who are strong academically are encouraged to participate. Students have gone to exchange programs in germany, Spain, France, Switzerland, and Austria.

At the Hawthorne Valley Farm, a biodynamic and organic dairy and vegetable farm in upstate New York, where the school has a close association, students examine the ecological implications of farming through visits to the farm and guest lectures.

Popular College Choices Amherst, Antioch, Barnard, Boston University, Columbia University, Maryland Institute College of Art, Middlebury, Oberlin, University of Chicago, The Rhode Island School of Design, New England Conservatory, Skidmore,

Sarah Lawrence College, Swarthmore, Smith, Tulane, Vassar, Wesleyan, Wellesley

Traditions   Annual Fall Fair and Spring Auction, all-school seasonal and holiday festivals, concerts, annual book fair, grandparents and special friends day, 5th grade Olympics, class plays grades 1–12, 6th grade farm trip, 7th grade outward bound trip, 8th and 12th grade class trip of their choice, end of the year class picnics, alumni reunions

Publications   Monthly bulletin for the entire school community
Upper School literary magazine: *The Key*
Student newspaper: *15 East*
Biannual alumni newsletter
Student yearbook

Community Service   20 hours per year for students grades 8 through 11, 12th grade has an internship of their choice

Hangout   The Nectar Coffee Shop, Viand, Central Park

Saint Ann's School

129 Pierrepont Street
Brooklyn Heights, NY 11201
(718) 522-1660
e-mail: admin@saintanns.K12.ny.us
website: www.saintanns.k12.ny.us

Coed
3's–12th grade
Not accessible

Dr. Larry Weiss, Head of School
Ms. Linda Kaufman, Assistant Head of School
Ms. Diana Lamask, Director of Admission

Uniform   None

Birthday Cutoff   None specified; readiness is stressed

Enrollment   Total enrollment: 1,050
Preschool total: 56
Kindergarten places: 30
9th grade places: 5–10
Graduating class: approximately 75

Grades   Semester system
No letter grades are given throughout the school; standardized tests are given each year to fifth and eighth grade students and the results are reported to parents
Departmentalization begins in 4th grade

Tuition Range 2005–2006 $15,750 to $22,500, Nursery–12th grade
No additional fees
A tuition refund plan is available
Private bus service (for an additional fee) is available from Manhattan; also accessible by subway or car

Financial Aid/Scholarship   15% of the student body receive some form of aid

Endowment $2,120,000

Diversity   17% children of color
30 Prep for Prep students enrolled as of Fall 2004

Homework   1st grade: none
2nd: ½ hour
3rd and 4th: 1 hour
5th and 6th: 1½ hours
7th and 8th: 2 hours
9th–12th: 3–4 hours
*The guideline is 20 minutes per class, but there is usually more

After-School Program   Open to current or new Saint Ann's students only
Kindergarten through 6th grade: 3:00 to 5:30 P.M. (6 P.M. if necessary)
Creative activities, computer, games, sports, study, art, theatre, music, and so on; an additional payment is required

Summer Program   Open to current or new Saint Ann's students (preschool through 8th grade); Six-week program that begins at the end of classes and continues through the end of July, offering creative activities, sports and field trips
Three-week gymnastics program
Soccer Program for grades 2–6
Two week science program for grades 6–8
Basketball Program for grades 2–6
Arts Program for grades 2–6

———

Saint Ann's School was founded with approximately sixty children in 1965 under the aegis of St. Ann's Episcopal Church. The rector of the church envisioned a school for gifted children, "with uniforms and a healthy dose of religion." Founding Headmaster Stanley Bosworth (known to all simply as Stanley), a former French teacher at the progressive (now-defunct) Walden School, was only thirty-five years old when he came to Saint Ann's. He came with his own vision: "It was my vow all those years ago that this particular school would somehow provide 10 percent of our nation's poets." It was Stanley's vision that prevailed.

In 1981, Saint Ann's was chartered by the New York State Board of Regents; in 1982 Saint Ann's was formally disaffiliated from the church. The sixties are long gone, Stanley's retired and Larry Weiss, formerly the Head of Horace Mann's Upper Division, has taken the reins, but one thing still remains at Saint Ann's, the philosophy that no student approaches the school without stars in his or her eyes.

Dr. Weiss wants to make Saint Ann's less "insular," according to a recent article in *The New York Times*. By that he means he would like to build relationships with other private schools in the area and with the neighborhood as well. So far, Dr. Weiss plans to teach a seminar on contemporary China.

Saint Ann's is a school where gym is called "Recreational Arts," where there are no grades, no class rankings and no rigid curriculum. Saint Ann's has produced award-winning playwrights as well as a Westinghouse Scholar. A parent said, "The unconventional tone of the school gives these kids a shared bond and a respect for the unconventional in life . . . these kids are not afraid to break the mold." Saint Ann's is a progressive, arty school for very bright children. "It's what Dalton used to be," parents say.

Located in Brooklyn Heights, now thoroughly gentrified, the school attracts many local families. Approximately one-quarter of the students come from Manhattan. Several years ago, the school renovated the basement of the main building and added a gym, a lecture room and an art gallery, plus five additional classrooms. More recently, the two-story dining room was redesigned to create two balcony rooms (which are used both as additional dining space and as classrooms). The entire area also doubles as a performing space. And, in '03–'04 the school opened The Farber Building, for first through third grade students affording more space for middle and high school students.

Getting in: The brochure states: "We admit the talented." Saint Ann's students must be self-motivated and have the ability and maturity necessary to handle freedom and rigorous academic requirements. They use a "holistic approach" when it comes to admissions. The admissions process is an eclectic one that considers both achievement and glimmers of special talent. Candidate profiles are cross-checked with ERB scores where appropriate. In addition to testing and interviewing the applicant, the admissions director will observe a child in his or her nursery school on occasion. Parents of applicants to the lower grades are interviewed with special concern for receptivity to the values of humanism and the arts. The admissions director provides parents with an opportunity to offer insights and/or additional information about their child that might help in making a decision. The appropriate division head also interviews Middle and High school applicants. Parents say that there is little of the "admissions anxiety" found at the Manhattan schools because "kids at Saint Ann's don't get their sense of self-worth from outshining others; there is very little glitter or glitz." Another parent said, "The atmosphere was informal and friendly." Saint Ann's maintains a wait list but there is not much movement on it.

Saint Ann's is not a member of ISAAGNY (Independent Schools Admissions Association of Greater New York) but does adhere to the same admissions notification and parent-reply dates as the other independent schools. The school's midwinter break is scheduled in February, a week before that of the public schools. Spring break is scheduled to coincide with Easter and Passover.

The typical Saint Ann's student is "bright, arty, concerned for others and confident." Is there a self-consciousness about being gifted? A parent says, "It has the effect of creating among the children a sense of community and specialness that overrides all other differences including ethnic background, family income and gender."

Although admittedly it is more of an accomplishment to make an award-winning scholar out of a mediocre student, Saint Ann's is nonetheless remarkably good at encouraging bright children to fully realize their potential. A mother told us, "All of my children's special talents—repeat, *all* of them—were nurtured, developed and tested in the very loving laboratory of Saint Ann's." One parent told us that her son's first grade teacher recognized that he had a talent for art. "She was so enthusiastic and encouraging that it brought out more than his ability to draw and paint—it also developed his interest in art history and a strong sense of himself." He is now in college majoring in a different subject but he is on the staff of the humor magazine, and art will be his lifelong avocation.

Aside from the excitement of teaching exceptionally able students, teachers say Saint Ann's is a great place to work because of the freedom and flexibility: "Teachers get to teach exactly what they want to teach; there is no rigid curriculum." In the Lower School most teachers have a special talent or interest; they are painters or writers, for example, "and the administration encourages these interests." A significant portion of the student body is made up of the children of faculty. The Middle and High School teachers are selected not because they have a master's in education but because they have expertise in a creative area: The drama teachers are playwrights and actors, the English teachers are writers and so on. Many of the teachers are young and "There is an enormous energy, excitement and commitment." Seventeen percent of the faculty are Saint Ann's alumni.

Parents: With respect to the parent body, one parent said she never felt that her bank account, background or lifestyle made a difference at Saint Ann's: "If I didn't fit in, I never noticed." Many fathers, such as those who work as full-time writers or illustrators or songwriters, are able to bring their children to and from school. One parent said, "Saint Ann's isn't interested in the parents; when you drop off your child, he becomes Saint Ann's child." Consequently, the Parents Association is not particularly strong. The same people have been running the Parents Association for several years. Parent events include Parents Night at school, cocktail parties, dance concerts, two Middle School and High School productions each year, voice recitals and instrumental concerts. Saint Ann's students act as hosts. There is a welcoming party for new parents at the school. Because the alumni body is so young (the first alumna graduated from Saint Ann's in 1970), alumni fund-raising was started only recently. Saint Ann's alumni keep in touch: The *Saint Ann's Times* reports on news of over four hundred alumni.

Program: Lower School at Saint Ann's is composed of grades kindergarten through third. Separation is handled gently. Parents say: "They are unbelievably sensitive." A parent can stay in the classroom if necessary. Kindergartners come for a playtime in the spring and begin with half/class half/day for the first day of school in the fall. The head of the Lower School, Gabrielle Howard, is outstanding; she has been at Saint Ann's since 1973, initially as a teacher. Cathy Fuerst is the head of the Preschool. She has served as a Lower School master teacher for eleven years, as an assistant to the Director of Development, and as Coordinator of the Lower School after-school program.

Classes are identified by teachers' names. In a kindergarten class of twenty children there is a master teacher and an assistant. Students in the Lower School address teachers by their first names.

The brochure says, "Reading is central." Writing, math, science, art, music and dance round out the rest of the Lower School schedule. Reading is taught with eclectic methods—"any way the child needs"— including phonics. By the end of first grade about 95 percent of the children are reading. A former Lower School teacher told us that "many first graders are reading Beverly Cleary or Roald Dahl, but some are still on *Mack and Tap*. But by the end of the first year most are on a second grade reading level." A parent told us that one shortcoming at Saint Ann's is if a student needs remedial help his parents must pay extra for it. "Parents must be aware of any learning difficulties their child is having," she said. There is no learning specialist on staff at Saint Ann's; however, several trained specialists are permitted to use the school premises for private instruction.

Parents say, "You have to get the daily and weekly information from your child but the school will let you know if your child isn't working up to his potential." The anecdotal reports are extensive. And the ERB and standardized tests are given during the year as objective measurements of aptitude and achievement. According to the brochure, these tests are used to see if students are at the proper level or need to be moved along.

Although the student body is a narrowly selected group of very bright children, the academic atmosphere at Saint Ann's is not one of cutthroat competition. "It's very nurturing and informal; kids are allowed to be who they are." For instance, parents say, a first grader can take a sixth grade math class and not feel out of place. (In fact, a first grader once did take sixth grade math; a teacher accompanied him to the class and stayed with him.) And of course there is no competition for grades because there aren't any. (On longer research papers students might receive a "good" or a "check", in addition to extensive comments.)

In the Preschool and Lower School, students leave their classrooms for "specials" in art, music, dance and recreational arts. Kindergartners also leave the classroom for dance. Beginning in second grade, students leave their homeroom class for math and in third grade for science and computer. Third grade is the last year of the classroom-based program; there are still blocks in the classroom. Formal instruction in computer begins in third grade. Third graders learn to type, use Hypercard, and even some programming. One Lower School group studying Greek mythology wrote an epic poem seventy pages long. Lower Schoolers produce one play or musical each year.

Middle School at Saint Ann's is equivalent to grades four through eight. It is up to the teacher whether or not students use their first or last names. Full departmentalization begins in the first year of Middle School (fourth grade), which requires a lot of maturity. Says a former Lower School teacher, "There's a lot of choice for a ten year old." Each fourth grader also has a locker with a lock.

The brochure says that "subject achievement and aptitude define placement, particularly in math and language groups. The makeup of English and history classes is largely determined by age." Sixth graders learn the structure of language. Formal language instruction begins in the seventh grade, and students can choose from Latin, Greek, French, Spanish, Chinese and Japanese. Science is part of the curriculum each year. Middle Schoolers take five years of science. Health issues are part of the curriculum.

One parent said, "My fourth grader is learning what I learned in college. In our conversations she talks about Greek and Norse myths and Latin."

The arts are considered academic subjects at Saint Ann's. The Middle School has its own literary magazine. Nancy Fales Garrett's playwriting course is so good that nearly every year a play by a Saint Ann's student is accepted for production by the Playwright's Horizons Festival's annual off-Broadway run in the fall.

Middle Schoolers perform in mixed-age plays and musicals; recent productions include *The Magic Flute* and *The Secret Garden*. A parent told us that when her son was in fifth grade, his drama teacher, an off-Broadway director (the kind that Saint Ann's delights in hiring), sparked his interest in performing and he eventually was selected as a member of a well-known theatre troupe.

Athletics are popular at Saint Ann's. There is girls' varsity softball soccer; basketball and volleyball. Boys play varsity soccer and junior varsity and varsity baseball and basketball. Coed teams include fencing, track and field. In the Middle School there is interscholastic competition in girls volleyball, softball, basketball, and soccer; boys' baseball, basketball, and soccer; coed track. There are gymnastics teams for Middle School girls. Classes are offered in team sports such as basketball, soccer, volleyball, softball and also in badminton, exercise and fitness, fencing, floor hockey, karate, weight training and yoga. There is plenty of school spirit exhibited at basketball games. Saint Ann's has several gymnasiums and uses nearby parks for playing fields.

In the Middle and High Schools milk, fruit, etc., are provided free of charge; lunch is available for an additional fee. Hot lunch is provided for the first through third grades.

The High School at Saint Ann's is composed of grades nine through twelve. There is a tremendous amount of freedom and choice in the High School at Saint Ann's so students must be self-motivated.

The teachers in the High School—all "masters" in their disciplines—

"love what they do and they communicate it to the students." The brochure describes the High School curriculum as "adventurous." Saint Ann's is progressive but the school is not embroiled in the multicultural debate rocking the public schools. Parents say the school stresses "Latin, writing, reading, theatre and playwriting." The school has a commitment to Western civilization and respect for the Western canon. (In this way it's not so different from a "traditional" school like Trinity.)

We observed an English class discussing Nabokov's *Lolita*. Some of the students had their feet up on their desks, others were sprawled or supine yet the conversation was electric. In a classroom nearby, a young attractive Spanish teacher gave her student a high five for a correct answer. The history class down the hall was studying the recent elections in Russia. History classes often have seminars on current events. A parent had praise for many teachers and for one standout, Victor Marchioro, who teaches "The Bible as Literature", described as "an unbelievably rigorous and unforgettable class." Also singled out for praise were Ruth Chapman, an art history/English teacher, and Angelo Belfatto an art teacher elected graduation speaker by the class of 2000. "It's worth insisting that your child take one of his classes just to read the evaluations he writes—you will not believe anyone could be so articulate about your child," said a parent.

Extracurricular activities keep Saint Ann's open seven days a week. Over the weekend the school may be used for play rehearsals, sports and yearbook meetings. There is a playwriting class for High School students and one for Middle School students and a playwriting festival each spring. Students can work on photography or literary magazines.

Students with a scientific bent can participate in the science research program in addition to the broad range of science courses offered. And several each year are selected for the Science Honors Program at Columbia University, and junior and senior math teams compete in the New York Interscholastic Math League.

High School students travel and work abroad. Visits to museums in New York City and foreign capitols, cathedrals in Europe, inaugurations in Washington, D.C., and model congresses at universities in the northeast corridor complement in-class curricula.

A parent of two Saint Ann's students told us: "My son had four years that were so spectacular in every way that college was a bit of a let down." Saint Ann's students are encouraged to strive for awards and honors (Saint Ann's produces numerous National Merit Scholarship

Finalists and AP scholars), and these accomplishments are conspicu-ously listed in the *Saint Ann's Times* each year. In addition, Saint Ann's students outshine their peers at other independent schools in the Johns Hopkins Center for Academically Talented Youth Competi-tion. (The CTY talent search is based on achievement on the PSAT and the SAT.)

Technology: The Director of Computers and Technology sup-plies an overview of the present and future role of computers at Saint Ann's, maintains the schoolwide network, coordinates computing activ-ities among the various departments, and runs the Computer Resource Center located in the Main building—a fully-equipped lab where teachers can bring classes to use programs such as A.D.A.M. for sci-ence, Civilization for history, and Geometers Sketchpad for math. A lab manager offers a wide range of courses for faculty so that teachers can keep up with their students' expertise. "We've attempted to make computers available and useful to all of our students and staff, from the third grade to the twelfth, and from the Head of School to the kitchen staff." Thus the Saint Ann's population is largely computer-literate.

The main library is fully computerized with Internet access. The school has a T1 high speed connection to the Internet in place and all students and staff have e-mail addresses and can create their own web pages if they wish.

Two newly renovated science labs are wired for network access. In addition to networked computers, the science labs have ten Power-Book computers and data acquisition instruments that enable students to conduct experiments and collect data in real time. The students then analyze the data on the spot as part of the lab.

The math department makes much use of computers as well. Stu-dents have published math papers on the school website. The Middle School Problem Solving class visits the Resource Center on a regular basis to obtain new problems and share solutions on the MATH-COUNTS website.

Ever aware of the arts, Saint Ann's has a multimedia computer lab in one of the music rooms, and the High School film classes make use of digital editing software.

Saint Ann's students apply to and are accepted at a broad spec-trum of colleges including the top Ivy League universities. Oberlin, a small liberal arts college in Ohio, is popular. A parent said, "The school devotes enormous energy to getting the students into the best schools—that means the best school for the child, not necessarily the parent."

Graduation is held in the Church of Saint Ann and the Holy Trinity. Caps and gowns are not worn but "Pomp and Circumstance" is played. According to tradition, the president of the board of trustees speaks as well as a member of the faculty. There are five student presentations that can be in any medium.

Popular College Choices   Princeton, Brown, Oberlin, Amherst, Bard, University of Michigan, Wesleyan, Yale, NYU

Traditions   Fun Run, Founders' Day, Senior Cruise, Grandparents Day

Publications   Middle School literary magazine
High school literary magazine
Photography or art magazine
Publications on a variety of subjects including: art, humor, nonfiction
Development office publication: *Saint Ann's Times*

Community Service Requirement   None

Hangout   On the steps in front of school

St. Bernard's School

4 East 98th Street
New York, NY 10029-6598
(212) 289-2878, FAX (212) 410-6628
website: www.stbernards.org

All boys
K–9th grade
Accessible

Mr. Stuart H. Johnson, III, Headmaster
Heidi R. Gore, Co-Director of Admissions
Anne S. Nordeman, Co-Director of Admissions

Birthday Cut-Off   None

Uniform   Kindergarten: Monday–Friday: students are required to wear khaki-colored trousers or shorts and St. Bernard's shirts; sneakers are worn to school; Grades I–IX: Monday–Thursday: navy blazers must be worn to and from school, Grades IV–IX wear polo, or oxford shirts or turtlenecks, khaki-colored trousers or shorts, sneakers for athletics only; starting in Grade III athletic clothing is provided by the school; Fridays: blazers, ties and oxford shirts required

Enrollment   Total enrollment: 372
K places: approximately 44

Grades   Kindergarten: Written reports in February and June; parents have a teacher conference in November
Grades I–III: detailed anecdotal reports in December and June
Parent conference in March
Grades IV–IX: Midterm reports in October; end of term reports in December, March and June

Tuition Range 2005–2006 $25,215 to $25,890, K–9th grade
Lunch, books, supplies, physical education and tuition refund plan are included

Financial Aid/Scholarship   16% of the student body received some form of aid

Endowment   N/A; reputed to be large

Diversity   Children of color represent 13% of the student body; the school enrolls students from Prep for Prep, A Better Chance, and the Albert G. Oliver program

Homework   Begins gently in the Junior School; (K–III); Grade I: Students read aloud to parents for twenty minutes each night
Grades II and III: reading and math assignments, finish work not completed in school, study spelling words, approximately 20–40 minutes
Middle and Upper School: regular homework in each subject, some homework can be completed in study periods, techers are available for help, approximately 1–3 hours

After-School Program   St. Bernard's boys in Junior School can participate in the Nightingale-Bamford Hobbyhorse after-school program; a wide variety of creative activities are offered
Afterschool sports at St. B's are available; the coaching staff supervises intramural games, including soccer, basketball, baseball, softball, lacrosse, and a tennis program for Grades II–IX
The Carpentry Club is available to boys in Grades II, III, V and VI

Summer Program   Summer sports camp from mid-June through mid-August

———

Although the school emblem shows a St. Bernard dog, St. Bernard's School was named after the rue St. Bernard, a street in Belgium. It is pronounced with the accent on the first syllable. Founded by John C. Jenkins, a young Englishman and Cambridge graduate, in 1904, St. Bernard's has always had an affinity for English traditions. It unselfconsciously calls its alumni Old Boys, and many of the devoted faculty still hail from Great Britain. But St. Bernard's is a kinder and gentler place than its British counterparts. Parents say there is a family feeling here combined with a crispness of attitude, with fun. A parent said "There's enough leeway so that the boys can be boyish."

Stuart Johnson, a Yale man, formerly a member of the St. Bernard's faculty who had also taught at Groton, was thirty-two when he was appointed to his post as headmaster. Mr. Johnson is described as "unpretentious, caring, witty and a bright and stylish writer" and it is said that he "writes wonderful messages in bulletins and follows the traditions set forth by the other heads." "He goes out of his way to know everyone," said a parent. "He even came to a lacrosse game in Greenvale!" Manners are very important; Mr. Johnson shakes each boy's hand each morning. Mr. Johnson listens to all complaints and dispenses "punishments without tears."

Getting in: Parents are advised to call for an application and brochure in September or October of the year before the child will enter kindergarten. St. Bernard's does not require any application fee. There is no birthday cutoff because they try to judge each boy on his own merits. Readiness is what is important. Boys in this year's kindergarten have birthdays spanning the entire year, including some younger boys with summer birthdays.

After the application is received by the school, they will call you to arrange a parent tour as well as a separate time for your child's interview. The tour, usually for two families at a time, is given by one of the co-directors of admissions and lasts about an hour and a half. Leave plenty of time for the tour because it is very thorough. After visiting parents meet privately with Mr. Johnson; questions are welcomed. A parent at St. Bernard's recalls that she took her time on the tour: "I loved that we had the opportunity to tour the school and meet with the headmaster before we decided to apply."

The co-directors visit as many nursery schools as possible to see the boys in their current setting. All boys have a thirty minute interview at St. Bernard's. You are told not to prepare your son for the individual interview. It is a formal evaluation but the boys usually enjoy themselves (thirty minutes of undivided attention!) while their nervous parents sit and wait. Reading material is provided for those parents who are able to concentrate. There is a strong sibling and legacy policy. There is not a typical St. Bernard's boy although they look remarkably similar walking up Madison Avenue in their blue blazers.

For the upper grades, applicants are considered on a rolling basis space permitting. Current transcripts, and ERB test results are required in addition to interviews.

Parents: A lot of Old Boys send their sons to St. Bernard's. Parents say the parent body is composed in part of "families with good values, 'Eleanor Roosevelt' types—women who work, even though they don't have to." One parent described the typical St. B parent as "an old New York family, with oil paintings of their ancestors on the walls and well-worn furniture." Certainly the tone of the parent body is "understated." Those who have means do not flaunt it. Although the ethos is WASP, families of all faiths are comfortable here.

Many parents who are prominent editors, writers or journalists send their sons to St. B's because of the school's emphasis on literacy. The beautifully written brochure says one of the basic premises at St. B's is "a regard for the beauty and power of English—in reading, writing, speaking, listening."

Class cocktail parties are held in the fall or winter and different families take turns as hosts. The event can be casual or catered; the Parents Association reimburses parents for their expenses. All parents are members of the Parents Association. It sponsors events such as the Book Fair, The Great Skate, an annual benefit, and a Raffle. The PA also publishes a newsletter, and all parents are required to walk on the school's safety patrol. On Parents' Night in the fall, mothers and fathers gather and are addressed by the headmaster and then meet the teachers. There is a special visiting day for grandparents in the spring.

In the words of one alumnus, "In the old days St. Bernard's was a hatchery for the progeny of millionaires." The scions of some of New York's old families still attend. (St. Bernard's is rumored to have one of the largest endowments among city independent schools.)

Program: Traditions are an integral part of life at St. Bernard's, and parents say the boys—and Old Boys—look forward to many of them. Every morning St. Bernard's boys shake hands with the headmaster and then with their teachers. Every afternoon they say good-bye to their teachers with another handshake. A school-wide assembly is held on Fridays. At assembly a hymn is sung, announcements are made and there is a program. After Christmas each grade I boy receives a hymn book with his name on it and the date that he received it, and he keeps it for the whole time he is at St. B's. Parents talk about the family feeling at assemblies, to which they are invited several times a year. Each boy gains experience in public speaking beginning in grade I. Each boy recites a poem or performs in a play at assembly. Topics at assembly range widely. There might be a group of Old Boys reminiscing about life at St. Bernard's in the fifties or a performance of music of the Middle Ages by the Interschool Orchestra.

There is a tradition at St. Bernard's involving a stuffed alligator given to the neatest class. At Friday assemblies the alligator is presented by one class to another with some original poetry or a song.

On your tour you will see desks arranged in traditional rows with the teacher at the front of the class speaking to the students. You might hear a student reciting a poem, or a nine year old reciting his multiplication tables, but don't be misled; although there is plenty of structure, there is flexibility and creativity within each classroom. Boys may stand upon their chairs, work on the floor in groups, sit in a circle and read aloud. "The combination of bright kids and unusual teachers makes St. Bernard's unique. The real beauty of St. Bernard's is its teachers," says Mr. Johnson. There is little turnover in staff at St. B, there are some eccentrics and there's a big age range. One parent described her sons' teachers as "warm, kind and intellectual." Another parent said, "Some teachers are rough and tough, but adored. Some teachers give the boys nicknames." Another parent said: "There are kids whose fathers had the same teachers, they are all well remembered, some revered, for generations." From fifth grade up all homeroom teachers are men.

A major expansion of the building is complete. The renovations include: a state-of-the-art gymnasium, science wing with new labs, a teaching theatre, two kindergarten classrooms with separate playdeck, and a carpentry room.

Junior School at St. B's is grades K–III. Parents told us that reading is expected to be under way by Christmas of first grade. Grade I boys are divided into two reading groups with much fluidity between them. Boys must read aloud to their parents, "From the first day of school boys get into the homework habit," says one parent. Homework is never unreasonable, but there is a certain amount expected every night.

There are reading specialists and math specialists on the staff of the special learning department. There is concern for the individual child. One mother told us her son needed a little extra help in math in first grade, and a St. B teacher who happened to be in the same summer community offered to work with him over the summer free of charge, so that he wouldn't have trouble with second grade math.

One mother spoke about the progress her son made in grade I: "It's a caring environment and they keep a close watch. My son is shy but they've helped him to socialize. Also, at first he couldn't write and now he writes pages; he also wasn't a team sports player and now he participates fully."

A typical grade I schedule: The day begins with an assembly in the gym and goes on to art, gym, library, science, sums, spelling, phonics, reading, math, recess, lunch, physical education, work-time/crafts and dismissal. The curriculum is well rounded, parents say, and there is time for physical activity every day, either on the outdoor play deck or in the fields of Central Park just a block away. There is at least a computer in every classroom, in addition to a large new computer lab, and the science labs for grades I through IX are very well equipped. The school-wide computer network supports a Windows-based system; boys have access to the Internet and other reference materials.

Third graders do a lot of written work. They study Greek mythology "and are very devoted to it," a parent said. Awards for best and most-improved handwriting are given in each class.

Music begins in first grade. If you are touring around Christmas-time, strains of "O Come All Ye Faithful" will float through the halls. Tryouts for the St. Bernard's singing group begin in fourth grade and most boys make it. Rehearsals are held twice a week before school. At performances, boys wear special ties and trousers.

Art is hands on, with an academic approach. One Christmas, boys made ornaments for the Florence Nightingale Nursing Home.

The Middle School is grades IV through VI. Fourth graders have a meeting before the school year begins to discuss the transition to Middle School.

Every homeroom performs at an Assembly; one recent year a fifth grade class did the story of Prometheus. A parent described the play as "pure entertainment" with St. Bernard's characteristic wit and English humor." The boy who played Hercules was the skinniest boy in the class, but he came out swaggering, with his sleeves rolled up. "The boys really loved performing!"

From time immemorial every fifth grader has written a ten-page research report on an animal, and, says a parent, "Every alumnus remembers his animal." They also do a unit on Native Alaskans in the winter and Native Americans in the spring. Latin begins in sixth grade.

The Garrett McClung Prize is a special award given in grade V for achievement. Six prizes are given out at the end of grade VI.

The Upper School consists of grades VII through IX. Special events during these years include the annual eighth grade Shake-speare production, directed by the headmaster. The play varies from year to year (in recent years it has been *The Tempest* and *The Taming of the Shrew*), and St. Bernard's boys play all roles. Another sixth grade tradition is a visit to Civil War battlefields in Virginia. There is an eighth grade debating society, an Upper School public speaking contest, and a Model Congress elective.

In grade VII *To Kill a Mockingbird* is read and in grade IX, Solzhenitzyn's *One Day in the Life of Ivan Denisovich*. Parents say the boys are very well prepared for the ongoing schools because of St. B's emphasis on reading and writing.

The student council is composed of elected members from grades IV through IX. The council meets each trimester and each class elects its own president, vice president and secretary. The entire council meets with the headmaster.

The entire school benefits from the handsomely renovated Jenkins Library, in which an oil painting of the stern-faced founder overlooks the stacks. There are shelves of O.E.D.'s and study carrels for the older boys as well as CD-ROMs and other research tools. A separate section of the library is reserved for the younger boys so that they do not disturb the concentration of the older boys.

Intramural sports competition begins in grade III. Ninety percent of boys from grade V through grade IX play on at least one team each year. There are varsity and junior varsity Red and White teams in all sports. St. Bernard's teams excel in soccer, lacrosse, and baseball. Ice hockey is offered in addition to the traditional sports.

Values are stressed throughout St. Bernard's and there is a code of conduct. In addition, one parent said, "High value is placed on both grades and awards." There are essay and composition prizes and a public speaking prize. At the final assembly numerous awards and prizes are given out; one of the highest awards is the Payne Whitney Honor Cup.

Consistent with the belief that "a good heart is finally more valuable than a well-stocked, well-trained head," community service at St. B's starts at the top with the headmaster, who is on the board of the Yorkville Common Pantry. Food drives are held at Thanksgiving, Christmas and Passover/Easter. In addition, each class does a project or community service work. Older boys visit the elderly at the Florence Nightingale Nursing Home or decorate the cafeteria or other common areas of the home for the holidays; the St. B's singing group performs or just visits informally. Other community service opportunities include the Environment Club (which has donated to a school in rural Ecuador), a recycling program, and bake sales for charities. There is usually a student-led response to a major disaster: For hurricane and earthquake victims, a well-decorated jar for contributions will be placed in the lobby and a check sent to a relief fund.

St. Bernard's imparts a palpable enthusiasm for learning, and the techniques for mastering any subject. An alumnus told us that the only times he wasn't at the top of his class were at St. Bernard's and The Harvard Business School. One parent said what surprised her the most about St. Bernard's was its warmth: St. Bernard's is not just for Anglophiles.

About one third of the graduates go to boarding school and the rest transfer to independent day schools in the area, after either eighth or ninth grade.

Traditions   St. Bernard's book of school songs, Friday assemblies, eighth grade Shakespeare play, sixth grade trip (Gettysburg), eighth grade trip (Ecuador), ninth grade trip (Paris), fifth grade animal report, passing of the alligator, Science and Technology Fair, Book Fair, Sports Day, Parents' Evening, Father's Dinner, Junior Old Boys' Lunch, Old Boys' Dinner, Grandparents' Visiting Day, Spring Concert, Christmas Carols

Publications   Yearbook: *The Keg*
Literary magazine: *The Budget*
Parents' Association Publication: *St. Bernard's Gazette*
Alumni Bulletin: *St. Bernard's School*

Community Service Requirement   No specific requirement but each boy must perform community service in a number of ways available through various programs within the school. There are also many opportunities to serve the local community: Yorkville Common Pantry, the Florence Nightingale Nursing Home, New York City Audubon Society, The Environment Club

Hangouts   Richie's Deli on Madison, the Italian ices man outside school

Saint David's School

12 East 89th Street
New York, NY 10128
(212) 369-0058, fax (212) 289-2796
website: www.saintdavidschool.org

All boys
Pre-Kindergarten–8th grade
Accessible (3 elevators)

Dr. P. David O'Halloran, Headmaster
Ms. Janet Sughrue, Director of Admissions
Ms. Julie Sykes, Director of Admissions

Uniform   Grades pre-kindergarten through omega (Kindergarten): collared or turtleneck shirts only, no jacket required, sneakers are allowed
Grades 1–8: tie and jacket (jacket can be any color); Bermuda shorts allowed in September and May, no sneakers

Birthday Cutoff   Children entering Kindergarten must be 5 by September 1
Children entering 1st grade must be 6 by September 1st

Enrollment   Total enrollment: 375
Pre-kindergarten places: 16
Kindergarten places: 45
Graduating class size: approximately 35

Grades   Trimester system
Pre-kindergarten through 3rd grade: detailed anecdotal reports and conferences
Letter grades begin in 4th grade
Departmentalization begins in 4th grade
First final exam is given in 7th grade

Tuition Range 2005–2006 $17,000 to $25,500, pre-kindergarten–8th grade
The cost for lunch, books, and athletics is included in the tuition
There is a 8-month tuition payment plan available to parents
A 10 percent discount is given on the tuition of the second child

of parents with three or more children in the school; there is a discount of 25 percent for the third child and 50 percent for the fourth and additional children

Financial Aid/Scholarship Approximately 10% of the student body receives some form of financial aid

Endowment N/A

Diversity 7% children of color
Prep for Prep students enrolled

Homework 1st: 15–20 minutes
2nd: 1/2 hour
3rd: 1 hour
4th and 5th: 1 1/2 hours
6th: 1 1/2–2 hours
7th and 8th: 2–2 1/2 hours

After-School Program The Saint David's after-school program is open to Saint David's boys only; an additional payment is required Grades 1 through 8: Monday–Thursday, 4:30–5:30 P.M.; various activities including sports, art, cooking, computer, woodworking, pottery, rocketry and chess

Summer Program The June Program for kindergarten boys during the last two weeks of June; an additional payment is required June Summer Sports program (9:00 A.M.–3:30 P.M.) for grades 1–8, two weeks in June: a variety of sports, games, activities and field trips; an additional payment is required March sports program for grades 1–8 either first or second week of spring vacation

———

Although Saint David's School, founded in 1951, is relatively young, it is interesting to note that the school has more traditions than most of the long-established East side boys' schools founded at the turn of the century. The school building, originally three private homes designed by Delano and Aldrich in 1919, retains much of the beauty, warmth and architectural detail of the period. Saint David's is a Catholic school for boys but the Saint David's community is inclusive;

about forty percent of the boys practice other religions, and the catalog states that Saint David's "is a family school in every sense of the word." Parents say Saint David's "offers a balance of academics, arts and athletics with a spiritual component." Saint David's is known for an emphasis on literature, languages, history and art "bolstered by practical anatomy, mathematics and a growing computer science department."

Saint David's was founded by lay Catholics and, according to the mission statement, Saint David's remains grounded in the traditions of that faith. Saint David's students are taught "to respect and learn from all religious traditions, to prize diversity and to develop the spiritual and ethical values necessary for successful moral decision making." One parent described Saint David's as a place where "the school and teachers work to develop boys who will be able to think critically about what life presents them with, and they do that by providing the boys with a foundation of ethical and moral instruction." One parent who is not Catholic and who recently relocated to New York City with her family from another country said she chose this school for her son because, considering the language and cultural differences, she felt Saint David's would provide "a challenging but nurturing academic environment with less pressure than at some other schools." Another parent said she chose Saint David's for "its heart, soul and mind."

Getting in: Applications should be filed by December 1st. After the application is filed (there is a $40 fee), tour and interview dates are scheduled. Individual tours of the school are given by parent tour guides. Applicants for grades kindergarten through seventh have a one-on-one interview with a teacher. Applicants for grades four through eight spend a day in a classroom. The directors of admissions say that a diverse group of boys is chosen from a variety of nursery schools; approximately fifteen schools are represented in a class of forty-five. Admissions at Saint David's is not stressful, and parents are made to feel comfortable about the process.

Parents: The parent body at Saint David's is described by a parent: "There is wealth and there are some limos but parents are far from ostentatious." Parents do dress well, and many wear suits to school events. An annual dinner dance is held in early March, which always includes a very successful auction. Parents mingle more informally at the frequent cocktail parties, teas, morning coffees, a theater benefit, and family skating at Wollman Rink.

Program: Saint David's has had remarkably few heads of school in its history; David Hume was headmaster for thirty-plus years. In

July 1992, Dr. Donald Maiocco became the school's fourth head-master and retired in June 2004. On July 1st, 2004, the school wel-comed Dr. P. David O'Halleran as the school's sixth headmaster. A native Australian, who can play the bagpipes, Dr. O'Halleran comes to Saint David's after a ten-year tenure at Allen-Stevenson and a stint as Headmaster of the Hilltop Country Day School in New Jersey. A guiding force in the school's "rededication to the humanities, Dr. Maiocco changed the names of the homerooms from A and B to Pi and Theta. The new school alma mater is sung to a Mozart melody." According to the catalog, "Saint David's is deeply committed to explo-ration of the civilizations that most shaped our own: Democratic Greece and Republican Rome." Latin is required in the fifth grade and becomes an elective in seventh and eighth grades.

Saint David's mission is "to provide the finest education available within the best traditions of the church." Religious instruction at Saint David's is based on an inclusive, not exclusive, Catholicism. Require-ments include: morning chapel, religion classes, mass (four times a year, third grade and up, held at the Church of St. Thomas More) and the celebration of Christian holidays. Preparation for First Commu-nion is optional. Religion classes are ungraded, and holidays of other faiths are also examined during the course of the year. The catalog states that "students of all faiths are encouraged to draw from their religious traditions for class discussions and assignments."

The chapel is the former library and contains a fireplace and ser-vant's bell in addition to pews. First and second graders attend chapel once a week for Bible stories. Third through eighth graders begin each day with chapel, at which hymns are sung and faculty members relate a personal story that reflects a particular moral or ethical lesson. These "chapel talks" can be humorous, serious, spiritual or merely enlight-ening, and range from an account of a close call with bears on a hiking trip to an explanation of the Book of Kells, an English teacher's description of the significance of the Jewish holidays to him or a well-loved member of the kitchen staff singing spirituals.

Saint David's calendar lists eight *fêtes de l'écoles* or celebration days. Each day is marked by a special program. There is a celebration for the founding of the city of Rome, and on every March 1, Saint David's Day, members of the school community bite a leek to sym-bolize their becoming a son or daughter of Saint David's.

The school recently added 6,000 square feet by renovating an adjacent building. The new building includes, a library/media center, two state-of-the-art science rooms, an expanded dining hall and more.

Lower School is composed of pre-kindergarten through third grade. There is one pre-kindergarten class of approximately sixteen students and three kindergarten classes (of fifteen students each.) The OMEGA Kindergarten class serves a useful purpose for boys who may be reading, but are young or need more time before first grade. The brochure states, "In the early years the school seeks a balance between work and play." A parent told us about a wonderful celebration in the Lower School for "Cinco de Mayo," a Mexican feast day: "They had a piñata, food and clothing from Mexico." One second grade project focused on how each boy could do his part to help save the earth. One year, the family of one of the second grade boys had lived in Japan and helped the class celebrate Children's Day with a Japanese Tea Ceremony.

In the Lower School basic skills are emphasized. Homework is introduced in first grade. Formal reading instruction also begins in this year with small group instruction. Manipulatives are used for math instruction. Math is tracked or grouped by ability starting in first grade. Fourth graders begin learning how to write a research paper. There is a computer in every classroom.

Drama, music and art are integrated into the academic curriculum. Lower School boys choose a famous painting to study. Parents look forward to the yearly first grade Christmas play. Students go outside their homerooms for instruction in pottery, woodworking, music, science and gym. Project Charlie, an anti-drug program, is taught in second and fourth grades. Sixth graders take a full health course called D.A.S.H. (drugs, alcohol, sex and health).

Lower School boys have a break midmorning for recess in the little gym, or they may go to the play yard. They change for sports in the afternoon. From kindergarten up, boys eat in the Lower and Upper School dining rooms. Lunch is served family style, and, said one mother, the boys are expected to eat what is on their plates. Parents praise Lower School Head Jane Warwick: "She knows each boy as an individual—his strengths and his weaknesses."

Sports at Saint David's begins with intramural competition in third grade. From grade 5 on there is All-Star Team competition with other schools, but a hallmark of the sports program at Saint David's is that all fifth and sixth grade boys get a chance to play at the varsity level; there are no team cuts at this age. The school's athletic facilities include a 16,000 square foot sports center located at 215 East 94th Street. The athletic director says, "a lot of attention is paid to skill development, and the coaching staff is strong," which enables the Saint

David's boys to compete with the best of them. The Red Team has fielded championship basketball and soccer teams. On Friday afternoons some faculty and boys sometimes go to the park for informal sports, or play pickup basketball in the gym. There are seasonal parent/faculty games and an alumni soccer match. The Player of the Week program recognizes outstanding performance in a game, enthusiasm or sportsmanship.

Another incentive for boys in the Lower School is the Saint David's armband, which is awarded at a monthly assembly to boys who did something special. The armband has been awarded for "recognition of academic excellence," for "neatness" or for "simply smiling." One parent said her son got it for mastering the "bird's nest" in gymnastics.

There is no Middle School at Saint David's: Grades four through eight are considered part of the Upper School. Letter grades begin in fourth grade. Boys begin lab science in fourth grade. Math continues to be grouped according to ability.

Latin, introduced in fifth grade, continues through eighth grade. In sixth grade boys can choose between French and Spanish. Fourth through sixth graders are taught the science of geography and they have a "map of the month" to study. April has been designated "Science Month" at Saint David's. Guest lecturers talk about the sonar systems in dolphins, the cardio-vascular system and advances in heart surgery and the impact of El Nino and the tsunami.

Drama continues to be incorporated into the curriculum. For example, Tom McLellan's fifth grade class stages a mock Revolutionary War battle, the Battle of Macgowan's Pass, in Central Park. Boys also take a field trip to Old Bethpage, Long Island. Class plays usually tie in with the history or English curriculum; past productions have included *Casey at the Bat*, *Philoctetes* and *The Pirates of Penzance*.

There are many opportunities for boys to practice public speaking: Sixth graders recite original poetry and eighth graders deliver research reports on art to students and teachers and give these reports to their peers at the Nightingale-Bamford. and sometimes give the chapel talks.

Opportunities for musical performance include handbell choir, recorder, Glee Club, Interschool orchestra, philharmonic and two ensemble performances with Brearley each year.

There is interaction between the grades in which students act as teachers. Eighth graders talked to third graders about Greek coins they had made; a fifth grade class addressed fourth graders about aspects of Native American cultures.

Visiting Day provides students an opportunity to interact with girls at the single-sex schools. They pick an activity such as library or music and go to a girls' school for the library or music hour in the fall. In the spring, they reciprocate and host the girls. Exchanges are matched by grade and age.

Boys in the Upper School are assigned many long-term projects in order to develop their time-management skills. Seventh and eighth graders have trimester exams. In addition to the humanities course there is an eighth grade course in comparative anatomy. The "Humanities" course is a survey of architecture, music and literature of three distinct eras: ancient Greece, Europe during the Renaissance and the United States during WWII. The course includes fundamental Greek and culminates in a 10-day study trip to Italy before the spring break. Eighth grade boys study Renaissance art and architecture in Rome, Siena and Florence.

Although there is a definite emphasis on the classics, Saint David's has increased its efforts to include in its curriculum the achievements of women and of members of a wide range of ethnic groups; the school strives for contextual understanding. Observance of Martin Luther King Day at Saint David's is not just a holiday but an opportunity for discussion of Dr. King's contributions across many subject areas. For instance, a discussion of the poetry of Langston Hughes might serve as a springboard for discussion of "Dr. King's impact on the moral consciousness of the American people and the world." Similarly, a study of Gandhi's influence on Dr. King's "I Have a Dream" speech is part of an Upper School study of the American civil rights movement.

Art is not an elective in the Upper School. Seventh and eighth grade boys receive letter grades in art, with the emphasis on attitude and effort, not talent. Some boys objected, some boys thought it would encourage them to take the arts more seriously.

Saint David's is proud of its honors math program for grades seven and eight. Students participate in the annual Math Bowl.

Outdoor education takes place on the week long annual seventh grade Cape Cod trip in October, during which boys are led on explorations by instructors from the Cape Cod Museum of Natural History. The sixth grade boys visit Camp Hi Rock in Massachusetts for two overnights to study the history and culture of an old whaling village.

Extracurricular activities in the Upper School include working on the school literary magazine *(The Canticle)* or the yearbook and playing on sports teams. The student council president (grades five through eight) is elected and he then selects his cabinet.

The Saint David's Social Action Committee participates in many community service projects, such as contributions to charity boxes, the Annual Thanksgiving Drive, Christmas gifts to the Graham-Windham home, and a sixth grade remote-control model car rally fund-raiser. Seventh graders make weekly visits to the Florence Nightingale Nursing Home.

At the end of their eight-plus years at Saint David's, the school magazine asserts that the boys will have "painted grapes and dissected frogs, studied Greek and conversed with computers." Graduation takes place at the Church of St. Thomas More in a nonreligious ceremony (boys wear ties and jackets). Awards are given in athletics, music, art and academic areas. The ceremony is followed by a reception with hors d'oeuvres and cocktails on the terrace at Saint David's. Afterwards, many families get together for dinner. Saint David's graduates attend a variety of day and boarding schools.

Traditions   Morning chapel talks, class plays, Math Bowl, History Bowl, weekly poetry recitation in Lower School, St. David's armbands, Player of the Week, fêtes de l'écoles, all-school Christmas concert, Gala Spring Art Show, clothing and book sales, seventh grade Greek play, Upper School Science Fair, Annual Dinner/Dance and Auction, faculty-father athletic contests, annual alumni soccer match, alumni Christmas party, eighth grade Art History lectures with Nightingale-Bamford School

Publications   *Saint David's Magazine*
Literary magazine: *The Canticle*
Lower School literary magazine
Yearbook

Community Service Requirement   7th grade nursing home visits are required; class projects; Upper School Social Action Committee coordinates community service activities

Hangout   Jackson Hole (hamburger restaurant)

St. Hilda's & St. Hugh's School
619 West 114th Street
New York, NY 10025
(212) 932-1980 FAX (212) 531-0102
website: www.StHildas.org

Coed
Toddlers–8th grade
Accessible

Ms. Virginia Connor, Head of School
Dr. Roxandra Antoniadis, Director of Admissions

Birthday Cutoff   September 1

Enrollment   Total enrollment: 365
  Toddler program places: 20
  Nursery places: 15
  Kindergarten places: 15
  Graduating class 2000: approximately 25

Tuition Range 2005–2006 $6,000 to $24,850, 2's (2 days)–8th grade
  All fees included, except for optional lunch for grades 3–8, $900

After-School Program   St. Hilda's & St. Hugh's After-School Program is open to children from other schools; a variety of creative and recreational activities; 3:00 P.M.–6:30 P.M.; an additional payment is required
  Vacation camps in December and March, for an additional charge

———

St. Hilda's & St. Hugh's is a coed Episcopal day school founded in 1950 by the Reverend Mother Ruth of the Community of the Holy Spirit, an Episcopal religious order for women. The faculty is entirely a lay faculty. Parents must complete an application before touring. After the tour, the child is interviewed. ERBs are required for Kindergarten. The school consists of a Lower Division for toddlers through third graders, and an Upper Division for grades four through eight. All students take art, music, drama, physical education and are required to perform community service both in and out of school.

The curriculum at St. Hilda's & St. Hugh's is traditional and integrated. There is a uniform requirement in grades one through eight, and teachers are addressed formally as "Mr. Smith," "Miss Jones." Although chapel attendance in first through eighth grades is required, the student body is diverse. French or Spanish is required from nursery on, Latin is required in seventh and eighth grades. The music and art program includes an English Brass Band and a theater arts program. Parents praise the warm, cohesive community.

St. Hilda's & St. Hugh's graduates attend a variety of secondary schools including the New York City specialized high schools (Stuyvesant and Bronx Science) and independent day and boarding schools including Horace Mann, Trinity, Nightingale-Bamford, Spence, Saint Ann's, Riverdale, Friends, Sacred Heart and Marymount.

St. Luke's School

487 Hudson Street
New York, NY 10014
(212) 924-5960, FAX (212) 924-1352
website: www.stlukeschool.org

Coed
Junior kindergarten–8th grade
Not accessible

Ms. Ann Mellow, Head
Ms. Susan Parker, Director of Admissions

Birthday Cutoff   Children entering junior kindergarten must be 4 by October 1
Children entering kindergarten must be 5 by October 1

Enrollment   Total enrollment: 200
Junior kindergarten places: 18
Kindergarten places: between 5 and 10
Graduating class: approximately 20
3 Prep for Prep students enrolled as of Fall 2000
7 Early Steps students enrolled as of Fall 2000

Grades   The Lower School is on a semester system (grades junior kindergarten–4); there are two parent conferences and two narrative reports
The Upper School is on a trimester system (grades 5–8); there are three reports and two conferences
Letter grades begin in 5th grade
Departmentalization begins in 5th grade

Tuition Range 2005–2006 $20,500 to $24,500, junior kindergarten–8th grade

Financial Aid/Scholarship   22% of the student body receive some form of aid

Endowment $600,000

Diversity 22% students of color

St. Luke's enrolls students from a variety of diversity programs including Prep for Prep, Early Steps and some others

Faculty Diversity Coordinator

Diversity Coordinator for Parents and faculty

Diversity Committees

Homework Begins gently in 2nd grade

2nd and 3rd grades approximately 30 minutes per night

4th grade 45 minutes–1 hour per night

5th and 6th grades 1½ hours per night

7th and 8th grades 2–2½ hours per night

After-School Program St. Luke's After-School Program: Monday–Friday, from 2:30 until 6 P.M.; a variety of creative and recreational activities; an additional fee is required; varsity intramural sports teams for grades 5–8; early morning dropoff at 8 A.M.

St. Luke's School was founded in 1945 and retains its affiliation with the Episcopal Church. The program is ecumenical but there is mandatory chapel from one to three times a week at the Church of St. Luke's in the Fields, a landmark building dating from 1822, rebuilt in 1985. Fifteen per cent of the students take communion.

Most classrooms in the West Village school face the two-acre enclosed tree-lined campus, affording good light and little street noise. The classrooms are spacious and bright. The school has a library, and media center, gymnasium, art, studio, small theater, music, computer and foreign language rooms, a science lab, and a large dining room. There are three out door play areas, and students use school facilities and local sports fields for junior varsity and varsity sports.

Getting in: Interviews are required for parents and children, and applicants for junior kindergarten and kindergarten must submit the results of ERB testing. Applications are due by December 1st.

Parents: There is a very active Parents Association. Parents help out in the admissions office, the library and with fundraising. Parents orchestrate grade-wide phone and e-mail chains as well as special events like welcome receptions and family dances.

Program: The school has a structured but relaxed atmosphere and offers a variety of educational approaches. St. Luke's has no formal dress code—dress is casual.

Interdisciplinary teaching is strong. The school is divided into two divisions: junior kindergarten through fourth grade; and fifth through eighth grades. Cooperative learning and small group instruction are a hallmark of the Lower School program. Technology is thoughtfully integrated in second grade. Upper School students learn strong academic skills, and are required to complete courses in English, math, social studies, foreign language, science, art, music, religious studies, physical education, library and technology. Group work and cooperative study continue with research assignments, science and technology labs. Students select either Spanish or French in fifth grade.

An outdoor education program includes a three-day trip to near the Delaware Water Gap.

Popular High School Choices Berkeley-Carroll, Brearley, Browning, Collegiate, Columbia Prep, Convent of the Sacred Heart, Dalton, Elisabeth Irwin, Fieldston, Fordham Prep, Friends, Hewitt, Loyola, Marymount, Nightingale-Bamford, Packer Collegiate, Poly Prep, Professional Children's School, Regis, Riverdale, Spence, Trevor Day, Trinity, Winston Prep, York Prep, Bronx Science, Brooklyn, Tech, LaGuardia, Stuyvesant, Hun, Kent, Millbrook, Northfield Mount Herman, Pomfret, Putney, Stony Brook, Westover

Traditions Chapel, Convocation, Jog-a-thon, Christmas Fair, Family Dance, Book Fair, Outdoor Education, Grade 8 Leadership Retreat

Publications Literary Magazine: *Portfolio*
Grade 5 Literary Newspaper: *Bookworms*
Lower School Literary Newspaper: *Wormlets*
Newsletter: *St. Luke's Times*

Hangouts Lilac Chocolates
Angelique
Cowgirl Hall of Fame
The Cupping Room Village
The Hudson Diner
Rivoli Pizza
Taylor's
The Factory Cafe

The School at Columbia University

556 West 110th Street
New York, NY 10025
(212) 851-4215, FAX (212) 851-4270
Admissions (212) 851-4216
website: www.theschool.columbia.edu
e-mail: info@theschool.columbia.edu

Coed
Kindergarten–8th grade
Accessible

Anne Burns, Acting Head of School
Luyen Chou, Associate Head of School
Dr. Marc Meyer, Director of Research and Curriculum
Anne Giaever, Director of Admissions and Personnel

Birthday Cutoff   Children entering kindergarten must be 5 by December 31st

Enrollment   Total enrollment: 335 in K–6 for the 2004–2005 school year
Kindergarten places: approximately 60

Grades   Trimester system; narrative reports with checklists, two in-depth parent/teacher conferences each year with an optional third conference at the end of the year.

Tuition 2005–2006 $24, 255, K–8th grade

Fiancial Aid/Scholarship   Approximately 97% of the student body receives some form of aid; the average scholarship awarded to families from the community is about $19,000

Endowment   Supported by the endowment and resources of Columbia University

Diversity   The student body is highly diverse and reflects the population of the neighborhood and community

After-School Program A variety of programs Monday through Friday from 3:30 to 5:30 P.M.; admission is based on a lottery, approximately 30 students per grade are admitted; there is an additional fee of $10 per day; financial aid is available

Summer Program Beginning in the summer of 2005, a recreational and academic enrichment program opens to members of the community for an additional charge

———

What started as The School Search Service at Columbia University for the children of Columbia's faculty has evolved into The School at Columbia University. The School, as it's simply called, recently opened its brand new doors. It focuses not only on attracting top faculty, but also on fostering diversity, education and community outreach.

Soon, The School will enroll 620 students in grades kindergarten through eight, and will serve some of the children of Columbia's faculty along with children from the Upper West Side (only from in Districts 3 and 5), selected through a random lottery.

The goal is to have a roughly 50/50 mix of children from Columbia families and children from the neighborhood. This is because the mission of The School is to serve as a recruitment and retention strategy for University faculty, to build community within the University and between the University and the neighborhood, and to serve as a resource and development lab for the New York City public schools. To build bridges to the neighborhood and produce materials and methodologies for the public schools, the demographics for The School have to be similar to those of a neighborhood public school.

Spearheaded by Dr. Gardner Dunnan of Dalton fame, (Dr. Dunnan was Headmaster at Dalton for 23 years), The School boasts the latest in technology—there are plasma screen TVs everywhere, even in the lobby—in a brand new 72,000 square-foot, five and a half floor facility. The School's building is adjacent to and connected through a common stairwell to a portion of Columbia's residential housing, making it ultra-convenient for some to get to school.

The School follows in a long line of other Columbia spin-off schools such as The Barnard School (now Horace Mann Lower Division) and the Horace Mann School (from Teacher's College), The Speyer School and The Lincoln School (no longer extant).

Unlike any other private school in the city, The School has the privilege of making use of the University's expansive facilities including, Butler Library, Dodge Physical Fitness Center, Baker Field, art studios, laboratories, fields, and the Earth Institute. In addition, University faculty members are regularly involved in the programs of The School.

Getting in: For families who are not affiliated with Columbia University but who live in Districts 3 or 5, applications are available through a lottery, and there's no application fee. Lottery forms are available on The School's website and at The School; the lottery is held in November. Members of Columbia's community can apply without entering the lottery but are enrolled through a "gentle" screening process using "service based" admissions. "Service based" means that as long as The School can serve a University affiliated child that child will be offered a spot *if* there is a space available at the appropriate grade level.

"Every West Side family should enter the lottery," advises Gardner Dunnan, the school's head. "It's a no brainer. If you win an application you don't have to apply, and if you do, it's an option." Of the approximately 1000 families in the lottery, The School admits a total of 30 to 40 children for kindergarten, and another 10 for grades one through seven. "We only interview fifty or so, so once you get an application you have a high probability of being offered a place at The School," explains Dr. Dunnan.

ERB's are not required, but evaluations from prior schools or programs are. Parents and children are interviewed separately on the same visit. On occasion, additional evaluations are requested and needed, The School will fund the cost.

Parents: Roughly one-third of all class parents have Columbia e-mail addresses, the rest are a mix. No fancy Fifth or Park Avenue cocktail parties here, but one on Central Park West may well be in the not too distant future.

The common goals of The School's PTA are, of course, to raise money and plan events, but also to work on community outreach and building relationships among The School and its neighbors.

"These are parents who have already made the commitment to diversity," remarks a parent of a second grader. "Play dates are easy, and so are the friendships," the parent says. "Almost all families live in the immediate area; friendships form along the lines of their interests."

The PTA is in full gear. They publish a newsletter, and have held a few events like a recent Q&A informational meeting.

Program: The School is a supportive, first rate learning environment, with a student/teacher ratio of approximately five to one; the focus is on the students. A parent of a second grader raves, "They know my child, they know what books he likes to read, and they know he likes history so they brought in some history books." Other parents praise teachers, too. "The faculty are extraordinary, experienced teachers that are responsive."

For some subjects, like dance, special teachers are arranged, often with a portfolio of skills. For its dance program, The School has a contract with Steps on Broadway, "a dance company that trains four-year-olds to seventy-four year olds," remarks Dr. Dunnan.

The creative, experimental and interdisciplinary program boasts a Child Study Team that evaluates and supports every child. Classrooms, called "pods," are common spaces that form the nucleus of each classroom. In kindergarten through fourth grade, children's learn math, science, culture and society, communication arts and technology, fine arts, wellness and fitness. In fifth through eighth grades, specific academic subjects, science and technology, math, humanities, fine arts, and wellness and fitness are often sequenced to provide a deeper understanding.

The latest in technology is omnipotent at The School—no black boards here—white boards and "smartboards" only. Moreover, there is a complete commitment to technology. Digital technology, multimedia materials and their applications, wireless connections and laptops are available, almost one for every student.

As a research and development center for the larger University, The School has a Center for Integrated Learning and Teaching (CILT) that sponsors and participates in research projects related to many aspects of a kindergarten through eighth grade program. Recently, CILT developed two experimental software programs that are currently in use. There's also plenty of professional development for faculty, including University sponsored research and academic collaborations, workshops and conferences.

Traditions Integrated Projects Week, Weekly All School Assemblies, fall and spring community events, Terry Fox Fun Run, Penny Harvest

Publications PTA monthly newsletter in English and Spanish

The Solomon Schechter School of Manhattan
50 East 87th Street
(corner of Madison Avenue)
New York, N.Y. 10128
(212) 427-9500
website: www.sssm.org
e-mail: sssm2@aol.com

Lower Elementary Division
Kindergarten–2nd grade
50 East 87th Street
(212) 427-9500

Upper Elementary and Middle School
Grades 3–8
15 West 86th Street
(212) 427-9500

Coed
Wheelchair accessible

Dr. Steven C. Lorch, Head
Elisa Marcus, Head of the Lower Elementary School
Gary Pretsfelder, Head of the Upper Elementary School
Daneet Brill, Director of Admissions

Uniform   K–5: Boys: navy or gray slacks, blue shirt (white on Fridays), navy sweater with crest
Girls: navy jumper or skirt or slacks, white blouse, navy sweater with crest
6–8: Boys: Khaki or navy slacks or corduroys, blue or white button down, turtlenecks or polo shirt, and navy sweater with crest
Girls: Khaki or navy slacks, corduroys or skirt, blue or white button down, turtleneck or polo shirt, navy sweater with crest

Birthday Cutoff   Children must turn 5 years old by December 31st; developmental readiness is the main consideration

Enrollment   140
Kindergarten places 36

Grades   Detailed anecdotal reports
K–5; anecdotal reports with checklists as well as a portfolio assessment for grades 3–8

Tuition Range 2005–2006 $21,800, (Tuition is based upon a sliding scale depending on parents' ability to pay)

Endowment   N/A

Financial Aid/Scholarship   55%

Diversity   8% students of color

After-School Program   Interscholastic sports teams in soccer, basketball and cross country, Homework Club, Drama Club, newspaper, Webwizards

Summer/Vacation Program   Vacation Arts Club

The Solomon Schechter School of Manhattan opened its doors in 1996 with a kindergarten and continues to grow, adding a new grade each year; the Lower School now has eight grades and enrollment is strong. The Solomon Schechter School is one of a network of over 70 Solomon Schechter schools throughout the United States and Canada, the first of which was established in 1951. Among these sister schools is the Solomon Schechter High School of New York, with which the school collaborates on a number of joint community initiatives. The two schools are separate entities, though there have been discussions from time to time about possible future affiliation.

The Solomon Schechter School of Manhattan was conceived in 1994 as an initiative of the United Synagogue of Conservative Judaism and the rabbis of the nine Conservative synagogues in Manhattan. During its formative period, a group of dedicated parents and community leaders came together to develop the school's mission and character. Elie Wiesel serves as Honorary Chairman of the Board of Trustees, Dr. Samuel Klagsbrun as Chairman of the Education Committee. Dr. Klagsbrun says that at the school "children learn to participate fully in modern society and contribute to our general culture while feeling completely at home in the Jewish world." The aim was to "establish a Jewish day school . . . where students will be given a rich understanding of their Jewish heritage, a fluent command of the Hebrew language, and a passion for Jewish learning. The goal is to nurture culturally aware, compassionate, and socially responsible individuals who will constitute the future leadership of the American Jewish Community."

Getting in: Parents must call for an application and schedule a tour. Tours are available in the Fall and Spring. Children entering kindergarten are interviewed in groups. When possible, nursery school visits are made. Older applicants meet with the Admissions Director and/or the Head of the Upper Elementary Division. The results of ERB or any other standardized testing should also be forwarded to The Solomon Schechter School. Finally, the parents come in to meet with the Head of School, Dr. Lorch. To fulfill the family education requirement, parents in the school must participate in a series of classes in Jewish life and texts but they are not required to know Hebrew.

Parents: One parent described the social mix as "An eclectic group who are down-to-earth and 'heimish,' " and diverse geographically and religiously (although all the children are Jewish). Parents help out in the office, go on field trips and volunteer in the classroom. The PA sponsors brunches, and an annual kosher food tasting evening, an Education Night and an annual retreat. All parents are members of the PA and invited to attend meetings.

Program: The Head of the Elementary and Middle School, Dr. Steven Lorch, who has degrees from Harvard and Columbia, has previously been the head of three other Jewish schools in North America, Australia and in Israel. According to Dr. Lorch, there are two language objectives for the kindergarten year: 1) that every child will read and write in English by the end of the year; and 2) every child will become proficient in Hebrew. "To achieve these objectives the classroom has to truly be an enriched bilingual environment."

The classroom teachers are bilingual (English/Hebrew) and work with the Early Childhood Director to design the curriculum. The classroom emphasizes experiential or active learning. There are early childhood materials, including blocks, as well as computers in the classroom. The classes often break into smaller groups for math activities, block building, computers, and so on.

A main feature of the program is an interdisciplinary (or thematic) approach to learning. Topics of study are chosen by the students on the basis of their interests and each topic is then investigated from a variety of perspectives: social studies, Jewish tradition, the arts, science, literature, mathematics, writing: all contribute to a rich and textured understanding of the topic at hand.

Reading is taught by combining elements of both Whole Language and phonics. Children use manipulative materials when learning math and sciences. Children are instructed by specialists in music and physical education twice a week. There is daily physical exercise, either on the outdoor play roof or in nearby Central Park.

Children are introduced to Jewish life through the Jewish Studies curriculum and Hebrew is taught using the natural method of language study. Religion plays a central role in the life of the school. Prayer, activities related to holidays, the observance of dietary laws and acts of kindness (charity) are stressed. Girls are offered full egalitarian privileges and participation.

Jewish issues and religious thought play a central role in the life of the school. Students study math, science, history, English, Bible, rabbinical thought, Hebrew and French or Spanish. Extracurricular courses and activities include the Bridges to Brotherhood, Blacks and Jews in Dialogue, Investment Club, City Lights (which brings students to special *High Five!* Performances), Solomon Society (student government), choir, drama, studio art, theater production arts, newspaper, yearbook, web design, festival and daily prayer planning committees. There are interscholastic sports programs offered in cross-country, soccer, volleyball, basketball and softball. Most of the school's Jewish rituals and holiday celebrations are entirely planned and carried out by the students in consultation with the school's rabbi.

Traditions   Monday and Thursday prayer in the Chapel (parents are welcome), Friday friendship circles, *Kabbalat Shabbat, Siddur* ceremonies, Family *Shabbaton* retreat, "Exhibitions" (Middle School presentations), annual concerts.

Publications   Weekly newsletter: *Daf Kesher*

393

The Spence School
Lower School
(Grades K–4)
56 East 93rd Street

Middle and Upper Schools
(Grades 5–12)
22 East 91st Street
New York, NY 10128-0657
(212) 289-5940, FAX (212) 289-6025
website: www.spenceschool.org

All girls
Kindergarten–12th grade
Accessible

Ms. Arlene J. Gibson, Head of School
Ms. Alice Shedlin, Director of Admissions

Uniform   Grades kindergarten–4: plaid jumper and white shirt, solid-color stockings, tights, socks
Grades 5–8: navy blue skirt, navy blue pants and white shirt
Grades 9–12: solid gray skirt or gray slacks, any shirt that has sleeves and covers midriff; no leg warmers, leggings or long underwear, low-heeled shoes only
Uniform is not required on Fridays
After fall trimester, seniors may petition to cease wearing their uniforms
Before the start of school uniform fittings are held at Spence
Gym outfits are given to the girls free of charge

Birthday Cutoff   Girls entering kindergarten must be 5 by August 31

Enrollment   Total enrollment: 621
Kindergarten places: approximately 52
9th grade places: 10–12
Graduating class size: approximately 40

Grades   Semester system in Lower School
Trimester system in Middle/Upper Schools

Grades kindergarten–4: checklist (skill acquired, developing skill, needs support, exhibits strength marked improvement)
Grades 5–8: letter grades begin in 7th grade, detailed anecdotal reports plus a checklist
Grades 9–12: letter grades and detailed checklist
Departmentalization begins in 6th grade
First final exam in 6th grade

Tuition Range 2005–2006 $26,000 to $27,300, K–12th grade
Additional fees: for lunch, Parents Association dues and miscellaneous supplies approximately $1,060 to $1,070

Financial Aid/Scholarship   Approximately 18% of the entire student body receives some form of tuition assistance, 23% in the Upper School
Financial aid accounts for 10% of the operating budget

Endowment $52.7 million (as of June 2003)

Diversity   24% students of color; 26% in the Upper School
8 Prep for Prep students enrolled as of fall 2003
2 ABC (A Better Chance) students
6 TEAK students
30 Early Steps students
Cultural Awareness Club
The Afro-Latino Alliance
Jewish Culture Club
Asia Society
Spence Women's Action Network (SWAN)

Homework   Kindergarten: none
1st and 2nd: approximately 10–20 minutes
3rd and 4th: 30–45 minutes
5th: 1 hour–1½ hours, plus reading assignments
6th: 20–30 minutes per subject per night plus reading assignments
7th–8th: approximately 2½–3 hrs
9th–12th: approximately 3–4 hrs

After-School Program   Second Act After-School Program: coed, open to students from other schools; a variety of creative and

enrichment activities for an additional charge; Monday–Thursday from 3:00–6:00 P.M., Friday from 2:00 to 4:30 P.M.
Middle School: interscholastic sports program
Upper School: varsity teams
Some club meetings and choir, drama and dance rehearsals for grades 5–12 are held after school; choruses rehearse during school periods except for select choir and glee club

Summer Program   Second Act June Program for students in grades K–4 there is an additional charge
Jump Start: a ninth grade one-week program for new ninth grade students
Early Start: a foreign language orientation program for new Middle School students

————

The Spence School, founded in 1892 as Miss Spence's School for Girls, is housed in elegant buildings on East 91st Street and East 93rd Street and offers a well-rounded, rigorous academic program, strong in performing arts, the sciences, visual arts and foreign language studies. Spence artfully combines the traditional and innovative; it was one of the first independent schools to use the computer in the lower grades, and multicultural perspectives add excitement and relevance to the traditional core of studies.

"Relevance" is a key concept at Spence. Spence's mission, "to inspire students to meet the ethical and intellectual challenges of life," is summed up in the school motto: "*Non Scholae Sed Vitae Discimus*: Not For School But For Life We Learn." Spence is committed to a diverse, academically talented student body. One parent said, "It's very fast paced; you need to have a child who can handle that."

In 1998, Head of School Mrs. Edes Gilbert retired; she was the last of a generation of Grand Dames who governed the prestigious Manhattan girls' school over the past twenty years. Arlene Joy Gibson was selected to lead Spence into the twenty-first century. Educated at Bryn Mawr College, Ms. Gibson's area of study is Latin America; she was a Fulbright Scholar in Political Science at the University of the Republic, Montevideo, Uruguay. An advocate of single sex education, Gibson was formerly headmistress of a girls' school in Summit, New Jersey, and she was founding President of the National Coalition of Girls' Schools. "What attracted me to Spence," Gibson told us, "was the relationship between the students and the faculty. The atmosphere, which I observed in the classrooms, was positively electric. Students were asking such intelligent and insightful questions that they stretched the thinking of the entire class, while teachers challenged students to probe ever deeper into the material. Everywhere, there was the excitement that comes from learning. Even in the youngest grades of the school, Spence truly forms a community of scholars."

Recently, Spence successfully completed a ten-year NYSAIS evaluation for reaccredidation. The Visiting Committee found the Spence traditions of rigor and inquiry, as well as its concern for meeting the challenges of diversity and the demands of a rapidly changing world to be strong. Also, the role of women is highly valued, and inextricably entwined with all aspects of the life of the school.

The new home for the Lower School (grades kindergarten through 4th) has more homerooms. The kindergarten spaces are larger and Lower School class sizes are smaller, about 16 per class. Computer and science labs are designed to serve the needs of Lower School girls. At 91st Street, the expansion of Middle and Upper School facilities includes a Foreign Language Media Lab, Visual Arts Center and a Black Box Studio as well as additional science labs. There are more meeting and conference spaces for students and teachers and a new gym.

Getting in: Spence is one of the few very selective schools where parents can have an individual tour and interview before they even apply. Admissions personnel told us, "No letters of recommendation, please." What are they looking for? "We are offering a place to a girl who will take full advantage of everything a Spence education has to offer." One parent was very impressed by the Upper School student who led her tour: "She was so open, obviously not scripted, and she answered all our questions, which indicated to me that Spence is proud of what it does, and the girls are not afraid to talk about it." Parents are given a card with the name of the young woman who led their tour so that they can contact her through the admissions office if they have any additional questions. Once the application is made, parents applying for kindergarten are given an appointment for their daughter's interview. In the Lower School, this takes place with a small group of other girls at the school. In the Upper and Middle Schools, the appointment is individual. Spence has a wait list.

One mother told us that there is no typical Spence girl: "What distinguishes Spence from the other girls' schools is that there is no norm here. The girls are individuals and all are enthusiastic about learning."

Parents: A parent described the parent body at Spence as dominated by two groups: "Those with well-worn, polished shoes (old money), and those with brand-new Manolo Blahniks (new money)." Another parent described the parent body as "some families who don't live on their salaries—attorneys, investment bankers, independent entrepreneurs." But the Upper School is more diverse. Many prominent Jewish families feel comfortable at Spence and the school's diversity has increased too. "But," says one parent, "ascension through the ranks of Spence's Parents Association requires a certain amount of social skill and savvy." Class cocktail parties or suppers are held at Spence. The Spring Event for new parents is a reception in the dining room at which fifth grade girls serve as hostesses.

Program: The Lower School curriculum is integrated where possible; drama and art are often incorporated. The girls spend lots of time in the big block area in the kindergarten classroom. Each kindergarten class has two teachers, and the class frequently breaks into small groups. Reading readiness begins in kindergarten using both Whole Language and phonics. There is a resource center for students who need support. A parent said, "Teachers reinforce learning through writing, speaking, observation, drawing." Classes write and illustrate their own books.

In kindergarten, students learn about world cultures (China, Korea, Puerto Rico, the Amazon) through through the lens of the family unit. Kindergartners do units on various countries for which they make passports and cameras, and as the teacher reads from a book about a country, a student says "click" and later draws a picture of the mental image she had "taken." The girls bring in items from other countries and create their own museum in a corner of the room.

In kindergarten parents are invited to spend a morning with their daughters sometime during the year to share a special talent or interest with the class. They also come in for Parents' Visiting Day. In one kindergarten class a parent came to talk about his trip to China. If parents have any questions, teachers are always available.

Computer classes are part of the curriculum in all divisions of the school. Alumnae from the late seventies remember an emphasis on computer even then. In grades kindergarten through fifth, LOGO, a computer graphics language, is taught. Keyboarding and word processing are taught in third grade. The Lower School has its own computer lab with Macintosh computers. There is a fully equipped Lower School science lab and two science teachers whose sole responsibility is to work with kindergartners through fourth graders. One computer science course is required in the Upper School.

In addition to academic subjects, first graders take courses in art, music, and physical education. Art, dance and drama teachers are working professionals. In the spacious art room we saw highly individualized stick puppets and masks. Throughout the social studies curriculum, the brochure states, there is a "special emphasis on the role of women in history and focus on the rich diversity of cultures," and social studies is coordinated with language arts, music and art.

Second graders are also introduced to chess with a semester devoted to learning the intricacies of the game. The Spence Middle School Chess Team took first place in their age group at the first National All Girls Chess Championship held in Chicago.

One year, for an integrated second grade unit on baseball, a parent told us, "For English they read the biography of Jackie Robinson, for art they studied baseball murals and created their own, in history they examined integration and baseball and in gym, they learned the essence of the game—they played it!"

Third graders participate in an immigrant project; they study a person or family from another country. They also study the history of New York and take many field trips to places such as Philipsburg Manor, Ellis Island, The Museum of the City of New York and the Natural History Museum.

"Simulations" enrich the fourth and fifth grade social studies curriculum. Art is incorporated into these simulations as well as research and writing skills. Fourth graders play the Economics Game, an activity in which the girls apply their mathematical knowledge to real world experiences. Each week the girls are paid a salary of $7.50. From that salary they must pay certain fixed expenses such as rent, food and taxes. Their variable expenses also include charitable donations and health expenses. To supplement their income, the girls write business plans, consult with the Better Business Bureau (their teacher) and set up their own businesses. Eventually the girls are able to invest in the stock market, just like Mom and Dad. As part of the fifth grade United States history unit, students imagine that they are colonists trying to survive in the New World. In the spring they take a "simulated" covered-wagon trip across the Western United States and construct detailed models of their wagon train.

Foreign language begins in third grade, with a choice between French and Spanish. One parent said games and songs are used to teach language in the early years. An optional second language can be elected in seventh grade.

Health education starts early and covers a variety of topics from nutrition to body image and anatomy to peer and family relationships. As part of the social and emotional learning curriculum, the fifth grade participates in the prepare/personal safety program. More important, parents say that self-confidence, self-esteem and leadership are constantly reinforced in the girls: "They are always supporting the girls in their choices and decisions," "The girls are self-confident from beginning to end."

Drama, dance and music are part of the curriculum in each grade. Kindergartners perform at the Holiday Pageant in December. Fourth graders perform a ballet. Lower School senior chorus is for third and fourth graders. The sixth grade chorus, a Middle School chorus and Glee Club are open to all. The Select Choir (which travels abroad) and three chamber ensembles in the Upper School are open by audition. There is an instrumental music program for grades one through twelve, and private lessons at Spence are in great demand.

The dance program is extensive: folk, jazz, ballet, in addition to physical education classes. One second grade mother said of her daughter's dance performance: "They were in unison doing these routines; we were all stunned." The Middle and Upper School dance company performs at Symphony Space each year.

All girls gain experience with public speaking. One parent said her daughter, who is normally reluctant to perform on stage, got up in front of the Lower School to read her own poem: "She never would have had the confidence if she hadn't been at Spence." The other girls were supportive. "There was no competitiveness. All the girls' poems were great."

To mark the transition from Lower School, Middle Schoolers (fifth through eighth grades) have their own newly renovated two floors, and their own uniform. The head of the Middle School told us "there is a real esprit de corps in Middle School; it has its own identity." Middle Schoolers have their own student council. The sixth grade is fully departmentalized and in the seventh grade letter grades begin.

Art continues to be integrated into the curriculum. The sixth grade class studies a unit on Egypt. The girls learned the names of the gods and pharoahs and all of their attributes and contributions and learned about Egyptian culture and religious beflefs. In math they studied the geometry of the pyramids. In art they made their own hieroglyphics. The Egyptian unit culminated with a visit to the Metropolitan Museum of Art to see the permanent exhibit on pyramids, the Sphinx, dynasties and relevant artifacts.

Eighth graders read *Jane Eyre, Romeo and Juliet* and a selection of poetry and American short stories. In history both Western and non-Western cultures are explored, and students hone their research methods. Seventh graders study the Middle Ages and the history of Africa and Islam.

The Middle School fields teams in basketball, softball, soccer, volleyball, track and field and swimming. These teams participate in interscholastic competition.

Middle Schoolers participate in community service projects through the Community Service Club for grades six through twelve and volunteer in the Lower School. Middle Schoolers perform in the annual eighth grade play with boys from neighborhood schools. Annual dances for seventh and eighth graders provide other opportunities to socialize with the opposite sex.

Contact among grades is important to Spence girls. Middle and Upper School students attend Wednesday morning assemblies together as well as their own assemblies. The Middle School has its own assembly on Tuesday mornings, the Upper School on Mondays. Mixing of grades occurs in the lunchroom: Upper School students eat all together according to their schedule, not by grade. The head of school and teachers eat with the girls. Field Day offers students on mixed teams a chance to work together with girls from other grades.

If you go straight through Spence from kindergarten to twelfth grade you are known as a "survivor." Attrition typically occurs after eighth grade when some girls go to boarding schools or, occasionally, to a coed day school. According to a survivor, "The work builds up in eighth and ninth grades and then increases again in tenth and eleventh, but if you're good at budgeting your time you don't notice."

The Upper School at Spence consists of grades nine through twelve. The Upper School is academically rigorous. Students who enter at ninth grade are required to ease their transition by attending the summer JumpStart Program, an orientation program that is free of charge. Girls with a problem subject can go to the Resource Center. "If necessary," says a student, "teachers will even look over your notes with you." Classes are kept small, about twelve to fifteen students. The average course load is five to six full credit courses. In addition to the usual core subjects, computer science, performing arts, speech and health are Upper School requirements, as are four years of foreign language or three of one language and two of another. Spence does not stress the AP program, but offers AP courses in foreign language, studio art, calculus, biology and physics. Many electives are offered to juniors and seniors and material covered is often as sophisticated as college level course work. Some electives include "Conflicts in the Middle East," Astronomy, Native American Literature, Computer Programming and Robotics. Students are required to take two years of lab science; most choose to take another advanced-level science course. In 2003, the Middle and Upper School science labs were completely renovated. A chemistry lab, a dedicated Middle School lab and a prep room for setting up experiments before class have been added. The physics lab has also been expanded.

Students say that a friendly teacher-student relationship at Spence makes their school unique. One reason for this is that teachers in the Middle and Upper Schools must teach a range of grades and as a result get to know the girls as they mature. Teachers also act as advisors to their students both as homeroom teachers and as faculty advisors to student-led clubs.

According to the brochure, in English a "special emphasis is placed on a cross-cultural study of literature so that students are exposed to a range of material outside the Western tradition that enriches their understanding of other cultures." An elective course in world literature is required. Senior Seminar and/or independent study are also available.

Clara Spence, visionary educator and founder of The Spence School, believed in a broad curriculum to meet the interests of the students. Today, many courses at Spence are developed based upon student interest or faculty initiative. Reflecting increased student interest, the history elective program in the Upper School includes "Conflicts in the Middle East," "Latin America: From Conquest to Independence," as well as Indian History and Japanese History. In a thoughtful course called "African-American Literature," students are introduced to the writings of the men and women who shaped contemporary black American culture: DuBois, Hurston, King, Baldwin, Malcolm X and others.

Students with proficiency in the arts can take advanced course work in studio art, photography and the performing arts.

Spence has wonderful opportunities for foreign language study abroad including "Adventures in Real Communication," open to tenth through twelfth graders, who can take a one- or two-month program in France, Spain or Latin America. There is the School Year Abroad option for eleventh and twelfth graders, the Swiss Semester in Zermatt for tenth graders, the San Patricio Exchange in Madrid for tenth or eleventh graders and for ninth graders, a one- or two-month spring program in Evreux, France. For those who prefer an experience closer to home, participation in the Maine Coast Semester in Chewonki, Maine, study at the Mountain School in Vermont in association with Milton Academy or the Island School Program in the Caribbean are offered.

An eleventh grader told us that after school most girls either do homework, participate in school clubs or go out with their boyfriends, who pick them up at school. "Athletics are popular, chorus is fabulous and so is the choral master. Attendance at dance concerts and Glee Club events is good," she said.

Ninth and tenth graders have privileges; they can leave school if they have parental permission. Eleventh and twelfth graders can simply sign out. Ninth and tenth graders share "the Pit," a lounge area contiguous with the ninth and tenth grade lockers. New junior and senior lounges were opened in 2004. They are carefully and thoughtfully located on the same floor as the College Counselor, the Registrar and the Upper School Dean. Senior privileges include not wearing their uniform in spring of senior year, coming in late on Fridays (if they don't have a class) and being allowed to use the elevators. "You'd think they'd never used an elevator before. They stop at every floor," says one parent.

There is an Upper School student council. One student council event is Color or Theme Days: Themes are picked, such as Western Day or Come As You Are Day, and the faculty dress up too. The Upper School student council is currently grappling with weightier issues such as reconsidering the school uniform and establishing an honor code.

There are numerous opportunities for faculty-led and student-led extracurricular participation at Spence. Faculty-led activities include dramatic productions, dance company, athletic teams and chorus, while student-led activities include drama club, Amnesty International, French club and Spanish club. Because of the size and unique nature of its community, many students have the opportunity to assume a leadership position in a club or activity by the time they graduate.

Commencement is held at the Church of the Heavenly Rest. Awards are given out at the Athletic Awards Banquet for athletic achievement and sportsmanship. The White Blazer Award is given to a student who is well respected in the athletic community, demonstrating determination, sportsmanship, cooperation, dedication and leadership. At Final Assembly external academic awards, such as National Merit Scholarships, are announced, but graduates no longer have the traditional Spence prizes for special academic achievements bestowed upon them. It is thought this will discourage excessive competition, according to the school. But one junior told us, "They didn't acknowledge the good work that everybody did."

When asked what embodies the spirit of Spence, Head of School Arlene Gibson replied: "The joy that is noticeable in the halls of the school."

Popular College Choices   Yale, Cornell, Princeton, Harvard, University of Pennsylvania, Wesleyan, Brown, Duke, Oberlin, Tufts, Vassar, Amherst, Columbia

Traditions   Opening Assembly, Lower School Halloween party, Lower School New Parents' Dinner, Lower School Field Day, spring drama, eighth grade play, eighth grade trip, skating party, Middle School Sing-Off Competition, Middle School picnic, Lower School holiday program, Father/Daughter Evening, Mother/Daughter Tea, third and fourth grade foreign language breakfasts, Grandparents' and Special Friends Day, Bias Awareness Conference, Mini Olympics, Hispanic Heritage Month Assembly, The Bridge, Dance Concert at Symphony Space, Middle and Upper School Concert, Book Fair, clothing sale, Choral group, Spence Boutique, student council 91st Street Fair, grade ten Interschool trip to Washington, D.C.

Publications   Newspaper: *Spence Voice*
Literary arts magazine: *Fingerprints*
Yearbook: *Threshold*
Newsletter on current political issues: *Spark*

Community Service Requirement   No specific number of hours: in grades 5–12 the board of the Community Service Club is made up of members from each division led by a student and faculty advisor; weekly meetings are held to plan a variety of fund-raising and volunteer activities such as tutoring projects in local public schools, food and clothing drives, visits to the elderly or homebound, work in soup kitchens or daycare organizations. The service club plans an annual Community Service Fair

Hangouts   Jackson Hole (hamburger restaurant around the corner on Madison), junior lounge, senior lounge

The Studio School

(Preschool through 4th grade)
124A West 95th Street
New York, NY 10025
(212) 678-2416

(5th through 8th grade)
115 West 95th Street
New York, NY 10026
(212) 678-2416
website: www.studioschoolnyc.org
e-mail: info@studioschoolnyc.org

Coed
Nursery (22 mos)–8th grade
Not accessible at 124A West 95th Street

Accessible at 115 West 95th Street
Ms. Janet C. Rotter, Head of School
Ms. Jennifer K. Tarpley, Director of Admissions

Birthday Cutoff   Children entering kindergarten must be 5 by September 1

Enrollment   Total enrollment: approximately 110
Nursery places (18 months–2½ years): 15, largest point of entry
Early childhood (3- and 4-year olds) places: approximately 10
Kindergarten and up: 5 to 6 places in K, as available in upper grades

Tuition Range 2005–2006 $4,670 to $24,055, Nursery through 8th grade
All fees are included

Financial Aid/Scholarship   15% of the student body receives some form of aid
Approximately $75,000 budgeted annually

Endowment   None

After-School Program   Extended day program until 5:50 P.M.; a variety of creative and recreational activities for an additional payment

Summer Program   Summer Camp from mid-June through the end of July; a variety of creative and recreational activities for an additional payment

---

The Studio School was founded in 1971 by Robert and Dolores Welber as a "one room schoolhouse" in Greenwich Village. Three years later Janet Rotter, a graduate of Bank Street, came to Studio as an assistant teacher. She is currently Head of the School, as she has been for the past twenty years.

In 1987 the school moved to a building on the Upper West Side which is leased from the adjoining synagogue. (The school has no religious affiliation.) In addition to several bright classrooms, the school has a well-equipped kitchen, a sunny yard, a library, and a large common room which also serves as the cafeteria and a toddler gym. In 2003, Studio added a Middle School by purchasing several brownstones across the street, and in September, 2004, Studio acquired the building adjacent to it that will ultimately become the future home of the school. The new facility, currently under renovation, will include larger classrooms, a new library, a music room, an art room, dance studios, a gym, greenhouse, lounges, community space, a science lab and offices. The Studio School has always emphasized a sound traditional curriculum combined with a developmental approach incorporating each child's social and emotional growth. The school has a neighborhood feeling and parent involvement is welcome.

Getting in: Parents can attend an open house/tour before applying. Tours are held every week in the Fall, beginning in October. Touring parents are given admissions materials, and interested parents must call to schedule an appointment for a family interview with the Director of Admissions after a completed application has been sent in. Children five and under are interviewed in small groups with parents. Older children attend a regular day of classes. ERB testing is requested for applicants age 8 and above.

Parents: All parents are encouraged to take advantage of the bimonthly Parent/Child Development meetings led by the school's Head, Janet Rotter. Trimester Group Curriculum meetings offer parents the opportunity to learn about their child's curriculum and ask questions; parent/teacher conferences are held three times a year. There's also a Parent Connection program by means of which current parents smooth the way for new ones.

Program: One of the founding principles of the Studio School is that children of all ages can learn from each other; the school still uses cross-age and cross-grade grouping. There is a teacher and an assistant in each classroom through second grade. Class groupings are carefully evaluated and reassembled each year.

"The school's emphasis is on learning how to think and create and not just fulfilling requirements," says Ms. Rotter. "Students learn that there is not just one way to get to the solution of a problem. Thinking, and the interaction between student and teacher, is the point." The school's curriculum focuses on the ways children learn, particularily on their individual learning styles. Trips both near and far enhance the program. Children can work independently within a group setting, focusing on the concepts and skills that will help them move on to the next level of development.

Attention is also paid to the emotional life of the students. A parent told us, "The teacher is very aware of my child's attitude towards her work. They work with her on the development of self-discipline, organization and self-evaluation in addition to teaching the curriculum."

Studio does not have formal grades; rather students are organized by age in mixed age groupings like "Sevens and Eights" instead of second and third grades.

A unique aspect of the Studio school curriculum is the Kitchen Science class. Each day a hot lunch is prepared (under the supervision of a chef and the Kitchen Science Teacher) by a team of students (ages three and up) and served to the entire school. Cooking combines skill work in math (measuring), reading and writing (recipes and menus), science (mixing different things together) and social studies (a group studying colonial America will prepare a lunch representative of that period).

The block room is used by all groups through the six and seven-year-olds. After "walking and exploring" the neighborhood, younger children will recreate what they saw in blocks. After a recent trip to the Brooklyn Bridge, the older children spent a week recreating it with blocks as a part of an in-depth study of the bridge. For physical education, toddlers play in the outside yard and have music and movement once a week, and elementary students (ages five and older) go to Central Park every day— weather permitting—and they have dance class once a week. Middle School students, jog around Central Park Reservoir, take calisthenics, play tennis, take yoga and compete in team sports.

Reading is taught using eclectic methods including Whole Language, sight words, basal readers, and phonics. Children are also read to every day. There is a cozy carpeted platform with cushions for independent reading in the hallway between nursery classrooms.

Reading and writing at Studio are inseparable and students have both subjects every day. Children ages seven and older have a Library Discovery class each week that includes poetry, fables, myths, short stories, folktales, biographies, autobiographies, essays and plays in developmentally appropriate ways. Children learn how to write, critique each other's work and interpret literary work. The year ends with an anthology of creative work of all the students who wish to participate. Middle School students, with the help of teachers, produce the anthology, editing, and proofreading and designing the layout and content while working on deadline. Computers are also used for research.

Math is taught sequentially beginning with block building and evolving to Algebra. Students are given open-ended problems that use manipulatives, puzzles, brainteasers that foster math and logic skills.

Studio's One World class combines social studies with science. Designed by Ms. Rotter, the One World class helps children gain perspective on the past and present and explore their relationship to the larger world and what it means to live in a global community. The class culminates with year-end independent projects that are shared with the school's community.

French, Spanish and Latin (for older students) are offered, beginning with songs in the early years and progressing to more formal instruction. French and Portuguese independent study programs are available.

The arts program permeates the entire school. The youngest children play with clay, crayons, paper and paints and singing and music are part of their daily lives at school. Older students can join the school's chorus, work with Orff instruments, recorders, and learn to read music. There are also weekly dance classes, and theater where students learn to write and perform their own plays, and work with other mediums such as paint, clay, charcoal, pencil, sewing, weaving, and photography.

Homework begins at age six (an assignment time is built into the school day). Grading begins in the middle elementary classes.

All students are required to complete a set number of hours student teaching, and an independent project before graduating. At graduation, students deliver individual speeches before receiving their diplomas.

Graduates   Attend various independent schools including: Saint Ann's School, Brooklyn Friends, Elisabeth Irwin, Ethical Culture/Fieldston, Friends, Horace Mann, Trevor Day, York Prep and various public schools like Beacon, Bronx Science and Stuyvesant.

Traditions   Back to School Orientation Night, Parent Development Meetings, Student Sponsored Halloween Party, Thanksgiving Feast, Winter Ice Skating/Picnic, Multicultural Festival, Auction/Gala, June Picnic, All School Graduation Party

Publications   Studio School Newsletter
Annual Anthology of Students Prose, Poetry, and Artwork

The Town School

540 East 76th Street
New York, NY 10021
(212) 288-4383
website: www.thetownschool.org

Coed
Nursery–8th grade
Accessible

Mr. Christopher Marblo, Head of School
Ms. Natasha Sahadi, Director of Admissions

Uniform   None for nursery and kindergarten divisions
Lower and Upper School girls: plaid kilt or navy jumper or navy and tan skirt; solid-colored collared or turtleneck shirt; girls may wear solid navy, gray or tan pants except on Fridays; sweaters, socks, leggings and tights may be worn in the colors of the plaid
Lower and Upper School boys: solid navy, gray or tan pants; solid-colored, collared or turtleneck shirt in the colors of the plaid
Friday is dress-up day for assembly: Girls wear skirts, boys wear navy jacket, white or blue shirt and tie
The first Tuesday of each month is a non-uniform day: Denim and sweat clothes may be worn

Birthday Cutoff   Children entering nursery school must be 3 by September 1
Children entering kindergarten must be 5 by September 1

Enrollment   Total enrollment: 385
Nursery places: approximately 18
Kindergarten places: approximately 26–32
8th grade graduating class: approximately 38

Grades   Trimester system
Letter and effort grades are given in the Upper School beginning with the second trimester of 5th grade
Departmentalization begins in 5th grade

Tuition Range 2005–2006 $13,500 to $26,500, nursery–8th grade

Tuition includes lunch, trips; Parents Association dues are $35 annually.

A tuition refund plan, extended payment plan and accident plan are available

Financial Aid/Scholarship   Approximately 14% of the student body receive some form of financial aid

Endowment $17 million

Diversity   11 Prep for Prep students enrolled as of Fall 2004; full time Director of Diversity; Diversity Curriculum Guide developed by the Town School Faculty Diversity Committee: a school-sponsored committee comprising parents, teachers and administrators, for the purpose of sharing multicultural interests, concerns and suggestions; monthly meetings are posted on school calendar; the committee includes members from the Parents Association and a Diversity Committee on Town's Board of Trustees

Homework   Because of the long school day, homework in the early years is kept to a minimum:

Kindergarten: occasionally

1st grade—HomeLinks twice a week

2nd: beginning in the second half of the year, about 15 minutes

3rd and 4th: 45 minutes–1 hour

4th, 5th and 6th: 1 hour–1½ hours

7th 8th: 2–3 hours

After-School Program   The Town School After-School Programs are Postscript and Clubhouse

Junior Postscript Program: for pre-K and kindergarten students, Monday through Thursday, 2:45–4:00 P.M., Friday, 12:30–1:30 P.M., a variety of creative and recreational activities; a fee is required

Postscript Program: for grades 1–6, Monday through Thursday 3:45–5:00 P.M., Friday, 1:00–2:30 P.M., with extended day option until 6:00 P.M.; activities include: fencing, basketball, computer, photography, woodworking, gymnastics, arts and crafts, CATS tennis, theatre; a fee is required

Clubhouse Program: a multi-aged option with rotating choices

daily, beginning at 12:00 until 6:00 P.M.
Intramural sports program
Interscholastic athletic competition for grades 5–8

Summer Program Summersault program for ages 3–9, open to children from the community, an additional payment is required

---

The Town School is a coed elementary school that ends with eighth grade. It overlooks the East River on quiet East 76th Street, opposite John Jay Park. The Town School emphasizes warmth and is sensitive to the developmental needs of young children. A traditional core of academic skills is taught using an innovative curriculum. The 1936 school brochure description of Town was accurate then and now: "Progressive but not radical . . . its object is to create an environment in which the child may develop the best that is in him and give him a thorough understanding of every subject he studies." Expectations are high but this is not a pressure-cooker environment. Because of the focus on the elementary grades, parents say there is an intimacy that provides an opportunity for leadership and the development of self-confidence. Students leave Town well prepared and well rounded.

Founded in 1913 by Miss Hazel Hyde and originally known as "Miss Hyde's School," The Town School acquired its present name in 1936 during the era of the town car and town house. The school motto roughly translates as "Be joyful in the pursuit of knowledge." Former head of school Fred Calder describes the committed faculty and administrators at Town School as "a group of people who [still] believe that the education of young children begins and ends with warmth, humor and good sense." Miss Hyde was known for attracting exceptional faculty who were very involved in running the school. To this day, the teachers at The Town School retain their influence through the "corporation" (known as "the members"), who serve as an advisory group to the Head.

Town School parents almost all agree that there is an emphasis on the process of learning rather than the rote accumulation of facts. Parents say, "Children learn how to think, and they learn that it's OK to be wrong or to fail."

In 1985 The Town School sold air rights to Glick Development Affiliates for $7 million. Some of this windfall went toward a capital improvement and maintenance fund, some toward the school's size-able endowment and a portion went into renovation and addition of facilities, including two new science labs for Lower and Upper School students, a new darkroom and a technology lab. Town students have use of their own auditorium, as well as a full-size gym. The school is uncluttered, clean and carpeted (no echoing hallways here). It's easy to see why children are comfortable here.

Getting in: There are no essay questions on the application. Parents may tour the school before they apply for their child. Many tour guides are members of the faculty, are very knowledgeable and don't mind answering numerous questions. At a later date, parents bring their kindergarten applicant in for a small group interview while the parents meet with the director of admissions.

Parents: The parent body at Town is relatively low-key. Says one parent, "These aren't all parents who went to private schools themselves." The Parents Association was founded in 1951. There is a monthly newsletter to inform parents about activities and meetings. Curriculum evenings and parent education seminars keep parents apprised of what's going on in the world of education and at Town (a recent panel discussed gender issues in elementary education). Head of School Marblo realizes that "parents [today] particularly need to discuss the challenges they face with their children." Activities for Town families include the Welcome Back Picnic in the Fall in Central Park, Science Night, the Book Fair Sports Night, a theater performance at each grade level and the Spring Benefit. One mother described the events she attended: "Everyone came, there were nice feelings, nothing was hyped up, just a wonderful, warm environment."

Program: Kindergartners have a fairly long day, from 8:15 A.M. until 2:30 P.M. Monday through Thursday and until noon on Fridays. First through eighth graders eat hot lunch at school; pre-kindergartners and kindergartners bring their own lunches. There are two kindergarten classrooms, each with two teachers. (All of the nursery and kindergarten division head teachers have a master's in Early Childhood Education.) In addition to the teachers, there are three language arts specialists and a school psychologist. The kindergarten rooms are situated at opposite ends of a short carpeted hallway where, during activity time, children from each class can play and socialize. Each kindergarten classroom has a block area, wood shop, listening corner, two computers, lots of pets and their own bathroom and kitchen. The children were busily working in small groups, some with clay or wood, some painting.

The Town School has traditionally celebrated the arts, and art is integrated into the curriculum at every level. Grades one through four visit the Lower School art studio once a week. Bas-relief self-portraits and still lifes in the style of Matisse were on display. There is a kiln for firing clay. Students frequently visit museums, and visiting artists come in to share their art, music, or drama expertise.

The music and dance curriculum begins in nursery when both are taught simultaneously. First and second graders learn the Orff method. Third graders learn to play the recorder. Private instrumental instruction is available both before, during and after school. Students who love to perform have the opportunity, and can work on costumes, scenery and stage managing as well. Children can perform at assemblies, and there are two full-scale musicals a year. The fourth grade musical typically has more than one lead: There were four Charlies for *Charlie and the Chocolate Factory* one year. There are Lower and Upper School choruses and a band. A highlight of the year is the annual eighth grade musical.

Unique to The Town School is the community based curriculum, used in kindergarten and developed by Town School teachers. It is a curriculum revolving around a year long study of how the neighborhood community mirrors the school community. It integrates language arts, science, math and the arts into a comprehensive educational program using field trips as the central core to build skills in observing, collecting and recording information.

The language arts program is literature based and by first grade students are writing in response journals daily. Invented spelling is used, but spelling skills are taught in second grade. First graders move out of the classroom for science in the Lower School science lab, library, gym, dance, music, art and Spanish.

Students from kindergarten through second grade have computers in their classrooms. By third grade students use the technology lab (which is equipped with PC's) where they learn keyboarding skills and word processing. Students learn to use software related to the language arts, math and social studies. By fifth grade students take a unit of math in the technology lab, writing workshop, and Internet research in science, social studies and foreign language.

Fourth graders study their own family unit, write letters to relatives, study their own country (countries) of origin and use this as a basis to learn about other immigrating groups. A book-publishing party is held in the spring. A multicultural curriculum is in place. The first grade examined the Cinderella myth from the perspective of different cultures, including Chinese and Egyptian. Assemblies often feature multicultural performers. Irish step dancers performed at one assembly and invited the students to come onstage and participate.

In math, using the University of Chicago Math Program, children learn to reason logically, see mathematical patterns and relationships, and understand the presence of math in everyday life. Manipulatives, math games and literature are woven into the curriculum to develop abstract mathematical thinking while reinforcing computational concepts. The Lower School science lab features scaled-down versions of the familiar black tables and stools; the curriculum stresses the process of inquiry. For instance, second graders studying the Northeast woodlands create a nature mural; each child researches a forest animal to add to the mural. Fifth graders studying oceanography use *The Voyage of the Mimi*, a computer companion program. There are numerous trips to reinforce laboratory learning: Third and fourth grade students travel to a working farm; fifth and sixth graders go to Camp Sloane, an environmental center in upstate New York. Seventh and eighth graders go to Blairstown, New Jersey, for an Outward Bound-type program.

Parents say that The Town School really "honors individual learning styles." Educators recognize that some children function better with lots of background noise and others appreciate a more quiet setting. (Outside the second grade classroom there is an inviting bench with pillows, perfect for quiet reading, and there are other nooks and crannies for small group activities.) Throughout the Lower School there is no tracking; collaborative units are used instead. Students might have a group lesson and then divide into smaller groups.

There is also recognition that children learn at different rates. Our tour guide told us: "They journey from first through fourth grades at their own rate, but by fourth grade they are all at the same place." The learning specialists at Town move into the classrooms, avoiding the stigma to certain children of being "pulled out" for remedial help.

Students use the full-size gym, one of four playroofs or John Jay Park playground, a wonderful resource right across the street. From kindergarten through fourth grade coed cooperative games and skills are stressed. In fifth grade, intramural competition begins. There is a full-size gym, and Upper Schoolers have two double periods a week for sports at Randall's Island. They have a very fine basketball, soccer, softball, and baseball programs. In the Upper School all students can participate in a variety of single-sex interscholastic sports. Parents say Town is a great place for girls who are interested in sports.

The Upper School at Town is composed of fifth through eighth grades. As in the Lower School, desks in the upper grades are grouped for collaborative learning. But fifth grade is an important transition year with new responsibilities and expectations. The fifth grade day is fully departmentalized and fifth graders begin to receive letter grades in the second trimester of the year. A half year of French and a half year of Spanish are introduced in fifth grade; Latin instruction begins in seventh grade. Support is provided: A special study skills course is built into the fifth grade curriculum to help students acclimate to the Upper School. Fifth through eighth graders take a "Lifeskills" program taught by a team including the school psychologist, a science teacher and the school nurse that covers decision making, AIDS, drugs and alcoholism prevention.

The social studies curriculum in the Upper School compares different cultures during the same time period or with the same theme. Fifth grade studies ancient Egypt, Greece and China; sixth grade studies Medieval Europe, Islam, and Japan. Seventh grade focuses on The Age of Discovery and Exploration and Pre-colonial America. The eighth grade studies the colonization of America through the Constitutional Convention.

Readings in English focus on the classics and are often related to the social studies curriculum within a spiral curriculum. Science continues to be experiential. The science lab is networked with the computer lab. Collaborative science projects require tremendous research and culminate in a science fair. Town School graduates place well in advanced science and math in the ongoing schools. Each year a number of students are accepted at Stuyvesant High School (one of the specialized New York City public high schools.)

Students have the opportunity to perform in class plays and in musicals. Fifth to eighth graders have an intensive trimester of art, music and dramatic arts. The eighth grade performs in a play as a graduation year culminating activity. Upper School students can work on the literary magazine, yearbook or newspaper. Student photographers help provide photographs for the yearbook.

Town School students have the opportunity to assume positions of leadership. The student senate is an elected body with co-presidents, co-vice president and class representatives. The senate plans assemblies and organizes social events and community service activities. The Town School has a relationship with Yorkville Common Pantry, and food and clothing drives are often organized on its behalf. There is an in-house recycling program.

Eighth grade is an important and exciting year at The Town School. There are many opportunities to be role models for the entire school and especially to younger Buddy Classes, lead the Student Senate, Assemblies and special events. The eighth grade musical is the culmination of years of musical training and performance. At graduation the William Lee Younger, Jr. Educational Award is given to "the student who flourished at Town [and] developed into an individual of fine character and dedication to excellence."

Discussion about ninth grade placement begins in the spring of seventh grade. A Placement Director and the Upper School Head work and support individual families. Many Town School graduates return to talk about their high schools. All eighth graders take a "Decisions" course, a learning experience that strengthens and prepares each student for high school.

A parent who has sent two children to Town (one is now at Trinity, the other attends an Ivy League college) says, "They care for each child as an individual and work with them until the children find something good in themselves. Kids admire kids with different strengths, and they cheer for each other. Although expectations for academic achievement are high, they care equally about the emotional and social development of each child." A parent says, "My child is known and understood as a whole person." Most Town School graduates choose to go on to the coed day and boarding schools. (We ran into Town grads at Trinity—two graduation speakers—and at Dalton—the Student Senate President.) A number also go to the specialized public high schools each year. The close-knit feeling at Town persists after graduation. Parents say: "There is a strong feeling of community. Students go back to school to visit their teachers."

Popular Secondary School Choices   Trinity, Dalton, Horace Mann, Fieldston, Columbia Prep, Riverdale, Spence, Brearley, Nightingale and Stuyvesant

Traditions   Fall Welcome Back Picnic, Book Fair, Spring Benefit, parenting lecture series, class trips for grades 3–8, 4th grade musical, annual 8th grade musical, alumni/ae reunions

Publications   Alumni/ae News: *Currents*
Annual report
Yearbook
Newspaper

417

The Town School Family News (monthly)
Literary magazine *Pen and Ink*
The Cry of the Wolf Eighth grade short story collection

Community Service Requirement   Community service begins in the nursery program. Every class has a buddy class in another division; the student senate organizes community service projects, often in conjunction with the Yorkville Common Pantry; during winter trimester, 5th–8th graders participate in a community service period once a week, going to a nearby soup kitchen and serving lunch to the homeless and so on; 8th graders also work with second grade students at P.S. 36 every Friday after school.

Hangouts   Bagels & Co., John Jay Park

Trevor Day School

Lower School
Early Childhood Division
(Nursery–Kindergarten)
11 East 89th Street
Elementary School
(1st–5th grade)
4 East 90th Street
New York, NY 10128
(212) 426-3355
FAX (212) 410-6507
e-mail: LSAdmissions@trevornet.org

Upper School
(6th–12th Grade)
1 West 88th Street
New York, NY 10024
(212) 426-3380 Admissions
FAX (212) 873-8520
e-mail: USAdmissions@trevornet.org
website: www.trevor.org

Coed
Nursery–12th grade
Accessible (Both Campuses)

Tom Tinker, Acting Head of School
Ms. Deborah Ashe, Director of Admissions, Lower School
Ms. Marcia Roesch, Director of Admissions, Upper School

Uniform Published dress code that emphasizes appropriate attire

Birthday Cutoff September 1

Enrollment Total enrollment: 750
Nursery places: 28
Kindergarten places: 56
Graduating class size: approx. 60

Grades Semester system with a trimester system in high school
Extensive written reports plus family conferences twice a year for
Nursery through 12

419

Letter grades begin in 9th grade
Full departmentalization by 5th grade
First final exam in 6th grade

Tuition Range 2005–2006 $17,100 to $28,275, Nursery–12th grade
No additional fees.
Families purchase laptops in 5th and 9th grades

Financial Aid/Scholarship   Approximately 17% of the students receive some form of financial aid, totaling $2.29 million
Percentage of financial award extends to the Afterschool program and to laptop purchase

Endowment $5.6 million

Diversity   Approximately 18 percent students of color
Students come from Early Steps, Albert G. Oliver Scholarship Program, A Better Chance, TEAK, and Prep for Prep

Homework   Kindergarten–1st: parent/child reading for 30 minutes
2nd: 30 minutes (reading, and 15 minutes of math and spelling practice)
3rd: 1 hour
4th: 1½ hours
5th and 6th: 1½–2 hours
6th–8th: 2–2½ hours
9th–12th: Up to 4 hours
(An additional 30 minutes of reading is expected each night for all grades)

After-School Program   Available for K through 12th grade for an additional fee, includes music conservatory, recreational activities and athletics with numerous team sports offered in the Upper School.

Summer Program   All programs require an additional payment
June sports program (ages 4–11), Trevor Day Students only
Summerday Camp: for 3–6 year olds; 5 weeks, 9 A.M.–12 P.M. for 3 year olds; 9 A.M.–2 P.M. for 4 year olds, and 9 A.M.–3 P.M. for 5- and 6-year olds

Trevor Day School, previously known as "The Day School," was founded as a nursery school in 1930 under the aegis of the Church of the Heavenly Rest. In 1971, The Day School, having grown into a primary school, became independent of the church. The rector of the church continues to serve ex-officio on the board of trustees but Trevor Day School has no religious affiliation or instruction. The school took the last name of long-standing board member, Paul Trevor, who had made many significant contributions to the school.

In 1991 Trevor Day School expanded further by purchasing the old Walden-Lincoln school building on West 88th Street and creating a high school division (grades nine through twelve). In 1992, the school connected its Early Childhood Division located on East 89th Street to its East 90th Street Elementary Division. Today, Trevor Day School is divided into the Lower School and the Upper School. The Lower School has two divisions: Early Childhood, nursery through kindergarten and Elementary, grades one through five. The Upper School, located at 1 West 88th Street, consists of the Middle School (grades six through eight) and the High School (grades nine through twelve).

Trevor Day School offers an eclectic blend of the old and the new. There is an elegant marble staircase in the limestone lobby of the East Side building suggesting that this is a staid traditional school, but don't be misled. Trevor Day School has incorporated many innovative features into a curriculum that stresses active learning: common rooms, Miniterms, family conferences and a policy of no letter grades until ninth grade.

The school's mission statement emphasizes cooperation and collaboration rather than competition as a motivational device.

Getting in: Trevor Day School offers information evenings and tours. Do call and ask for these dates. Once they have applied, parents come to the school twice, once for a parent tour and once with their child. Children applying for kindergarten are met in the lobby of the 89th Street building and go upstairs for choice time and to work at a table with age-appropriate materials. One parent who said that she barely survived the admissions process in general, commented that "Trevor was wonderful at handling the shy, quiet child, both through admissions and in the classroom."

On a separate date parents are taken on a tour of the school and then meet with a member of the admissions staff for about thirty minutes. Parent representatives and admissions staff lead the tour groups and they are very informative as well as candid. Nursery applicants are not separated from their parents, but are engaged by a teacher while the parents talk to a member of the admissions staff. Recommendations are optional. Kindergarten visits are held on Saturdays to help ease the stress of parents and children. Trevor families come from all over—the East and West sides, downtown, and in the boroughs.

Families applying to the Upper School, grades six through twelve, are scheduled for tours and interviews in the Fall and early winter. Small group tours for parents and students are either preceded or followed by an individual interview for each student and his parents. Parent admission representatives lead Middle School tours, members of the student admissions committee lead High School tours.

Parents: Parents describe the parent body at Trevor Day as a "mixed but cohesive group of East Siders, West Siders, Jews, WASPs and families of color. But the parents, along with the students, teachers and administrators, all share a strong enthusiasm for the school." All parents are automatically members of the Parents Association, which sponsors community-building activities, such as the two-week-long program "Everybody Reads at Trevor Day School," and runs several fund-raising events including the very popular Auction and Fall Festival.

Program: Trevor Day School is composed of four divisions, Early Childhood, Elementary, Middle and High Schools. The Early Childhood Division consists of Nursery, Pre-kindergarten and Kindergarten. The nursery program is half a day, five days a week. Pre-kindergarten ends at 2 P.M., Monday through Thursday (3 P.M. after February), and noon on Friday. The kindergarten day at Trevor Day School runs from 8:40 to 3:00 P.M., Monday through Thursday, and until 2:00 on Friday. There are four kindergarten classes, each with twelve to fifteen children, a head teacher and an assistant teacher. Our guide told us that "the homeroom is an extension of the home." The smallish square classrooms are neat, well-equipped, clean and carpeted and each has its own bathroom and a locker for each child. Pre-kindergarten and kindergarten students visit the library weekly in half groups, where parent volunteers read to children and help them select books. Foreign languages (French and Spanish) are introduced in Nursery. Pre-Kindergartners and kindergartners visit the well-equipped art and music studios twice a week in half groups; they participate in physical education and roof time (on the padded playroof), daily, in half groups and as a class, and there are specialists in physical education, foreign language music and art. Lower Schoolers go to a well-equipped art room staffed by a full-time teacher and an assistant. Their expressive and very individual work is permanently displayed throughout the 89th Street building a part of a school-wide Art Show.

Parents say kindergarten at Trevor Day School is "academic" but nurturing and "takes into account the varying rates of development of the children." Along with traditional skills the children gain a sense of security. "The development of self-esteem is important," say parents. "They know each child is cut from a different cloth." The curriculum is structured but not too much so. In Pre-kindergarten and kindergarten the classes split into half groups for traditional academics, including reading and math Pre-kindergartners and Kindergartners begin working with math manipulatives and math games, using big books, practicing letter sounds, writing in their journals using approximate spelling and handwriting skills.

A group of focused children was sitting in chairs in a row learning letter sounds, but parents say, "There is very little recitation or rote learning, it's not learn or else—it's learn at your own pace."

The Elementary Division consists of grades one through five. Hot lunch is offered starting in grade 1. Classroom life in this division is informal but the day is structured. The school believes that children should feel free to make mistakes: "We'd rather have a child take chances, do something daring." In order to free children from the constraints of working for grades, there are no letter or number grades until ninth grade. Students in nursery through eighth grade receive narrative reports, with extensive checklists, sometimes as long as three to four typed pages, and also receive regular feedback from teachers. Family or cooperative conferences starting in pre-kindergarten and continuing through the High School are a feature unique to Trevor Day School. Students participate in the family conference whose goal is to emphasize the idea that the students share the responsibility for their own education. Teachers and parents remain in close contact throughout the year.

There are three homerooms in the first and second grades with two teachers in each class of about eighteen children. There are several computers in each first grade classroom. But by third grade students are divided into four small homerooms with about twelve students and one teacher, adjacent to a common room. The common room at Trevor Day School is considered the nucleus of the learning community—a place where students can do homework, use the computers, play chess or learn independently with the guidance of faculty. Time-management and a cooperative teacher-student relationship are two themes central to the school's philosophy. Homework assignments begin in second grade. Assignments are usually posted by the teacher. Students can complete some of their homework in school during common room time, which is part of their daily schedule.

Parents say there is more social interaction with the entire grade during the early years because groups are mixed, not tracked. One parent said of a new student, "He was so happy at Trevor Day School that he wanted to spend weekends there!"

Classroom life in this division is informal but the day is structured. Reading and math groups might be as small as four to eight children. Third grade uses literature and word processing as part of the writing experience while the children continue to practice their handwriting in workbooks. During math some of the class used Cuisenaire rods, some were doing math with numbers on a blackboard and some were sitting or lying on the floor working with manipulatives or math games. The students in all three groups were actively engaged. The Investigation Colloquium Method is used to teach science, emphasizing "child-directed exploration and interpretation." First graders study the science of Central Park; second graders, life cycles (which includes plants and mealworms); third graders, environmental science; fourth and fifth grade students use a newly renovated science lab and work collaboratively.

The computer program at Trevor Day School begins in the nursery school in the classrooms; all of the classrooms have computers. Third and fourth grade have a mobile laptop lab and wireless classrooms while fifth grade students have their own laptops. In the fall of 1996, Trevor Day School became the first private school in Manhattan to join the Microsoft/Anytime Anywhere Learning program. All students in grades five through twelve use laptops for inquiry and learning. (Families purchased them outright; there is a payment plan.) Students generally take them for granted. The goal of this program is for the computer to become a "transparent" tool, like paper and pencil. "I use the laptop in every class," said a seventh grader. "In English to write essays and take notes on classroom reading, in history, foreign language and science to take notes and do homework, in math for writing assignments and graphing."

Social studies topics begin with community and interdependency, and students learn early on an awareness and respect for difference. Topics broaden from a study of family history to units on immigration and ethnic diversity in New York City and the history of Manhattan

Island. The third grade studies Native American populations. Fourth graders begin a two-year sequence in American history.

Music and movement are an integral part of the curriculum. Study begins with the Orff, Kodaly and Dalcroze methods and students start learning to play recorders in third grade. A video called "Growing Musicians" is available to view on the school's website.

Grades four and five are partially departmentalized. The homeroom teacher, who is also a subject teacher, serves as advisor to approximately twelve children. Students make use of a central common room with glass-fronted classrooms on the perimeter. There are three common room periods a week as well as a daily quiet reading period.

The "Miniterm" is first introduced in grades four and five. This is a three-week period during which academic electives occupy the morning while afternoons are reserved for classes that take students beyond the traditional subjects. Sometimes, Miniterm is devoted to an original musical, a production that relates to "the lives and experiences of the students, using material taken from various literary sources as well as the students' own work." Music and dance from other cultures are often incorporated. Throughout the year there are opportunities for students to gain confidence in public speaking and to participate in plays. A parent said, "Nobody is ever excluded. Everyone is in the plays, and no one is made to feel inferior."

Fourth and fifth graders have an extended day once a week for physical education at Randalls Island.

After four years of studying both French and Spanish each year, third graders now choose to specialize in one language for the next three years.

Parents praise the art program, which stresses each child's individual expression, as well as the attainment of skills. According to the head of the Lower School art department, "Children need to be who they are. If one is an artist, he is given a lot of credit for becoming an artist." From an early age, Trevor Day School students learn to use and maintain a variety of art materials from a central supply area. By fourth grade they are working on projects in various media, including drawing, painting, collage, 3-D paper, ceramics and printmaking. Starting in Middle School, students can do film and computer animation, and graphics and photography in the school darkroom.

The Middle School is composed of grades six through eight. The Middle School common room is the center of student and teacher activity. The homeroom/advisor system changes somewhat in the

Middle School. Nine to ten students share an advisor and meet together at the start of each day. The advisor actively supports each student's intellectual and social growth, acting as an advocate and academic counselor as well as the primary contact for both family and and school. In addition, each student meets individually each week with an academic advisor. There are still no grades in the Middle School (until ninth grade) but students do self-assessment and continue, when they meet individually with their advisor each week, to receive feedback in the form of "accountability reports." These reflect not only the content and quality of the student's weekly course work, but also the student's emerging understanding as well as critical thinking skills.

The Middle School has its own three-week-long Miniterm, during which students take academic electives in the morning and rehearse for a gala musical in the afternoon, take short courses and participate in special arts offerings. Students are involved in all aspects of putting on this full-scale production. Miniterm reinforces community spirit at Trevor Day School, with everyone working toward a common goal in different capacities. Health education is introduced during Miniterm, which includes an AIDS curriculum.

The teaching of English in the Middle School is literature based. Students write, edit and produce finished drafts. Much time is spent on the mechanics of grammar and vocabulary building. Group discussion and collaborative learning activities dominate the classroom experience. In sixth grade students are assigned "considerable homework in reading and writing." Seventh graders focus on essay writing, critical thinking and oral expression. Eighth graders engage in "formal literary analysis of classic adult literature" while continuing to improve their essay-writing skills.

Foreign language study continues in sixth grade with either French or Spanish.

The Middle School history curriculum begins with geography in sixth grade which lays the foundation for World History in seventh and eighth grades.

Science in the Middle School utilizes a laboratory format. Emphasis is on the scientific method. By the end of eighth grade, all students have covered the basics of biology, physical science and chemistry.

In mathematics, critical thinking, problem solving and competency are stressed. All eighth graders take "Algebra I."

Participation in the arts is not optional at Trevor Day School.

All sixth graders take a rotational Arts Workshop series, sampling the arts available to seventh and eighth graders. Electives include "Video Workshop", "Designing for Illustration" and "Photography."

Middle Schoolers may select from vocal or instrumental electives in music. There is a Middle School chorus. Students interested in dance can participate in Choreolab, which meets after school and puts on an annual student dance concert.

Community service is a vital part of the Middle School. There are numerous food, toy and clothing drives. Seventh and eighth graders may volunteer to serve either in the Trevor Day School Community, or outside of school.

Middle Schoolers spend a week with their grade as part of the outdoor education program. Grade levels focus on themes such as cooperation, collaboration and leadership.

Physical education is required three times a week. After school there is a range of intramural and interscholastic sports. Parents say that no child is ever cut from a team. If you show up and participate, then you are considered a member of the team. But a participant in the physical education programs says, "We deemphasize competition in gym until 3:00 P.M. and then we don't like to lose." Between 35 and 40 percent of the Middle and High School students participate in after-school sports programs.

The High School is composed of grades nine through twelve. The High School building has a working theatre, music rooms, a dance studio, a full-size basketball court, darkrooms, ceramics studio and an audiovisual studio. The High School library has 15,000 volumes, a microfiche and is computerized. Trevor Day School renovated its science floor and updated the science program.

The High School includes a student-faculty center that serves as an extension of the formal classroom. It functions as a meeting space for teachers and students, is equipped with a laptop computer, and, like the entire school, has access to a wireless network.

Twenty-two credits are required for graduation. This includes three math, three science, three language, four English, three history and nine trimesters of the Arts. Students complete the three-year science requirement in an innovative science program that offers a coordinated course of biology, chemistry and physics each year for three years. At the end of three years, students have completed the equivalent of a year in each of the three subjects. Advanced courses in computer science, foreign language, English, history, mathematics and the sciences are offered. Letter grades are introduced in ninth grade and are sent home twice a year with written reports. All high school students are required to complete eighty hours of community service over their four years.

Highlights from the English curriculum include: "Asian-American Literature," "Rites of Passage," "19th and 20th Century Literature," "Romantic Poetry," "African American Literature," "Irish Literature," "Tennessee Williams and his Contemporaries," "Hemingway and His Circle," "Jane Austen and the Romantic Novel," "The Playwright-Poet," "Philosophical Literature," "Images of Women," "Gender and Shakespeare," "The Art of the Short Story," "Baseball and Literature," "British & American Drama Since 1950," "Marquez and his Contemporaries," etc.

Ethical Foundations is a two-year program that is required for all ninth and tenth grade students. The three-part course covers health, nutrition and wellness, human sexuality, social justice and ethical decision making.

Trevor Day School students participate in their graduation, putting on a performance with a song or a tribute. The strong sense of community at Trevor Day School persists after graduation. A parent of two alumnae says, "There's a warmth among the children, a camaraderie that continues even though some go on to different schools. They're still friends."

Cynthia E. Bing, former president of the Board of Trustees, describes the school's unique approach: "There is an adult presence that is not obtrusive. Students are encouraged to take the initiative but there are plenty of adults around to help them make [wise] decisions." Parents and alumni say that the emphasis on independent learning and time management pays off in college.

Popular College Choices   Bard, Bowdoin, Brown, Columbia, Connecticut College, Cornell, Emory, Mount Holyoke, NYU, Oberlin, Sarah Lawrence, Skidmore, Smith, Tufts, University of Michigan, Washington University, Vassar and Wesleyan

Traditions   Fall auction/dinner, head of school's fund-raising party, clothing sale, class parties, Fall Festival, parent workshops, Parent Partners, Friday assemblies, potluck dinners, High School Conference Day, miniterm musical productions, Music Conservatory student recitals, family/faculty concerts, Choreolab dance production

Publications   Yearbook
   Newspaper: *The Dragon*
   Magazine: *Trevor*
   Student literary magazine: *The Flame*
   Foreign language newsletters

Community Service Requirement   80 hours—20 hours per year
   in high school

Hangout   Common Room and High School Center (open and
   supervised until 5:30)

Trinity School

139 West 91st Street
New York, NY 10024
(212) 873-1650
website: www.trinityschoolnyc.org

Coed
Kindergarten–12th grade
Not accessible

Mr. Henry C. Moses, Headmaster
Ms. June Hilton, Director of Admissions, K–4
Ms. Jan Burton, Director of Admissions, 5–12

Uniform   Lower School: For boys, Trinity polo-style shirt or turtleneck, chinos or corduroy pants, walking shorts may be worn in warm weather, no jeans or gym shorts. Sweater or navy blazer, no sweatshirts. Tied shoes or sneakers
For girls, white uniform blouse, white or navy turtleneck, long or short sleeve Trinity polo-style shirt. Tan or navy pants, Bermuda shorts may be worn in the warm weather, no jeans or gym shorts. Sweaters or navy blazer, no sweatshirts. Shoes or sneakers, appropriate legwear.
Dress code in Middle School (grades 5 through 8): no jeans, short skirts or shorts permitted; skirts or slacks and neat collared shirts are preferred; hats cannot be worn in class
Dress code in Upper School (grades 9 through 12): jeans and sneakers may be worn; clothing must be neat, clean and socially appropriate

Birthday Cutoff   Children entering kindergarten must be 5 by September 1

Enrollment   Total school enrollment: 975
Kindergarten places: approximately 60
Graduating class size: approximately 110

Grades   Semester system
Kindergarten–5: detailed anecdotal reports and checklists
Departmentalization begins in 5th grade

Letter grades begin in 6th grade
First final exam is offered in 7th grade

Tuition Range 2005–2006 $26,890 to $28,390, K–12th grade
Additional fees: approximately $1,300 for lunch; cost of trips may range from $100 in the Lower School to $800 in the Upper School; $25 accident insurance required
$400 for graduation expenses

Financial Aid/Scholarship   Approximately $3 million available
17% of the student body receives financial assistance

Endowment   Approximately $25 million

Diversity   55 Prep for Prep students enrolled as of fall 2004 (The Prep for Prep program is housed at Trinity School); 25 Early Steps students
Trinity School has a Black Affairs, Women's Caucus, Jewish Affairs, Gay-Straight Alliance, Asian-American Alliance and a Diversity Leadership Coalition

Homework   Kindergarten: None
1st grade: minimal, beginning in second half of 1st grade
2nd: 15–20 minutes (some homework given Monday is due on Friday); nightly silent reading
3rd: 30–45 minutes (spelling quizzes and tests)
4th: 45 minutes–1 hour
5th and 6th: 1–2 hours
7th and 8th: 2–3 hours
9th–12th: 40 minutes per subject, approximately 3–4 hours

After-School Program   K–6: After-school program for an additional fee, a variety of creative and recreational activities
Some clubs meet after school
Intramural sports for 7th and 8th graders
Interscholastic sports in the Ivy Preparatory League (boys) and the Independent School Athletic Association (girls)
Extended day program

Summer Program   June Program
Trinity Day Camp: a variety of creative and recreational activities, including swimming; Trinity students have priority in

enrollment and there is usually a wait list; an additional payment is required

————

Trinity School was founded in 1709 as the first public charity school in New York City. While Collegiate claims to be the oldest school, Trinity claims to be the oldest *continually operated* school in Manhattan, as it remained open throughout the British occupation of New York City during the Revolutionary War. Trinity was a coed school until the mid-nineteenth century, when the city withdrew its support from charity schools. According to the school's brochure, Trinity then reincorporated as a private boys' school, eventually moving uptown alongside the town houses of the well-to-do on Manhattan's Upper West Side. At this time Trinity modeled itself on the English public (private) schools like Harrow, Eton, Westminster and Winchester. Trinity was a single-sex traditional school until the sixties. One alumnus said that "the Kennedy days marked the fall of the 'preppie' era at Trinity."

Beginning with the Upper School in the seventies, Trinity School again became coed, and by the late eighties was coed throughout. Trinity is a traditional school with "West Side" style; this is the key to the school's popularity. Many dualities are present in Trinity: highly selective admissions but generous financial aid, a diverse student body, with an emphasis on classical education, all bound by a respect for Trinity's traditions, a Protestant ethos amid the mostly Jewish and Hispanic residents of the Upper West Side.

Headmaster Henry C. Moses, former dean of freshmen at Harvard, replaced Christopher Berrisford in 1991. Parents say Moses, who gives speeches at Chapel and has been seen in school plays, is approachable and cares about the students.

The Headmaster and Trustees are committed to diversity at Trinity. Trinity's annual report recently boasted that Trinity has a "truly diverse" lower school: "Our goal is a school population that reflects our city's. "Approximately one-third of the students in the Lower School are children of color. The Parents Association has its own Diversity Committee to support this commitment, and meetings have been held with parents to discuss their concerns and also to encourage them to help with recruitment of children from diverse backgrounds. Trinity's Multicultural Coordinator works accross divisions, with students, parents, and faculty. Parents publish a diversity newsletter for all families.

Despite the name Trinity, compulsory weekly Chapel and the presence of an Episcopalian chaplain, Trinity School strives to be inclusive; the school is popular with Jewish families. Scheduled holidays include Rosh Hashonah, Yom Kippur, Christmas, Passover and Good Friday. There is the traditional all-school Christmas Chapel with a candlelit procession, a holiday fair and a Lower School Christmas program, and also a Chanukah Chapel. Beginning in first grade all Lower School students attend Chapel once a week and often sing as a group in Chapel. The program is interfaith, and one parent said the religious component is not as prominent as the ethical and moral aspects. For example, on Valentine's Day her child's class read their own work aloud, and one child read a story about being friends forever. Chapel speakers in the Upper School might include a senior faculty member or a protester from Tiananmen Square. In the brochure, Headmaster Henry C. Moses says, "I hope the Chapel will always be a place of quiet reflection for all." All students take introductory religion courses in fifth and sixth grade. Eleventh and twelfth graders can choose among seven electives, including "Morals and Ethics" and "Religion and Literature," to fulfill their one-semester religion requirement.

Getting in: There are three open houses in the fall. Parents of kindergarten applicants are advised to send in their completed application along with the $60 application fee as soon as possible to be granted an interview at the school. A wait list for interviews has been maintained in recent years. Kindergarten tours are extensive and are given by Lower School parent volunteers, and interviews are on separate days. Children do not tour. In my opinion, the gentle-mannered Director of Admissions, June Hilton, is the best part of Trinity's admissions process. The child goes next door with the tester while you go into Ms. Hilton's office for a conversation. Your child will join you in half an hour so ask your important questions quickly. Your four-year-old may have questions of his/her own (most likely "Can we go home now?") but this is to be expected. There is a play area for children should parents wish to spend additional time in conversation. Don't send your child to Trinity to be coddled. A parent said, "Trinity is a tough, no-nonsense school, but they really care about the kids."

Trinity requests a recent photograph of your child, so have some good wallet-size pictures ready. Do not cancel your interview appointment with Trinity unless your child really is ill. The demand for kindergarten places is high; you might not get another appointment time. According to one nursery school director, "They like to see both parents." Once admissions decisions have been made, Trinity has an active wait list, and there is a strong sibling policy.

Although occasionally places are available in grades one through eight, ten and eleven, the main entry points after kindergarten is grade nine. Each family is interviewed individually and has a student guide for the tour of the Upper School. Interviews begin in late September and end in mid-January. There are three Open Houses in the Fall, and throughout the process there are opportunities to meet and talk with faculty members. After a candidate has been accepted, he or she visits classes.

Parents: The style at Trinity is traditional but not formal. "It's a very relaxed atmosphere for a traditional school," a parent told us. There is no typical parent. This is definitely not a celebrity school although there are more than a few. There is a multicultural mix along with a fair share of East and West Side powerhouses. Many East Side parents said the one thing they would change is that they would move Trinity to the East Side of Manhattan. One parent said the school is financially mixed. There is money, but "by and large it's low-key." School dinners are held in the Trinity cafeteria. Parents Association meetings are scheduled so that all parents can attend, and there are meetings between the Parents Association and the Trustees. Parents of entering kindergarten students attend a May reception and ninth grade parents attend dinner parties at parents' homes.

Separation is handled gently. The kindergarten schedule is staggered in the beginning, and parents walk children up the stairs to their classroom. After a few weeks parents say goodbye at the bottom of the steps and the students go up by themselves. They shake hands with the teacher at the end of the day. Lower School Principal Rosemary Milliman greets the children in the morning. Parents say Milliman is always asking parents for input on how to improve the school. Lower School parents are kept informed about school and classroom events by the LS newsletter, "The Tuesday Newsday."

Program: There are three kindergartens with two teachers each, approximately twenty students in each class. The children go out of their classrooms for music, gym, swimming (on the premises) and art. There is swimming, gym or turf time daily and a new play area for kindergartners with age appropriate equipment. In first grade the three kindergartens split into four smaller classes with approximately fifteen children in each; each class has a head teacher and an assistant. Parents say that this is a great advantage academically: "Students receive a lot of individual attention—they are really focused on developing important reading and math skills early." The approach to teaching reading is eclectic, with a multi-disciplinary approach. June Hilton says, "We use many approaches to accommodate different learning styles." The Writing Workshop includes creative writing and reading stories aloud. Trinity seeks to instill a love for reading with programs such as D.E.A.R. (Drop Everything and Read). Kindergartners deliver their own "Sunny Day Newspaper" weekly. The marvelous Lower School library at Trinity is inhabited by larger-than-life stuffed figures from children's classics: Clifford the Big Red Dog and some of Maurice Sendak's "Wild Things."

By second grade, expectations are greater. One parent told us she was afraid to go out and leave her second grader with the babysitter because he wouldn't be able to do his homework. New material is never introduced in homework assignments. Reading and math groups are formed according to ability. Foreign language (French or Spanish) is introduced in the Lower School. Formal computer instruction in the computer lab begins in kindergarten. Kindergartners and first graders are taught in their classrooms. At many points in the Lower School the curriculum is integrated. For example, second graders study Native Americans of the Eastern Woodlands in social studies, and in music they present a festival of Native American song, story and dance for parents.

There is support for different learning styles, and a staff of specialists works with the homeroom teachers. At Special Services Night parents meet the team of specialists who provide remedial instruction. As in many independent schools, some tutoring is initiated by the parents. At Trinity a breakfast was held with the school psychologist and parents to discuss academic pressure but a consensus was not reached. We were told "Some parents think there is too much pressure and some think there is too little, depending on how their child is doing." While academic achievement is appreciated in the Lower School, one parent said, "You don't have to be brilliant to be happy at Trinity. There is a spectrum of intelligence." One mother whose daughter is struggling with the academics, but bubbling with enthusiasm for Trinity nonetheless, was told by her child, "I'm really learning a lot this year!"

One of the highlights of the tour is the Lower School science room, which looks like a Woods Hole laboratory with aquatic life tanks around the room and charts, specimens and waders hanging on the walls. Howard Warren, Lower School science head, oversees a hands-on science program. Warren received a Governor's Environmental

Study Citation for his memorable beach cleanup with third graders (who do a unit on the environment). Warren takes the fourth graders wading into Jamaica Bay to collect specimens, which they bring back and put into the tanks, study and release at the end of the school year.

Music is an area of strength at Trinity. Twice weekly, beginning in kindergarten, students use the Orff, Kodaly and Dalcroze methods to learn rhythm and singing skills. Every class performs music, ranging from psalms sung in chapel to rap songs about the fifty states. The Adventures in Strings Program gives fourth graders the option of studying violin or cello and continues through fifth and sixth grades. There is a Lower School and Middle School orchestra.

Trinity reorganized and consolidated the lower Middle (grades five and six) and upper Middle Schools (grades seven and eight) into one Middle School serving grades five through eight. The Middle School is housed in its own bright, newly renovated wing and features a Middle School technology resource center. The school now has two full size gymnasiums. Departmentalization begins in Middle School. Modern language instruction, begun in the Lower School, continues in grades five through eight. Latin instruction begins in grade 6. Students who need reinforcement take a study skills course in which they meet with a learning specialist in small groups. Middle Schoolers participate in the Pythagorean Contest. In athletics, Middle Schoolers choose between coed kickball and football on the Astro Turf and Sports Club (interscholastic or intramural sports competition). Required swimming classes continue through eighth grade. There are informal "chalk talks" born out of the Project Charlie anti-drug program in Middle School.

The Upper School at Trinity is composed of the ninth through twelfth grades. After the architectural grandeur of the Lower School, Trinity's Upper School (Hawley Wing) with its cinderblock walls and bustling corridors has the feeling of a suburban public school. There are no bells in the Upper School. The Upper School library has Proquest and Newsbank, and students can work in carrels or on computers. Computers are networked throughout the school.

Approximately forty-five new students enter at the ninth grade. Trinity is a popular high school choice for students at the single-sex schools who want a city coed day school.

To ease the transition into high school and integration of new students into the class, ninth graders take an orientation trip to Frost Valley in the Catskills, with senior leaders and faculty, and continue to meet once a week during the school year with their Frost Valley groups.

Contact between students in the three divisions occurs formally at all-school events several times a year. Currently, twice a week, ten to fifteen seniors eat lunch with kindergarten students, other seniors help fourth graders put on plays about Greek myths, several juniors and seniors work with Lower School students on math enrichment, and Upper and Middle School students meet in programs like Kids Helping Kids to discuss social issues. The Black Affairs Club meets with and mentors children of color in the Lower School.

The graduation requirements at Trinity are similar to those at the other rigorous high schools. Students take a minimum of five or six academic courses in grade nine. In grades ten through twelve, they must take a minimum of four, but almost all students take more. Seniors may choose from a variety of electives, including "Journalism," "Economics," "Gender and Politics." English is required but seniors choose from seven different options each semester. About seventy percent of the seniors are enrolled in advanced science. A new interdisciplinary course taught by teachers of chemistry and religion is offered in ninth grade.

Some classrooms are set up in traditional rows or seminar style with oak lectern desks, but in English, history, modern languages and religion, the desks are arranged in a circle or the tables in a rectangle to promote discussion.

Trinity maintains its traditional emphasis on the Classics, the study of Latin and Greek. The school's course guide asserts that the classics are "a rigorous and significant part of the curriculum." "The best Latin program in the country," says one student. The study of DWAMs (Dead White Ancient Males) really comes alive at Trinity. Advanced reading in elegiac poetry and Ovid's *The Art of Love*, a provocative and satirical portrait of love in ancient Rome, is offered. Advanced students can participate in The Virgil Academy, in which students read a book of the *Aeneid* in tutorial and later take part in public examination by professors and colleges. In addition to Latin and Greek, students can continue study in French or Spanish. The English department requires Upper School students to read five books over the summer. Ninth graders begin the year with a six-week Writing Workshop to perfect their essay-writing skills. Recent eleventh and twelfth grade English electives have included "Existentialism: The Search for Meaning," "What's Going on in Poetry Right Now," "How to Tell a War Story," and "Four African Authors: Race and Related Matters."

After a solid grounding in modern European and American history, seniors can choose from the following electives (these vary from year to year): "Prejudice in America" (women and nonwhite ethnic minorities), "The Postwar World, 1945–1965" and "U.S. History, 1965–1984," and Economics.

In keeping with the commitment to diversity at Trinity there has been much discussion about the need to incorporate more views of nonwhite ethnic minorities and women into the Upper School curriculum. At the first alumni panel (with faculty), part of a Faculty Professional Day, the theme was "Perspectives in Multiculturalism and Education." Five recent Trinity graduates talked about the need to broaden the curriculum with more diverse viewpoints, and one student said that although they visited many cultural sites in New York City including, of course, the Metropolitan Museum, "We should have taken trips to the Schomburg Center along with the Guggenheim Museum."

Honors courses exist only in mathematics and modern languages. Although not all advanced courses follow the AP curriculum, AP Prep courses are offered to prepare students for the exam. Science requirements are biology plus one year of another laboratory science. Science electives include "Psychology," "Marine Biology," "Astronomy" and advanced courses in biology, chemistry and physics. The computer science department offers courses in word processing, Web Programming and AP Computer Science.

High school students can do advanced independent work in addition to the required four academic subjects. Advanced work is graded pass/fail and doesn't count as a credit toward graduation. Seniors, however, may enroll in an independent study in a specific discipline such as German literature, chemistry or studio art, but they must also take four other courses. Seniors receive a letter grade for their independent study program.

The arts and theatre programs at Trinity are extensive. Theatre at Trinity is exciting. Every year there is a major musical production and a Cabaret. I saw a rehearsal for *Fiddler on the Roof* in the Chapel; another year it was *Carousel.* The Theater IV play production course allows students to direct any one-act play of their choice. These spring productions are very well attended.

Adjoining visual arts and ceramics studios are large and bright. Students make good use of New York City's museums. Students can take beginning through advanced photography for credit. There is room for individual initiative in the arts at Trinity. In fall of 1991 a small group of students with a keen interest in films and filmmaking organized the first New York National High School Film Festival and received 215 entries from across the country. Prizes were awarded. The Festival has become an exciting annual event.

When they're not studying, students can relax in the Swamp (a seating area off the main lobby) or on the other side of the lobby. There is no student lounge as such. There is a no-smoking zone around the school. Students can leave campus as early as the second half of freshman year.

Three representatives from each grade serve in the student senate (serving grades nine through twelve). The Senate recently voted to install a Snapple or soda-vending machine but this was not permitted. Homecoming, run by the student senate, takes place at varsity and junior varsity games in the winter. At other times during the year the senate gives out hot chocolate.

There are numerous clubs. The most popular, we were told, is the "Free Tibet" club, with over 200 members.

There is no community service requirement, but most Trinity students participate in at least one community service activity. Often an entire grade will do a project together, for instance, clean an area of Riverside Park or give a variety show to make money for hurricane victims. The Student Volunteer Service Organization (SVSO), born in the sixties, continues to coordinate a range of student volunteer activities, such as Santa's helpers, the Thanksgiving program for senior citizens, You Gotta Have Park and the March of Dimes Walkathon.

In recent years, AIDS has been important issue on campus and there were numerous discussions at Trinity among parents and students about AIDS. "Although abstinence is preferred," said one mother, "we have to be realistic."

The athletic program at Trinity is wide ranging and strong. Some teams begin two-hour morning practice sessions at 6:00 A.M. Games are held after school and some are well attended. Soccer, lacrosse and swimming are a few of Trinity's best teams, but students say "this is definitely not a rah-rah school."

At graduation, awards are bestowed upon Trinity seniors, in recognition of excellence in nearly every area. The three students with the highest grade point averages in each grade receive the Hawley Prizes. Important non-academic awards include: the John Hanley Prize for community service and the Annelle Fitzpatrick Award for gentleness of spirit. On Prize Day in May, all academic departments announce the students in grades nine through twelve, who are recipients of endowed prizes, including four prizes that have been given annually since 1890—the Eaton Prize for Classics, the Alumni Prize in English, the Rector's Prize in Religion, and the Eaton Prize for Senior Mathematics. At a formal induction ceremony in the spring, students with outstanding academic records are elected to the Cum Laude Society, the high school equivalent of Phi Beta Kappa. There are some students who compete for these prizes, but the *real* source of competition, one alumnus told us, is college placement.

Graduation exercises, complete with academic gown, are held in a church at 96th and Central Park West. A Baccalaureate service, planned by the seniors, is held the night before graduation at Trinity Church, the original site of the school, near Wall Street. By tradition, the graduation speaker is the parent of a senior.

Popular College Choices   Yale, Harvard, Brown, Princeton, University of Pennsylvania, Cornell, Wesleyan, Stanford

Traditions   Holiday Fair, Spring Benefit, Virgil Academy, Reunion Weekend, Cabaret, Theater IV productions, senior and first grade Halloween Costume parade, Multicultural Fair

Publications   Yearbook: *The Bruner*
Literary magazine: *Columbus*
Newspaper: *Trinity Times*
Photography journal: *Malinconico*
Trinity School magazine: *Trinity Per Saecula* (Trinity through the Ages)
The Lighter Side of Journalism– *Enquirer*
French Literary Magazine– *Correspondances*

Hangouts   The Swamp (a small seating area in the rear of the Upper School lobby), the Food Zone (seating in the lobby where students can eat), the McDonald's at 91st and Columbus

United Nations International School

24–50 Franklin D. Roosevelt Drive
New York, NY 10010
(212) 684-7400, FAX (212) 684-1382
website: www.unis.org
e-mail: admissions@unis.org

Coed
Kindergarten–12th grade
Accessible

Dr. Kenneth Wrye, Director
Mrs. Anne Lowenstein, Director of Admissions

Birthday Cutoff   Children entering kindergarten must be 5 by August 31

Enrollment   Total enrollment: 1,510
Kindergarten places: 85
Graduating class size: 95–105

Grades   Semester system
Number grades begin in 7th grade
Full departmentalization by 7th grade

Tuition Range 2005–2006 $18,000 to $20,000, K–12th grade
Additional fee for new parents, $1,500 per family

Financial Aid/Scholarship   12% of the student body receive some form of financial aid; $762,573 has been awarded

Endowment $14,633,062

Diversity   Students at UNIS come from over 100 countries.

After-School Program   Open to UNIS students only
A variety of creative and recreational activities from 3:00 P.M. until 6:00 P.M.; an additional payment is required
Varsity and junior varsity teams

Summer Program   The six-week UNIS summer program is open to children from UNIS as well as from the community, nursery through 12th grade; a variety of creative and recreational activities as well as English as a Second Language are offered; an additional payment is required

———

UNIS is housed in a modern, spacious building overlooking the East River. A large garden forms the tranquil core of the building. For younger students the school has a fully equipped, multi-level playground. UNIS was founded in 1947 by a group of United Nations parents to provide their children with an international curriculum and to inspire in its students the spirit and ideals of the UN. Today, UNIS is open to all New York City families. Students at UNIS represent over one hundred countries; the faculty and staff represent over seventy different nationalities.

UNIS is organized into four schools: The Junior School is for kindergarten through fourth grade students, the Middle School is composed of fifth through eighth grade, and the High School, "Tutorial House" is for ninth through twelfth grade students. There is also a kindergarten through eighth grade campus in Queens. Each school has its principal and staff, who insure a smooth transition from school to school. Dr. Kenneth Wrye is the Director. Dr. Wrye is a U.S. citizen and was formerly head of the Copenhagen International School.

Getting in: UNIS offers spring and fall tours (led by current parents) for prospective applicants; students in fifth grade and above are welcome to accompany their parents on the tour. Once an application has been filed, the school will contact parents to set up an interview date and parents can tour at this time. Children applying to kindergarten through fourth grade are observed in an informal play group of four or five. While the children are playing, their parents meet as a group (approximately twenty parents) for a Q. and A. session with the school principal and admissions staff. All English speaking students are required to submit results of ERB testing. Teacher recommendations are required unless the student's school report includes comprehensive teacher's comments; personal recommendations are welcome but not required. The school is sensitive to applicants from other cultures and countries and is familiar with all of the different national systems. Each year one or two places in each grade are held open for children of incoming U.N. diplomats. Forty-four per cent of parents are affiliated with the U.N.

Program: The curriculum is designed to provide for direct interaction by the children with the world around them. The children are encouraged to think for themselves, while working cooperatively in small groups. In the Junior School, academics are stressed in an integrated program that includes music, art, French, Spanish, science and computer science taught by specialists. Creativity is encouraged.

UNIS recognizes that the Middle School years are critical ones for social, emotional and intellectual growth. The curriculum builds upon the basics learned in previous years, adding new subjects and additional language options. In English, Middle School students read world poetry and explore works of literature from many countries and cultures. UNIS places high value on the teaching of modern languages. French and Spanish are offered from kindergarten, and beginning in seventh grade eight languages are taught by native speakers with beginning, intermediate and advanced classes available. English as a Second Language is a separate course.

The curriculum of the "Tutorial House" (High School) balances electives and required subjects. In grade 10 students can pursue a special talent or interest, whether it be math, science, languages, writing, the humanities, music or art. The program culminates in the International Baccalaureate Diploma Program (IB), study for which takes place during the last two years of high school. The vast majority of UNIS students take the full IB program. Students with high grades can sometimes receive up to one year of advanced standing at American universities. Eighty-five percent of graduates choose to attend colleges in North America.

UNIS has an articulated computer studies program. Technology is integrated into classroom instruction in many different subject areas. We saw computers in all of the classrooms and there are four computer labs. The school is networked, connecting all classrooms and bridging the Manhattan and Queens campuses. The school is connected to the Internet through a T1 line.

There are numerous opportunities for leadership throughout the school. Students can be elected to Student Council as early as grade two. Members of the Student Councils of all four schools meet periodically with their principal and with the director to discuss issues of concern.

The UNIS athletic program includes twenty-nine varsity and junior varsity teams.

The annual UNIS/UN conference is an exciting annual event. This conference is held in the UN's General Assembly Hall and requires months of planning and research by UNIS students and students from the more than fifty participating schools from around the world.

443

Popular College Choices   Brown, Columbia, Cornell, Harvard, MIT, Parsons School of Design, University of Michigan, NYU, Tufts, Vassar, Yale, McGill, London School of Economics

Traditions   United Nations Day, Winter and Spring Concerts, UNIS/UN Conference, Theater Workshop, English Writing Weekend at Bard College, Theory of Knowledge Weekend, Science Weekend, Math Weekend, Senior Trip, Sports Carnival, Sports Banquet, International Book and Craft Festival, World Outreach to Needy People.

Publications   Yearbook
Upper School Newspaper: *UNIS Verse*
Student Council Newsletter
Junior School Newsletter
3 Literary Magazines

Community Service Requirement   An important aspect of student life is community service, either in-house or at an approved public service agency in the metropolitan area.

Village Community School

272 West Tenth Street
New York, NY 10014
(212) 691-5146

Coed
5/6's (kindergarten)–8th grade
Accessible

Ms. Eve Kleger, Director
Ms. Jennifer Trano, Director of Admissions

Birthday Cutoff   Children entering kindergarten must be 5 by December 31

Enrollment   Total enrollment: 312
  5/6 (kindergarten) places: 35 to 40
  Graduating class size: 32–34
  7 Prep for Prep students enrolled as of September 2004

Grades   Semester system in the Upper School
  Lower and Upper Schools: detailed anecdotal reports and conferences twice a year
  Full departmentalization begins in 6th Grade

Tuition Range 2005–2006 $21,550 to $22,780, 5/6's–12/13's
  Additional fees: for books, approximately $500

Financial Aid/Scholarship   25% of the student body receive partial financial aid

Endowment   The school has recently begun to build its endowment.

After-School Program   After School at VCS: for children ages 5 and above; open to children from other schools; Monday–Friday 3:15 P.M. to 4:45 P.M.; activities include sports, arts and crafts, music, theatre and dance; an additional payment is required
  A play group is available until 6 P.M.

445

Summer Program VCS has a summer camp from mid-June through July open to students from other schools; an additional payment is required

---

Village Community School was founded in 1970. VCS's building, with its high ceilings, wide stairwells, and a newer sky-lit library was originally a public school one hundred years ago. VCS is governed by an elected Council which is composed of parents, faculty and alumni. There's a large outdoor play yard and a free-standing wood shop. In 2003, the school completed construction of a new five-story building that houses eight classrooms, a gym, auditorium, and a rooftop play area. VCS is fully networked with computers in every classroom, and also has wireless access for laptops. All classrooms are now carpeted and air conditioned.

No ERB testing is required for kindergarten admissions (it is required for second grade and above). There are two divisions: The Lower School is composed of ages five through ten. The Upper School is composed of grades six through eight. VCS has interage (flexible) class groupings until sixth grade. There is no uniform. VCS does not have a cafeteria and students must bring their own lunches.

VCS has a friendly, relaxed atmosphere but the curriculum is highly structured. Students address their teachers (as well as the director) by their first names. Parents say that in the Lower School VCS is very nurturing; in the middle years the expectations are more demanding. Spanish is introduced in the 7/8's and continues until 9/10's. Latin is taught to all sixth grade students; seventh grade students can continue Latin or can choose Spanish or French for their remaining two years at VCS.

VCS admits families from Early Steps and Prep for Prep; children of color make up twenty percent of the student body.

VCS graduates attend a variety of city high schools including the specialized public schools, NYC independent schools and boarding schools.

York Preparatory School

40 West 68th Street
New York, NY 10023
(212) 362-0400
www.yorkprep.org

Coed
Grades 6–12
Accessible (elevator)

Mr. Ronald P. Stewart, Headmaster
Mr. Chris Durnford, Principal
Ms. Maryll Feild, Director of Admissions

Uniform   There is a dress code; students wear a York Prep polo shirt in white or navy, Monday through Thursday; Friday is a "free dress" day within certain guidelines

Birthday Cutoff   None

Enrollment   Total enrollment: 310
   6th grade places: 20
   9th grade places: 20–25
   Average graduating class size: 60

Grades   Semester system
   Numerical grades begin in 6th grade
   Grades reported weekly to parents via an open on-line grading book
   Tracking system by academic subject

Tuition Range 2005–2006 $25,900 to $26,400, 6th–12th grades
   Additional fees: for books, activities, and student insurance, $1,600

Financial Aid/Scholarship   Approximately 33% of the school receive some form of aid
   $600,000 in financial aid was distributed in 2003–2004

Endowment   None

After-School Program   Jump Start; Scholars Program Varsity and junior varsity team competition in the Interschool League

An active intramural program
Academic clubs meet after school
All teachers remain after school for extra-help classes
Extracurricular activities include: dance, chess, cooking, drums, chorus, drama, literary magazine, newspaper, environmental awareness, fiction writing, folk music, guitar, jazz ensemble, mock trial, math, science, etc.

Summer Program An academic enrichment program is offered from mid-June–July for an additional charge for York Prep students. Week-long sports and study skills camps are held in August

---

York Prep was founded in 1969 by its present Headmaster Ronald Stewart and his wife Jayme Stewart. In 1997 the school moved from its former location on East 85th Street into its current home on the Upper West Side, a handsome seven-story granite building formerly occupied by the Hebrew Union College. After completing a "boiler to roof" renovation, the school, crisply painted in yellow and blue, reflects the can-do optimism exuded by the Oxford-educated headmaster, and his wife, Jayme Stewart, who has been Director of College Guidance since the school's inception.

York Prep is a proprietary (for-profit) school, owned and operated by the headmaster. The school is run like a high class Mom and Pop organization: The Stewarts oversee every aspect of the school which operates free of the politics of a board of trustees. Liv Tyler and Kelly Klein are two of the school's glamorous grads; so is James de la Vega, a graffiti artist (recently profiled in *The New York Times*), who grew up in El Barrio, studied art at Cornell and now teaches at his alma mater, "occasionally taking his students on a tour of Harlem street art."

When you enter the school, a regulation sized basketball court serves as the backdrop to the reception desk. Two uniformed security guards stand nearby. On closer inspection one turns out to be an effigy. York Prep values both athletics and a sense of humor, both of great advantage when managing adolescents, as the Stewarts, who have three grown children, know well. Participation in athletics and other extracurricular activities is encouraged here; a component of the school's philosophy is "putting children in situations of success." A parent told us: "It's a very nurturing school, the teachers are great; it's the perfect alternative to one of the real high-powered schools; an excellent private school education."

The schoolhouse has two modern science laboratories, a library/media center (with beautiful Shaker-style windows), lounge, technology center, performance and art studios, and a sprung hardwood floor gymnasium with weight and locker room facilities. The classrooms are light and airy, carpeted and climate controlled. The classrooms are wired with a T-1 line and students and staff have e-mail addresses. In addition, all classrooms are linked to the school's in-house television station, WYRK, which gives students interested in television, broadcasting, journalism, and production, the opportunity to showcase their talents.

Getting in: Open houses for parents are offered regularly by the Headmaster and the Admissions Department. Upon request, parents can tour the school individually with the Associate Director of Admissions, before filing an application. Applicants and their parents have an interview meeting and the applicant is invited to spend a day visiting the school. York Prep admits Prep for Prep students.

Program: Headmaster Stewart believes that a student must be offered a real opportunity for success, and that is a major factor in student motivation. York Prep's curriculum provides a strong foundation in the traditional core subjects of a liberal arts education. For a small school, it offers an impressive range of courses with electives in most fields for qualified students and a growing number of AP courses in History, Math and foreign languages. Beginning in seventh grade each subject area is divided into at least three tracks (homogeneous ability groups). These tracks are fluid; students whose skills improve will move into the next track enabling students to experience success while always being challenged to work beyond their "comfort level." Each student's program is constantly evaluated for proper placement within the tracking system to ensure the right balance of challenge and support is maintained in all subject areas.

"York Prep's system of academic support has helped many students who've been 'over-faced' [at other schools] rediscover the thrill of learning," says Stewart. For gifted students, York Prep provides the challenge of its top track courses leading to AP courses. In addition to the tracking system and individual assistance given to students, the school uses a study skills and learning strategies program of its own design that is taught in every grade and every subject.

For students who are more academically able York offers a

Scholars Program that requires students to meet every two weeks with the program Director. The three year program culminates in a Degree with Honors.

The school has always provided academic support and accommodation for students with different learning styles and educational needs. The Jump Start program is an individualized and intensive program that works to strengthen reading comprehension and writing skills. This program also imparts organizational and study skills. It was created to help students develop independence not only with day-to-day tasks but also with respect to long range goals. There is an additional fee for the Jump Start program. York Prep also offers an ESL program with daily English-language instruction and tutorial assistance.

Seniors and advanced eleventh graders who qualify may either take courses at Columbia, New York University, or Hunter College, or independent study and advanced placement courses.

Communication between parents and the school is frequent. "The teachers and staff have their fingers on everything that's going on; if my son was having a problem I could ask the principal to 'keep an eye on him today' and they will," said one parent. In 2003, York began using Edline, an online website that provides current grades, class news, and other information in a private way.

Teachers take full advantage of the school's Lincoln Center location in addition to visiting museums, theaters and the Wall Street area.

A wide range of sports is offered at York and the full trophy cases are proof of their success. York Prep competes in the Independent School Leagues, the Private Schools Athletic Association and the Manhattan Independent Schools tennis and golf leagues. Students can choose from competitive or non-competitive basketball, softball, soccer, swimming, track, tennis, cross-country track, aerobics, gymnastic, golf and weight training. Horseback riding at the Claremont Stables is a feature of York Prep's extra-curricular program, as are ski weekends and trips to Europe and Washington, D.C. The range of clubs and activities changes each year according to student interest.

York Prep students volunteer their time at more than 150 non-profit organizations, including the American Red Cross, the ASPCA, the Legal Aid Society, and so on. Some students surpass the required hours of the Community Service Program.

Stewart says, "Each child needs a feeling that he can do something well—whether it's athletics or something else. We tell them 'you pick it, we'll support you.' " This philosophy is carried all the way through to graduation. York Prep is very successful at college placement thanks to the expertise of Jayme Stewart, author of *How to Get Into the College of Your Choice* (William Morrow & Co., 1991). Ms. Stewart encourages students to make realistic choices. Her thoroughness and tenacity as a student advocate pay off because more than 85% are accepted at their first choice school.

Popular College Choices   Barnard, Bowdoin, Brown, Colgate, Boston University, Cooper Union, Juilliard, George Washington, University of Michigan, Cornell, University of Pennsylvania

Publications   Literary Magazine: *Genesis*
Yearbook: *The Legend*
Newspaper

Community Service Requirement   100 hours

ADDITIONAL SCHOOLS

Beekman School
(Grades 9–12)
220 East 50th Street
New York, NY 10022
(212) 755-6666
FAX (212) 888-6085
website: www.beekmanschool.org
Total enrollment: approximately 97

Beth Jacob Parochial School
(Orthodox Jewish, Grades
    Kindergarten–8)
142 Broome Street
New York, NY 10002
(212) 473-4500
FAX (212) 460-5317
Total enrollment: 130

Claremont Preparatory School
(Grades K–8)
41 Broad Street
New York, NY 10004
(212) 232-0266
FAX (212) 232-0284
website: www.claremontprep.org
Opening, Sept. '05
Total enrollment: approximately
    300

Frederick Douglass Academy
(Grades 6–12)
2581 Adam Clayton Powell
    Boulevard
New York, NY 10039
(212) 491-4107
FAX (212) 491-4414
website: www.FDAI.org
Total enrollment: approximately
    1100

King's Academy
(Grades Nursery–12)
2341 Third Avenue
New York, NY 10035
(212) 348-7380
FAX (212) 348-0515
Total enrollment: approximately
    200

**Manhattan Christian
    Academy**
(Grades Pre-kindergarten–8)
401 West 205th Street
New York, NY 10040
(212) 567-5521
FAX (212) 567-2815
Total enrollment: 280

Manhattan Day School (Orthodox)
(Grades Nursery–8)
310 West 75th Street
New York, NY 10023
(212) 376-6800
FAX (212) 376-6388
website: www.mdsweb.org
Total enrollment: 450

Mestivta Timereth Jerusalem
(Orthodox Jewish, Grades
    Kindergarten–12)
145 East Broadway
New York, NY 10002
(212) 964-2830
FAX (212) 349-5213
Total enrollment: approximately
    150

Montessori School of New York, Inc.
(Nursery 2 year-olds–14 year-olds)
347 East 55th Street
New York, NY 10022
(212) 223-4630
FAX (212) 644-7057
website: www.montessori
schoolny.com
Total enrollment approximately 100

Northeastern Academy
(Grades 9–12)
532 West 215th Street
New York, NY 10034
(212) 569-4800
FAX (212) 569-6145
Total enrollment: approximately 177

Saint Spyridon Greek Parochial School
(Greek Orthodox, Grades Pre-kindergarten–8)
120 Wadsworth Avenue
New York, NY 10033
(212) 795-6870
FAX (212) 795-6871
Total enrollment: 300

Saint Thomas Choir School
(Boarding for boys only, Grades 4–8)
202 West 58th Street
New York, NY 10019
(212) 247-3311
FAX (212) 247-3393
website: www.choirschool.org
Total enrollment: 40

Yeshiva Rabbi S.R. Hirsch
(Orthodox Jewish, Grades Nursery–12)
85–93 Bennett Avenue
New York, NY 10033
(212) 568-6200
FAX (212) 928-4422
Total enrollment: approximately 500

Yeshiva University High School for Boys
(Orthodox Jewish, Grades 9–12)
2540 Amsterdam Avenue
New York, NY 10033
(212) 960-5345
FAX (212) 960-0027
website: www.yuhsb.org
Total enrollment: 325

RESOURCES FOR CHILDREN WITH LEARNING DISABILITIES

When parents are first told that their child has been diagnosed with a learning disability they are heartbroken. They feel as if they've done something wrong that might have caused or contributed to their child's disability. Then they start shaking the family tree for any relatives who might have had a learning problem—was it your brother, grandmother, aunt or cousin who had so much trouble in school? Parents start to think that their child is the only one struggling and then they worry about the erosion of their child's self-esteem.

Learning disabilities are diagnosed in children with a wide range of IQ's; very bright children can have LD's that aren't diagnosed until later in their schooling because they came up with ingenious strategies to compensate for their deficiency. Skilled educators will usually see red flags early on, in pre-kindergarten or earlier. Most primary schools have early intervention specialists on staff, including speech therapists. Keep in mind that individual schools have different timetables for developmental skills. With a wide age range within classrooms, children will be at different points of development throughout their school years.

If you are concerned about a "developmental lag" at any point, don't be afraid to ask the teacher if she thinks you should have your child evaluated; if her answer isn't satisfactory, go to the division head or guidance counselor with your concerns. If you're still not sure why your child isn't doing grade level work the first order of business is to get a psycho-educational evaluation to determine exactly what the problem is and what you can do about it. The Parents League and the organizations listed below can refer you to a qualified tester. Word of mouth is also a good way to find one. The best bet is to find a tester who is also trained in neurology. The test is long and is usually given in two-hour segments, morning and afternoon, over a couple of days. Reports are detailed and sophisticated.

The best grades for testing children are: first grade (an important year for acquiring learning skills), fourth grade (skills are consolidated and more independent learning is expected); seventh grade (so you can better assess high school options), tenth grade (because now is the time to make critical high school decisions, like qualifying for extended time on SATs.) Medication is sometimes prescribed for children with related attention disorders to help them focus, settle down, and get to work.

Re-evaluate and re-test every three to four years. Your child's school should be apprised of any testing you do outside, and provided with the results so they can best work with your child. Remember this is a partnership. Alice Goldman, who has run parent workshops and seminars on learning disabilities for The Parents League, offers a comforting thought, "If a child is completely evaluated and a learning disability has been identified, there is often a sense of relief and it is much easier to set a course of remediation." Once the right type of intervention and programming are in place, learning becomes enjoyable again.

Schools for children with learning disabilities are small in size and highly structured. Classes in a therapeutic setting vary in size from six to twelve students per class with an assistant as well as additional sessions with various specialists who work with students one-on-one. Often, these schools will have mixed-age groupings of students because many learning disabled children learn at different rates that don't correlate with their ages. These programs really work and are worth all the time and money that you will invest. Many children who attend a specialized school are mainstreamed back into a regular educational environment, often the goal of many of these schools. (See, for example, The Little Room, *supra* page 111.) Students who stay in their present schools may require extensive and costly tutoring after school. Don't expect your child's private school to provide all the services he'll need, but most schools will provide study skills programs and extended time for tests and exams. Keep your chin up and take heart, many children with learning disabilities have gone on to wonderful colleges, (including the Ivy League) and have successful careers.

Here are some of the schools in the New York City area that educate children with learning disabilities, and/or psychological, social, behavioral or emotional issues. With the exception of the Parkside School, most of the schools listed below are very similar. The Parents League can also provide a listing of schools for children with developmental and learning disabilities. There are many success stories out there and here are some of their alma maters:

The Churchill School
310 East 30th Street
New York, NY 10016
(212) 683-3105
FAX (212) 722-1387
website: www.churchillschool.org

Coed
Ages: Kindergarten–12th grade
Total enrollment: approximately 400

The Churchill School serves children who have average to above average cognitive ability whose learning in a mainstream classroom is compromised by a learning disability. This may be a language processing or reading disability, perceptual and/or motor weakness or attentional issues. Churchill cannot meet the needs of students with primary emotional and social issues. Students with dyslexia, a reading disability, respond to the multisensory small group instruction at Churchill. For students with Attention Deficit Disorder with Hyper-Activity (ADHD), not in itself a learning disability, Churchill may not necessarily be the right school.

The high school opened in 2004 and offers a Regents' Curriculum.

The Gateway School of New York
236 Second Avenue (between 14th and 15th Streets)
New York, NY 10003
(212) 777-5966
FAX (212) 777-5794
website: www.gatewayschool.org

Coed
Ages: 5–12 years
Total enrollment: 62
When Gateway was founded in 1965, it was one of the first schools in New York City to work exclusively with children who had learning disabilities. The aim of The Gateway School is to remediate and mainstream children who have moderate to severe learning disabilities.

The Gillen Brewer School
1190 Park Avenue
New York, NY 10128
(212) 831-3667
FAX (212) 831-5254

Coed
Ages: 3–8 years
Total enrollment: 50

The Gillen Brewer School started as an early childhood program and evaluation site, and now extends up through second grade. Parents are very pleased with the school. The program serves children who have a wide variety of learning issues and developmental delays.

The Mary McDowell Center for Learning
20 Bergen Street
Brooklyn, NY 11201
(718) 625-3939
FAX (718) 625-1456
website: www.marymcdowell.org

Coed
Ages: 5–11/12 years
Total enrollment: 125

The Mary McDowell Center for Learning educates children with developmental delays and learning disabilities. A good resource for families who live in Brooklyn.

The Parkside School
48 West 74th Street
New York, NY 10023
(212) 721-8888
FAX (212) 721-1547

Coed
Ages: 5–10 years
Total enrollment: 80

The Parkside School's program serves children who have a wide range of language-based learning difficulties. The school offers a well-designed comprehensive array of academic and other support services. This very supportive program offers a highly structured, multisensory curriculum that inspires children and makes learning fun.

Robert Louis Stevenson School
(Serves children with learning disabilities and attention deficit
    disorders,
    Grades 7–12)
24 West 74th Street
New York, NY 10023
(212) 787–6400
FAX (212) 873-1872
website: www.stevenson.school.org
Total enrollment: 58

Stephen Gaynor School
22 West 74th Street
New York, NY 10023
(212) 787-7070
FAX (212) 787-3312
website: www.sgaynor.com

Coed
Ages: 5–13 years
Total enrollment: 150

The oldest school in New York City, (founded in 1962) for children who have dyslexia, ADD, visual spatial and/or non-verbal learning disabilities. Stephen Gaynor is highly respected in the community and does an excellent job of mainstreaming children who have a wide spectrum of special needs.

West End Day School
255 West 71st Street
New York, NY 10023
(212) 873-5708
FAX (212) 873-2345
website: www.westenddayschool.org

Coed
Ages: 5–12/13 years
Total enrollment: 45

This school helps children with a wide range of special needs. The staff works closely with each family to ameliorate the problems that affect their lives. There's a social work component incorporated into the program that has been very successful in helping many families.

Windward School
Windward Avenue
White Plains, NY 10605
(914) 949-6968
FAX (914) 949-8315
website: www.windwardschool.org

Coed
Grades: 1st–9th
Total enrollment: 300

Windward is located in Southern Westchester, and offers a multisensory program for children with language-based disabilities and average to superior IQs. Windward's staff is extremely skilled at remediating children to achieve their full potential and then mainstreaming them.

Winston Preparatory School
126 West 17th Street
New York, NY 10011
(646) 638-2705
FAX (646) 638-2706
website: www.mail.winstonprep.edu

Coed
Grades: 6th–12th
Total enrollment: 220

Winston Prep is an individualized program for junior and senior high school students who have learning differences. The goal of Winston's program is designed to maximize independence and self-reliance. Class size is about 12, and every student has one-to-one instruction, called Focus, in English and math daily. Athletic and other extracurricular activities are available after school. Winston sends the majority of its students on to college. Teachers are trained in a variety of methods, and are knowledgeable about how to teach children with learning issues.

The Learning Resource Center at Columbia Grammar and Preparatory School
5 West 93rd Street
New York, NY 10025
(212) 749-6200
website: www.cgps.org

Coed
Grades: Kindergarten–12th (the school goes from Pre-K–12)

This is *not* a school for severely learning-disabled children. The program is designed for high achieving students who need extra support. CGPS's

Learning Resource Center is well established, organized and structured. According to the school they "will provide some degree of professional skills and remediation on a temporary basis." Roughly, ten or more well-trained professionals staff the Learning Center, and enrollment is limited to only approximately forty students school-wide (The school has about 1,000 students.) There is an additional cost for any student in the Learning Center of approximately $21,500 per year. (*Supra* page 180.)

The Quest Program at The Dwight School
291 Central Park West
New York, NY 10024
(212) 724-2146 ext. 212

Coed
Grades: Nursery through 12th

Dwight is also not a school for children with learning disabilities. However, the school has a small program (approximately fifteen percent of the student body is enrolled) for students who have minor learning difficulties and need extra support in the classroom. The Quest Program is set up so students do not have to go to a tutor every day and can still participate in a full college preparatory curriculum. The Quest Program has an upper and lower division and resembles in a way the Parisian system with lots of mnemonics, repetitive learning and drills. The program is flexible enough so that students who need help in one subject area can get it, without compromising their schedules, it also serves students with a range of abilities. Parents are kept apprised of their children's test results in reading and writing. The additional fee for the program averages approximately $15,000 per year, depending on the amount of sessions needed. (*Supra* page 214.)

A complete listing of educational resources in the New York City area for children with learning disabilities can be obtained from:

The National Center for Learning Disabilities, 381 Park Avenue South, Suite 1401, New York, NY 10016-8806, (212) 545-7510 or 1-(888) 575-7373 ext 210, website: www.LD.org
NCLD is a voluntary, not-for-profit organization founded in 1977 by Carrie Rozelle. NCLD operates a national information and referral service and is the nation's only central, computerized resource clearinghouse committed solely to the issues of LD.

The Learning Disabilities Association of New York City Telephone Referral Service: Weekdays from 9 A.M. to 5 P.M., (212) 645-6730, FAX (212) 924-8896, website: www.LDANYC.com
This nonprofit organization is an affiliate of the Learning Disabilities Association of America. Trained counselors will explain how to recognize symptoms, and offer referrals to community based agencies in the New York City area. The Learning Disabilities Association also provides printed material and conducts workshops.

Other resources for information about LDs:

The International Dyslexia Assocation, 71 West 23rd Street, Suite 1527, New York, NY 10010, (212) 691-1930, FAX (212) 633-1620, website: www.nybida.org
This is the New York branch of the International Dyslexia Association, which advocates a multisensory approach for teaching children with dyslexia. They offer a free telephone referral service to parents looking for information on testing, schools, trained remediators, psychologists and other professionals. The International Dyslexia Association also sponsors an annual two-day conference on a topic of interest to parents, a conference for teenagers and parent support groups. A yearly membership is available.

The Parents League of New York, Inc., 115 East 82nd Street, New York, NY 10028, (212) 737-7385, website: www.parentsleague.org
The Parents League sponsors a workshop and provides information and referrals about learning disabilities to member parents. Mrs. Alice Goldman, an adviser with the Parents League, is particularly knowledgeable about which schools specialize in which type of LD.

Resources for Children with Special Needs, 116 East 16th Street, 5th floor, New York, NY 10003, (212) 677-4650, FAX (212) 254-4070, website: www.resourcesnyc.org, e-mail address: info@resourcesnyc.org
Resources for Children is a nonprofit information, referral, advocacy, training and support center for programs and services for children (from birth to age twenty-one) with learning, developmental, emotional or physical disabilities. Resources for Children publishes a family support guide listing camps and summer programs for children with special needs.

The Churchill Center, 310 East 30th Street, New York, N.Y. 10016, Tel: (212) 683-3105
An outreach center for services and programs for children and adolescents with attention and/or learning problems.

Advocates for Children of New York, Inc., 151 West 30th Street, 5th floor, New York, NY 10001, (212) 947-9779, FAX (212) 947-9790, website: www.advocatesforchildren.org
Advocates for Children works to protect and extend the rights of children with learning and/or developmental disabilities in public schools.

National Dissemination Center for Children with Disabilities, P.O. Box 1492, Washington, D.C. 20013-1492, (800) 695-0285, website: www.nichcy.org

Advisors to Benefit Children, 60 East 83rd Street, New York, N.Y. 10028, Tel: (917) 837-3064, FAX (212) 628-7165, website: www.advisors ny@att.net
Beth Gordon, a Harvard Business school graduate and parent of a special needs child and her associates help parents sort through complex choices that face families who have children with special needs.

And see the New York City Department of Education's website, www.nycenet.edu/offices/spss/sei/ctm for public school programs.

PUBLIC SCHOOL OPTIONS

Many parents agonize over the choice of public or private school education for their children. If sending their children to private school would be a tremendous financial burden on families already stretched to their limits, it is very important not to add additional pressures. Parents should resist societal pressure and use common sense to make the right decisions for their family. Children might be better off with a parent who is accessible, rather than one who is working 24/7 to make tuition payments. Select public schools offer a top-notch education at a rock bottom price and parents who get involved in their child's school can really make a difference.

The public schools are experiencing a revitalization as a result of a number of factors: More families are making the decision to raise their children in the city, and the cost of a private school education is well beyond the reach of many families.

The New York City public school system, the largest in the nation, offers a truly diverse student body, enrichment programs for gifted students, magnet/option programs*, bilingual immersion programs, collaborations with the city's major cultural institutions, corporate grants for whatever is new and exciting in education is happening in New York City's public schools. Be aware that there is tremendous variation among individual schools in terms of philosophy, physical plant, magnet grants, enrichment programs, extracurricular activities and parent involvement. There are traditional schools as well as smaller "option" schools. Much has changed since Chancellor Joel Klein has taken the reins at the new Department of Education.

The two questions parents ask most often concern class size and safety in the public elementary schools. For grades K–3, class size is "limited" to twenty-five students but can go to twenty-eight or more in some schools. For grades 4–6, the maximum class size is generally thirty-two, but can go beyond that. Student-teacher ratios vary from school to school because some schools have student teachers and parents often pay for extra para-professionals to staff classrooms. Regional and district superintendents say "there are fair, firm and consistent rules of discipline in effect at all the elementary schools. Every

*Option or alternative schools are schools of choice that are at the forefront of the educational reform movement. They are small, director-managed schools with a clear guiding vision and specific philosophical, thematic and curricular commitments. Although they are located in regular school buildings, they are autonomous. Staff, parents and students elect to attend these schools. Admission is by application or lottery, which often can be obtained from the schools. Parents must contact each school since application requirements and notification dates vary from program to program.

elementary school should have a guard in front who requests identification from visitors.

The standard time to preregister for the public school in your catchment area or zone (immediate neighborhood) is May of the same calendar year your child will be attending school (register in May of 2005 for Fall of 2005). But, like private schools, be advised that many New York City public school gifted and talented programs require an application process that begins in the Fall *prior* to the calendar year that a child would attend the school.

How to Begin Finding Out About New York City Public Schools

1. **Department of Education's website:** www.nycenet.edu This website provides the most current and accurate information about the city's public schools. The Department of Education has an additional website for a continuum of special education and other services: www.nycenet.edu/offices/spss/sei/ctm
2. **New York City's Best Public Elementary Schools**, **New York City's Best Public Middle Schools** and **New York City's Best Public High Schools,** all by Clara Hemphill, et al.
3. *www.insideschools.org* is a website with information about many public schools. The website is based at Advocates For Children, a Manhattan non-profit organization.
4. **Center For Educational Innovation/The Public Education Association (CEI/PEA)**, 28 West 44th Street, Suite 300 New York, NY 10036, (212) 868-1640,
   This one hundred year old organization which merged with CEI in 1999, is an advocate for high quality schools for all of New York City's public school children. The CEI/PEA's Education Information Center provides timely and useful information to parents and the public about public schools.
5. **The Manhattan White Pages**
   In the center of the telephone book is a section called the Blue Pages that contains a directory of New York City government offices. Under the heading Education, you will find a listing of all the Manhattan public schools, elementary through high schools.
6. **New York Charter School Resource Center,** website: www.nycsrc.org, (888) 343-6907; The Department of Education's website for charter schools, www.nycenet.edu/charterschools/charter.profiles.html

Call the elementary school or middle school directly to request a tour. A representative of the Parents Association usually conducts these tours and can answer many of your preliminary questions. A school might have an excellent reputation but you should see the school with your own eyes and let the principal/teachers describe the school's philosophy to you. Some alternative/option schools *require* a parent tour before application.

Students who live within a zone, or regional district have first priority for enrollment in neighborhood elementary schools, followed by students who live outside the zone but within the district. Student may also attend a school outside their zone providing they qualify and space is available. Contact the district office of the desired school for variance information.

Free busing on a Department of Education School bus to a school outside the student's zone is no longer provided; although busing *is* provided for students attending a gifted and talented school within the student's district. Students may obtain a bus pass for New York City buses.

PROGRAMS FOR GIFTED AND TALENTED STUDENTS

Tracking (ability grouping) within grades at the elementary level, an educational practice familiar to many baby boomers, has fallen out of favor these days. However, many parents still prefer their "bright" children to be with other children of similar ability. In the past, many middle-class families made financial sacrifices to send their children to prestigious private schools where they would receive an enriched educational program. The burgeoning gifted and talented programs (also known as talented and gifted or "TAG" programs) within the New York City public schools are an attempt to lure white, middle class parents back to public education. Getting a child into Hunter Elementary is as prestigious as gaining admission to the most selective independent school. Like the private (independent) schools, most of the TAG programs require parents to apply on behalf of their children one year prior to the year of enrollment. While some of the public TAG programs still have a "cutoff score" (they will only accept students who score above a certain percentile on an I.Q. test; the Stanford-Binet V is the most commonly used test) in District 2, a screening process (which includes an interview with the child) has replaced I.Q. testing. New York City public school TAG programs fill up quickly and waiting lists are maintained. All of these programs are free of charge.

Many of the programs for talented and gifted students are contained within the public elementary and middle schools. A few programs are housed separately (The Laboratory School for Gifted Education, Hunter College Elementary). Because the gifted and talented programs are not all alike—there are different models and different approaches—parents are advised to tour them.

I.Q. Testing

Hunter Elementary and some of the gifted programs require I.Q. testing, and the Stanford-Binet V is the most widely used test. Testing must usually be done after July 1 of the year of application at an approved testing site. The results are shared with the parents and sent to the program. The usual fee ranges from $225 to $345 or more, but "accommodation can be made for families who are in need."

A good source on I.Q. testing for the various TAG programs is Victor Toledo, director of the **National Training and Evaluation Center**, 15 West 84th Street, New York, NY 10024 (off Central Park West), (212) 877-4480

Hunter College Elementary provides a listing of approved testing agencies with the application.

The Programs

The programs highlighted below are only *a few* of the most sought after elementary and middle school programs for gifted and talented students available in Manhattan public schools. For information on TAG or alternative programs in your zone, contact your district office. (Keep in mind that the birthdate cutoff for public schools is December 31.)

The Hunter College Campus Schools:
Both Hunter College Elementary and Hunter College High School are located at 71 East 94th Street (94th and Park), New York, NY 10128 (212) 860-1262, Kindergarten admissions (212) 860-1405

Hunter College Elementary, Hunter Elementary is administered through Hunter College of the City University of New York. The school is tuition free and serves as a laboratory for the study of education. Admissions to kindergarten are open only to Manhattan residents. At seventh grade they take applicants from all five boroughs. Kindergarten and seventh grades are the only points of entry. However, there is an active wait list for kindergarten applicants. You must apply for your child one year in advance of enrollment—apply to kindergarten the year your child is four. Call for specific birthday cut-off dates. Application deadlines are usually around November 1st. Applicants to seventh grade are tested in sixth grade. Parents are advised to call or write for an application in September of the year prior to the year of enrollment. For kindergarten, parents must make a testing appointment for the Stanford Binet V at an approved testing center. (The usual fee for the Stanford Binet is $225 but it can be waived.) Students are interviewed in a group at Hunter Elementary. One recent year the cutoff for the Stanford Binet was 98th percentile and above but this score varies from year to year. There is a second round of admissions; typically, about 100 children compete for 32 places. Children are individually interviewed by a psychologist while anxious parents wait in the library. Reply dates are usually the first week of February.

Hunter College High School, Website: www.hchs.hunter.cuny.edu (212) 860-1259 information, (212) 860-1261 for admissions.

Seventh grade is the *only* point of entry to Hunter High School. Entrance is based solely on performance on the Hunter entrance exam taken in the sixth grade. Each year there are approximately 2,000 applicants for 240 places; there is a slightly lower cutoff for students of economically disadvantaged status and thirty places (of the 240) are reserved for these applicants. In order to sit for the January exam, sixth grade students must have the principal of their school submit a certification package to Hunter High by the first week of November. To qualify, students must score in the top percentiles in reading and math on *any* standardized test taken in fifth grade. The cutoff varies from year to year. There is a $40.00 fee.

The Anderson Program, at Public School 9, 100 West 84th Street (at Columbus Avenue), New York, NY 10024, (212) 595-7193 (same FAX #) Website: www.Andersonps9.org

The Anderson Program accepts applications from all five boroughs for kindergarten through eighth grade. There are two classes per grade. Applications can be downloaded from the website. Admission for grades kindergarten to fifth require the Stanford Binet V IQ test; and middle school applicants must score the top scores, like double 4s, on the math and ELA standardized tests. There are also additional in-house tests required for middle school.

Delta Honors Program at Booker T. Washington Middle School, MS 54, 103 West 107th Street, New York, NY 10025, (212) 678-5855, Grade 6 through 8

This honors program housed inside a dreary public school building sends approximately eighty percent of its students onto all the best private and public schools. Founded in 1986, Delta Honors students are admitted on the basis of test results, teacher recommendations, and an interview. Most accepted students score at least in the 90th percentile or higher, but must live in the district. The program is broad, thoughtful and interdisciplinary and even though the facility may seem scary to some parents, the quality of the program makes up for whatever else is lacking.

New York City Laboratory School for Gifted Education (Lower Lab), 1700 Third Avenue (between 95th and 96th Streets), New York, NY 10128, (212) 427-2798, FAX (212) 423-0634

The Lab School "operates on the premise that gifted education need not be elitist." The Lab School serves kindergarten through fifth grades. There are two classes per grade. Applications must be submitted one year prior to enrollment. Call in early October for a group tour appointment. The application requires a preschool skills checklist and a teacher evaluation. When the file is complete, the child comes in for an hour-long performance based interview with four other applicants. Note: Students in Lower Lab must apply to the Upper Lab School as they would to any other gifted/option Middle School program. Admission to Upper Lab is not automatic.

New York City Laboratory School for Collaborative Studies (Upper Lab School), 333 West 17th Street, New York, NY 10011 (212) 691-6119, FAX (212) 691-6219, website: www.nyclabschool.org

The Upper Lab consists of grades six through twelve. Total enrollment is approximately 950. The Upper Lab School is rigorous and academic, but non-traditional; emphasis is put on collaborative and interactive approaches to learning. The Middle School has consistently scored in the top five in reading and math scores in the city. The majority of students come from District 2, but a small number are accepted from out of the district. Applications should be filed by mid-December of the year prior to enrollment. The largest point of entry is at sixth grade. Sixth and seventh graders are required to take a teacher-designed math problem solving test and a teacher-designed essay test; both are administered at the Upper Lab School. Ninth grade is the second largest point of entry. Applicants for ninth grade use the normal high school application process, but applicants must have a solid academic background and should have completed one year of Spanish. "We look at grades and courses." College courses are offered in the eleventh and twelfth grades and internships are available in eleventh. Students can take college level courses at area universities including NYU, Borough of Manhattan Community College, Hunter and Parson's School of Design.

THE PUBLIC HIGH SCHOOLS

The Specialized High Schools

There are four specialized high schools; all of them require an entrance examination or audition. Stuyvesant High School, Bronx High School of Science and Brooklyn Technical High School, known as "the science schools," emphasize mathematics and science studies. The New York State Education Law requires a written examination for admission to the science schools. The three schools are different from one another; applicants must take the entrance exam at their first-choice science school. In addition, there is the Fiorello H. LaGuardia High School of Music and Art and the Performing Arts, for which applicants must audition.

The general timetable for admissions to the specialized high schools is similar to that of many private schools; for specific schools check with each one.

September: Call for a handbook and application
November: Applications are due in early November
December: Exams are offered to students in either 8th or 9th

grades one year *prior* to the year of enrollment. The exam is taken at the candidate's first-choice school.

March: Notification of acceptance

THE MATH/SCIENCE INSTITUTE
345 Chambers Street
New York, NY 10282
(212) 312-4816
FAX: (212) 312-4815

In March 1995 former Public Schools Chancellor Ramon C. Cortines announced the creation of an 18-month preparatory program designed to groom able seventh graders from diverse backgrounds for admission to one of the three specialized science high schools. Participating students attend various parochial, public and independent private schools. Housed at Stuyvesant High School, the program has expanded. Recommendation to the program must be made by the student's current school principal. The Math/Science Institute has summer sessions and various 7th and 8th grade programs. In addition to test preparation, students take various courses in literature, writing, math, science and research skills.

Bronx High School of Science

75 West 205th Street, Bronx, New York, NY 10468, (718) 817-7700

Total enrollment: approximately 2,600 students. Students come to Bronx Science from every borough. The Bronx Science yellow school bus can be seen travelling up and down Manhattan's avenues. The school population is approximately 40% of Asian descent. Bronx Science students have opportunities for independent research. There is a Holocaust Study Center and Museum, nine foreign languages are offered, and there are partnerships with NASA, The Bronx Zoo, Rockefeller University, Stevens Technology and so on. The handbook says, "Bronx Science is the nation's all time leader in the Westinghouse Science Talent Search." The school has five alumni Nobel Laureates. Extracurricular activities include over 60 clubs, numerous school publications, orchestral and vocal music programs, and 30 athletic teams; a nationally acclaimed speech and debate team; mock trial, and a full-scale theatrical production each year.

Brooklyn Technical High School

29 Fort Greene Place (South Elliot Place at DeKalb Avenue), Brooklyn, NY 11217, (718) 858-5150

Total enrollment: approximately 4,000 students. The student body is diverse. The brochure states that Brooklyn Tech excels in the areas of engineering, math and science and computer science. During ninth and tenth grades students take an academic core of studies and are introduced to engineering, computer science and lab science through hands-on experiences in well-equipped laboratories. At the end of sophomore year, students select a major area of concentration which they begin in eleventh grade. All tech students are prepared to follow any course of study at the college level, but are particularly well versed in their major area. Brooklyn Tech has over 100 clubs and fields varsity and junior varsity teams in handball, fencing, football, swimming, baseball, soccer and basketball.

Stuyvesant High School

345 Chambers Street, New York, NY 10282, (212) 312-4800, website: www.stuy.edu

Total enrollment: approximately 3,000 students. Stuyvesant High School occupies a brand-new high-tech building in lower Manhattan. In addition to advanced courses in mathematics and the sciences, students can select from a wide range of electives. Advanced Placement classes in biology, chemistry, physics, foreign language, mathematics, English and social studies are offered. Stuyvesant's extracurricular offerings are broad. There are over 100 clubs, a symphony orchestra, dance band, choral and ensemble groups, thirty-two athletic teams, fifteen student publications and an active student government. The school has an Olympic-size swimming pool.

Fiorello H. LaGuardia High School of Music and Art and Performing Arts

108 Amsterdam Avenue, New York, NY 10023, (212) 496-0700

Total enrollment: approximately 2,500. LaGuardia is the high school featured in the movie *Fame*. It is the only public high school in the world that offers a complete academic program along with professional-level training in the arts. Because of the dual nature of the program, LaGuardia students can expect to put in very long days. Admission to this high school is based on an individual audition in dance, drama, instrumental music, vocal music or art. Only New York City residents are eligible. The handbook describes what is needed for the audition.

OTHER RESOURCES

1. **The National Association of Independent Schools (NAIS)**, Office of Public Information, 1620 L. Street NW, Washington, D.C. 20036, (202) 973-9700, website: nais.org. The website has a database of over 1,000 schools and other information.

   NAIS is a voluntary organization to which accredited independent schools may apply for membership. The primary function of NAIS is to serve its over 1,200 member schools. NAIS does not accredit independent schools but does issue guidelines, chart trends, sponsor workshops and publish information on issues relevant to the independent school community from diversity to boarding schools. Many of these publications are available on the school's websites.

   Parents who are interested in learning more about boarding schools can call The Association of Boarding Schools (TABS) Answer Line, (202) 966-8705,

2. **Educational Testing Service (ETS)**, Rosedale Road, Princeton N.J., 08541, (609) 921-9000.

   The Educational Testing Service publishes informational pamphlets on many issues related to independent schools.

3. **Reading Reform Foundation of New York**, 333 West 57th Street, Suite 1L, New York, NY 10019, (212) 307-7320, FAX (212) 307-0449

   The Reading Reform Foundation of New York, founded in 1981 by a group of reading specialists and interested citizens, is a non-profit literacy organization based on the belief that almost every child, regardless of social and economic background, can learn to read, write and spell if taught by effective methods (with an emphasis on the use of phonics). Reading Reform Foundation offers graduate level courses all year 'round in the teaching of reading, writing and spelling, holds conferences, conducts workshops for parents and sends skilled teaching consultants into public schools throughout the city to work with classroom teachers.

4. **The Council for Spiritual and Ethical Education**, (404) 355-4460 1-(800) 298-4599, website: www.csee.org

   The Council for Spiritual and Ethical Education (CSEE) is a nondenominational organization composed of approximately 425 member schools the majority of which are secular coed day and boarding schools located in the northeastern states.

   CSEE is independent of any religious body and does not impose any one point of view. According to the brochure "It is the

481

only national, interfaith, professional organization meeting the moral and religious needs of independent schools." CSEE conducts workshops and directs conferences on values, ethics and religion education.

CSEE has been actively promoting community service in schools for many years and sponsors conferences that feature community service workshops.

New York City Independent Schools that are Members of CSEE:

The Allen-Stevenson School
The Browning School
The Buckley School
The Caedmon School
The Cathedral School
Collegiate School
Convent of the Sacred Heart
Grace Church School
Horace Mann School
Marymount School of New York

The Nightingale-Bamford School
The Packer Collegiate Institute
Saint David's School
St. Hilda's & St.Hugh's School
St. Luke's School
The Spence School
The Town School
Trinity School

5. **The Catholic Center,** Office of Superintendent of Schools, Education Department, 1011 First Avenue (between 55th and 56th) (18th floor), New York, NY 10022, (212) 371-1000

For $8, The Catholic Center will mail its complete directory of elementary and secondary schools. A list of Catholic high schools only will be mailed to you free of charge.

6. **The National Coalition of Girls' Schools,** Meg Milne Moulton or Whitney Ransome, Executive Co-Directors, 57 Main Street, Concord, Massachusetts 01742, (978) 287-4485, FAX (978) 287-6014, website: www.ncgs.org

The National Coalition of Girls' Schools has 103 member schools in North America (both public and private). Its members share a commitment to the values and advantages of an all-girl's education. They conduct research, gather data, and sponsor forums for leading girls' and womens' groups; NCGS publications, including: *Choosing a Girls' School* (a directory of girls' schools), *Raising Confident, Competent Daughters*, and

What Every Girl in School Needs to Know, and *Girls and Technology*, are available by mail order.

7. **American Association of University Women (AAUW)**, 1111 Sixteenth Street N.W., Washington, D.C. 20036, 1-(800) 326-AAUW (2289) (membership information and to locate a local branch of AAUW), (202) 785-7788 (general) or 1-(800) 225-9998 (for a copy of *How Schools Shortchange Girls* and *Separated by Sex: A Critical Look at Single-Sex Education for Girls*). Members' Help Line 1-(800) 326-2289.

In 1992 the AAUW Educational Foundation released the report *How Schools Shortchange Girls* which challenged myths about the education of girls in the public schools and uncovered disturbing evidence of new barriers to their learning. In March 1998 the AAUW released a report that finds separating by sex is *not* the solution to gender inequity. *Separated by Sex: A Critical Look at Single-Sex Education for Girls* is controversial and well worth reading. Recently, AAUW published *Tech-savvy: Educating Girls in the New Computer Age*. The AAUW has been working toward eliminating the educational, financial and legal barriers faced by women and girls for over 125 years. Parents can request free of charge useful guides for assessing gender bias in their children's schools—the *School Assessment Guide* and *Growing Smart: What Works for Girls in School*.

8. **The Association of Teachers in Independent Schools in New York City and Vicinity, Inc. (ATIS)**, (212) 472-3572

ATIS was found in 1914 to ensure that teachers in private schools were properly paid and protected. Today the incorporated, non-profit organization continues its support of educational professionalism and increased opportunities for private-school teachers. ATIS sponsors several workshops for teachers throughout the year as well as the annual conference—book exhibit. ATIS publishes a newsletter that reports news of schools represented by the association, and in the spring contains a list of school positions available.

9. **The Interschool Faculty Diversity Search**, (212) 501-0031

The Search is an organization whose purpose is to enlarge the pool of talented candidates of color for faculty and administrative positions in participating schools. Although the Search is administered by Interschool (a consortium of eight Manhattan independent schools) many more schools (over 20) participate.

10. **The Guild of New York Independent Schools**, Dr. James Dawson, Chair, Professional Children's School, (212) 582-3116

    The guild is an informal association of approximately fifty-two heads of school (from schools located in all five boroughs) who meet approximately twice a year at the Cosmopolitan Club, and may meet elsewhere as well, to discuss common concerns within the independent school community (such as medical benefits for faculty) and to coordinate their calendars (vacation schedules, opening and closing dates). They do *not* discuss tuitions. The guild does not provide information to parents about individual schools.

11. **NYC-Parents in Action Inc.**, P.O. Box 287451, Yorkville Station, New York, NY 10128, (212) 987-9629

    NYC-Parents In Action, Inc. is a nonprofit, voluntary organization incorporated in 1979 as a parenting education program in response to growing alcohol, marijuana and other drug use among minors and their parents. Rumors circulate that certain schools have more drug and/or alcohol abuse than others. The truth is that a portion of the student body at all the New York City independent high schools (and boarding schools) does experiment with alcohol, drugs and/or sex. NYC-PIA provides information, parent education, seminars and workshops and provides trained facilitators for parent-organized discussion groups. The Parent Representative program provides a link to the parent body within the independent schools. NYC-PIA publishes a newsletter. In cooperation with the Parents' League, NYC-PIA sponsors Teen Scene—a candid discussion of teen life in the city by a panel composed of students from various independent and boarding schools.

12. **New York State Education Office of Non-Public Schools**, New York State Education Department, Non-public School Services Team, Room 481 Education Building Annex, Washington Avenue, Albany, New York 12234, (518) 474-3879
    New York State Education Office of Information, Reporting and Technology Services, (a division of the State Education Office that compiles statistical information), Room 863, Education Building Annex, Albany, New York 12234, (518) 474-7965

    Upon request, the Department of Information, Reporting and Technology will send a statistical breakdown for each school based on an extensive questionnaire. Information includes the number and type of computers the school owns, which foreign languages are taught and the ethnic and religious composition of the student body and faculty. (Most of this information can be obtained more easily from the school's brochure or directly from the school.)

ACCREDITING ORGANIZATIONS

The New York State Board of Regents authorizes both the New York State Association of Independent Schools and the Middle States Association to accredit schools. According to the National Association of Independent Schools, "Accreditation is a process of peer evaluation that certifies that schools meet certain generally accepted standards of educational quality defined by an independent entity." Each of the independent schools sets forth its accreditation in its brochure. Tradition determines which organization accredits the school. NYSAIS deals primarily with the independent schools in New York State, whereas Middle States accredits many independent as well as public schools in the Middle Atlantic states. Note: NYSAIS and Middle States do not provide parents with information about specific schools—do not call them to find out which school is the best for your child.

How does it work? Both NYSAIS and Middle States evaluate a school based on its philosophy (or mission) and how well the school puts its philosophy into practice—is the school doing what it says it does? This evaluation process takes place every ten years or so. The first step in the reaccreditation process is a year-long self-study. Next, the school is evaluated by a team of recognized evaluators, which often includes heads of other independent schools. The evaluating team makes recommendations for improvement, and the school is requested to provide an action plan for implementing these changes. Accreditation is granted if the self-study, evaluation and planning reports reveal that the school meets the standards for accreditation. Accreditation is granted for a period of ten years. After approximately eight and a half years, the school begins another self-study and the cycle is renewed.

1. **New York State Association of Independent Schools (NYSAIS)**, 12 Jay Street, Schenectady, NY, 12305 (518) 346-5662, FAX (518) 346-7390, website: www.nysais.org, Executive Director: Fred Calder

NYSAIS is a voluntary association of approximately 160 independent nursery, elementary, middle and secondary schools in New York State whose enrollment is about 60,000 students. NYSAIS publishes a useful pamphlet entitled "Choosing a School: A Guide for Parents." One of its main activities is advocacy for independent education.

2. **The Middle States Association of Colleges and Schools**, 3624 Market Street, 2nd Floor Annex, Philadelphia, PA 19104, (215) 662-5600 or 5610

The Middle States Association established standards that are administered by the three accreditation authorities under the auspices of the Middle States Association: the Commission on Elementary Schools, the Commission on Secondary Schools and the Commission on Higher Education. The Middle States Association is a nonprofit organization established in 1887 to set standards for American education. Middle States publishes information on school standards and the accreditation process.

Index of Schools and Programs

490

Index to Websites